CW00828505

AN INTRODUCTION TO INDIAN CHRISTIAN THEOLOGY

AN INTRODUCTION TO

INDIAN CHRISTIAN THEOLOGY

R. H. S. BOYD

ISPCK
1994

This edition is jointly published by the Indian Society for Promoting Christian Knowledge, Post Box 1585, Kashmere Gate, Delhi-110006 and Indian Theological Library, Trivandrum, Kerala.

First published, 1969
Revised Edition, 1975
Reprinted, 1979
Reprinted, 1989
Reprinted, 1991
Reprinted 1994

Printed at Printsman, 18A/11, Doriwalan, New Delhi-110 005.

FOR FRANCES

FOREWORD

I feel greatly honoured to have been asked by my good friend Dr. Robin Boyd to write a foreword to this important book, *An Introduction to Indian Christian Theology.*

The theological schools in India have not yet got out of the habit of considering the history of the Church in India as an appendage to the history of Western Christian missions and the story of Western missionaries. It is only recently that Church historians have begun to recognise the fact that, while foreign missions have played an integral part in their life and growth, the history of the Indian Churches is best understood and interpreted as an independent story. It is the story of a people's dynamic corporate response to the challenge of the Gospel of Christ and of their living and growing in constant dialogue with the religious and ethical environment of India. We do not have, however, any history of the Church in India which takes this new recognition seriously. When there is no Indian Church History in the proper sense of that term, there cannot be any history of Indian Christian Theology. For living theology is the manner in which a Church confesses its faith and establishes its historical existence in dialogue with its own environment. If the Indian Church is understood merely as a product of Western missions, then Indian theology will only appear as an appendage to Western theology. Now that we are beginning to discover that the Indian Church has a history of its own, we are also beginning to discover an Indian Christian theology with its own history.

Robin Boyd breaks new ground in two important respects. First, he has brought to light the continuity of the hidden stream of living theology which has been flowing in India. Second, he has sought to see it as a function of the mission of the Church in India and evaluate it in terms of the future of that mission. We have had studies of Indian theologians; but in these studies they were made to stand out and apart from the life and mission of the Indian Church, more or less as unexpected freaks of nature. In the present survey they are standing solidly within the flowing stream of the Church. More than this, till now most of the studies of types of Indian theological thinking were undertaken by men who were eager to evaluate them in terms of Western theological schools and categories. Indeed theologians like Oosthuizen and Wagner studied Indian theology on the assumption that it must justify itself before Western theology. There are occasions when Boyd also is tempted in this direction. But he does not yield; he warns himself and others against it, and affirms that Indian theology must be judged in the light of the mission of the Church in India, and need not be brought to any other bar of judgment. This is a welcome departure.

I am not arguing for the isolation of the Indian Church or its theology from the impact of ecumenism and its criteria. Isolation is impossible, and undesirable even if it were possible. But ecumenism should not be confused with foreign imposition; at its best, ecumenism India is concerned with the theological tools relevant to fulfil the mission of the universal Church in the Indian situation.

The criticism one hears so often, that Indian Christians have not yet produced any theology, only means that they have not produced *summae* or *Church Dogmatics*. But living theology, which arises as tools for confessing the faith and fulfilling the mission in specific situations, is often fragmentary and partial in character. It is the raw material for systematic theology. It is foolish to underrate it simply because it has not resulted in systems, Systematisation may have been an important aspect of theological development; and in the past such systematisation was deemed necessary to build up and carry forward a tradition of theological teaching. Today we have realised the deadening effect of total systems of thought on human creativity in any field of life; and we are justly suspicious of premature systematization and synthesis. I am not sure whether the Church in future will give the same weight to theological systematization as it did in the past. In any case, even if theological systematization is considered necessary for theological development, it can have only a secondary value. Dr. Boyd is right in refusing to confuse the reality of theological existence with the development of theological systems.

I have always felt sad that the books in the *Christian Students' Library* have not drawn on the theological insights of the pioneers here surveyed, and that Indian students training for pastoral and theological ministry in the Indian Church have been given no opportunity to come to grips with them. I am happy, therefore, that Robin Boyd's book is the first book in the new *Indian Theological Library* series. One hopes that the Indian character of at least the books in this series will be jealously guarded. Surely the time has come for Indian theological schools and agencies of Christian education in India to take Indian Christian theology more seriously.

Bangalore
19 March 1969

M. M. THOMAS
Director
Christian Institute for the Study of Religion and Society

PREFACE TO THE SECOND EDITION

In this second edition I have tried to remedy some of the omissions of the first edition—the 'Vedic theology' of K. M. Banerjea, for example, and the work of A. G. Hogg. I have given a fuller treatment of some of the writers already briefly touched on, such as Manilal C. Parekh, Dhanjibhai Fakirbhai and Raymond Panikkar, and have also given a brief account of the work of K. Subba Rao, Swami Abhishiktananda, and Klaus Klostermaier. The most extensive new material is that on Dr. M. M. Thomas, who so kindly wrote the foreword to the first edition.

To make the printer's task easier, and to limit the cost of publication, it was decided to leave the thirteen chapters of the first edition virtually unaltered, and to concentrate the new material in what is really a 'postscript'—Chapters XIV to XVII. Thus the conclusions of the book—to be found in Chapters XII and XIII—remain as before, though I would ask the reader to give special attention to the new treatment of the problem of 'levels of existence' which I have attempted in pp. 308-310. This method of procedure has resulted in the Indexes to the new material being printed separately, rather than being incorporated into the earlier material.

I had hoped that the second edition would bring the book up to date, but unfortunately that has not proved possible as the additional material was completed in 1972 and publication has been unavoidably delayed till 1975. I must apologise, therefore, for statements like that on p. 322 which notes Jayaprakash Narain's retirement from politics, but not his reinvolvement!

Printing difficulties inevitably arise when an author finds himself several thousand miles away from his publisher, and for this reason some errors have occurred in the numbering of footnotes, especially on pages 290-293, 311-320, and 324-330. The correct reference will frequently be found by consulting the footnote *before* that signified by the number in the text (and this will sometimes be found at the foot of the previous page). The author and publisher apologise for this blemish.

I should like to thank those who have made this second edition possible, especially my wife and daughters, and my friends at the Christian Literature Society, Madras, Mr. T. K. Thomas and Mr. D. Packiamuthu. I hope that in its new form the book will prove helpful to those who want to think out and express their faith in a way that is true to the Gospel and true to India.

Melbourne,
22nd May 1975

R. H. S. BOYD

PREFACE

This book is based on a thesis presented in 1966 for the degree of Doctor of Philosophy of the University of Edinburgh in the Faculty of Divinity. I am conscious of its many omissions, and of sections where a much fuller treatment is required—for example the interesting 'Vedic fulfilment' theology of K. M. Banerjea almost a century ago, and the contemporary work of Dr. Raymond Panikkar whose massive contribution I have presumed to assess on the strength of a single book published in English. My aim has been, however, to provide a working introduction to Indian Christian theology, setting it so far as possible in its historical and cultural context, and tracing the more obvious lines of development. It is my hope that this book may stimulate others to produce more adequate studies, and to carry forward the work of Christian theology in India.

I wish to express my gratitude to all those who have helped and encouraged me, and especially to the following: my supervisors Professors T. F. Torrance and John McIntyre of the University of Edinburgh; Principal R. B. Desai of the Gujarat United School of Theology, Ahmedabad; Principal J. R. Chandran of the United Theological College, Bangalore; the Very Rev. Dr. A. A. Fulton of the Presbyterian Church in Ireland; Mr. M. M. Thomas of the Christian Institute for the Study of Religion and Society, Bangalore; Mr. A. C. Dharmaraj of the National Christian Council, Nagpur; Mrs. K. Leonard of the Central Library, Selly Oak Colleges; Dr. Maurice Creasey of Woodbrooke College, Selly Oak; the Rev. A. D. Manuel and Mr. T. K. Thomas of the Christian Literature Society, Madras; the Rt. Rev. Bishop A. J. Appasamy; Dr. K. Baago. I also wish to thank my colleagues and students at the Gujarat United School of Theology, Ahmedabad; and above all my wife, who made the book possible.

Ahmedabad R. H. S. BOYD
8th March 1969

CONTENTS

Chapter I

INTRODUCTION

For many years western theologians have been accustomed to look forward to the day when the Indian Christian Church will begin to make its distinctive contribution to ecumenical theology. Bishop Westcott believed that the most profound commentary on the Fourth Gospel was still to be written, and that it could not be written until an Indian theologian would undertake the task.[1] Always this hope has been placed in the future, and it has been tacitly assumed that this characteristic Indian theology has not yet begun to emerge. Even Indian theologians themselves have adopted this tentative view, regarding their writings more as the preparation of the ground, the *prolegomena* to theology rather than the stuff of theology itself. The pages of Chenchiah abound with expressions like, 'Indian Christian theology can only arise when . . .'—and other writers even apologise for the fact that the Indian Church has not yet produced a single heresy, and only one serious controversy, that on the status and use of the Old Testament.[2]

This deliberately-fostered impression that Indian theology has not yet emerged is reinforced by other factors. There is no doubt that to an outside observer the Church in India seems to be dominated by western attitudes and modes of thought. In church architecture, church organisation, church services, church music and church publications, western forms and attitudes still seem to predominate. The ancient Syrian Church of Kerala is little known in the north of India, and even in it theological thought tends to wear a western aspect. The feature of Indian Christian life and witness which has become more familiar than any other to western observers is the church union movement and the liturgical developments associated with it, and publications in this field, however great their intrinsic worth, have tended to be framed in western theological terminology and modes of thought, even when the writers were Indian.

Again, the teaching given in theological colleges throughout India has been, and still is, dominated by western theology, as

[1] E. Asirvatham, *Christianity in the Indian Crucible* (1957), p. 118.
[2] V. E. Devadutt, 'What is an Indigenous Theology?' in *Ecum. Review*, Autumn 1949.

a glance at any syllabus will show. The result is that the preaching of the average Indian minister or evangelist reflects the western theological categories in which he has been trained. It is a common experience to hear western visitors say, after attending a church service in India, 'It was all so familiar; how touching to hear the same old hymns sung in a different language!' There are, as we shall see, many exceptions to this tendency, yet the charge has often been made against Indian Christianity, and still is made, that it denationalises a man and uproots him from the cultural heritage which is his by right.

Many efforts have therefore been made—and not just in recent years, as is sometimes imagined—to make the Church 'indigenous' in its life and worship. In the Syrian Church this effort is perhaps not needed, for it has been 'indigenous' for longer than the Church in Britain or Germany. But there have been experiments in many other areas—churches built in Indian architectural styles,[1] Christian *āshrams* or religious communities, and of course—from the earliest days of western missionary activity—the use of Christian lyric hymns in Indian metres and sung to Indian tunes accompanied by Indian instruments. There have been Indian Christian poets in every area, and Indian Christian ascetic *sādhus*. All these have had their importance, and all have helped to mould the pattern of Indian Christian life. Over the years many millions of Indian Christians have lived, prayed, studied the Bible, worshipped together and witnessed by the quality of their life and their devotion. They have found many opportunities of expressing their Christian faith in truly Indian ways. Yet the question remains—is there a truly Indian expression of theological thought?

Today it is manifest that a body of Indian theological writing exists which demands serious attention. This is not to say that there is any single authoritative system, an Indian *Summa Theologica* or *Institutes of the Christian Religion* or *Kirchliche Dogmatik* which might become the basis for a 'subordinate standard' for the Indian Church. In the days of Tertullian, of Clement and Origen and of the Antioch-Alexandria controversy, there was no such *Summa* and yet no one would assert that there was no theology. A distinctive Indian theology has indeed emerged, in a remarkably rich diversity of forms and modes of thought, related—as was the theology of Origen and

[1] Cf. J. F. Butler, 'The Theology of Church Building in India' in *Indian Journal of Theology* (IJT), V/2 (1956), and VIII/4 (1959).

Augustine—to the main philosophical schools of the surrounding culture. In the following pages it will be our task to unravel the origins and examine the structure of this theology.

A factor which has tended to discourage the emergence of a formulated Christian theology in India is the widespread dislike, among both Hindus and Christians, for anything 'dogmatic'. This attitude has received considerable encouragement from the writings of Dr. S. Radhakrishnan who has criticised the Christian religion because of its tendency to fix its doctrinal categories.[1] Hindus tend to think of Christianity—perhaps with some justification—as an authoritarian religion which lays down certain dogmas as essential, and demands uncritical acceptance of them as the prerequisite of salvation. Jesus is accepted as a great religious teacher and inspiring leader perhaps even as an incarnation of God, but the creeds, confessions and doctrinal statements of the organised, institutional Church are felt to be alien to the Indian religious and cultural tradition, and in fact to represent a somewhat low form of human religious development.

Some Indian Christian theologians have taken this criticism to heart, and have themselves attempted to avoid 'dogmatic' theology, while at the same time making radical criticisms of such traditional doctrines as the Christological formula of the Council of Chalcedon. There is a tendency—influenced perhaps more by the Hindu inclination to regard experience (*anubhava*) as of primary importance in revelation than by western theologians like Schleiermacher or Otto—to make direct experience of God and of Christ the primary criterion in theology, and to give little or no importance to official credal statements, even those of the undivided Church of the first five centuries. At the same time these writers have felt obliged to discuss most of the classical Christian doctrines, and in the process have given clear expression to their own views. We shall therefore attempt, in our study, to give some thought to the question of the necessity and validity of credal statements, and of the extent to which a particular formulation of belief must be regarded as binding on the Church in all ages and in all places.

We shall find that Indian theologians have related themselves to a number of Hindu philosophical systems, and we must ask about the possibility and legitimacy of this type of relationship. Western theology has never been able to dissociate itself from

[1] See, e.g., S. Radhakrishnan, *The Bhagavadgita* (1948), p. 142: 'The absolute character of theological doctrine is incompatible with the mysterious character of religious truth.'

philosophy, from the time of the Platonism of Justin Martyr onwards. Plato lies behind Augustine, Aristotle behind Aquinas and even Calvin; right down to the days of idealism, existentialism and logical positivism, no theologian, not even those like Barth who have tried to break free from philosophy, has succeeded in dissociating himself from the philosophical presuppositions of certain schools. In the West, the philosophy with which theology has been associated has not necessarily been Christian philosophy; theologians have felt the need, in their systematic statements, of using the language and the thought-patterns of a Plato, an Aristotle, a Kant, a Hegel, a Gogarten, a Buber, a Wittgenstein. So far as an Indian theologian like Chenchiah is concerned the formula of Chalcedon, with its underlying philosophy of substance and accident, is pure pagan Aristotle. Why then should an Indian theologian feel bound by formulae which have no essential relationship to the Christian revelation? May it not be possible for Indian theologians, while remaining faithful to the biblical 'deposit', to work out their apologetic and their systematic theological statements in the terminology of certain schools of Hindu thought? We shall find that this process has in fact been extensively carried out, and we must try to estimate how far it has been successful.

As we reflect on the process by which Christianity in the early centuries became acclimatised in the Greek world, and by which it made use of certain categories of Greek thought, we are struck by the double fact of its acceptance of 'secularised' Greek philosophy and philosophical terminology, and its complete rejection of Greek religion and mythology. Over a long period Greek religion was gradually secularised. Philosophy was separated from what had once been a religio-philosophic unity. The religious content—which had already been deeply influenced by secularisation right from the time of Aristophanes and Euripides—developed into a cultural, literary, artistic entity, 'incapsulated' and isolated, except in the Orphic and mystery traditions, from that living, existential faith which transforms men's lives. The mediaeval monks who concealed their copies of Virgil in the thatch of their cells, and read them surreptitiously when religious authority was not looking, were not reverting to Graeco-Roman paganism, but were simply seeking an artistic, cultural outlet and stimulus of which their monastic life deprived them. The old gods died, but their ghosts passed into the literary and cultural heritage of Europe, and it was the Church, strangely enough, which preserved them. Greek religion was isolated from philosophy, secularised, preserved, and eventually became incorporated, at the Renaissance, into modern European culture. Christian poets, philosophers, painters and even theologians have not hesitated to use 'incapsulated' Greek religion and mythology in their works. From Milton to T. S. Eliot, and even to theologians like Reinhold Niebuhr, the types and stories of Greek religious mythology have provided a background and illustration for Christian exposition. Christian culture has seldom banished the Muses and the Graces, and the stuff of Greek tragedy has at times served to expound and to deepen our understanding of the work of Christ.

Is a comparable development of Hinduism likely? The usual answer is to say that Hindu philosophy and religion are more closely interwoven than were Greek. Whereas Greek philosophy was often almost entirely secular, Hindu philosophy *is* religion, and Śankara and Rāmānuja are regarded as great religious figures as much as philosophers.

And yet it is an obvious fact that there is at present a rapidly-moving process of secularisation going on within Hinduism. Outwardly this tendency can be seen in the creation of the secular state in India. The official abolition of caste, and the increasing tendency to make legislation uniform and so valid for all communities, in distinction from the earlier communal laws, is an indication of the lessening grip of religious sanction, and its replacement by universal, secular legislation. Simultaneously, the process of general secularisation, which has been going on steadily since the days of Ram Mohan Roy a century and a half ago is still gaining momentum, and recent studies have revealed that the present generation of educated young people is almost as secularised as its counterpart in the West, and has little knowledge of, or interest in, the traditional piety of popular Hinduism, or even in its more philosophic forms. For many people today the chief medium for the assimilation of Hindu religious mythology is the cinema, where epics and musicals based on the great stories and dramas of Hinduism are a favourite spectacle. The current popularity of similarly spectacular biblical films in the West does not lessen the fact that this form of Hinduism is almost entirely secularised and 'incapsulated' and is of cultural rather than of deeply religious significance.

Philosophical Hinduism would seem to have cut itself off very largely from the traditional mythology. The writings of Sri Aurobindo, or of Dr. Radhakrishnan, though using the terminology of the traditional philosophical systems, do not use 'mythology' except perhaps for the purposes of illustration.

Philosophical Hinduism has been fairly thoroughly 'demythologised'. This is not simply the victory of monism or *advaita* over the conception of a religion of devotion to a personal God. It is to a very large extent a victory of demythologised Hinduism over the myth-filled tradition.

It would seem, therefore, as though Hinduism were already well started on the path followed by Greek religion. And so we are led to the question of whether or not it is legitimate for Christian theologians to use and adapt the categories of what still purports to be *religious* Hinduism, and yet is already very largely secularised. What, indeed, is the real meaning of the word 'Hindu'? Does it describe the fully mythological Hindu religion? Does it describe certain philosophico-religious systems? Or is it simply a synonym for 'Indian culture'? We shall find that some Indian Christian theologians, notably Brahmabandhab, have believed that Christianity was not incompatible with cultural, secularised Hinduism. We shall have to attempt to follow up the implications of this point of view.

The Indian Christian theologian, like all true and effective theologians, has two chief concerns. The first is to remain faithful to his experience and knowledge of Jesus Christ, who is the centre of his life, and this involves him in loyalty to those sources through which he has come to know and love Christ. Secondly, he is concerned to interpret and proclaim his understanding and experience in such a way that other men may come to the same knowledge. In order to do this he must proclaim Christ and the significance of Christ in such a way that his contemporaries and compatriots may fully understand the message, and this involves him in the problems of effective communication and persuasive proclamation. It is his duty to seek to remove all hindrances to the effective proclamation and the full reception of Jesus Christ by his fellow men. We must, therefore, in this enquiry, estimate the success of Indian Christian theologians in the work which they have undertaken, noting at the same time some of the evidence of history about similar approaches and similar situations in the past.

Important and integral as the Muslim contribution to Indian culture has been, we are here restricting ourselves to the relation of Christianity to the *Hindu* cultural and religious background.

The aim of our enquiry is, then, to trace the origins of Indian Christian theology, to assess its meaning and significance, and to draw from it what encouragement and insight we can for the task of the Church's mission not only in India but in every land and culture in the world.

Chapter II

SOME SOURCES OF THEOLOGICAL TRADITION

The Syrian Tradition

A most ancient and venerated tradition of the Indian Church says that the Apostle Thomas came to India, landing in Malabar in 52 A.D.[1] Whatever the truth of this may be, there is no doubt that the Christian Church has been established in South India from very early times, probably from the third century and possibly considerably earlier. Tradition further says that in 345 A.D. a Syrian Christian merchant called Thomas of Cana brought a group of Syrian settlers to Malabar. Nestorian missionaries and settlers also came to India, probably from about the end of the fourth century, during the golden age of the Nestorian missions to Asia.[2] The so-called 'Nestorian' Church, known also as 'the Church of the East' was in fact the Church of Persia, with an origin going back beyond the Nestorian controversy, and its tradition appears to have become the dominant one in South India in the period before the arrival of the Roman Catholic missionaries at the beginning of the sixteenth century.

The arrival of Vasco da Gama at Calicut in 1498 opened a long and tragic chapter in the history of the St. Thomas Christians.[3] The Franciscans who arrived in 1500 found a Christian Church under the care of four Nestorian bishops, but it was not long before the Roman Church began a determined effort to win their allegiance, aided by Pope Leo X's establishment in 1514 of the *Padroado* which gave to the Portuguese rights over the Christians of the East. Among the numerous methods adopted to win the Christians away from their Persian loyalty was a maritime blockade which cut off the supply of bishops from overseas, a blockade which was finally broken only in 1665 with the arrival of a bishop of the Syrian Church under the jurisdiction of the See of Antioch. Meantime the struggle between the Roman hierarchy and the St. Thomas Christians had been a bitter one. In 1599, at the Synod of Diamper, all the members of the ancient churches, with the honourable exception of 30,000

[1] For a good account of the Syrian Church see L. W. Brown, *The Indian Christians of St. Thomas* (1956).

[2] John Stewart, *Nestorian Missionary Enterprise—the Story of a Church on Fire* (1928).

[3] For a Roman Catholic view of these events see Cardinal Tisserant, *Eastern Christianity in India* (1957).

Nestorians, submitted to Rome. The Syrians chafed under the Roman yoke, however, with its unfamiliar liturgy, doctrines and practices, and in 1653 came the famous 'Revolt of the Coonen Cross' when they came out in open rebellion and, holding a rope tied to an ancient stone cross, took a solemn oath to sever all connection with the Roman Church. It was after this revolt that the blockade was at last broken and a non-Roman bishop arrived. By this time the St. Thomas Christians had apparently little interest in the theology or allegiance of their bishop, provided he was not Roman, and this one, Mar Gregorius, was in fact a Jacobite, not a Nestorian, but they gladly welcomed him and the Syrian Church has been Jacobite ever since.[1]

There is no need here to follow the later history of the Syrian Church, for example in its complicated relations with the Church Missionary Society in the 19th century, which led to the formation in 1887 of the reformed Mar Thoma Church. From the theological point of view the important fact is that the ancient Syrian Church of Kerala includes in its history a number of different traditions, notably those of the Persian Church, commonly referred to as Nestorian, and of the Syrian or Jacobite Church. It might be expected that the Syrian Church, with its long Indian tradition behind it, would have evolved a distinct type of theology which could be a guide and inspiration to Indian theologians of other, more recent, traditions. It must be admitted, however, that this has not been the case, and that it is only comparatively recently, and under the influence of western theology, that theological writers of note have begun to emerge. The explanation of this is to be found in the fact that the Church existed for centuries in the midst of an alien, Hindu environment, and as a result became somewhat introspective, fitting into the caste-pattern of society as a special caste but with little if any idea of its responsibility for the evangelism of its non-Christian neighbours. In addition, the language of the liturgy was Syriac, which most of the people could not understand. The liturgy was preserved indeed, and was the focus of the people's Christian life, but such conditions, together with the lack of a vernacular (Malayalam) translation of the Bible until the early 19th century, could not make for theological interest or discussion.[2]

[1] The name 'Jacobite' applied to the so-called 'monophysites' of Syria comes from Jacob Baradai, Bishop of Edessa (d. 578), who organised their Church after the expulsion of Severus, Patriarch of Antioch, by Justinian in 518 and his excommunication in 536.

[2] L. W. Brown, *op. cit.*, p. 213.

Although the Syrian Christian community has been culturally closely integrated with Indian society, there has been little or no attempt to work out a theology in Indian terminology which might be used as an instrument of evangelism, for until comparatively recently there was no evangelistic urge. Thus the theology of the Syrian Church, found as it is mainly in the liturgy and in formularies for ordination and consecration, has remained entirely Syrian, based on the Syriac language, and, despite its age-long sojourn on Indian soil, theologically as far removed from Indian thought as is Roman or Protestant theology.[1]

We shall leave aside the question of the theology of the Indian Church in Nestorian times, as no records are available,[2] noting merely that there is still a small Nestorian Church in South India and that India has never ceased to be conscious of this ancient Nestorian association. Instead we shall consider briefly the influence on Indian theology of the characteristic Syrian Christology.

The Syrian Orthodox Church is frequently called 'Jacobite', and 'Jacobite' is usually equated with 'monophysite'. And in the history of dogma monophysitism is associated with the heresy of Eutyches, who held that the human nature of Christ was absorbed into the divine, and who was condemned by the Council of Chalcedon in 451. Yet although the Syrian Church rejects the formula of Chalcedon with its affirmation that in Christ two distinct natures, divine and human, are found in one 'Person', it equally rejects and condemns Eutyches. A modern Indian Syrian writer, E. M. Philip, holds that the early Syrian fathers like Severus of Antioch who died in 538 were not so very different in what they believed from the Chalcedonian party, though they condemned the words 'acknowledged in two natures' as savouring of Nestorianism.[3] When they maintained that in Christ there was only one 'nature', they did not mean this in a Eutychian sense, but in fact came close to the western idea of a single 'Person' in whom two natures, though distinct, are united. The 'one nature' which they affirmed was, writes Philip,

> A one-nature formed by the hypostatic union of divinity and humanity, substantially and inseparably preserving the properties of the natures without mixture and without confusion. It must

[1] For a theological discussion of the Syrian liturgies see K. N. Daniel, *A Critical Study of Primitive Liturgies, especially that of St. James* (2nd edn., 1949).

[2] L. W. Brown, *op. cit.*, p. 294.

[3] E. M. Philip, *The Indian Church of St. Thomas* (1950), p. 368 f.

be observed that both the Council of Chalcedon and the Syrian Fathers upheld the same view in respect of the union of natures and the Incarnation. What the Council really condemned was the teaching of Eutyches, in his conception of the character of the union, viz., that in our Lord the natures were so united that *one of them absorbed the other.*[1]

The Chalcedonian formula, Philip feels, fails in effect to safeguard the true unity of Christ's Person, or 'nature', and he quotes the comment of a sixth century Jacobite writer, Mar Philexinos, Bishop of Mabug:

> We anathematise and set aside the Council of Chalcedon, because in the one Lord Jesus Christ, the only begotten Son of God, it separates the natures and the properties and the actions and the heights and the humiliations and the divinities and the humanities, and thinks of Him as two, and brings in *Quaternity*, and worships the simple Son of Man.[2]

Syrian theologians feel that their understanding makes clearer the newness and uniqueness of Christ, without reducing either his divinity or humanity. Here is how the matter is put by a Syrian theologian of the mid-nineteenth century, E. Philipos:

> The Syrians believe that *the nature in Christ is one:* that the two natures were united with one another; because in Christ the two natures were mingled together—the nature of the Godhead and the nature of the manhood—like wine with water. And whereas it is said that there is one nature in Christ, it is for the confirmation of the unity of the two natures one with another.[3]

It is clear that the modern Indian Syrian theologian V. C. Samuel has every right to ask, in connection with men like Severus of Antioch, 'Were they Monophysites?'[4]. And in the Syrian Church's traditional attitude to the Council of Chalcedon we can detect the seeds of the conviction in the minds of many Indian theologians that the Chalcedonian formula is not the only way of expressing a true Christology. In other words, in Indian theology today the formula of Chalcedon cannot be accepted as a *sine qua non*, for there are those who, with a long tradition to support them, question its terminology. It may also be that in the idea of the 'one-natured Christ', the 'wine

[1] *ibid.*
[2] *op. cit.*, p. 374.
[3] E. Philipos, *The Syrian Christians of Malabar* (1869), quoted in L. W. Brown, *op. cit.*, p. 292.
[4] V. C. Samuel, art. in IJT, XI/1 (1962).

mingled with water', there is a foreshadowing of a conception which is found fully developed in Chenchiah's theology of Christ as the 'new' factor, 'not mere hyphenated God-man' the *ādi-puruṣa* of the New Creation.[1]

The Indian Syrian tradition calls for much theological explication and scholarship, especially in the field of liturgy, and today there are many signs that this ancient Church is responding to the challenge, as in the work of the scholars we have mentioned. Our references to this tradition will be comparatively few, but it must never be forgotten that its presence is constantly felt, not only in the South but throughout India, in all the thousands of places where its adherents, distinguished or humble, are witnessing to their ancient yet ever-burning faith.

De Nobili

We have mentioned the beginning of full-scale missionary work in India by the Roman Catholics in the early 16th century. In 1542 the great Jesuit pioneer Francis Xavier arrived at Goa and worked energetically and successfully in India till 1552 when he left for China and his death. We need not here enlarge on the evangelistic methods used by him and his Portuguese Jesuit companions and followers. The pattern followed was that of close adherence to Roman Christianity as found in the West, accompanied, unfortunately, by the threat or use of the force of the Portuguese crown. The *Padroado* had laid down the Christianising of India as one of the aims of the imperial expansion, and so a link was early formed between evangelism and imperialism which was to do a great disservice to the work of the Church in India.

It was to such a westernised, un-Indian Church that Roberto De Nobili came as a young Jesuit missionary in 1605.[2] He immediately concluded that he could never come close to the people of India by living a European life, and so decided to act the role of a Christian *saṇyāsi* and to adopt the appropriate garb and style of living. He managed to find a Brāhman willing at the risk of his life to teach him Sanskrit, and so became the first European to master the language of the Hindu Scriptures. The idea that the study of the Vedas, which had hitherto been guarded jealously from the eyes of foreigners, should become 'the chief means of converting these people'. was a new and startling one. De Nobili hoped to master both the Vedas and

[1] *ādi-puruṣa*: original man.
[2] Vincent Cronin, *A Pearl to India: The Life of Robert De Nobili* (1959).

the Vedānta and so to use Indian philosophy and philosophical language as a vehicle for conveying Christian theological truth. Further reading and discussion with his Brāhman teacher convinced him that he could not base an apologetic directly on either the Vedas or the Vedānta, in the way in which Aquinas is based on Aristotle, yet his study helped him to make some very interesting literary attempts to present Christian theology in a form which would be intelligible to the Brāhmans of Madurai. He had become convinced that if the Church in India were to survive it must have its own clergy, educated as far as possible according to Indian traditions, and so made plans to open a Brāhman seminary with a five-year course in Christian philosophy:

> He wanted his future priests to present Christianity to the Indian people in their own languages, not in a jargon in which all religious terms were Portuguese; to be well trained in Christian theology but also experts in the religion of the Hindus around him; to depend for support and protection on their own countrymen, not on foreigners.[1]

The money for building the college was delayed, yet De Nobili never abandoned his scheme. He asked permission from Rome to take Sanskrit instead of Latin as the liturgical language for the new Indian Church. It is unlikely that such permission was given, but highly interesting that De Nobili should have made the suggestion.

De Nobili was not the first pioneer in Christian writing in Indian languages and true Indian style. That honour goes to a remarkable English Jesuit called Thomas Stephens who had arrived in Goa in 1579 and settled in the peninsula of Salsette, near the present city of Bombay.[2] Realising the hold that the popular vernacular *Purāṇas* had on the minds of the people he composed a Christian *Purāṇa*, a long poem narrating the stories of the Old and New Testaments, written in colloquial Marathi with an admixture of Konkani. With this example before him De Nobili composed a *Life of Our Lady* in Sanskrit verse, canticles for marriages and funerals, and a summary of Christian doctrine in a hundred Sanskrit *ślokas*. Even more important than these, perhaps, were his writings in Tamil, the most significant of which was the large catechism known as *Gnanopadesam* (Teaching of Knowledge), a summary of Christian doctrine

[1] Cronin, *op. cit.*, p. 168.
[2] *ibid.*, p. 174.

which he kept revising and enlarging until it grew to five volumes, 'a veritable *Summa Theologica* for the Indians'.[1] He also wrote various books for the edification of new Christians, such as *Gnana Sancheevi* (Spiritual Medicine), and a number of controversial books in which Hindu doctrines were discussed and refuted, the best known being *Punar-janma-ākshēpam* (Refutation of Rebirth).

De Nobili's methods of work were indigenous and highly original, and he is greatly to be commended for his study and use of Sanskrit and Tamil. We should not imagine, however, that his writings really represent an experiment in 'indigenous theology', using Hindu terminology for the exposition of Christian doctrine, for indeed his attitude to religious Hinduism is entirely negative, and he writes to refute. To give a single example, here is how he writes with regard to the practice of repeating the name of a god in order to obtain forgiveness of sin:

> This prescription for the removal of sin is from the Devil. He teaches them that repeating the name 'Siva' thrice will remove all the sins of the past and the present . . . [and that] repeating the names 'Rama' and 'Krishna', worshipping in their temples, taking bath in Kaveri, wearing sacred ash on the forehead, and *Rudraksha* around the neck will remove . . . sins.[2]

In a similar way he argues against and ridicules the doctrines of rebirth, *karma* and of the *avatāra* or divine incarnation, without making any attempt to give them a Christian reinterpretation.

His positive exposition of the Christian faith is equally conservative. For example, in one of his shorter catechisms, *Gnanopadesam Twentysix Pirasangangal*, he reproduces the Thomist arguments for the existence of God, devotes considerable attention to expounding a non-biblical Mariology and purgatory, and touches only slightly on the death of Christ. In other words, De Nobili's Sanskrit and Tamil works, interesting as they are as experiments in coining new words and phrases to replace the Latin theological vocabulary, in effect simply reproduce the current Tridentine theology and make no real attempt to use

[1] J. L. Miranda, *The Introduction of Christianity into the Heart of India or Father Roberto De Nobili's Mission*, Trichinopoly, 1923, p. 22. For this and for much of the information which follows I am indebted to D. Yesudhas, 'Indigenization or Adaptation? A Brief Study of Roberto De Nobili's Attitude to Hinduism', in *Bangalore Theological Forum*, Sept. 1967, pp. 39 ff.

[2] *Gnanopadesam Kurippidam*, p. 43.

Hindu terminology and thought-forms to express the Christian faith.

His achievement—and it was a great achievement—is to be seen in his understanding and adaptation of Hindu customs and ceremonies, in his pioneering study of Sanskrit and Tamil and in his initiation of the essential task of evolving a Christian theological vocabulary for Indian languages. For this contribution Indian Christian theology will always be indebted to him.

We shall limit ourselves to this brief mention of De Nobili as it is our intention to deal primarily with Indian, not missionary, theologians. For the same reason we shall merely mention in passing one who, coming to India 100 years after De Nobili, in 1710, attempted to restore De Nobili's work. This was Joseph Constantius Beschi, who wrote a famous Tamil epic on the life of Joseph, *Thembavani*, in which many Hindu theological conceptions are used as vehicles of Christian teaching.[1] After the work of these missionary pioneers the effort to use the language and ideas of the Vedas and the Vedānta as a direct means for conveying and expounding Christian doctrine was not seriously undertaken again by Christian theological writers until the time of the Christian *bhakti* poets of the 19th century.

The Protestant Tradition

By the early years of the 17th century a different kind of Christian 'presence' had begun to make itself felt in India through the arrival of the various western trading companies. Long before the arrival of Portuguese, French, Dutch or English, the Armenians had established their trading posts in such centres as Calcutta, Surat, Madras and Bombay, from where they carried on extensive trading by the overland route; and where they settled they brought their priests and built their churches. The East India Company, which had established its first 'factory' at Surat in 1608, waited fifty years before appointing a chaplain, and the responsibility of the chaplains who were eventually sent was limited to the care of the representatives of the Company.[2] The lives of many Europeans in India did little to commend their religion to the Indians who observed them, and when Protestant missions eventually began their work they had to overcome much

[1] D. Rajarigam, *The History of Tamil Christian Literature* (1958), p. 19 f.
[2] W. S. Birney, 'Early Anglican Worship in Hindustan, 1658-1672' in *Bulletin of the Church History Association of India*, Nov. 1966, p.3.

opposition whose roots could be traced to the unsavoury living and overbearing manner of those who were assumed to be Christians. The Company chaplains were not encouraged to preach the Gospel to Indians and it was not until 1813, when the Company's Charter was renewed, that a separate diocese was established in Calcutta and permission was given for missionaries, as distinct from chaplains, to work in the Company's territory. The tension in the Anglican Church between the chaplains, whose first duty was to the British community, and the missionaries who had come to proclaim the Gospel to the people of India, remained for many years.[1] For the British, as for the Portuguese, the official connection between the State and the Church did not assist the building up of a truly Indian Christian tradition.

The history of Protestant missions in India begins with the landing of the Lutheran missionaries Ziegenbalg and Plutschau at Tranquebar on 9th July 1706.[2] Ziegenbalg was a scholarly man and a firm believer in the basic principle of Protestant missions that first priority must be given to the translation of the Scriptures, and by 1711 he had completed the translation of the New Testament into Tamil. Although the Italian Jesuit Beschi mocked at Ziegenbalg's Tamil, there is no doubt that Ziegenbalg had his priorities right when he made this his first task. It was by no means his last, however, for he was unwearied in his researches into Hinduism and indeed caused some consternation at the mission's headquarters in Halle by his sympathetic account of Indian religion. In 1710 he wrote:

> I do not reject everything they teach, rather rejoice that for the heathen long ago a small light of the Gospel began to shine . . . One will find here and there such teachings and passages in their writings which are not only according to human reason but also according to God's Word.[3]

A new era in Protestant missionary work in India was inaugurated in 1793 by William Carey of Serampore, who, like Ziegenbalg, soon found himself grappling with the problems of Bible translation.[4] He and his colleagues eventually set up at Serampore what might almost be called a Bible factory with many different linguistic departments, and succeeded in translating

[1] M. E. Gibbs, 'The Anglican Church in India and Independence' in *Bulletin* of CHAI, Feb. 1967, pp. 45 ff.

[2] E. Arno Lehmann, *It Began at Tranquebar* (1956).

[3] *ibid.*, p. 31. v. infra p. 88.

[4] George Smith, *The Life of William Carey* (1885).

the Bible, in whole or part, into more than thirty languages. For many of the languages they thus established the basic vocabulary of Christian theology, though it is true that in some regions better translations by local missionaries almost immediately superseded the Serampore versions.

This work of establishing the biblical vocabulary is of the greatest importance in any language. But in India, where there is such a rich theological vocabulary ready to hand, it has never been simple to find clear and readily-understood terms to coincide with Hebrew and Greek words. Practically all the terms which would seem most natural to use have already got a meaning, fixed in relation to Hindu religion or philosophy. Some word must be chosen, however, and in the course of years it becomes familiar to Christian people, for whom it gradually acquires specific Christian overtones. The Christian community becomes familiar with and ultimately devoted to the language of the most familier translation, and any efforts to revise or modify this vocabulary are strongly resisted. But the words so used are by no means so clear and unambiguous to the Hindu who may read the Bible. He may find the language barbarous and uncouth, some of the terms quite unintelligible, and the significance of others may be only too clear to him, but not in the sense intended by the translator. To take an example, Dr. John Wilson, the famous Scottish missionary who arrived in Bombay in 1829, wrote an article in 1830 in which he argued strongly against the Christian use of the word *svarga* for heaven, on the grounds that its meaning is limited to the sensual heaven of Indra.[1] He suggested instead the use of the neutral word *devaloka* ('the abode of God'). It is, however, the word *svarga* which has in fact gained universal acceptance, while today there is a marked antipathy in Christian theological circles to the use of the word *deva* for God, as it is often used in the plural in Hinduism to denote gods and demons. It is still true, however, that the word *svarga*, when first read in the New Testament by a Hindu, may create a quite wrong impression.

Through the work of Carey and his many successors the Bible has become the treasured possession of Protestant Christians all over India, and these vernacular translations have been a primary instrument of evangelism. Yet the 'foreignness' of these translations has been held against them by non-Christians and has restricted their effectiveness. It has become one of the

[1] *Oriental Christian Spectator*, Nov. 1830. Wilson founded this journal within a year of his arrival in India!

tasks of Indian Christian theologians to provide a more effective biblical terminology, and the tendency in recent translation work has been to adopt a much more positive attitude to terms with a Hindu background.

Along with Bible translation and the daily preaching of the Gospel the early Protestant missionaries busied themselves with writing and printing, in the various Indian languages, pamphlets and books expounding Christian doctrine, refuting—often in very polemical fashion—the claims of Hinduism, and adducing the proofs of natural theology as 'evidences' of the truth of the Christian religion. Such publications, together with the preaching of the Word, the distribution of the Scriptures, and occasional set disputations with non-Christians such as those used by John Wilson in Bombay,[1] comprised the 'Christian theological approach to Hinduism' of the day.

A different type of missionary work, and one destined to bear much Christian fruit in its earlier stages, and to have a widespread if less obvious result over many years, was meantime being pioneered by Alexander Duff in Calcutta and Wilson in Bombay. Shortly after his arrival in Calcutta in 1830[2] Duff determined to develop higher education through the medium of English, thus coming down definitely on the English side in the famous Anglicist-Orientalist controversy of the time and anticipating the well-known Macaulay Minute of 1838. It was the hope of Duff and those who thought like him that secular education in English would prove an effective *praeparatio evangelica* by undermining the religious structure of Hinduism in the light of modern knowledge; and indeed in the early days in Calcutta there were some notable high-caste converts from Hinduism. But a counterbalance to the work of the missionaries, and of evangelically-minded Company chaplains like Henry Martyn and Claudius Buchanan, was provided by the simultaneous flood of rationalist literature which began to pour into India from an England where the Christian Church itself was torn by the struggle between Arians and Trinitarians. The final effect of these two opposed influences from the West tended to be the creation of admiration for the life and teaching of Jesus, accompanied by an attitude of rationalism and the rejection of dogmatic religion of any kind. The atmosphere of the early decades of the nineteenth century was however, especially in Bengal, one in which a definite encounter between the Christian and Hindu faiths

[1] E. G. K. Hewat, *Christ in Western India* (1950), pp. 77 ff.
[2] E. G. K. Hewat, *Vision and Achievement 1796-1956* (1960), pp. 67 ff.

could take place.[1] Strangely enough it is not to any Christian that we turn to find the pioneer of a line of theological enquiry and statement which has continued to develop until the present day, but rather to a famous Hindu who came into contact with the Serampore missionaries. His name was Ram Mohan Roy.

[1] For a good account of the background see K. Ingham, *Reformers in India, 1793-1833* (1956) ; and for the encounter itself, M. M. Thomas, *The Acknowledged Christ of the Indian Renaissance*, 1969.

Chapter III

THE GOSPEL AND THE INDIAN RENAISSANCE

Ram Mohan Roy (1772-1833)

Raja Ram Mohan Roy may be said to be the first Indian to have written seriously and extensively on Christian theological themes.[1] His is a name which is highly honoured in the history of India, for he was the pioneering Hindu social reformer without whose enthusiastic advocacy many reform measures, such as the abolition of *sati*, might have been long delayed. It is not without reason that he is sometimes called 'the Father of modern India'. His work merits careful consideration, for many of the theological attitudes which he outlined have become widely accepted in India.

He was a Bengali Brāhman who, finding no satisfaction at home for his religious longings, set off at the age of fifteen and wandered as far as Tibet. His early studies included Persian and Arabic and he became thoroughly familiar with the faith of Islam, which strongly influenced him in the direction of the unity of God and the meaninglessness of idol-worship. The turning point in his life came in 1811 when he was the unwilling witness of the *sati* of his brother's wife. This incident made him vow to devote his life to the overthrow of this and similar abuses. In this work the two chief sources of his inspiration were the *Upanishads* and the moral teaching of Christ. His study of his own Hindu scriptures deepened his conviction of the unity of God, while of Christianity he wrote:

> The consequence of long and uninterrupted researches into religious truth has been that I have found the doctrines of Christ more conducive to moral principles and more adapted for the use of rational beings than any other which have come to my knowledge.[2]

It was Christian ethics rather than Christian dogma which attracted Ram Mohan Roy, and he saw no reason why a compromise should not be possible between his own Hindu monism

[1] There is an extensive literature on Ram Mohan Roy. See Bibliography under M. C. Parekh; N. C. Ganguly. For a more comprehensive bibliography see Otto Wolff, *Christus unter den Hindus* (1965), pp. 15, 16. There is a general account in J. N. Farquhar, *Modern Religious Movements in India* (1918), pp. 30 ff. See also M. M. Thomas, *op. cit.*

[2] Farquhar, *op. cit.*, p. 32.

based on the *Upanishads*, and the morality of the Sermon on the Mount which so greatly attracted him. In a series of pamphlets he began openly to attack Hindu polytheism and Brāhmanical religion in general, and tried to rouse his fellow Hindus from their 'dream of error' so that they could contemplate 'the unity and omnipresence of nature's God'.

His study of Christianity led him to publish, in 1820, a book entitled *The Precepts of Jesus*. This is a collection of extracts from the four Gospels covering the greater part of the teaching of Jesus, and was primarily intended to enlist the Hindu intellectual in the cause of the moral reform of Hindu society. It is significant that of the 82 pages of extracts only the last four are devoted to the Fourth Gospel. The clear teaching of this Gospel on the unity of the Son with the Father did not appeal to Ram Mohan's unitarianism and it is interesting that he omits John 10 : 30, 'I and my Father are one', a verse which was destined to exercise a fascination for most later Hindu students of the New Testament. He gives a typical defence of his neglect of John :

> 'It is from this source that the most difficult to be comprehended of the dogmas of the Christian religion have been principally drawn'. Here 'is erected the mysterious doctrine of three Gods in one Godhead, the origin of Mohummedanism, and the stumbling-block to the conversion of the more enlightened among the Hindoos.'[1]

Some contemporary Christians no doubt saw in this book the beginning of a change for the better in the Hindu attitude towards Christianity, but the Serampore missionaries thought otherwise and in the pages of their journal *The Friend of India* a controversy with Ram Mohan developed, to which he replied in a series of *Appeals to the Christian Public*.[2] The missionary attack concentrated on showing that Christianity is not just a religion of monotheism and morals, but that at its centre lies faith in Jesus Christ as divine, and in his work of atonement. In his first *Appeal*, in reply to these attacks, Ram Mohan Roy gave his reasons for separating the teaching of Jesus from Christian theology, while in the second and third appeals he carried the argument further, asking whether indeed the characteristic doctrines of Christianity—the Trinity and the atonement—have Scriptural warrant.

[1] *An Appeal to the Christian Public in Defence of 'The Precepts of Jesus'* by A Friend to Truth (Calcutta, 1820), p. 22.

[2] *Second Appeal* (1821), printed by the Baptist Mission Press, Calcutta. *Final Appeal* (1824). The Mission Press refused to print this. For an account of the controversy, see Thomas, *op. cit.*, pp. 1-38.

At this time Ram Mohan Roy was in touch with Unitarians in England and America, and succeeded in winning to his side one of the Serampore missionaries, William Adam. Indeed much of his theological writing is reminiscent of that of rationalists and unitarians in the West at that time, and has little that is specially Indian about it. He rejects ' revealed ' doctrines such as those of the Trinity and the two natures of Christ, and is interested rather to maintain the position of natu ral theology. God is for him the Absolute and so any kind of personal knowledge of Him is ruled out. A letter to his American friend Henry Ware makes his general position very clear:

> Nothing can be a more acceptable homage or a better tribute to reason than an attempt to root out the idea that the Omnipresent Deity should be generated in the womb of a female, and live in a state of subjugation for several years, and lastly offer his blood to another person of the Godhead, whose anger could not be appeased except by the sacrifice of a portion of himself in human form. So no service could be more advantageous to mankind than an endeavour to withdraw them from the belief that an imaginary faith, ritual and observances, or outward marks independently of good works can cleanse men from the stain of past sins and secure their eternal salvation.[1]

The words ' independently of good works ' show Ram Mohan's concentration on ethics to the exclusion of anything savouring of dogmatism, ritual or even faith as distinct from works.

In 1815 Ram Mohan had established a society called the *Ātmiya Sabhā* (Spiritual Association) for the propagation of his religious views. Then in 1821 a ' Unitarian Mission ' was formed with William Adam, with services in English. This proved unsuccessful, so in 1828 a more distinctly Indian society was formed, called at first the *Brāhma Sabhā* and eventually the *Brāhma Samāj*, a society which was destined to play an important part in the reform of Hinduism, first under its founder and later under Keshab Chandra Sen.

The religious services of the early Brāhma Samāj included the reading of passages from the Upanishads and the singing of specially composed theistic hymns in Sanskrit and Bengali. The word *Brāhman*, which signifies the Supreme Being of the Vedānta philosophy, is used for God, and the trust deed of the Samāj's place of worship, opened in 1830, makes clear the conception which Ram Mohan had in mind. The building must be used

[1] *English Works of Raja Rammohun Roy*, Pt. IV, Calcutta, 1947, p. 44, in 'A Letter on the Prospects of Christianity'.

for the worship and adoration of the Eternal Unsearchable and Immutable Being who is the Author and Preserver of the Universe but not under or by any other name, designation or title peculiarly used for and applied to any particular Being or Beings by any man or set of men whatever.[1]

Ram Mohan Roy sailed for England in 1830 on a visit which brought him great fame and popularity. He hoped to return to India for further service of his people but died in Bristol in 1833. His name is revered in India as a great patriot and pioneer of social reform.

* * * *

We shall now turn to a brief consideration of his treatment of four of the fundamental Christian doctrines, for many of the attitudes which he adopted have become very familiar in India, and are still influential in Hindu-Christian relations.

The Person of Christ

Ram Mohan's attitude to Christ is one of reverence, as for a great teacher and 'messenger' of God, but he denies that the title 'Son of God' attributes divinity and writes:

> The epithet 'Son' found in the passage 'Baptizing them in the name of the Father, and of the Son, etc.' ought to be understood and admitted by everyone as expressing the created nature of Christ, though the most highly exalted of all creatures.

It is clear that Ram Mohan is here taking up an Arian position, which is not surprising in view of his monistic background, his Islamic studies, and his association with western unitarianism, and that too at a time when the Arian controversy was at its height in England, Ireland and elsewhere. He quotes many scriptural passages to prove what he calls 'the natural inferiority of the Son to the Father'[2] and holds that Jesus is merely delegated with power from God, but does not possess this power intrinsically. The unity with the Father implied in certain Johannine texts is merely 'a subsisting concord of will and design, such as existed among his Apostles, and not identity of being[3]'. He does indeed accept the title 'Son of God' and other scriptural titles of Christ, but always in a qualified sense, implying that each one is a special gift conferred by God, rather than his by right. Jesus is

[1] Farquhar, *op. cit.*, p. 35.
[2] *Second Appeal*, p. 12.
[3] *ibid.*, p. 19.

the 'Son of God', a term synonymous with that of Messiah, the highest of all the prophets; and his life declares him to have been, as represented in the Scriptures, pure as light, innocent as a lamb, necessary for eternal life as bread for a temporal one, and great as the angels of God, or rather greater than they.[1]

Strangely enough Ram Mohan accepts the doctrine of the Virgin Birth, though taking care to divorce it from any belief in the personality of the Holy Spirit as that would, he felt, involve 'the Godhead's having had intercourse with a human female'[2]. In line with this, he does not deny the miracles of Christ, even the resurrection, but insists that they are unimportant, and points out that in India, where so many other miracles are believed, they carry little weight in Christian apologetic.

His argument for the rejection of the belief that Christ's nature is divine as well as human reveals the common Hindu (as well as gnostic) conception that God can have no direct connection with matter:

> Were anyone to insist that the term 'God' applied to Jesus should be taken in its literal sense, and that consequently Jesus should be actually considered God in the human shape, he would not only acknowledge the same intimate connection of matter with God that exists between matter and the human soul, but would also necessarily justify the application of such phrases as 'Mother of God' to the Virgin Mary.[3]

The implication is that either of these conceptions would be totally unacceptable to those Hindus whom one might hope to convince of the divinity of Christ.

The Work of Christ

The saving work of Christ, Ram Mohan Roy believed, is accomplished through his teaching, and his death is simply the supreme illustration of those precepts whose communication was 'the sole object of his mission'[4]. The ideas of vicarious suffering and of sacrificial death are rejected, and Ram Mohan uses his arguments simultaneously to attack the doctrine of the two natures. God for him is impassible, so that if Jesus suffered in his divine nature this would be highly inconsistent with the nature of God, which is 'above being rendered liable to death

[1] *ibid.*, p. 69. The qualifications on light, lamb, bread will be noticed!
[2] *ibid.*, p. 88.
[3] *ibid.*, p. 110.
[4] *ibid.*, p. 58.

or pain '. If on the other hand Jesus suffered vicariously in his human nature, the innocent for the guilty, this is in turn inconsistent with the justice of God. Jesus did indeed suffer, innocent as a lamb, that ' symbol of innocence subjected to persecution '[1], but Ram Mohan considers unscriptural the attempt ' to represent human blood, or that of God in human form, as an indispensable atonement for sin '.

The plan of salvation is for him a very simple one. ' This do and thou shalt live ', said Jesus, and the following of his precepts is ' the best and only means of obtaining the forgiveness of our sins, the favour of God, and strength to overcome our passions and to keep his commandments.'[2]. If we repent we receive forgiveness and there is no need for an atoning death, though we are greatly helped by the supreme example of the Cross. Jesus, he writes,

> exposed his own life for the benefit of his subjects, purged their sins by his doctrines, and persevered in executing the commands of God even to the undergoing of bodily suffering in the miserable death of the Cross, a self-devotion or sacrifice of which no Jewish high-priest had ever offered an example.[3]

If we fail to follow Jesus' teaching—as we inevitably shall—the solution lies in repentance, which is ' the most acceptable atonement on our part to the All-merciful, when we have fallen short of that duty '. This is the nearest that he approaches to a doctrine of repentance, faith, grace and forgiveness.

The Holy Spirit

As a unitarian Ram Mohan Roy is unable to accept the Holy Spirit as a Person of the Godhead, or as possessing personality or deity at all, and he devotes a chapter of the second *Appeal* to ' The Impersonality of the Holy Spirit '. The Spirit represent for him the holy influence and power of God but he denies any self-existent or distinct personality. The Spirit is that influence of God from which we may expect direction in the path of righteousness.[4] It is the power of God through which Mary conceived the child Jesus. But this Spirit is not to be thought of under any particular form:

> If we believe that the Spirit, in the form of a dove, or in any other *bodily shape*, was really the third person of the Godhead, how

[1] *ibid.*, p. 68.
[2] *First Appeal*, p. 10.
[3] M. C. Parekh, *Rajarshi Ram Mohan Roy* (1927), p. 88.
[4] *Second Appeal*, p. 86.

> can we justly charge with absurdity the Hindoo legends of the divinity having the form of a fish or any other animal ?[1]

Ram Mohan's programme of reform required just such a charge against the legends of Hinduism.

The Trinity

Throughout his active life Ram Mohan Roy regarded 'the Trinitarians' as his opponents, though we are told that when he visited England in 1830 and compared the spiritual life of Unitarian and Trinitarian Churches he felt somewhat inclined to change his mind.[2] Much of his life had been devoted to a polemic against Hindu polytheism and idolatry, and he felt that to include Christ and the Spirit as 'Persons' in the one Godhead was a reversion to something primitive, a yielding to the polytheistic trends of the Greece and Rome of the early centuries as against the clear monotheism of Judaism, of which he had made a careful study.

God, then, is the sole object of worship. Jesus may in a certain limited sense be regarded as Son of God or Mediator, the messenger who explains the will of God, while the Spirit is the influence of God. Those who accept the Christian revelation should, he says,

> profess their belief in God as the sole object of worship, and in the Son through whom they, as Christians, should offer divine homage, and also in the holy influence of God, from which they should expect direction in the path of righteousness.[3]

The words 'as Christians' here are significant, as they imply that Ram Mohan believed that Christ was a worthy channel for Christians to use in their approach to God, but that there might be other channels for those brought up in other traditions.

Before the time of Ram Mohan Roy there had been objectors to the work of the Christian missionaries. But he is the first to raise serious theological objections, and in the process to propose his own version of Christianity, on the basis of a rationalist and monist interpretation of the biblical evidence. He would have liked to make Christianity into a unitarianism with strong emphasis on the ethical teaching of Jesus. It is an ideal which has continued to be held by many until the present day, for William

[1] *ibid.*, p. 90.
[2] Parekh, *op. cit.*, p. 169.
[3] *Second Appeal*, p. 85.

Adam was not the last to be attracted to a Hindu interpretation of Christianity. Nevertheless the testimony of C. F. Andrews should not be forgotten, that some leading Bengali Christians acknowledged that they owed the beginnings of their faith in Christ to the study of *The Precepts of Jesus*.[1]

Keshab Chandra Sen (1838-1884)

Ram Mohan Roy died in 1833 and for some years the Samāj was without a leader of outstanding calibre. Then there emerged Debendranath Tagore (1817-1905), father of the poet Rabindranath Tagore. From the point of view of the dialogue with Christianity, however, the next great leader was Keshab Chandra Sen, whose work we must now consider.[2]

Sen was a man of spiritual fervour and great oratorical powers who joined the Brāhma Samāj in 1857 at the age of nineteen. He developed a great enthusiasm for the life of Christ, so much so that many missionaries expected that he would seek Christian baptism and regarded him as an influence of the greatest importance on the side of Christianity, while many Hindus thought that he had in fact gone over. This impression was no doubt created by his attack on the caste-system, which Ram Mohan Roy had never deserted, and by his manifest and steadily growing interest in the Person of Christ.

The Brāhma Samāj as organised by Sen was very much on the lines of a Christian Church, and indeed after the passing of the Brāhmo Marriage Act in 1872 the Samāj stepped right outside the pale of Hindu society. At the same time Sen's thought and practice tended to develop more and more along the lines of his own inspiration (*ādeśa*) and this inspiration, moulded especially by the warm emotional *bhakti* of the medieval Bengali saint Caitanya, gradually took the place of the principle of rationalism so beloved of Ram Mohan Roy. Step by step also, following his private interpretation of Christianity and the light of his own genius, Sen introduced ritual practices into the Samāj. Ram Mohan Roy had been strongly opposed to ritualism or anything savouring of sacrifice in the worship of the Samāj, yet Sen in his later ' Church of the New Dispensation ' developed a system of asceticism, rituals and sacraments, including baptism

[1] C. F. Andrews, *The Renaissance in India* (1912), p. 113.

[2] P. C. Mozoomdar, *The Life and Teachings of Keshub Chunder Sen* (1887). M. C. Parekh, *Brahmarshi Keshub Chunder Sen* (1926). Farquhar, *op. cit.*, pp. 41-73. Sen's chief theological publications in English are included in *Keshub Chunder Sen's Lectures in India* (London, 1904). (Cited as *Lectures*).

and a form of communion, in which the elements were rice and water. It can be seen from these developments that his outlook became progessively more and more self-centred, though he never set himself on a level with Christ, as J. N. Farquhar has suggested in an unguarded paragraph.[1] He did, however, come to see himself and his fellow ' apostles of the New Dispensation ' as being in a line of succession which stretched through Moses, Christ and Paul, and his Church was the third ' dispensation ', which fulfilled and transcended those of the Old Testament and the New. He died in 1884 at the early age of forty-six.

Sen was a controversial figure in his own time. Many Hindus regarded him as a Christian, while most Christians—partly because of his constant criticism of the Church—thought of him as a mere eclectic. Yet despite all the inconsistencies of his thought he is a key figure in the development of Indian Christian theology and his writings deserve to be treated with the greatest respect and seriousness. Here was a man, regarded by many as the greatest Indian of his time, who came more and more under the spell of Christ and responded to him in his own way. The western trappings of the organised Christianity of his day alienated him and yet beyond the externals he could see a vision of Christ himself, and the story of his life is the story of a pilgrimage with Christ in the course of which he gradually came closer to orthodox Christianity. Christ became the centre of his life and the guiding force in all his thinking, yet he steadfastly refused to allow that thinking to be forced into a western mould. It is an undeniable fact that many of the conceptions and categories which have become familiar in the writings of later Indian theologians were first stated by Sen, who yet would never acknowledge the name of ' Christian '.

There is something tremendously attractive and touching about Sen. He is the pattern of the Hindu seeker, of one who has found the pearl of great price but is reluctant to sell all that he has in order to buy it. There is no denying the reality of his experience of Christ and the genuineness of his effort to express his experience and his knowledge in terms of his own well-loved Indian tradition. For an understanding of the way in which Indian thinkers have responded to Christ and sought to interpret their experience it is essential to be familiar with the approach of Keshab Chandra Sen, and we shall look at his treatment of some of the leading issues, as he dealt with them in his famous series of annual lectures to the Samāj.

[1] Farquhar, *op. cit.*, p. 64. Parekh corrects Farquhar's error; Parekh, *op. cit.*, pp. vii ff.

Christ the Logos

Christ was the centre of Sen's religious experience, yet his spiritual pilgrimage had begun from the Brāhma Samāj, whose God was the undifferentiated Absolute *Brahman*, and from time to time he retains this title. But just as the advaitins had never hesitated to describe even *Brahman* as *Sat*, *Cit*, *Ānanda* (being, intelligence, bliss), so for Sen God is always triune, and he moves away from Ram Mohan Roy's unitarianism. 'I have seen and felt God in his triune nature', he writes, claiming that his personal experience of God is of the Trinity.[1] Later we shall consider in more detail his conception of the Trinity as *Sat*, *Cit*, *Ānanda*, but first let us look at his striking picture of the creation where, in language reminiscent of the Chandogya Upanishad, he shows the work of Christ as the pre-existent Logos:

> Here the Supreme Brahma of the Veda and the Vedanta dwells hid in himself. Here sleeps mighty Jehovah, with might yet unmanifested . . . But anon the scene changes. Lo! a voice is heard . . . Yes it was the Word that created the universe. They call it Logos . . . What was the creation but the wisdom of God going out of its secret chambers and taking a visible shape, His potential energy asserting itself in unending activities?[2]

With the act of creation there commences an ongoing process of creative evolution whose agent is still the Logos and which continues through and beyond the evolution of man. And as the Logos is at the beginning, so at the end of the process stands the Logos, through whom all men are called to rise to the stature of sonship:

> The Logos was the beginning of creation, and its perfection too was the Logos,—the culmination of humanity is the Divine Son . . . But is the process of evolution really over? . . . If sonship there was, it was bound to develop itself not in one solitary individual but in all humanity. Surely universal redemption is the purpose of creation.[3]

The Logos, then, who in eternity lay as it were asleep in God, is the Word of Creation, *Cit* (intelligence, wisdom), ever at work in the development of the created world, and in the fulness of time being born as man in Jesus of Nazareth.

[1] *Lectures* II, p. 10. Lecture on *That Marvellous Mystery—The Trinity* (1882).

[2] *ibid.*, p. 11. Cf. *Chand. Up.* 6. 2. v. infra p. 74.

[3] *ibid.*, p. 14.

What is the relation to humanity of this eternal Logos, this *Cit*-Christ? In the first of his series of annual public lectures, *Jesus Christ : Europe and Asia*, delivered in 1866, Sen has a good deal to say about the humanity of Jesus. He calls him 'the Son of a humble carpenter' and speaks of his growth as human rather than divine, though he was 'above ordinary humanity' and had 'almost superhuman wisdom and energy'[1]. In another passage he uses the words 'Christ was a man', but this humanity is immediately qualified by the adjective 'divine'[2]. So *divine humanity* becomes the category which for Sen best describes the nature of Christ. In a remarkable passage which foreshadows some of the theological developments of the next 90 years he expounds the nature of Christ's divinity in a form of the kenotic theory, taking as his starting point that *locus classicus* of Indian Christian theologians, 'I and my Father are one', a text which he regards as the corner-stone of Jesus' thought about himself:[3]

> When I come to analyze this doctrine I find in it nothing but the philosophical principle underlying the popular doctrine of self-abnegation . . . Christ ignored and denied his self altogether . . . He destroyed self. And as self ebbed away, Heaven came pouring into the soul. For . . . nature abhors a vacuum, and hence as soon as the soul is emptied of self, Divinity fills the void. So it was with Christ. The Spirit of the Lord filled him, and everything was thus divine within him.[4]

Jesus, then, by his utter abandonment of self, by his *kenosis*, by living only as 'the Man for others'—to anticipate Bonhöffer's phrase—becomes filled with God. Sen goes on to use another concept which has recently become popular once more—that of transparency. Jesus, he writes,

> manifested this divine life in man as no other man had ever done before. There is Christ before us as a transparent crystal reservoir in which are the waters of divine life. There is no opaque self to obscure our vision. The medium is transparent, and we clearly see through Christ the God of truth and holiness dwelling in him.[5]

[1] *Lectures* I, p. 8.
[2] *Lectures* II, p. 25.
[3] *Lectures* I, p. 369. Lecture on *India asks : Who is Christ?* (1879)
[4] *ibid.*
[5] *ibid.*, p. 373. Compare J. A. T. Robinson, *Honest to God* (1963), p. 73: 'Jesus reveals God by being utterly transparent to him, precisely as he is nothing "in himself".'

Clearly Sen believes that Christ's union with the Father is not a material or metaphysical one but rather one of deep communion, a mystical rather than an ontological union, and indeed he goes on to compare this relationship to that of the believer with Christ, thus blazing a trail that was to be followed by many later theologians. Jesus, he feels, sought to extend to others that spiritual oneness which he had with the Father: 'As Thou, Father, art in me, that they also may be one in us'. Christ's fundamental theology, he affirms, can be summed up in two phrases, 'I in my Father' and 'You in me'. It is no accident that these phrases are the New Testament's closest approximation to some of the *mahāvākyas* of the Vedanta—*tat tvam asi* ('Thou art that') and *aham Brahma āsmi* ('I am *Brāhman*'). Here we can see a pioneer Indian theologian wrestling to express the meaning of Christ's dual relationship to God and to man in terms which will be intelligible to his Hindu friends.

Sen's close friend and disciple P. C. Mozoomdar wrote a book with the title *The Oriental Christ*.[1] This book is an elaboration of one of Sen's most typical insights, the fact that Christ is of Asia, not of the West. Despite the ancient Syrian tradition in South India most of Sen's contemporaries thought of Christianity as a religion of the West, closely associated with European imperial power. Sen never tires of pointing out that not only Christianity but all the main religions of the world are oriental in origin, and that in many ways it is easier for an Asian than a European to understand the life and teaching and character of Jesus. 'And was not Christ an Asiatic?' he asks.[2] The West, he feels, has reduced Christianity to a series of 'lifeless dogmas and antiquated symbols', while the East realises that what is needed is a living encounter with the living Christ, whose very humanity is guaranteed, as it were, by his Asian-ness. In an illuminating phrase he writes, 'How Mary-like was Jesus' Jesus too, like his mother, is of the East.

The Work of Christ

Sen's writings on the work of Christ show a considerable development of thought as the years go by, always in the direction of fuller Christian orthodoxy. Beginning from his special interpretation of the kenotic theory—that Christ by self-forgetfulness and self-denial emptied himself of 'self' to the point where 'divinity filled the void'—he stresses the force of Christ's

[1] Boston, 1898.
[2] *Lectures* I, p. 33.

moral example and influence, yet in his later lectures he has quite a lot to say specifically about such topics as atonement, sacrifice and the Cross. We shall attempt to look briefly at one or two of his emphases.

In his earlier utterances Sen regards Christ's work as an example of moral influence. In a phrase strangely prophetic of Barth he speaks of Christ as 'the Journeying God' who, according to the divine plan, sets out from his Father, 'the Still God', to bring salvation to men. He comes, and in his love for the men of the far country he destroys self, denying himself in taking the form of a servant and so becoming transparent to God. He gives a living demonstration of the two fundamental Christian principles of forgiveness and self-sacrifice and through the moral influence of this self-sacrificing love accomplishes his work for mankind in an act of 'supernatural moral heroism'. Sen writes:

> I have always regarded the Cross as a beautiful emblem of self-sacrifice unto the glory of God . . . The vast moral influence of [Christ's] life and death still lives in human society.[1]

The conclusion which he draws from this is that we too, in imitation of the wonderful example of Christ, should sacrifice ourselves for the good of our country and of the world, and so find regeneration and sanctification. Through Christ, 'as through a brother's example, fallen humanity rises sanctified and regenerated'[2].

There is a link in Sen's thought between Christ's nature as 'divine humanity' and his work of inspiring men by his example of loving self-abnegation. Christ through his *kenosis* has become transparent to the divine, and through him—by the power of the Spirit—our humanity can be exalted and changed into the pattern of his:

> In him we see human nature perfected by true affiliation to the Divine Nature . . . He shows us not how God can become man nor how man can become God, but how we can exalt our humanity by making it more and more divine.[3]

Sen is very conscious of the fact that the salvation offered in Christ, this exalted and changed humanity, is not just for individuals but for all men, for the whole creation. Christ the

[1] *Lectures* I, p. 7.
[2] *Lectures* II, p. 27. (1882).
[3] *ibid.*, p. 20.

journeying God has come to earth in order that through him and through his obedience all men might realise their sonship. At this stage in his development Sen is interested chiefly in universal or cosmic rather than in individual salvation, and his exposition of the process by which men come to share in Christ's work is most interesting, providing as it does a foretaste of an argument which was to be elaborated in a Hindu setting by Sri Aurobindo, and in Christian terms by P. Chenchiah in India and Teilhard de Chardin in Europe. Right from the time of creation God's plan is that men should become like Christ, and through the coming of Christ into the world this 'Christification', in Teilhard's phrase, has become possible even for sinful men. Sen writes:

> The problem of creation was not how to produce one Christ, but how to make every man Christ. Christ was only a means, not the end. He was the 'way'.[1]

The process of Christification appears to have been for Sen a sort of automatic evolution. Christ himself represents the finished product of this evolutionary process, but through the power of the Spirit men too are given the possibility of becoming like him, and so evolving to a divinely human nature in conformity with God's original purpose:

> The Father continually manifests His wisdom and mercy in creation, till [men] take the form of pure Sonship in Christ, and then out of one little seed-Christ is evolved a whole harvest of endless and ever-multiplying Christs.[2]

It is not easy to understand precisely what Sen's meaning is here. Is he implying, as is implied by later writers like Chenchiah or Dhanjibhai Fakirbhai, that Christ is the 'new Man' and that we are called to be 'new men' in him by a process of mystical union which may be described as 'reproduction' (Chenchiah) or 'multiplication' (Dhanjibhai)? Or is he rather restating the Vedantic *mahāvākya* 'I am *Brāhman*' (*aham Brahma āsmi*)? It is difficult to be sure, but at least it is clear that Sen sees the process as one of evolution and growth, and that it is by the power of the Spirit that our lives can be so conformed to Christ and transformed.

In his last great lecture, delivered in 1883, Sen moves beyond these two conceptions of moral influence and 'multiplication' to a position much closer to orthodox theories of atonement and

[1] *ibid.*, p. 15.
[2] *ibid.*, p. 16.

mediation, and though recognising the reluctance of his predominantly Hindu audience to accept such terms as atonement, substitution and even blood, he uses and expounds them. Jesus is 'the atoning medium', the one who brings God and man together so that they may be 'at one'. In exercising this atonement Christ can also be described as Mediator, though one receives the impression that the work of mediation is more a corollary of his divinely human nature than the result of any one particular mediatorial act. Christ is a 'mediating link between man and God'.[1] In a rather strange illustration he describes those Benares boxes where each box as it is opened is found to contain another, and so on in a long series. So too, he says, as man seeks to reach God he has to pass from his own humanity to the 'invisible supreme essence', and this is only possible through Christ, who thus performs 'a necessary logical mediation'.[2] We cannot reach the Godhead 'except through that pure Sonship which environs and encloses it. . . . In this sense Christ is our Mediator.'[3]

Here we see a certain reluctance to deal with the significance of the death of Christ as distinct from his nature, but this reluctance is finally overcome and we find some moving passages explaining the suffering of Christ in relation to the removal of the sin of the world, in which the orthodox language of substitution is used:

> [Christ] substituted himself for the world, and at once heaven and earth, hitherto two, became one. The substitution is a grand fact. Its moral grandeur who can comprehend? . . . Believe in this substitution, and we are all one in Christ. . . . In his atoning blood the most polluted of all ages and climes find a place. . . . Behold, I am reconciled to all through the blood of him crucified. Fellow-countrymen, be ye also reconciled through him.[4]

It is difficult not to be moved by these words, one of Sen's last public utterances, in which he appeals to all his fellow-countrymen, of whatever religion, to accept by faith Christ's death and the atonement it brings for those who receive it. We can see here how, with his deep personal experience of love for Christ, he is trying to move forward from a mere theory of moral influence, and finally finds his way closer and closer to an

[1] *ibid.*, p. 35.
[2] *ibid.*, p. 34. Compare the Hindu psychology of the five 'sheaths' (*koša*), v. infra p. 79.
[3] *ibid.*, p. 35.
[4] *ibid.*, pp. 91-94

orthodox view of the atonement. We can see why Brahmabandhab Upādhyāya believed that Sen, had he lived longer, would have joined the visible Church.

The Doctrine of the Trinity

Like Ram Mohan Roy, Sen had many contacts with western unitarians; yet we find that his thought moves steadily in the direction of full acceptance of the doctrine of the Trinity. His final position is expressed with great power in a lecture which he gave in 1882 entitled *That Marvellous Mystery—the Trinity*. Sen seems to have been the first thinker to expound the meaning of the Trinity in relation to the famous definition of *Brahman* as *Saccidānanda* (*Sat*, *Cit*, *Ānanda*), and in so doing he began a tradition which has been followed by such later thinkers as Brahmabandhab and Monchanin. He expounds his understanding of the conception under the figure of an equilateral triangle. The apex, he writes,

> is the very God Jehovah, the Supreme Brahma of the Vedas. From Him comes down the Son in a direct line, an emanation from Divinity. Thus God descends and touches one end of the base of humanity, then running all along the base permeates the world, and then by the power of the Holy Ghost drags up regenerated humanity to Himself. Divinity coming down to humanity is the Son; Divinity carrying up humanity to heaven is the Holy Ghost. This is the whole Philosophy of Salvation.[1]

Following this description of the work of the different Persons of the Trinity he gives a sort of table of equivalents or parallels, beginning with the Christian Trinity and ending with *Saccidānanda*:

Father	Son	Holy Spirit
The Creator	The Exemplar	The Sanctifier
The still God	The journeying God	The returning God
'I am'	'I love'	'I save'
Force	Wisdom	Holiness
True	Good	Beautiful
Sat (Truth)	*Cit* (Intelligence)	*Ānanda* (Joy)

His explanation of this correspondence between *Saccidānanda* and the Trinity is interesting:

[1] *ibid.*, p. 16.

The Trinity of Christian Theology corresponds strikingly with the Sachidananda of Hinduism. You have three conditions, three manifestations of Divinity. Yet there is one God, one Substance and three phenomena. Not three Gods but one God. Whether alone, or manifest in the Son, or quickening humanity as the Holy Spirit, it is the same God, the same identical Deity, whose unity continues indivisible amid multiplicity of manifestations . . . Who can deny that there is an essential and undivided unity in the so-called Trinity? Were I to contemplate the mystery of that marvel of Christianity, the Trinity, in solitary communion, I would close my eyes and, lost in wonder, rapt in solemn silence, I would point my finger thus,—Above, Below, Within; The Father, above, The Son below, The Holy Ghost within.[1]

We can detect a tendency towards modalism here, in the words 'conditions' and 'manifestations', as well as a reluctance to accept the Chalcedonian conception of three Persons in one God. But Sen had all the Brahma Samāj's antipathy to polytheism and the Christian formula must have appeared to him as verging on tritheism, for that is the implication when one uses the word 'Person' in its normal English sense—which is the natural thing for any Indian thinker to do—or when one attempts to use the various Sanskritic translations which have been suggested, such as *vyakti* or *puruṣa*. Sen is perhaps here feeling his way towards a completely new and fully Indian formulation of the mystery, in terms of *Sat*, *Cit*, *Ānanda*. And it may be that the road here marked out by him and later followed by others will prove more effective for the Christian mission in India than concepts derived from Greek philosophy, the Roman theatre or even from modern western personalism.

The Church

Sen's 'Church of the New Dispensation' has already been mentioned. Despite his great personal devotion to Christ he never felt himself attracted towards the Christian Church as he saw it in India, or on his visit to England in 1870. Indian Christians seemed to him to be denationalised and isolated not only from the Hindu religion but from Indian culture. He felt it impossible to join such a church and besides he was already a member and indeed an *ācārya* in the Brahma Samāj. Nevertheless his interest in Christianity and his devotion to Christ led him to incorporate into his branch of the Samāj many features

[1] *ibid.*, p. 17.

taken from the life of the Christian Church, and ultimately these became a normal part of the life and practice of the body which he named 'the Church of the New Dispensation'.

Sen thought of his Church as the ultimate development of religion. For many people in India, as for Dr. Radhakrishnan today, the establishment of a 'world religion' has been a cherished ideal, and Sen in his effervescent enthusiasm attempted to found just such a religion which, though modelled chiefly on the Christian Church and explicitly centred on Christ, yet claimed for itself the best of all the great religions, as is shown by its emblem which included the Cross of Christ, the trident of Siva and the Muslim star and crescent. He regards the New Dispensation as intimately connected with the Holy Spirit, as it were the end-product of the process of spiritual evolution which the Spirit has been inspiring ever since the creation. He writes:

> Behold the beauty of this chain of logical sequence from Adam to Christ and from Christ down to the modern times. Now all prophets and reformers, all Scriptures and dispensations are linked together in the unity of a vast synthesis. . . . Bring into a focus these scattered dispensations, and you will at once find their harmony in science, their unity in truth and God.[1]

Sen's eclecticism cannot be disguised but he himself makes it clear that it is what he calls 'Christian eclecticism', in which Christ himself becomes the touchstone by which every doctrine or practice must be tested:

> All that dishonours Christ it disclaims. Whatsoever is Christian and pure and holy my Church rejoicingly glorifies. . . . I do firmly believe that whatsoever is true and good and beautiful is of Christ. . . . Nay, I would go further, and declare Christ to be the Centre of this Broad Church.[2]

Before criticising these sentiments we should remember that Sen is not writing 'Indian Christian theology'. He is speaking before a great concourse of people, most of whom are Hindus. His Church should not be thought of simply as a piece of practical syncretism, for in fact it kept developing more and more in the direction of Christian orthodoxy, to the great alarm of his Hindu and Brahmo friends. It should rather be regarded as the effort of a highly gifted man to interpret the nature of the Church in a way that made sense to people with a Hindu cultural

[1] *The Brahmo Samāj*, Calcutta, 1886, pp. 363-5.
[2] *Lectures* II, pp. 85-6.

background. Here once again Sen touches on a point which is crucial for the development of Indian theology, for many of those who came after him, baptised though they were in the Christian Church, have eventually taken up a position very remote from its actual corporate life. The list includes such distinguished names as Brahmabandhab Upādhyāya, Sādhu Sundar Singh, V. Chakkarai, P. Chenchiah, and Manilāl C. Parekh. Sen, in his typically enthusiastic way, rather than simply criticising the organised Church as he found it, tried to turn the Brahma Samāj into a Christian church. It is not surprising that he failed and that today comparatively little trace remains of the Church of the New Dispensation, yet the experiment is not without theological interest, both as an illustration of the response of a great Hindu who was 'gripped by Christ'[1] and also as a demonstration of some of the factors which make it difficult for a Hindu to accept the Christian Church as it is found in India.

The Hidden Christ

While Sen was highly critical of many aspects of Hinduism, and especially of polytheism, he had a deep affection for the faith in which he had grown up and constantly sought to relate Christianity and Hinduism in a meaningful way. He is not unaware either of the lofty ethical monotheism of Judaism and the activist tradition of Islam. Christ, he was sure, had come to fulfil all that was best in all of these faiths, to fulfil the Hindu dispensation as well as the Mosaic. Years before J. N. Farquhar gave expression to the concept of fulfilment Sen writes:

> Behold Christ cometh to us as an Asiatic in race, as a Hindu in faith, as a kinsman and a brother, and he demands your heart's affection. . . . He comes to fulfil and perfect that religion of communion for which India has been panting, as the hart panteth after the waterbrooks. . . . For Christ is a true Yogi, and he will surely help us to realise our national ideal of a Yogi.[2]

And so he asks his Hindu friends to turn to the Christ who is already with them, the Christ who is hidden in their Hindu faith, using words which give clear expression to the thesis which has recently been restated with great cogency by Raymond Panikkar and others:

> Christ is already present in you. He is in you, even when you are unconscious of his presence. . . . For Christ is 'the Light that

[1] Cf. S. Estborn, *Gripped by Christ*, London, 1965, pp. 9-20.
[2] *Lectures* I, pp. 388-9.

> lighteth every man that cometh into the world.' . . . He will come to you as self-surrender, as asceticism, as Yoga, as the life of God in man, as obedient and humble sonship.[1]

Following up this idea he sees Christ, as did Justin Martyr, in all that is good in every philosophy and religion. Christ is present in the hearts of men of all religions, waiting only to be seen, realised, unveiled:

> In every true Brahmin, in every loyal votary of the Veda on the banks of the sacred Ganges, is Christ, the Son of God. The holy word, the eternal Veda dwells in every one of us. . . . Go into the depths of your own consciousness, and you will find this indwelling Logos. . . . The real recognition of Christ has taken place in India. . . . only the nominal recognition remains.[2]

Sen's idea of a world religion is not a merely syncretistic one, like Radhakrishnan's. Certainly he wishes to draw on the riches of all traditions, and certainly he longs for the unity of all men. But always at the centre of his visions of evolution and union there stands the figure of Christ. Christ provides the key to the development. Men of different faiths should now unite, Sen believes, in that Kingdom of Heaven which has no sectarian dogmas, whose cardinal principles are the love of God and the love of man, and which unifies all mankind in one man—Christ the Son of God.[3] Such a unification of all men in Christ was Keshab Chandra Sen's aim in all his writings and in his Church of the New Dispensation. His own personal experience of Christ led him to see that only in him can all men be united, and that the world-religion of the future, if it is ever to come, will be one which places Christ firmly in the centre, so that all men may be one in Christ, the true Man.

Ram Mohan Roy and Keshab Chandra Sen were the first two Hindu reformers to meet and face the challenge of Christianity. Certain parts of that challenge, in particular the ethical teaching of Jesus, they accepted with enthusiasm. They were also, especially Ram Mohan Roy, serious in their detailed, scholarly attempt to understand the Christian faith. But the interpretation which they provided, though interesting and ingenious and full of hints which were later to be taken up by others, both Christian and non-Christian, was fundamentally different from the Christian faith as handed down in the Bible

[1] *ibid.*, pp. 391-2.
[2] *Lectures* II, p. 33.
[3] *ibid.*, p. 95.

and received by the Church. A modern Indian theologian, Dr F. Muliyil, has written:

> These movements did not have their beginning in faith, but in unbelief. From the point of view of the Church in India it is the story of a great rejection.[1]

When we recall Sen's deep personal experience of Christ we may dissent from this judgment in its total disavowal of these thinkers, and may indeed even wonder if it was part of God's way of working in India that a man of Sen's calibre should hammer out ideas which would be left for others to use as instruments of Christian theology.

[1] F. Muliyil: 'An Examination in the Light of NT Doctrines of the Treatment of Christian Theology in Modern Reformed Hinduism, as illustrated by the Brahma Samāj.' Unpublished Oxford D. Phil. Dissertation, 1952.

Chapter IV

'THE RATIONAL REFUTATION OF HINDUISM': NEHEMIAH GOREH

Nehemiah Goreh (1825-95)

While Keshab Chandra Sen was evolving his own interpretation of Christianity in the Church of the New Dispensation, there had arisen a man of a very different stamp, a champion of Christian orthodoxy who was to publish a classical refutation of the six systems of orthodox Hinduism and engage in a long polemic with the Brahma Samāj. His name was Nilakaṇṭha Śāstri Goreh.[1] He took the Christian name of Nehemiah, and in later life, after his ordination in the Anglican Church, became widely known as Father Goreh. Already before his conversion he had achieved a considerable reputation as a Sanskrit scholar and exponent of traditional Hinduism, and, with the possible exception of Paṇḍita Ramābāi, he was probably of all Indian Christians the one most deeply versed in Hindu learning. His life story and his extensive writings are of the greatest interest for they show the struggle of a sensitive soul to find the truth, and later to refute the Hinduism of his contemporaries, both orthodox and reformed, while at the same time striving to demonstrate that the Christian faith fulfils the needs and longings of the Indian mind and heart. In some ways his reaction to the Hinduism in which he had grown up may be described as negative, yet he never ceased to be consciously and constructively Indian, not merely in his way of life but in his expression of theological thought.

Nilakaṇṭha Śāstri belonged to a Chitpavan Brāhman family from Maharashtra but grew up in Benares where he was carefully trained in the ways of strict Śaivite orthodoxy. He early showed his theological independence by transferring his allegiance to the Vaisṇavite tradition, having come to the reasoned conclusion that it was supported by more ancient authority. His first contact with Christianity came through the street-preaching of a CMS missionary, William Smith, to whom he listened not from sympathy for Christianity but rather from 'a desire to dedicate his powers of intellect to its destruction'[2].

[1] C. E. Gardner, *Life of Father Goreh* (1900). Balwant A. M. Paradkar, *The Theology of Nehemiah Goreh*, CISRS—CLS, Madras, 1969. There is a brief account of Goreh in Rajaiah D. Paul's *Chosen Vessels* (1961).

[2] Gardner, *op. cit.*, p. 38.

Smith treated him with imagination and sympathy, and soon Nilakaṇṭha was grappling with the study of the Bible. After a long and very difficult period of reasoning and doubting, and much opposition including beating, drugging and the abduction of his wife, he was baptised in 1848. Within a year he was widowed for the second time (his first wife having died while he and she were both children) and his only child Ellen Lakshmi Goreh was adopted by a missionary family and grew up to be a Victorian hymn-writer of some note.[1]

Goreh visited England in 1853 as tutor to the young Maharaja Dhulip Singh, and while there met many prominent people, including Queen Victoria. He had an interesting encounter with Max Müller whom he decided to be an unreliable guide to Hinduism because of his undue sympathy for all things Hindu, while Müller in turn found it hard to understan why a Hindu pandit should become a Christian.[2] While in England Goreh attended some theological lectures at the CMS Institution at Islington and made a special study of Paley's *Evidences* and Butler's *Analogy*,-books which made a lasting impression on him and confirmed him in his conviction that Christianity, while it is a religion of revelation, must be capable of standing up to that same critical rational evaluation which it applies to other religions.

After his return to India in 1855 his modest but clear and winning testimony was directly instrumental in the conversion of a number of highly educated young men, Hindu, Muslim and Parsi, some of whom later became well known leaders in the Christian Church. He was not without his own doubts—'doubts about the truth of Christianity itself, doubt about the divinity of Christ, doubt about the mode of baptism'[3]—and indeed it is plain that he ultimately became somewhat unbalanced psychologically, with constantly recurring scruples; yet it was his special gift and vocation to help in overcoming the intellectual doubts and difficulties of enquirers. His biographer comments:

> The doubts were scholastic, not devotional. His subtle intellect was ever striving to prove by natural reasoning what he firmly held as a matter of faith. Such were the efforts of medieval schoolmen to demonstrate points of Christian faith by rationalistic arguments.[4]

[1] She became a friend of Frances Ridley Havergal, and wrote the hymn, 'In the secret of His presence, how my soul delights to hide'.

[2] Gardner, *op. cit.*, p. 98.

[3] *ibid.*, p. 96.

[4] *ibid.*, p. 102.

It was, indeed, *fides quaerens intellectum.* Goreh's faith and his devotion to Christ never falter, but he always doubts his own worthiness and never attains to real joy in believing. He is constantly seeking for intellectual certainty, for positive 'evidence' of what he believes, and as constantly is disappointed, though he is able to remove the doubts of many others.

In 1857 Goreh, who had hitherto been well within the evangelical tradition of the CMS met Dr. William Kay, Principal of Bishop's College, Calcutta, who introduced him to the writings of the Fathers and also of the Tractarians, and whose own saintly and ascetic life made a deep impression on him. He moved further and further in an Anglo-Catholic direction and in 1867 severed his connection with the CMS. Hitherto he had remained a layman, but in 1869 he was ordained deacon, and in 1870 priest. In the same year he entered into correspondence with Fr. R. M. Benson, founder of the Society of St. John the Evangelist, and partly at least as the result of his request the Society opened work in India in 1874. Goreh was convinced that the most effective way of carrying out evangelistic work in India was through an ascetic religious brotherhood, and the corporate life and spiritual discipline of the Cowley Fathers attracted him greatly, though he eventually found that western methods of devotion and discipline were not entirely suitable for his own needs. In 1876 he sailed again for England in order to serve his novitiate at Cowley. He never became a professed member of the Society, as he concluded that he had no vocation but his superiors wisely gave him wide freedom to work according to his own ideas and, despite later scruples and difficulties about keeping the Rule satisfactorily, he remained a novice of the Society till his death in 1895.

Partners in Dialogue

It was in 1860 that Goreh published his best known work, '*Shaddarshana Darpana ; or Hindu Philosophy Examined*, by a Benares Pandit'[1]. An English translation entitled *A Rational Refutation of the Hindu Philosophical Systems* was published in 1862 and for many years continued to be regarded as a standard work on Hinduism, the third edition being published as recently as 1911. The book is, as its name implies, a detailed logical

[1] The title literally means *Mirror of the Six Systems*, i.e. the six traditional Hindu systems of philosophy—Sāṁkhya, Yoga, Nyāya, Vaiśeṣika, Mimāṃsa, Vedānta. The English title was later modified to *A Mirror of the Hindu Philosophical Systems*.

examination of the main Hindu systems, in which Goreh with ruthless reasoning makes of each point a *reductio ad absurdum.* Here we can see him bringing his powers of mind to bear on the first of a number of partners in dialogue—perhaps for him 'beloved opponents' would be a better nomenclature—with whom he was to engage in discussion over many years, in this case the adherents of the traditional systems of Hinduism, from whose orthodox ranks he himself had come.

He finds the Nyāya and Vaiśeṣika systems the most reasonable of the six as, unlike the Sāṃkhya and Mimāṃsa, they do posit a God, and, unlike the Vedānta, do not identify God and the soul. But he finds none of the systems satisfactory and carefully refutes such ideas as that of salvation meaning emancipation from ignorance rather than sin ; the permanence of the soul ; the origin of the world from a material cause, be it *prakriti* (Sāṃkhya), atoms (Nyāya) or *māyā* (Vedānta) ; the desirability of refraining from all works, no matter whether good or evil ; the belief in transmigration ; the idea of salvation as absorption in *Brahman* etc. In his treatment of the Vedānta, which is of special importance, he gives a very interesting analysis of the three different types of existence—true, practical and apparent[1] —posited by *advaita* thinkers. This section is in fact a very effective critique of that traditional Hindu epistemology which seeks to establish the fact that *Brahman* alone truly exists, that the soul is *Brahman*, and that all else is illusory.

We shall consider some of these points in more detail later. Here we shall only say that although this book sets out primarily to be a critique of Hinduism, it in fact gives Goreh many opportunities of stating the Christian point of view, and in a very interesting way we can watch the development of a positive Christian statement at each point where he criticises a particular Hindu doctrine. His theology develops entirely in relation to his apologetic task.

In 1867 Goreh had his first meeting with his famous younger contemporary Keshab Chandra Sen and the encounter was the beginning of a dialogue with the adherents of the Brahma Samāj which continued till the end of Goreh's life. They were introduced by a missionary, J. R. Hill, who was struck by the contrast between them, 'Keshab handsome in person, confident and agreeable in deportment, with a ready flow of rhetoric ;

[1] *paramārthika, vyavahārika, pratibhāśika.*

Nehemiah diffident, thoughtful, reticent'.[1] Goreh was astonished to find that Sen had not read Paley's *Evidences*, and indeed had not given anything like as much study and critical thought to the establishment of his theological position as Goreh had to his. He immediately felt called to make a special study of the Brahma Samāj and a large proportion of his later writing consists in apologetic directed to the 'Theists' as he called the members of the Brahma and Prārthnā Samāj.[2] His basic argument is to say that the ideas about the nature of God which the Brahmos have accepted, and which have led them to reject orthodox Hinduism, can be proved to come from the Bible and from no other source; therefore it is the rational duty of the Brahmos to accept the *whole* revelation of the Bible, and not just those parts which suit them and which can be accepted without the danger of social ostracism.

Goreh at first had great hopes that the Brahmos might yield to his arguments, and as the years went on he frequently talked to them, held disputations with them, and wrote tracts and pamphlets for them, but with disappointing results. He could not understand how their reason could take them as far as a rejection of traditional Hindu orthodoxy and acceptance of 'theistic' principles, without leading them on to the fulness of the catholic faith. Nevertheless the apologetic writings which are the outcome of this dialogue are of great interest and he has not unjustly been compared to the Alexandrian Fathers, whom he resembles in his great output of such literature.

That his ministry was effective is shown by the fact that he was the instrument for the conversion of one of the greatest of all Indian Christians, Paṇḍitā Ramābāi.[3] Like Goreh, Ramābāi was a Chitpavan Brāhman, and as a child became a noted Sanskrit scholar through the instruction of her father, Anant Śāstri. On his death she rapidly achieved fame as a woman pandit. After a happy but tragically brief married life she became even more famous as a pioneer of women's rights. The friendship which she had formed in Calcutta with Keshab Chandra Sen and other leading reformers led her to become a member of the Prārthnā Samāj when she went to live in Poona. Here she came in contact with the Wantage Sisters, to whose community she went on her visit to England in 1883. In England her interest in Chris-

[1] Gardner, *op. cit.*, p. 135.

[2] The Prārthnā Samāj ('Prayer Society') is an organisation similar to the Brahma Samāj, based on Bombay and functioning in Western India.

[3] Paṇḍitā Ramābāi Sarasvati, 1858-1922. The best biography is Nicol Macnicol, *Pandita Ramabai* (1926).

tianity grew, but her keen mind had still many intellectual doubts and it was at last a long letter from Goreh which resolved these and led her to receive baptism, convincing her that the position of the Samāj was untenable and that only in Christ could she find certainty. She wrote to a friend:

> You will be glad to know that I have become a catechumen. Fr. Goreh preached to me from India. His humble, sweet voice has pierced my heart. Oh what a mighty power of preaching he has! I think no one would have had the power of turning my heart from the Brahman religion but Fr. Goreh.[1]

Later, during her stay in America from 1886-89, Ramābāi made many friends among the Unitarians, and for a time her inclinations ran in that direction. Once again Goreh came to the rescue, and his booklet *Proofs of the Divinity of Our Lord, Stated in a Letter to a Friend*, published in 1887, was in origin a letter to Ramābāi.

In addition to his dialogue with the orthodox traditionalists and with the theists of the Brahma Samāj, Goreh made clear his views on the great tradition of devotion to a personal deity known as *bhakti*. Coming as he did from a Marathi family it was natural for him to make a special study of Tukārām, the great *bhakti* poet of Maharashtra, who was later to have such an influence on the Christian poet Tilak. But though in his pre-Christian days Goreh had turned from the Śaivite tradition to that of the Vaiṣṇavas with their teaching on the divine incarnations (*avatāras*) and though he felt that this belief in incarnation was a *praeparatio* for the Christian faith, he could find little to attract him in the *bhakti* tradition, and never attempts, as Appasamy was to do, to adapt it as a vehicle for a Christian *bhakti mārga*. He felt that the character of Krishna took away the positive value of the *avatāra*-conception by divorcing incarnation from morality, and did not seriously consider the allegorising interpretation which later became common under the influence of Christianity. Indeed, Goreh's attitude to the *bhakti* saints like Tukārām in Maharashtra and Caitanya in Bengal (who so deeply influenced Keshab Chandra Sen) is a negative one. He felt that they had not in fact *reformed* Hinduism, as they did not bring in any substantially new elements. The same old worship of Kriṣhna persisted in them and they were, for him, no more enlightened than traditional popular

[1] Gardner, *op. cit.*, p. 275. See also Ramābāi's own booklet *A Testimony* (1917), p. 10.

Hinduism, although the Brahmos—particularly the New Dispensation—tended to look to them as prophets and 'great men'. Goreh thought of them as mere revivalists rather than reformers:

> They revived *bhakti*, that is, ardent devotion, not to the true God of whom they were ignorant, but to Krishna, Rama, etc., whom they, like all Hindus, ignorantly believed to be God.[1]

* * * * *

We shall now look a little more closely at some of the more important issues dealt with by Goreh in the *Rational Refutation* and elsewhere. We must remember that he had come to accept western 'catholic' orthodoxy in full—the Athanasian Creed was his special delight !—and that it is from this base that he is arguing with his Hindu friends. The special interest of his approach derives from his intimate knowledge of the Hinduism he is 'refuting', and his deep desire to express his own faith in terms which his Hindu and theist friends will understand.

God, Creation and the Nature of Existence

All the Hindu systems deny the idea of creation from nothing, and Śankara's *advaita* ultimately denies the reality of creation at all, though acknowledging that creation has taken place on the mere *vyavahārika* or practical level. Goreh therefore lays great stress on the importance of the Christian doctrine of *creatio ex nihilo*, as he sees clearly that this is something quite new in India. It is indeed one of the crucial issues which Christian theology in India has to face. The word *sriṣṭi*, which is commonly translated 'creation', really signifies merely the giving of form to some substance or material cause which was already in existence. According to the *Nyaya* system this previously existing material cause is the supreme atom or *paramāṇu* ; in the Sāṃkhya system it is *prakriti*, the primordial substance, nature, 'originant' or 'evolvant', to use Goreh's own preferred translation ; while in the most famous of all the systems, Śankara's *advaita*, creation is the product of *māyā*, illusion. Thus 'all Hindu systems hold that the ultimate material cause of all effects is without a beginning and that 'the stream of the world has been flowing on from eternity'[2], so that the world itself is in effect eternal. As against this Goreh firmly holds the revealed

[1] N. Goreh, *Christianity not of Man but of God* (1888), p. 32.
[2] *Rational Refutation*, p. 41.

Biblical doctrine of *creatio ex nihilo*, which alone gives full sovereignty to God.

In an interesting section of the *Rational Refutation* Goreh investigates the Vedānta (*advaita*) theory of different types of existence, which is a matter with a fundamental bearing on the doctrine of creation. This is perhaps the most detailed and scholarly study of Vedāntic epistemology which has yet been made by an Indian Christian theologian, and it is worth our pausing to examine it in some detail. Unlike Brahmabandhab forty years later, who attempted to use the concept of *māyā*, freshly interpreted, to assist an alliance between Christian theology and *advaita*, Goreh firmly rejects the Vedāntic theory of knowledge and creation, seeking to demonstrate its invalidity in a *reductio ad absurdum*. The argument is devoted to proving the irrationality of believing that the created world is false and that *Brahman* is all.

Advaita Vedānta posits three sorts of existence—*paramārthika* or true existence, which can be posited of *Brahman* only; *vyavahārika* or practical existence, which includes the world, human souls, and the personal God or *Iśvara*; and *pratibhāśika* or apparent, illusory existence. The classical example which illustrates these types of existence is that of the snake and the rope. A man sees what he thinks to be a snake. On closer investigation, however, it turns out to be merely a rope. The snake then, which for a time existed in his mind, has only *apparent* existence. The rope, an ordinary object of everyday experience, has *practical* existence. Yet the true *advaitin* knows that such practical experience is also illusory, and that ultimately the rope is not real either, for only *Brahman* truly exists. Yet for the *advaitin* there is a sense in which there really *is* existence at each of these levels. This whole three-tiered epistemology is designed to prove three things: that the world is illusory; that *Brahman* alone exists; and that the soul is *Brahman*. Thus the world, souls, and even *Iśvara*, the personal God, are granted only a limited kind of existence, which indeed is regarded as false, that is, as existence which in fact is not, but, owing to mistake or ignorance (*māyā*, *avidyā*) *seems* to be. This is an important belief for *advaitins* for, as Goreh says,

> however they may designate the world's existence, if they concede that the world really exists, then Brahma does not remain without a second; and the consequence is duality.[1]

[1] *ibid.*, p. 162.

For the Vedāntin there are not simply three modes of epistemology or three different classes of objects. The distinction is taken right into the realm of being, and there are three separate kinds of existence. Thus *Brahman* must be described as 'really real', while a rope, or a person, or God Himself, is 'unreally real'. And it is only the Vedāntin who can distinguish the real from the unreal, for to others *all* seems real. For the benefit of these lesser mortals, of course, the Vedāntin allows a complete world of practical (*vyavahārika*) existence, and here we find 'an omniscient and omnipotent Iśvara, framer and ruler of the external world',[1] a world evolved, not from *prakriti* or primordial nature, as in the Nyāya sytem, but from *māyā*. Yet this whole world, and so the whole of creation, and the personal God himself, are ultimately unreal, and it is only beyond them that the real, *paramārthika* level lies, where '*Brahman* is true; the world is false; the soul is *Brahman* himself, and no other'. The world's existence, then, is not its own but *Brahman's*; it is the *vivarta* or 'illusory effect' of *Brahman*, and on the practical level may be called the *pariṇāma* or evolution of *māyā*.

Goreh has now brought the argument to the point at which he feels he can demonstrate its absurdity; the world has been shown to be false and illusory, and at the same time it is said to be *Brahman*. This is a logical inconsistency, which must be rejected.

In a similar way he deals with the Vedāntic doctrine of God. Only *Brahman*, they hold, really exists, and *Brahman* is ultimately without attributes (*nirguṇa*), for *saguṇa Brahman* (*Brahman* with attributes) exists only on the practical level. Hence the creator God, the personal *Iśvara*, is 'unreally real' or rather false. It is only to be expected, then, that the *advaita* monists should regard the Christian conception of God as inferior to their own:

> They suppose that we, at the best and furthest, stop short at Iśvara, and make no approach to the pure Brahma beyond. But they do not consider, that such a Supreme Spirit as they contend for cannot be proved to exist.[2]

Goreh goes on to show that *nirguṇa Brahman*, for the very reason that he is void of qualities, reduces to zero, and so his existence cannot be proved. The traditional arguments for the existence of God, on which, following Paley, Goreh puts consider-

[1] *ibid.*, p. 175.
[2] *ibid.*, p. 197.

able weight, cannot apply to ***nirguṇa Brahman***; if ***Brahman*** is out of relation to the world, how can we arrive by inference at a conviction of his existence?[1] Even the famous definition of *Brahman* as *Saccidānanda*, which the advaitins accepts, does not raise the deity above zero:

> Their Brahma is only nominally intelligence and bliss. He is intelligence that cognizes nothing, and bliss without fruition of happiness. What hope is there, that the soul would be happy, if it came to such a state as this?[2]

Christians, however, who believe in a personal God who has created the world out of nothing can, he believes, prove the existence of the Creator, though not that of a Being (*Brahman*) who transcends him. The Christians' God is truly the world's Creator and Upholder, supporting it by his divine will, and in fact this Creator-God is the highest, than whom nothing higher can be proved. *Iśvara* is really a higher conception than *Brahman*.

The concept of *māyā* can be seen to play an important part in the Vedāntic theory of creation and existence, and in view of the way in which a later writer, Brahmabandhab, was to seek to use this concept in a positive way, we may note how Goreh refutes it as a false way of interpreting reality. The following paragraph, in which he uses 'ignorance' as a translation of *māyā*, is a good example of his logical method, as well as of his style of prose:

> On hearing, that the Vedāntins regard ignorance as the cause of the world's appearing to be true, one would, of course, suppose, that this ignorance was understood, by them, to be itself true. For if ignorance did not actually exist, how could the world, which they hold to be a nonentity, have appearance? When a man mistakingly sees a snake in a rope, the snake is called false. At the same time, that man's misapprehension is not said to be false, but true. The Vedāntins, however, maintain that ignorance is false. We ought, therefore, to inquire, how it is reckoned false, and what is gained to the Vedānta system by so reckoning it.[3]

[1] *ibid.*, p. 221. Some modern scholars feel that Śankara has been distorted by his later followers and that in fact *nirguṇa Brahman*, as Śankara himself understood it, can be 'the most personal being'. See R. V. De Smet, 'Categories of Indian Philosophy and Communication of the Gospel' in *Religion and Society*, Sept. 1963, p. 22.

[2] *Rational Refutation*, p. 274.

[3] *ibid.*, p. 347 (1911 edn.)

His conclusion is that what depends on falseness must itself be false, and that so the whole *advaita* view of the nature of God, of creation, and of our knowledge of them both, proves unusable.

Man and Sin

According to the orthodox systems of Hinduism the soul of man (*ātman*) is eternal, and is in reality identical with the Supreme Soul (*paramātman*) or *Brahman*. Looking at the creation on the practical level it is held that 'God made the world in order to requite the good and evil deeds of souls',[1] that is, that God brings the world into existence, through *māyā*, to be the instrument of *karma*, rather than creating both it and men out of his sheer free will and good pleasure. The Christian view of the soul as being created by God for fellowship with himself is in direct contrast to the Hindu teaching that on the 'practical' level the soul has existed as soul from eternity, and yet is ultimately identical (on the 'true' level) with *Brahman*. This identity of the soul with *Brahman* Goreh challenges:

> It is a maxim of the Vedānta, that 'The soul is Brahma itself, and nothing other'. How, I would ask the Vedāntins, can this be? For they assert, that, on the one hand, soul errs by reason of ignorance; and that, on the other hand, Brahma is, in essence, ever pure, intelligent, and free, and can never for a moment be otherwise. Still, they maintain that the soul is Brahma; and, with interest to reconcile their contradiction, they resort to the most elaborate mystification.[2]

The logic of his argument is not easy to answer, except by a new interpretation of *māyā*, such as that attempted by Brahmabandhab.

Goreh's own understanding of the nature of the soul, and of man himself, is very different from this. He takes a more serious view of sin than most Indian theologians, in the sense that he never tries to minimise the positive evil power behind it, and sees it to be bound up with the corruption of man's whole nature. Hinduism here fails to draw a clear distinction, for from the point of view of *karma* virtue as well as vice is a cause of bondage and so the Hindu systems tend to lose the distinction between the two, and to advocate release from all works, whether good or evil:

[1] *Rational Refutation*, p. 113.
[2] *ibid.*, p. 33.

> Sin and virtue are acknowledged, indeed, from the standing point of practical existence ; but, nevertheless, they come to be, in truth, nothing.[1]

In refuting the counsel of the Nyāya and Vaiśeṣika systems, that man should seek to abandon all works, whether good or evil, Goreh gives a clear statement of his own understanding of the nature of sin :

> Your solicitude to shun good works is quite superfluous ; for, so corrupt is the nature of man, that, let his works be ever so good, still there cleaves to them much of evil and imperfection ; and he is incapable of a single good work wrought with purity of body, speech and heart. . . . In the sight of God, who knows everything without and within, these very works are tainted with evil.[2]

While orthodox Hinduism thus reduces sin to zero, the theism of the Brahma Samāj is found to be little better. It regards sin as a sort of natural evil like disease, which can be healed by remedial treatment. For Goreh, the fact that Christianity recognises the reality and seriousness of sin, and provides a means to overcome them, is an overwhelming proof of its effectiveness. And this conviction springs from his own experience, for it was the thought of the fearfulness of sin which first drew him to Christ. He might seem, indeed, to devote a disproportionate amount of his writing to the doctrine of eternal punishment, on which he wrote a tract of 126 pages ! He gives the explanation :

> It was the doctrine of everlasting punishment, which shook my soul from the very bottom, and forced me to come away, at any cost, from the path of error, and resolve in my mind to strive with all my might to leave off sin and follow holiness and virtue.[3]

His exposition of the necessity of eternal punishment is developed in reply to an anonymous Brahmo tract—possibly by Keshab Chandra Sen—entitled *Atonement and Salvation*, in which the author argues that (*a*) we *deserve* punishment for our sins, but that (*b*) God punishes us *for our welfare*. Goreh feels that this view underestimates God's justice. Sin is no 'illness'

[1] *ibid.*, p. 275. Goreh is writing in 1860, long before Vivekānanda and Gāndhi had reinterpreted the meaning of work and service.
[2] *ibid.*, p. 141.
[3] N. Goreh, *A Letter to the Brahmos from a Converted Brahman of Benares* (2nd edn. 1868), p. 52.

deserving a remedial medicine; it is moral wrong which must suffer the just consequences, and so men who have

> made themselves proof against the influence of Divine Mercy, and incapable of turning towards God and virtue, cannot but remain subject to the punishment due to their ever-enduring wickedness for ever and ever.[1]

In his own tract Goreh is led from this statement of the nature of justice and punishment (which perhaps owes at least something to the doctrine of *karma*) to an exposition of God's love and of the way of salvation and of the benefits of Christ's passion mediated to us in the eucharist. For this is the road which he himself had travelled. He was, indeed, a rather 'fearful saint', but his fears did lead him to salvation, even though they kept recurring in moments of weakness all through his life.

The Meaning of Salvation

In the *Rational Refutation* Goreh points out what he believes to be the inadequacies of the Hindu conception of salvation—inadequacies which are common to all the systems. Man's soul, it is held, is in bondage to ignorance (*māyā, avidyā*), because the soul has come to identify itself with the mind, the senses and the body. To engage in either evil or good works is a sign of this bondage. Salvation (*mokṣa, mukti*) is emancipation from this bondage, and such emancipation can be secured only through 'right apprehension' or knowledge (*jñāna*), that is, the recognition by the soul that it is distinct from mind, sense and body. Such *jñāna* is to be obtained by the study of the *śāstras* and with the help of a *guru* or preceptor, and gives a man the 'immediate cognition of his own soul'.[2] Emancipation or salvation, then, is something negative rather than positive; it is simply 'immunity from misery, and is not a source of any happiness whatsoever'.[3]

The realisation that the soul is separate from the body leads on to the realisation of its identity with the supreme soul (*paramātman*) or *Brahman*. But even this identity, especially in the Nyāya and Vaiśeṣika systems, is largely without content. It is simply, he writes, 'to lose the faculties of apprehension, will,

[1] N. Goreh, *On Objections against the Catholic Doctrine of Eternal Punishment* (1868), p. 16.
[2] *Rational Refutation*, p. 28.
[3] *ibid.*, p. 34.

and all manifestations of sensibility, and to become like a stone',[1] and the attainment of such a state of insensibility cannot be called true emancipation or *mokṣa*.

His verdict on the Hindu type of salvation is that it cannot deal effectively with man's real problem, which is to get rid of his sins and of their penalty. The Christian conception of *jñāna* is very different, and has an immediate practical bearing on man's deepest needs. It is the knowledge which enables one

> rightly to apprehend God, and oneself, and one's wretchedness, and the way of escape from it, and what man ought to do, and what he ought to forbear.[2]

Such *jñāna*, however, is beyond the power of man to attain by his own efforts, and comes only as the gift of God's grace through Christ's incarnation. The Christian, like the Hindu, does believe that the highest goal of man is union with God, and that there is a means for attaining this, but it is God alone who can provide the way. Goreh writes:

> The doctrine that God, out of His amazing love to man, made Himself so low as to become Man, by assuming our nature, and opened the way for uniting man to His Humanity, through the sacraments, and, through His Humanity to unite man even to His Divine Nature (not in the way that the Vedanta teaches, for that is impossible), and to exalt him thus to a height so great as to surpass conception, and to communicate to him Divine Righteousness and holiness—this doctrine, I say, is calculated to sanctify and to elevate our souls in such a way as mere Theism knows nothing of.[3]

In this passage, published in 1887, we see Goreh's later view that the benefits of Christ's passion are to be appropriated primarily through the sacrament of Holy Communion. And indeed it is in an exposition of the eucharist that we find his fullest and most impressive statement on the subject of how salvation has been secured for us, how we are to appropriate it, and how it fulfils the deepest longings of Hinduism. In the eucharist, he writes, we behold the Lamb of God,

> sacrificed for us once for all on Calvary, who comes, we know not how, with His fresh wounds and with His precious Blood overflowing to drown and annihilate our sins therein, in His amazing

[1] *ibid.*, p. 152.
[2] *ibid.*, p. 108.
[3] N. Goreh, *Proofs of the Divinity of Our Lord, stated in a letter to a Friend* (1887), p. 36.

Love, to meet us, to be received by us, to dwell in us, yea, to unite us with Himself, and through Himself with the Father. He, as the Mediator between God and men, being one in nature with His Father in His Godhead having taken our flesh, and giving that very flesh to us in the Holy Eucharist, and thus uniting us with Himself even in nature through that flesh, though not personally, (we still remain distinct *in person* from Him) but mystically (therefore the Church is wont to call herself His mystical Body) yet really and truly, and thus through Himself unites us to the Father, yea, makes us 'partakers', as the Scripture says, 'of the Divine Nature'. O Glorious Gift! O Amazing Love! May we, the sons of India, say, that the unity with God, Whom our fathers delighted to call 'Sat Chit Ananda Brahman', after which they ardently aspired, but in a wrong sense, for in that sense a creature can never be united with the Creator, yet after which they ardently aspired, God has granted us their children to realize in the right sense? Was that aspiration and longing, though misunderstood by them, a presentiment of the future Gift? I indeed have often delighted to think so.[1]

This is a magnificent and moving passage, showing something of the positive orthodoxy and power of persuasive expression, as well as the sympathetic insight into Hinduism which is the other side of Goreh's rational criticism.

Praeparatio Evangelii in Hinduism

We have seen that Goreh's dialogue with Hinduism was largely a negative one. Yet it would be a great mistake to imagine that he was merely a westernised Indian Christian, de-nationalised and out of sympathy with his own cultural tradition. The reverse is true. No one could ever have called him westernised. He refused to adopt western dress—even clerical dress—and always lived a life of the utmost simplicity and asceticism in the Indian sense, keeping only as much of his salary as was necessary for his minimum requirements. It is true that he was a staunch Anglo-Catholic who fully accepted the Tractarian position on Church, Ministry and Sacraments, and could be extremely critical of 'dissenters', with whom he once refused to sit on a Hindi Bible Revision committee![2] Yet the western trappings of the Church repelled him, even when channelled to him through the asceticism of the Cowley Fathers. Like Keshab Chandra Sen he attached importance to the fact that Christianity was in its origin Asian not European, and urged his countrymen to accept it as such. He writes:

[1] *On Objections* (1868), pp. 41-2.
[2] Gardner, *op. cit.*, p. 290.

No one should call it a foreign religion, and yet if any people have a greater right to call it theirs than other people they are the Asiatics.[1]

He was a saint, and his saintliness was much more typical of the East than of the West. He was also, as we have seen, a severe critic of the rationalism and scepticism which seemed to be the most characteristic western influence then at work in Indian society.

He loved his Hindu fellow-countrymen, felt at home in their society, and was convinced that in some unknown way God had been preparing their hearts and minds to receive the Christian revelation. Indeed he came to the conclusion that a genuine orthodox Hindu was more open to the Gospel than the more sophisticated Brahmo or rationalist who had been thoroughly westernised and secularised. He writes:

But a genuine Hindu is rather prepared to receive the teaching of Christianity... Providence has certainly prepared *us*, the Hindus, to receive Christianity, in a way in which, it seems to me, no other nation—excepting the Jews, of course—has been prepared. Most erroneous as is the teaching of such books as the *Bhagvadgita*, the *Bhagvata*, etc., yet they have taught us something of *ananyabhakti* (undivided devotedness to God), of *vairagya* (giving up the world), of *namrata* (humility), of *ksama* (forbearance), etc., which enables us to appreciate the precepts of Christianity.[2]

This is an interesting and even touching sentence, for in using the pronoun 'us' Goreh here ranges himself alongside his Hindu brothers, while the four qualities he mentions are ones which he himself had learnt from Hinduism, and which had helped to make him the true Christian saint he was. They are indeed distinguishing marks of the best Indian Christianity.

He goes on to point out that there are certain ideas in orthodox Hinduism which are not found in rationalism and which point beyond themselves to their fulfilment in Christ. Such ideas are the acceptance of the possibility of miracles, and above all the idea of *incarnation*. These conceptions can and should be regarded as a *praepartio evangelii*, and he testifies to his own experience:

I gave up the Hindu religion because I came to see that it was not a Religion given by God. The errors of it I condemn. But I never found fault *in idea* with its teaching that God becomes

[1] N. Goreh, *Christianity not of Man but of God* (1888), p. 59.
[2] *Proofs of the Divinity of Our Lord*, p. 75.

Incarnate. Indeed, many stories of Krishna and Rama, whom the Hindu religion teaches to be incarnations of God, used to be very affecting to us. . . . And thus our countrymen have been prepared, to some extent, to appreciate and accept the truths of Christianity.[1]

In an interesting passage dealing with the Hindu understanding of incarnation he is able to quote Tertullian on his side, and indeed his own rather negative approach has perhaps more in common with Tertullian than with the more accommodating Clement. In his *De Resurrectione Carnis* Tertullian, while expounding the meaning of the resurrection of Christ, shows how Christ unfolds the hidden secrets of past ages. Transferring the argument to the doctrine of the incarnation, Goreh writes:

> Tertullian speaks of the Resurrection. His teaching is equally true of the Incarnation, of which there was a dim mysterious expectation among the nobler minds of antiquity. He [i.e. Christ] showed the meaning of those anticipations and gave the answer to those doubtings, and satisfied those yearnings and shadowy foretastes of truth, which expressed themselves in the imaginary incarnations dreamed of by poets and philosophers. He proved the truth of the anticipations, not only by his preaching, but also by his history. He was and is substantially and in fact all that they had dreamed and infinitely more.[2]

Christ is here clearly indicated as the fulfilment of the longings of Hinduism. We have already seen how Goreh saw in the Christian's faith-union with Christ, experienced in the eucharist, the fulfilment of the ancient Hindu longing for union with *Brahman* as *Saccidānanda*. God has not left himself without witnesses in Hinduism, and he has placed in the hearts of his Hindu people that 'divine light' which can guide them to the truth:

> May God, in His infinite mercy, grant, my dear countrymen, that you quench not the divine light which He has lighted in your breasts; that, on the contrary, you may follow its leading; that you meekly and patiently try, by it, the Christian Scriptures; that you take hold on their priceless promises; and that, in the end, you may inherit, as your everlasting portion, the joy of the Heavenly Kingdom.[3]

[1] *ibid.*, pp. 76-77 (footnote).
[2] *On Objections*, p. 81 (footnote).
[3] *Rational Refutation*, p. 280 (the peroration of the book)

The 'divine light' to which he refers is no doubt, for him the light of reason, and it was to reason that he turned as the instrument of his theology. Yet he urged the use of reason in order to look beyond reason to revelation, and to discern in the best traditions of Hinduism many pointers towards that True Light which shines in Christ.

Chapter V

NOTHING BUT THE HIGHEST: BRAHMABANDHAB UPĀDHYĀYA

Before we consider the next great figure on the Christian theological stage, Brahmabandhab Upādhyāya, we must glance briefly at one or two outstanding leaders of the later reform movements of 19th century Hinduism. We shall merely mention in passing the founder of the Ārya Samāj, *Swāmi Dayānanda Sarasvati* (1824-1883), as his attitude to Christianity was totally negative.[1] The Ārya Samāj is still today a force to be reckoned with and its anti-Christian polemic has not mellowed, but, as Goreh pointed out clearly while Swāmi Dayānanda was still living, its exposition of the Vedas, on which it claims to be based, will not stand up to any strict exegetical tests.

The Brahma Samāj and the Ārya Samāj affected only a very small proportion of the vast Hindu population of India, and as yet no leader had arisen to give renewal and cohesion to the traditional structure of Hinduism, which appeared to be being undermined from different directions. *Sri Rāmakrishna* (1836-1886) provided just such leadership.[2] A man of great simplicity and little formal education, he found it possible—sometimes after long struggle and asceticism—to obtain 'realisation' in the adoration of the different deities of the *bhakti mārga*, and later mastered the way of *advaita*, attaining the state of *nirvikalpa samādhi* or complete absorption in *nirguṇa Brahman*, the unqualified Absolute. Having participated in the whole gamut of Hindu religious experience he turned to Islam, and then to Christianity, when he had a vision of Christ and experienced union with him. We are told that

> Christ merged in Rāmakrishna, who forthwith lost his outward consciousness and became completely absorbed in the *savikalpa samadhi* in which he realised his union with Brahman with attributes. After this experience Rāmakrishna remained firm in his conviction up to the last days of his life that Jesus Christ was an Incarnation of God.[3]

[1] Farquhar, *op. cit.*, pp. 101 ff.
O. Wolff, *op. cit.*, pp. 106 ff.
[2] Farquhar, *op. cit.*, pp. 188 ff.
[3] *Cultural Heritage of India* (Belur Math, Calcutta), Vol. II, p. 494.

As a result of this experience Rāmakrishna was led to propound his theory of the equality of all religions, a message which was taken up enthusiastically by his disciple Vivekānanda, and has now come to be widely accepted in India. Here is how Rāmakrishna states his view:

> I have practised all religions—Hinduism, Islam, Christianity, and I have also followed the paths of the different Hindu sects. . . I have found that it is the same God towards whom all are directing their steps, though along different paths. . . . The tank has several ghats. At one Hindus draw water in pitchers, and call it *jala*; at another Mussalmans draw water in leathern bottles and call it *pani*; at a third Christians do the same and call it *water*.[1]

Rāmakrishna, whose teaching was given largely through a series of simple and attractive parables and stories, infused new life into traditional Hinduism, winning the devotion of modernists like Keshab Chandra Sen as well as of thousands of pious orthodox Hindus. His later life, till his death at the age of 50 in 1886, was devoted to teaching those who came to hear him, and demonstrating the many and various ways in which he claimed to have found realisation.

Rāmakrishna's successor, *Swāmi Vivekānanda* (1862-1902) was in many ways a contrast to his *guru*.[2] He had received a thorough western education, graduating from Calcutta university in 1884, and absorbing much of the materialism then current. When Ramākrishna died in 1886 Vivekānanda was the obvious person to succeed him as leader of the band of disciples. Right from the beginning we see his eagerness to regard Rāmakrishna as an incarnation of God, and also to appropriate some of the methods and terminology of Christianity. He refers to Rāmakrishna as 'the foremost of divine Incarnations', and sees his own position as being to Rāmakrishna what Peter or Paul was to Christ.

A brilliant speaker and a man of great charm, Vivekānanda created a sensation when he appeared at the 'World Parliament of Religions' in Chicago in 1893. The theme of his addresses was that India had discovered a principle of priceless worth to the whole world—the gospel of the harmony of all religious; and in the West he found a ready audience. On his return to India

[1] *ibid.*, p. 518.
[2] J. R. Chandran, 'A Comparison of the pagan Apologetic of Celsus against Christianity as contained in Origen's *Contra Celsum* and the neo-Hindu attitude to Christianity as represented in the Works of Vivekānanda.' (Unpublished thesis, Oxford, 1949.) Wolff, *op. cit.*, pp. 126 ff. Nalini Devdas, *Svāmi Vivekānanda*, CISRS, Bangalore, 1968.

he founded the Rāmakrishna Mission in 1897. The mission centred in the life and teaching of Rāmakrishna, and envisaged a close fellowship of members of different religions who recognised their faiths to be different manifestations of the one eternal religion whose purest form was *advaita* Vedānta.

We have seen earlier how the Hinduism of Ram Mohan Roy and of Keshab Chandra Sen was transformed by their contact with the Christian faith, and how Sen's life was indeed dominated by his encounter with Christ. In the writings of Vivekānanda and his followers we find something very different, an attempt to force Christianity into a Vedāntic mould, and on Vedāntic terms. The result is that, while Sen's work opened up many avenues of thought which Christian theologians have been able to explore and use, Vivekānanda's writing leads only deeper and deeper into Hinduism. He was born into an India where Christianity had already become familiar and so less challenging. He regards Christianity from the lofty eminence of *advaita*, and, though he is interested enough to study and discuss Christian doctrine, he persistently tries to make it conform to his own pattern of thought. It can be said with some truth that the distinguished line of Hindu thinkers who have followed him, Rabindranāth Tāgore, Mahātma Gāndhi, Sri Aurobindo and Dr. Radhakrishnan, have adopted the same approach, and so have not come into a dynamic and fruitful relationship with Christianity in the way that Sen did. Indeed, although Vivekānanda served himself heir to the Brāhma Samāj as well as to Rāmakrishna, Sen's true spiritual successor was neither his biographer P. C. Mozoomdar nor his friend Rāmakrishna's disciple Vivekānanda, but the Christian Brahmabandhab Upādhyāya.

We shall not attempt a detailed examination of Vivekānanda's treatment of Christian doctrines, but it is instructive to look at one or two of his typical attitudes, on such subjects as creation, sin and our union with God.

He holds, for example, that there can be no creation, nor any personal God who brings the world into existence *ex nihilo*. The world is rather 'evolved' from God, as a spider spins its web out of its own body, since a doctrine of creation is incompatible with the immutability of God. If the *ātman* or soul is created it must also be perishable, which is impossible. The dominating *advaita* idea that the *ātman* and the *paramātman* are one is irreconcilable with the Christian doctrine of creation which sees man as God's fallen creature in need of redemption.

Vivekānanda's optimistic and indeed ebullient estimate of human nature is well-known, and shows scant sympathy for the

Christian idea of sin. He constantly exhorted his countrymen to rise to their full moral stature, to be 'lions not sheep'. With this optimism went a denial of the reality of sin, and indeed it was sin to call a man a sinner. 'Sin' was simply ignorance and weakness caused by the hypnosis of *māyā*.

> Essentially all ideas of imperfection and sinfulness are hallucinations since man is of the substance of God himself.[1]

We have already noticed the attraction of the fourth Gospel for many Indian writers, both Hindu and Christian, and Vivekānanda continues the tradition and gives it added impetus. He selects certain texts—'I and my Father are one' (John 10 : 30); 'The Kingdom of God is within you' (Luke 17 :21); and 'In Him we live and move and have our being' (Acts 17 : 28)—and from these tries to derive the Vedāntic principle of the mystical identification of the individual soul and the ultimate *Brahman*. His assumption is that Christ experienced absorption in the Absolute, *Brahman*, and similarly we, with him, can be so absorbed. The intimate and personal faith-union of the believer with Christ is thus eliminated, and the distinction between the three Persons of the Trinity is denied. In Dr. J. R. Chandran's words :

> Vivekānanda approached the Bible with the assumption derived from [Hindu] metaphysics that ultimately there is no distinction between the self which was in Jesus and the other individual selves, and whatever is predicated about Jesus is applicable to each individual self.[2]

The Johannine understanding of the words, 'I and my Father are one' is, on the contrary, that the historic Jesus is truly God. We may quote the illuminating comment of Bishop Appasamy :

> This utterance has appealed to the religious heart of India which, because of the monistic point of view so largely familiar to it, has defied all reasonable laws of exegesis and has interpreted the passage to mean that Jesus, always one with God, realised in a luminous moment this supreme identity. But we must remember that Jesus always lived in whole-hearted trust and faith in the Father. He did not consider Himself as identical with God.[3]

[1] Quoted in J. R. Chandran, *op. cit.*
[2] *ibid.*
[3] A. J. Appasamy, *What is Moksa ?* (1931), p. 2.

Vivekānanda's assumption was that *advaita* monism provides the key to the exegesis and evaluation of the Christian scriptures—a principle carried out in practice in the two Biblical commentaries published by his follower Sri Parānanda.

Sri Parānanda's Commentaries

The first of these, a full-scale commentary on St. Matthew's Gospel, was published in England in 1898, and was followed in 1902 by one on the Fourth Gospel, in which the author makes out that St. John was a Hindu following the Śaiva Siddhānta doctrine![1] An examination of these commentaries reveals the fact that they are not really a straight exposition of the text, but an attempt to make the Gospel conform to the pattern of Vivekānanda's *advaita* teaching. Where the text cannot be made to yield a Hindu meaning it is declared to be unsound. This is an interesting example of an attempt to make the Christian Gospel a part of Hinduism; to absorb and reinterpret it, not merely in an Indian manner but as part of the Hindu system.

The method may be clearly illustrated by taking one or two typical exegetical comments. For example on Matthew 6 : 12 ('Forgive us our debts') we find the following 'expansion':

> And let that communion be so complete as to efface all differentiating sense of 'I' and 'Thou', or of obligations left undone by me. Mayest Thou, O Lord, graciously *annul* the relation of debtor and creditor, and make me *one* with Thee.

Here is the note on Matthew 11 : 28 ('I will give you rest'):

> *Rest*. This is identical with Peace. When thoughts run down to a perfect calm and sleep does not intervene, Peace of the Kingdom of God is attained.

And on Matthew 20 : 28 ('To give his life a ransom for many'):

> This figure employed by Jesus is, that he taught the soul its condition of captivity and awakened in it a desire for freedom, and then gave his own body to the captor as a consideration for the release of the soul. All this figurative language means that in order that 'lost' souls may regain the Kingdom of God, he had to teach them objectively (by sanctifying his life) the subjective truth that self-effacement, or forsaking all the rudiments of the flesh, was essential to obtain God.

[1] Sri Parānanda, *The Gospel of Jesus according to St. Matthew, as interpreted to R. L. Harrison by the Light of the Godly Experience of Sri Parananda.* (1898).
Sri Parānanda, *An Eastern Exposition of St. John* (1902).

These passages are the nearest that Parānanda comes to a doctrine of the atonement. The suffering of Christ is merely an object-lesson to teach us the necessity for 'self-effacement' and the forsaking of the 'flesh'. As we progress in knowledge (*jñāna*) we leave behind the body and its distractions and so, finding unity with the Absolute, 'regain the Kingdom of God'. We are reminded of Keshab Chandra Sen's teaching on the self-abnegation of Christ being reflected in the life of the believer.

It is plain that Parānanda's commentaries are not in fact Christian commentaries at all, but rather attempts to prove that Christianity is nothing other than *advaita* Hinduism, and fully capable of absorption within the Hindu system. It is somewhat of a relief to turn to another thinker who, though no less 'Indian' than those we have just been studying, and thoroughly familiar with their work, yet approached the Christian faith from ***within*** and, starting from a deep personal experience of Christ and the Church, struggle to work out a theology in Indian terms.

Brahmabandhab Upādhyāya (1861-1907)

Bhavāni Charan Bānerji, to give him his original name, was born in 1861, a Bengali of Brāhman family.[1] As a boy he came under the influence of Keshab Chandra Sen, whom he later affirmed to be the greatest man that modern India had produced. From early boyhood he became warmly attached to the Person of Christ, and this love was nurtured by his contacts at the Scottish General Assembly's Institution in Calcutta where he studied, and by his intimacy with Sen and P. C. Mozoomdar. Another Christian influence in his early life was that of his uncle, the well-known Rev. Kāli Charan Bānerji, one of the earliest and greatest Christian nationalists of Bengal. In 1887 he became a member of the Church of the New Dispensation.

In 1888 at the age of twenty-seven he went as a Brahmo teacher to Hyderabad in Sindh, and there, chiefly through his friendship with two CMS missionaries, Redman and Heaton, gradually became convinced of the truth of the resurrection of Christ and of his co-eternal Sonship.[2] He was baptised in 1891, affirming at the same time that he did not thereby join the Church of

[1] B. Animananda, *The Blade : Life and Work of Brahmabandhab Upadhyaya* (Calcutta : n.d. but probably c. 1947).
F. Heiler, *Christliche Glaube und Indisches Geistesleben* (1926), pp. 65 ff.
F. Heiler, *The Gospel of Sundar Singh* (1927), pp. 248 ff.
A. Väth, *Im Kampfe mit der Zauberwelt des Hinduismus* (1928). This is the fullest critical study of Brahmabandhab.

[2] Animananda, *op. cit.*, p. 36.

England. Before the end of the year he had become a Roman Catholic, being given conditional baptism, and choosing the name Theophilus, which he translated as 'Brahmabandhab', 'the friend of *Brahman*'.

Even before his open profession of Christianity he had been interested in the possibility of reconciling 'pure Hinduism and pure Christianity':

> To preach Christ as the eternal Son of God, as the Logos in all prophets and saints before and after his Incarnation, and as the incarnate perfect Righteousness by whose obedience man is made righteous.[1]

This ideal he admits to be the direct fruit of the influence of Sen, many of whose theological ideas we shall later recognise in the work of Upādhyāya. From his earliest days as a Christian his deep knowledge of Hinduism, and especially of the Vedānta, led him to study the Christian revelation in relation to the deepest insights of Hinduism, and unlike Goreh he became convinced that the best way of bringing home the Christian faith to Indian thinkers was by using the categories of the Vedanta. He writes:

> Indian thought can be made just as useful to Christianity as Greek thought has been to Europe. . . . The truths of the Hindu philosopher must be 'baptized' and used as stepping-stones to the Catholic Faith. . . . The European clothes of the Catholic religion should be laid aside as soon as possible. It must assume the Hindu garment which will make it acceptable to the people of India. This change can only be effected by Indian missionary Orders who preach the Sacred Faith in the language of the Vedanta.[2]

Here we see the ideal of De Nobili asserting itself once more, and Upādhyāya was conscious of the Madurai tradition. In 1894 he donned the ochre robe of a *sannyāsi*, seeking and eventually obtaining the permission of the authorities of his Church for his experiment, although he did not belong to any order, nor was he ordained. In the same year he founded the monthly journal *Sophia*, which continued till 1899 and provided him with a platform for publicising his views. The name *Sophia* was carefully chosen as indicating the Wisdom of God, revealed in Christ the Logos who alone can lead the wise to true Wisdom. This was a highly creative period of Upādhyāya's life. He travelled and lectured, defending the Christian faith against the attacks

[1] *ibid.*, p. 38. These words were written while he was still a Brahmo.
[2] Heiler, *The Gospel of Sundar Singh*, p. 248.

of theosophy (for Mrs. Annie Besant was then a power to be reckoned with, and had many followers), developing his own distinctive explanation of doctrine in terms of Vedāntic thought-forms, and giving himself in love and self-sacrifice to the education of his people and the service of the poor and needy. At this period his relations with the Church authorities were cordial and he was given every encouragement to follow up and publish his ideas.

He was already a Christian *sannyāsi* and had gathered round himself a few like-minded companions, but he longed to establish a *maṭha* (monastery) which might become a centre for new spiritual experiments, a source of Christian life which was yet closely linked with the old Hindu ideal of a group of ascetics living together in poverty and following a life of contemplation and study. Here there would be an opportunity to express the heart of the Christian faith in a new way, using terms and concepts and practices which would attract the Hindu world instead of alienating it like so much of the missionary work of the West. He found a site near the narrow gorge of the Marble Rocks on the river Narmadā at Jabalpur, and looked forward eagerly to the beginning of the experiment. But official opposition to Upādhyāya's advanced views was growing within the Roman Church. It was felt that he was going too fast, that the scheme was ill-advised and not sufficiently thought out. No official approval was given, and the plan was reluctantly dropped. It was the beginning of a conflict with the Church authorities which was to become more and more painful and end only with the death of Upādhyāya.

In 1900 he moved from Jabalpur to Calcutta, and for a time worked closely with the poet Rabindranath Tagore in developing the famous *āshram* at Śāntiniketan. His journalistic activity continued and increased, and he began to turn more and more to Śankara's non-dualism as an instrument for expressing Christian doctrine. In his earlier days as a Christian he had been drawn towards the 'Vedic theology' of K. M. Banerji,[1] and had opposed the use of Śankara's Vedānta by Christians, but now he came to the conclusion that this was Indian teaching at its highest, and began to attempt the very difficult task of an alliance between Christian truth and *advaita* philosophy. It is in this effort that his most brilliant and profound thought can be seen.

[1] v. supra, p. 57, footnote.

At the same time he became more and more involved in the developing national struggle, into which he threw himself with all the fervour of his nature, and indeed outside Christian circles most Indians today remember him chiefly as a patriot, one of the first, if not the first to have advocated complete political independence for India. One result of his political activity was a widening of the rift between him and his Church, which resulted in the banning of his journal *Sophia* (by this time a weekly), and of *The Twentieth Century* which succeeded it.

In 1902-03 he paid a visit to Europe, living as a *sannyāsi* and spending his time mainly in England. Though he found friends in Oxford and Cambridge, as well as in London where he met Von Hügel, his European experiences tended only to increase the bitterness which he felt against the West for its political, cultural and intellectual domination of his country.

Some of his activities after his return made even his closest Indian Christian friends doubt his orthodoxy, while his missionary acquaintances more or less took it for granted that he had severed his connection with the Church. In a school which he ran for Hindu boys he encouraged the pupils to take part in the veneration of Sarasvati, goddess of learning. He also defended the propriety of Hindus worshipping Krishna as an *avatāra*, though he maintained a clear distinction between an *avatāra* and the unique *incarnation* of Christ. Finally, he took part in a ceremony of *prāyaścitta* or ritual atonement, in repentance for the 'defilement' which he had incurred by travelling overseas and eating food with foreigners. Some of his Christian friends assumed that by this ceremony he intended to leave the Christian faith and return to Hindu society.

Yet Upādhyāya maintained that he remained a Christian, and gave a clear explanation for each of these acts. He felt that he was *culturally* a Hindu, while being at heart a Christian. In Europe he had seen statues and pictures of the Muses and Graces: why should not Sarasvati, as the figure of learning personified, be venerated by Hindu pupils in an institution of learning? So too Krishna is seen not as the love-God of popular Hinduism but as a historical figure from Indian history and as the mouthpiece of the sublime teaching of the *Gitā*, who has a true message for the people of India. Even the ceremony of *prāyaścitta* had for him no implication of re-admission into the Hindu religion, though it did indeed mark his ritual re-entry into a society from which he had felt himself cut off.

On 10th September 1907 Upādhyāya was arrested by the

British Government on a charge of sedition. He appeared in court, not in 'the saffron garb of liberty'[1] but in plain Bengali dress and wearing the sacred thread of a Brāhman to indicate his solidarity with Hindu society. Shortly afterwards he had to enter hospital for a hernia operation, and although the operation seemed successful, complications set in and he died in hospital, still a free man, at the age of forty-six.

Brahmabandhab Upādhyāya is a towering, stormy figure in the political and literary history of Bengal. What are we to say about his work as a theologian? Fr. Alfons Väth, who has written the fullest study to appear so far,[2] gives the verdict that Brahmabandhab failed—failed in his attempt to pioneer a new Christian theology, failed even to found a new secular school of purified Vedāntic thought.[3] Yet perhaps time will show that Upādhyāya succeeded. It is not that he has produced a definitive *Summa Theologica*, but that rather—like Bonhöeffer whose work was similarly left incomplete—he has begun new lines of thought and suggested new possibilities of interpreting the Christian Gospel in an Indian setting. It remains for us to examine his teaching on a number of points in order to understand what the task was which he undertook, and how far he succeeded in accomplishing it.

Christianity and Hinduism

We have seen how in his youth Upādhyāya was a great admirer of Keshab Chandra Sen. He believed that Sen had been truly Christ-centred, but thought that his successors in the New Dispensation had deserted his teaching. Upādhyāya similarly felt, not that all religions were equal, as his friend and contemporary Vivekānanda was preaching, but that in Christ and in him alone all religions must find their fulfilment and so be reconciled with one another.

Christianity, it seemed to him, had come to India, or at least to Bengal, as a western religion, with its purity hidden under a series of unfamiliar terms and structures. But these western forms were neither the only possible ones nor were they final:

> The development of the Christian religion has not come to an end. It will grow, blossom and fructify till the end of time. Indian soil is humid and its humidity will make the ever-new Christian

[1] Ānimānanda, *op. cit.*, p. 169.
[2] A. Väth, *Im Kampfe mit der Zauberwelt des Hinduismus* (1928).
[3] Väth, *op. cit.*, p. 216.

Revelation put forth newer harmonics and newer beauties, revealing more clearly the invincible integrity of the Universal Faith deposited in the Church by the Apostles of Jesus Christ. The Hindu mind and heart, coming under the dominion of the One, Holy, Apostolic and Catholic Church, will sing a *new* canticle which will fill the earth with sweetness from end to end.[1]

We can see here how strongly Upādhyāya is convinced that the 'integrity' of the faith committed to the Church must not be tampered with. It is rather the western elaboration of that 'deposit' which is misleading and which should be replaced by an Indian thought-system, above all by that of Śankara. He writes:

> The Hindu mind is extremely subtle and penetrative, but is opposed to the Greco-Scholastic method of thinking. We must fall back on the Vedantic method, in formulating the Catholic religion to our countrymen. In fact, the Vedanta must be made to do the same service to the Catholic faith in India as was done by the Greek philosophy in Europe.[2]

This, then, was Upādhyāya's task, and we shall shortly see how he attempted it in the field of various doctrines. But first we must turn to another very important issue, his view of the relationship of Hindu culture to Hindu religion. He was convinced that it is possible to be a Hindu and a Christian at the same time, yet by this he did not imply a process of syncretism, but rather a separation of religious from cultural Hinduism. He expresses his view very unambiguously:

> We are Hindus so far as our physical and mental constitution is concerned, but in regard to our immortal souls we are Catholic. We are Hindu Catholics. . . The test of being a Hindu cannot therefore lie in religious opinions.[3]

Writing towards the end of his life in *Sandhyā*, a Bengali daily paper which he edited, he says:

> Our *dharma* has two branches: *samaj dharma* and *sadhan dharma*. . . . We are Hindus. Our Hinduism is preserved by the strength of *samaj dharma*. While the *sadhan dharma* is of the individual, its object is *sadhan* and *muktee* (Salvation). It is a hidden thing and one to be meditated upon. It has no connection whatever with

[1] Ānimānanda, *op. cit.*, p. 68.
[2] *ibid.*, p. 74.
[3] *ibid.*, pp. 71-f.

society. It is a matter known to the *guru* and *shisha* only. A Hindu, so far as *sadhan* goes, can belong to any religion.[1]

Upādhyāya is here writing at a time when he was deeply involved in the national struggle and felt impelled to identify himself as fully as possible with his country, Hindustan, the land of the Hindus. We may take issue with his separation between a man's religion and his life in society. And yet there is a very important point here, for he is saying in effect that it is possible to accept *cultural* Hinduism without accepting Hinduism as religious truth. There is a clear parallel in the development of Greek culture. Originally it was closely linked with Greek religion. Gradually the bonds were loosened, philosophy became a separate discipline, mythology became part of literature rather than religion, and finally Greek religion died, while *cultural* Hellenism, philosophic, scientific, literary and artistic, merged with the Christian tradition and is still very much alive today. May it not be that Upādhyāya has here for the first time isolated a fact of the utmost importance for the development both of the Christian Church and of Indian—of Hindu—culture ?

Saccidānanda Brahman

Upādhyāya had grown up in the tradition of the Brahma Samāj in which, ever since the time of Ram Mohan Roy, God had been described by the neuter word *Brahman*, which signifies the unconditioned Absolute, beyond all qualifications, beyond even the concept of personality. As we have seen, however, this conception of God had been greatly developed by Keshab Chandra Sen, who had been convinced that in Jesus of Nazareth we see the God-man, divine humanity, and had in consequence seized upon the only attempt of the Vedānta to describe *Brahman*, the conception of *Sat*, *Cit*, *Ānanda*, and found in this an inspired interpretation of the Christian doctrine of the Trinity. Upādhyāya, who had chosen the name of Brahmabandhab (friend of *Brahman*) for himself, eagerly seized upon this conception as providing a key for the fulfilment of his great desire to reconcile Hinduism and Christianity in the Person of Christ. Both before and after his conversion he had made a detailed study of Roman scholastic theology which he appears to have accepted in its entirety, and the order and completeness of Thomism

[1] Ānimānanda, *op. cit.*, p. 200. *Dharma* can be translated by ' religion ' or ' duty ' ; *samaj dharma* is ' social obligation ' and *sādhan dharma* refers to religious life. ' *Guru* ' and ' *shisha* ' : master and disciple.

appealed to him greatly, while making him long for a similarly comprehensive yet fully Indian system which would discard Thomism's western thought-pattern. We need not be surprised therefore to discover that his fascinating and penetrating use of the Vedānta is based ultimately on a theological sub-structure which is little different from traditional scholasticism, at least in the earlier phases of his work.

Perhaps the best starting place for a consideration of Upādhyāya's teaching on God and the Trinity is the wonderful hymn on the Trinity as *Saccidānanda* which he wrote in Sanskrit and which, better than all his writings, illuminates his beliefs and shows the deep devotion behind them.[1] The hymn begins with a verse of worship of the Trinity, *Saccidānanda* (Being, Consciousness and Bliss), and then goes on in the four following verses to describe successively the work of the three-fold unity, of the Father, the Son and the Spirit.

I bow to Him who is Being, Consciousness and Bliss.
I bow to Him whom worldly minds loathe, whom pure minds yearn for,
the Supreme Abode.

He is the Supreme, the Ancient of days, the Transcendent,
Indivisible Plenitude, Immanent yet above all things,
Three-fold relation, pure, unrelated,
knowledge beyond knowledge.

The Father, Sun, Supreme Lord, unborn,
The seedless Seed of the tree of becoming,
The Cause of all, Creator, Providence, Lord of the universe.

The infinite and perfect Word,
The Supreme Person begotten,
Sharing in the Father's nature, Conscious by essence,
Giver of true Salvation.

He who proceeds from Being and Consciousness,
Replete with the breath of perfect bliss,
The Purifier, the Swift, the Revealer of the Word,
the Life-giver.

This is a magnificent hymn, and the deeper it is studied the more its Christian orthodoxy stands out, despite the use of Hindu terminology. Much of the language has Scriptural

[1] This appeared in the monthly *Sophia*, Oct. 1898. The Sanskrit text is available on the flyleaf of *Swami Parama Arubi Anandam : Fr. J. Monchanin —A Memorial* (1959). The English translation is, with slight alterations, that printed in the *Prayer Book and Hymnal* published for the 38th International Eucharistic Congress in Bombay, 1964 (Hymn No. 2).

echoes, though the vocabulary is not that of most Bible translations—Father, Supreme Lord (*Parameśvara*), Word, begotten, Breath, Purifier, Revealer of the Word, Life-giver. Where the terminology is derived from Hinduism—*Sat*, *Cit*, *Ānanda*, 'the seedless Seed of the tree of becoming', 'perfect bliss'—it is fully as expressive as, and indeed more vivid than the Greek or Latin-derived words which might have been used instead. What the Bible says about the triune God, and what the Church teaches, can be felt behind this hymn whose atmosphere is yet so very Indian. The conception of *Saccidānanda* cannot exhaustively define the nature of the Trinity. But when imaginatively used as here, especially with Brahmabandhab's rich combination of ideas from Scriptural, Greek and Hindu sources, it seems definitely to provide for the Hindu a 'stepping-stone' towards the full understanding of the Christian doctrine. Indeed it throws fresh light on the doctrine for those who have been brought up in a purely western theological tradition.

Upādhyāya did not find it impossible to combine the Thomist idea of God as pure Being with the Vedāntic conception of *Brahman*. He accepted the usefulness of the traditional theistic arguments for the existence of God and held that logically a man must become a theist before becoming a Christian, and that a common foundation of natural theology can be laid for all theists, on which the supernatural superstructure of the Christian faith can afterwards be erected. 'We hold with the Vedantists that there is one eternal Essence from which proceed all things', he wrote.[1] This pure Being is identical with *Brahman*:

> Brahman is Being Itself. He alone is identical with His own Being while creatures have no right of being, but have a merely participated and dependent existence.[2]

But *Brahman* is very far removed from the mere abstract pure Being of the rationalists, whom Upādhyāya severely criticises. God is 'Divinity *per se*', living in 'the supreme felicity of self-colloquy'. This is the *Brahman* of the Vedānta. Yet perfect and self-sufficient as he is, he is not unknowable or unapproachable, Upādhyāya believes, and he shows what he means in a review of a collection of sonnets entitled *Naivedya*, published by his friend Tagore in 1901. He writes:

> The keynote of the sonnets is the direct, personal relation with the Infinite. There are some who argue that as the Infinite is not

[1] Ānimānanda, *op. cit.*, p. 71.
[2] *ibid.*, p. 83.

easily approachable, the finite should be worshipped tentatively as the Infinite by the less spiritually advanced. Is the Infinite really unapproachable? If it had been so, Reason would be an anomaly. The perception of the Infinite is the dawn of Reason...

The crowning idea of *Naivedya* is to see God in God, Unrelated, Absolute, divorced from all relations. Who does not see in this the ancient Vedantic aspiration of attaining to *Nirlamba Brahmajnan* (knowledge of God as He exists in Himself)? Man knows Him through relations as the great Related One, but His bliss beatific does not consist in His correspondence with creatures but in the colloquy of His depthless profundity with His boundless expanse where all varieties are merged into an incomprehensible, synthetic unity.[1]

So Upādhyāya turns to what he regards as the highest possible Hindu conception of God, that of *Brahman* or *Parabrahman* or *nirguṇa Brahman*, for to stop short at anything less than this, any mere personal God or *Iśvara*, would amount to an admission that the God whom Christians worship is less than the All-highest. Nothing but the highest will satisfy Brahmabandhab.

Is there then no place for *saguṇa Brahman*, for the *Iśvara* of personal theism? For Upādhyāya anything connected with *Iśvara* is definitely on a lower level than the highest religion. To this plane he relegates popular Hinduism, with its worship of one's chosen deity, *iṣṭa deva*, and those who like Ramakrishna claimed to have had a vision of God are regarded as having reached only a comparatively low level of religious experience, for 'no man hath seen nor can see God'. As a good Roman Catholic he believes that the ultimate end of man is to pass beyond the abstract knowledge of God's divinity to 'the immediate vision of the Divine Essence'.[2] There can be no reality in the conception of *Iśvara*, who, as the Creator or demiurge, belongs to the realm of *māyā* rather than to true existence. In other words we can never hope to find ultimate peace, to have full knowledge (*jñāna*) of God, until we know Him as he really is, as *nirguṇa*. Any devotion or mystical union which stops short of this is inadequate.

It might appear that such uncompromising emphasis on the 'attributelessness' of the Godhead makes it impossible for us to predicate anything of God; must Christian Vedāntins also say only *neti, neti*? The answer to this question is found in

[1] *ibid.*, p. 101.
[2] *ibid.*, Appendix II, p. v.

Brahmabandhab's understanding of the doctrine of the Trinity in terms of *Saccidānanda.* Even Śankara was prepared to describe *nirguṇa Brahman* in this way. How much richer, then, the understanding of the Godhead given through a Christian Trinitarian exposition of *Saccidānanda*, as we see it demonstrated, for example, in the hymn which we have quoted? Brahmabandhab is not a Hindu drawing an interesting parallel between *Saccidānanda* and the Trinity. Rather, having come himself to know God in Christ, his own personal experience of God is triune, and he finds the Vedāntic teaching fulfilled here in a more meaningful way even than in Śankara. And so, for the benefit of his countrymen, he is led to explain the mystery of the Godhead, the *real* meaning of Brahman, in terms of the Trinitarian *Saccidānanda.* This mystery can be known only through revelation. Śankara indeed had understood something of the Trinity-in-Unity, but the true meaning of *Saccidānanda* is given only in the Christian revelation.

The crucial problem which he has to face is that of the origin of the Second and Third Persons of the Trinity. How can God, who is 'unrelated' (*nirguṇa*), have a Son? What is the inner meaning of the traditional phrase 'eternal generation'? He finds his solution, as Sen had done, in the nature of *Brahman* as *Cit*, Thought, and in the fact that though God is 'unrelated without' he may yet be 'related within'. God, existing from all eternity, has self-knowledge, and the origin of the *Cit*-Logos, who is likewise eternal, is to be found in this self-cognition of God:

> The differentiation of the Divine Self as subject and object can be served by no other medium than the Undivided, Infinite Substance which is Pure Knowledge. . . . It is knowledge and nothing but knowledge which can distinguish the Knowing Self of God from His Known Self. Jesus Christ has told us that there is a response of knowledge in the Godhead. God knows His own Self begotten in Thought and is known in return by that Begotten Self. . . God reproduces in knowledge a corresponding, acknowledging Self-Image, and from this colloquy of Reason proceeds His Spirit of Love which sweetens the Divine Bosom with boundless delight.[1]

It will be noted that this whole passage is very reminiscent of the language of Keshab Chandra Sen, and also catches echoes

[1] *The Twentieth Century*, 1901, pp. 116, 117.

of the Upaniṣads.[1] It is also a deeply Christian exposition of *Saccidānanda*. Upādhyāya feels that the Vedāntic teaching on God as *Saccidānanda* is true and helpful as far as it goes, but that it reaches its completion, its 'finale' only in the full Christian doctrine of the Trinity, which has been given to the Church by revelation. This doctrine, however, must be explained to Hindus in terms with which they are familiar, and in this very process of explaining the Christian faith through concepts drawn from another tradition light will be shed on the inner meaning of Christian truth itself.

Creation and Māyā

The problem of creation, of the relation of the created world to God, of the many to the One, is perhaps the most difficult in Indian philosophy. The *mahāvākya* of the Vedānta, *tat tvam asi*, with its assertion 'thou art That', postulates the identity of the believer, and ultimately of the whole creation, with God, *Brahman*. The personalist school of Rāmānuja attempts to solve the problem by saying that the world is related to God as the body is to the soul, so giving to it a definite reality and leaving the way open for a two-way personal relationship between man and God.[2] Yet the major strain of Hindu thought, and the one which is most widely accepted by Hindu thinkers today, is that of Śankara who holds that *Brahman* alone is real, and everything else is illusion, the product of *māyā*. We ourselves, like the world, are part of *Brahman*, and the object of religion is that we should, through knowledge, *jñāna*, get rid of our ignorance, *avidyā*, which is the product of *māyā*, and so come to realise our true identity with *Brahman*.

In his earlier days, as we have seen, Upādhyāya felt that it was impossible to use Śankara's *advaita* as an instrument of Christian theology. Later, however, realising that Śankara's system represented Hindu thought at its highest, at least in the minds of most Hindus, he decided to make the effort to use *advaita* as the philosophical basis of the system which he felt called to establish. The greatest problem facing him was that of creation, and he tackled it boldly by giving a new and original

[1] v. supra p. 28. Compare the description of the origin of multiplicity in the *Chandogya Upaniṣad*, 6 : 2 :—

> In the beginning this world was Being, one only, without a second. It bethought itself: 'Would that I were many! Let me procreate myself!

[2] v. infra on Appasamy, pp. 126 ff.

interpretation to Śankara's teaching on *māyā*. Väth and others have felt that this attempt was unsuccessful and that it took Upādhyāya far away from Christian orthodoxy, yet it is probably the most original and penetrating contribution which he made to Indian Christian theology and is worth careful study. Upādhyāya was determined that if Hindu philosophy were to be used to 'hew wood and draw water'[1] for Christian theology, then only the purest water and the strongest wood were good enough, and those, he was convinced, were to be found in Śankara rather than in any other system. How is God related to the world? 'By *māyā*', said Śankara. 'By *māyā*, then', said Upādhyāya, and proceeded to give his own interpretation of *māyā*, relating it to Thomist and Hegelian conceptions.

The traditional Vedāntic teaching asserts that God or *Brahman* is *Sat*, Being, and that everything else in the world is *asat*, non-being. Upādhyāya now expounds this as meaning that while God, as *Sat*, is *necessary* being, creation (*asat*) is not mere nothingness, but rather is being which is not self-existent, which does not *necessarily* exist, that is *contingent* being.[2] He describes *asat* as 'that which is, but has no right to be; what was, what is, but, does not exist of necessity—in the language of the scholastics, a contingent being'[3]. It seems that Upādhyāya is here attempting to interpret the idea of *creatio ex nihilo* in terms which will be consistent with scholastic theology, and will yet be acceptable or at least intelligible to advaitins. 'Not-being' (*asat*) becomes another way of saying 'nothing'. The process of creation is then the emanation, caused by Being (*Sat*), of derived being from non-being (*asat*).

Clearly some further explanation is needed of the process by which contingent being emerges from *asat* and Upādhyāya brings forward his explanation in an exposition of *māyā*. He writes:

> Māyā is what St. Thomas calls 'creatio passiva'—Passive Creation. It is a quality of all that is not Brahman, and is defined by the Angelic Doctor as 'the habitude of having "being" from another and resulting from the operation' of God.... The Vedāntists affirm all that is not Brahman to be *Māyā*, in the sense of illusion, and they are right, because creatures, in themselves, apart from Brahman, are indeed darkness, falsity and nothingness (tenebrae, falsitas et nihil) as St. Thomas teaches.[4]

[1] Ānimānanda, *op. cit.*, p. 67.
[2] *ibid.*
[3] *ibid.*, p. 82.
[4] *ibid.*, p. 83.

It is clear that *māyā* is here something more dynamic than mere illusion. It is the divine power by which the finite, created world comes into existence, a world which has *being*, though not indeed necessary being. Upādhyāya thus advances a stage further, following traditional Hindu terminology, and characterises *māyā* with the name *śakti* or power. He writes :

> Māyā . . . is the fecund Divine Power (Sakti) which gives birth to multiplicity . . . It is eternal but its operation is not essential to the being of God. By it, non-being (asat) is made being (sat). By it, that which is nothingness by itself is filled with the richness of being. By it darkness is illumined with the flow of existence. It is Māyā indeed.[1]

Māyā is, then, the divine power which brings finite creatures into being. Yet in popular parlance *māyā* has another, more common meaning, that of blindness or illusion, as when men say that they live ' under the spell of *māyā* '. Upādhyāya seeks to give a positive, Christian content even to this aspect of *māyā*. God's creative activity through *māyā* projects the individual as it were outside his true self, which is to be found only in God, for ' our hearts are restless till they find rest in Thee '. So man, in his natural, sin-bound state, finds himself separated from God, living by himself and turned in on himself. It is *māyā* which keeps him thus apart from God, and yet it is that same *māyā* which keeps his heart restless and makes him long to return home. Thus *māyā* has a double aspect, first creating man, and then showing the illusoriness of all man-made pleasures, so ' preventing the *jiva* from resting in himself or in anything finite '[2].

Thus Upādhyāya sees *māyā* not simply as the creative power of God but also in a sense as his prevenient grace which awakens in our hearts the desire to return to him. He does not, however, seek to identify *māyā* with any particular Christian concept, but rather to use it as he finds it in Śankara and to interpret it in a way which will bring him close to the teaching of Aquinas on contingent being. The interpretation of *māyā* as *creatio passiva* is the vital point in Upādhyāya's attempt to restate the Christian

[1] Ānimānanda, *op. cit.*, p. 84. *Śakti* can be used quite neutrally to mean force or power, and in current Christian usage in India is one of the words normally used for the power of the Holy Spirit. In Hinduism it is frequently used to indicate the female consorts of deities, who often personify the power of those deities. In Bengal, *Śakti* is used especially of the goddess *Kāli*, who in turn frequently symbolises the ' Mother ' or Motherland, as in Bankim Chatterji's famous national song *Bande Mātaram* (' Reverence the Mother ').

[2] *ibid.*, p. 86.

doctrine of creation in terms familiar and intelligible to Vedāntic Hindus.

The attempt is open to criticism from two sides. Vāth believed that Upādhyāya was guilty of a forced interpretation of Śankara, quite different from that accepted by all Hindus of his time. Yet surely it is the mark of a great constructive theologian that he can take common philosophical conceptions and transform them, making them vehicles for quite new theological ideas, as indeed Aquinas did for Aristotle. A second, and perhaps more telling criticism is that it is sad that Brahmabandhab should have exercised so much ingenuity and shown such deep insight merely to bring us to the point of departure of Aquinas. All through his expositions one feels that the Angelic Doctor looms too large and the Bible too small. If only he had been free to take the 'deposit' of the faith as he found it in the Bible, or even in the undivided Church of the first four centuries, and then to carry out the work of a Clement or an Origēn, what a wonderful work might have been accomplished. But he felt that his mission was to be to the India of the 20th century what Aquinas was to the Europe of the 13th, and the result was undoubtedly a curtailment of what he might have achieved.

Christ the God-Man and Logos

To introduce Brahmabandhab's teaching on the Person of Christ we can once more do no better than to quote one of his fine Sanskrit hymns—the *Hymn of the Incarnation*:[1]

The transcendent Image of Brahman,
Blossomed and mirrored in the full-to-overflowing
Eternal Intelligence—
Victory to God, the God-Man.

Child of the pure Virgin,
Guide of the Universe, infinite in Being
Yet beauteous with relations,
Victory to God, the God-Man.

Ornament of the Assembly
Of saints and sages, Destroyer of fear, Chastiser
Of the Spirit of Evil,—
Victory to God, the God-Man.

[1] *The Twentieth Century*, 1901, pp. 7-8, where the poem appears in Sanskrit with Brahmabandhab's own English translation. The version here given is that printed in C. F. Andrews, *The Renaissance in India* (1912), Appendix VIII, and is very close to Brahmabandhab's.

Dispeller of weakness
Of soul and body, pouring out life for others,
Whose deeds are holy,
Victory to God, the God-Man.

Priest and Offerer
Of his own soul in agony, whose Life is Sacrifice,
Destroyer of sin's poison,—
Victory to God, the God-Man.

Tender, beloved,
Soother of the human heart, Ointment of the eyes,
Vanquisher of fierce death,—
Victory to God, the God-Man.

Here once more one is impressed by the Christian orthodoxy of the implied theology, couched as it is largely in Hindu terminology. Christ is the Image of God (*Brahman*) and in him the eternal Word (intelligence, *Cit*), the fulness of the Godhead, dwells. In the refrain victory (*jai*) or glory is ascribed to him who is the true *Nara-Hari* ('Man-God'). He is infinite, the upholder of the universe, and yet is born of a Virgin; though he is 'infinite in being' (*nirguṇa*), yet he is also 'with relations' (*saguṇa*) and so personal and knowable.

His work also is described. His deeds are holy, showing the essential connection between God and morality, and here perhaps there is an implied contrast with the deeds of Krishna. He pours out his life for others, in agony of soul, giving himself as sacrifice, he who is both priest and victim. In language which recalls the Śaivite story of Śiva drinking poison to save the world, we are told how Christ destroys the poison of sin, himself drinking that bitter cup to the dregs in order that he may win the victory over death, destroy fear, and overcome Satan, the spirit of evil. And in all this we see only his love—'Tender, beloved, soother of the human heart'.

Upādhyāya is at his best when describing the work of Christ in poetical language, rich with Biblical and Indian concepts and images. When he attempts a closer definition he is perhaps less successful, but his way of describing how the divine and the human are related in the Person of Christ is full of interest. He never wavers in his conviction that Jesus Christ is fully God and fully man, 'the transcendent image of *Brahman*' but also 'Child of the pure Virgin', and to express this fact of the two natures united in the one Christ he often uses for him the name *Nara-Hari* or 'man-God'. The second element of this word, *Hari*, is in fact a proper name, used for the god Viṣṇu, and for this reason many Christians have taken exception to Brahmabandhab's using it in this way. It is, however, commonly used in Hindu circles simply as a synonym for God, for example in Gandhi's well-known use of the word *Harijan* (' people of God ') for the untouchables, and it is no doubt in this sense that Brahmabandhab intended to use it. This, as we have seen, is the word used in the refrain of the hymn on the Incarnation— Victory to God, the God-Man '—and Upādhyāya frequently uses for himself the *nom-de-plume* ' Narahari Dās ' (servant of the God-Man) to indicate his devotion to Christ.

At the same time Upādhyāya follows the lead of Keshab Chandra Sen in regarding Christ as the divine Wisdom, the *Cit* of *Saccidānanda*, and the title of his magazine *Sophia* reflects this understanding of the Person of Christ as Logos. Writing for the pupils of his school in Calcutta he says :

> God is Sat-Cit-Ananda. Every aspect of God should be worshipped, but being students we quite naturally worship in Him the aspect of Cit, Intelligence, Knowledge, Wisdom. . . The Hindu pierces the veil of the world and honours in God the Intelligence that ordered the Chaos into Kosmos.[1]

Lest we should think that by using the word ' aspect ' he implies that Christ is simply a ' mode ' of the Godhead in a Sabellian sense he continues :

> Sophia, according to the Catholic Faith, is more than an aspect of the Godhead. It is the Word of God, the Son, who became man for our sake and died for us on the Cross.[2]

When he goes on to give his explanation of how the two natures of Christ are united in one Person, Upādhyāya gives a very interesting excursus into Indian psychology. His final solution is not very different from that of Keshab Chandra Sen, but the argument is a very striking one :

> According to the Vedanta human nature is composed of five sheaths or divisions (*kosha*) . . . .[3] These five sheaths are presided over by a personality (*ahampratyayi*) which knows itself. This self-knowing individual (*jiva-chaitanya*) is but a reflected spark of the Supreme Reason (*kutastha-chaitanya*) Who abides in every

[1] Animānanda, *op. cit.*, p. 121.
[2] *ibid.*, p. 122.
[3] These sheaths (*kośa*) are : (1) physical (*annamaya*) ; (2) vital (*prāṇamaya*) ; (3) mental (*manomaya*) ; (4) intellectual (*vijnāmaya*) ; (5) spiritual (*ānandamaya*).

> man as the prime source of life and light. The time-incarnate Divinity is also composed of five sheaths ; but it is presided over by the Person of Logos Himself and not by any created personality (*aham*). The five sheaths and the individual agent, enlivened and illumined by Divine Reason. . . make up man. But in the God-man the five sheaths are acted upon direct by the Logos-God and not through the medium of any individuality.[1]

Upādhyāya is here attempting to reproduce, with Vedāntic terminology, the position of what he understands to be Catholic orthodoxy. The fact that the solution is close to that of Apollinaris whom the early Church held to be heretical should not rule out this method of approach which has as good a claim to validity as one which uses an outdated Greek psychology. Here we see a man who is striving, like Leontius of Byzantium or John of Damascus, to secure an orthodox Chalcedonian position, seeking to avoid both monophysitism and Apollinarianism yet tending in the direction of the latter. He would probably have found himself in agreement with the position of these two theologians as summarised by H. M. Relton :

> The human nature of the God-Man was from the beginning inseparably united with the Divine Nature, and in virtue of that union received from the Logos-personality its personality and thus its completeness.[2]

The interest of his statement, however, lies in the fact that he has given a clear description of the interrelation of the divine and human Christ without using western terms, either ancient or modern.

Avatāra *or Incarnation ?*

The personalist strand of Hinduism, and especially the Vaiṣṇava tradition, holds that God, *Iśvara*, from time to time comes down to earth as an *avatāra*, in order to save man in his need. The word *avatāra* comes from a root meaning 'to descend', and according to the Vaiṣṇava tradition Viṣṇu descends as an *avatāra* such as Rāma or Krishna when his intervention becomes necessary. The classical statement of the doctrine is found in the *Bhagavadgita*, where Krishna says to Arjuna :

> Whenever there is a decline of law, O Arjuna, and an outbreak of lawlessness, I incarnate myself. For the protection of the good,

[1] *The Twentieth Century*, 1901, p. 7.
[2] H. M. Relton, *A Study in Christology* (1917), p. 90.

> for the destruction of the wicked and for the establishment of the law I am born from age to age.[1]

The question at once arises whether or not Christian theologians should use the word *avatāra* as a synonym or a substitute for 'incarnation', and it is a question to which different Indian theologians have given different answers, as we shall see. Keshab Chandra Sen, standing within the Brahma Samāj tradition, was vehemently opposed to the custom of referring to Jesus as an *avatāra*, sternly calling it 'the lie of Christian avatarism'[2]. Upādhyāya, from his standpoint on the side of Śankara, similarly rejects the use of the word *avatāra* for Christ. There is only one Incarnation, that of Christ, for he is unique and in him God himself, *Parabrahman* than whom there can be none higher, becomes incarnate.

Having thus made secure the position of Christ as the unique Incarnation of God, Upādhyāya somewhat startlingly goes on in his later writings to allow a certain validity to the claims of Krishna, not as an incarnation of *Brahman*—for that position belongs to Christ alone—but as an *avatāra* of Viṣṇu. This is undoubtedly a strange development, one which involved Upādhyāya at the time in a controversy with J. N. Farquhar, and which has been enough to damn him unread in the eyes of many Christians ever since.[3] Why should he wish to champion Krishna in this way? The answer to the question is probably twofold. As a dedicated nationalist who felt that his country and its whole religio-cultural heritage was being obliterated by the West, Upādhyāya felt called to defend many beliefs and practices which in his earlier days he would have rejected. Secondly, his view of the possibility of separating Hindu religion and culture and ultimately of secularising the religious content of Hinduism made him feel that so long as Christ's uniqueness was safeguarded it did not much matter if respect or veneration were paid to Hindu deities. His attitude toward the Hindu personal deities was to treat them as great historical figures, or to 'moralise' them, or to do both. Thus he defends the historical existence of Krishna, and, because of the lofty teaching of the *Gita*, claims him as a

[1] *Gita* IV, 7:8, translated by D. S. Sarma.

[2] *Lectures* II, p. 38.

[3] Ānimānanda, *op. cit.*, p. 123. Upādhyāya was replying to Farquhar's critique of Krishna's historicity in his book *Gita and Gospel* (1904).

great moral leader. The undoubtedly immoral stories of the *Purāṇas* are interpreted allegorically.[1]

It must be admitted that Upādhyāya's position here is a dangerous one, and yet there is logic in it. Hindu religion for him is something precious, not to be lightly thrown away; and if some of his countrymen are in any case going to follow it, then it should be purified, and in that purification he can help. As a Roman Catholic he believes in natural theology, and Hinduism represents natural theology—'the highest rational philosophy'—and indeed a natural theology with a richer content than that of the West and one which rises to a higher peak since in its doctrine of *Saccidānanda* it raises man to the rational knowledge of God as not merely existent but triune. Within the framework of that natural theology Krishna appears as an incarnation of Viṣṇu, who is himself a personal manifestation of the supreme impersonal *Brahman*. Thus Krishna is at several removes from God, and appears only in time and space, not having any existence apart from that. In other words he belongs to the realm of *māyā*, of contingent being. Christ on the other hand is beyond *māyā*, for he is God himself, living in the eternal dialogue of the Trinity. He too appears in history as the man Jesus, but his personality is eternally in the Godhead. Thus Krishna the *avatāra* does not constitute a threat to Christ the Incarnation. In a blunt but vivid phrase Upādhyāya says, 'Christ is like the sun and Krishna. . . a juicy ball!'[2]

There is no doubt that Upādhyāya gives to Hindu theism—both *advaita* and also personal theism—a considerable validity in its own field. He is concerned that the reality of the religious experience of millions of Hindus for hundreds of years should not be denied. Yet at best Hindusim is for him a stage on the journey to something more ultimate, and the final stage is found only in Christ.

The Indian Church

In his earlier days as a Christian Brahmabandhab seems to have accepted the discipline of the Roman Catholic Church gladly, but later he had many conflicts with authority and on one occasion even encouraged his publisher to take a court case

[1] It is still common to find people treating the stories of the *Purāṇas* allegorically. Dr. Radhakrishnan notes the tendency, but himself solves the problem, as does Upādhyāya, by rejecting the Puranic account of Krishna (*Indian Philosophy* II, p. 496).

[2] Ānimānanda, *op. cit.*, p. 128.

against the Church authorities. Unlike many Indian Christians he did, however, readily recognise the need for a visible, organised Church and for the regular ministry of the Word and sacraments, although towards the end of his life, when deeply involved in political activities, he was somewhat irregular in his attendance at Church. He died very suddenly in hospital, without receiving the last rites of his Church, and his body was cremated by his Hindu friends. The obituary notices which appeared in his own daily *Sandhyā*, however, spoke of him clearly as a Christian and his most intimate friends, like Ānimānanda, never had any doubts about his desire to remain, not merely a Christian, but a loyal member of his own Church.

In none of his writings do we find any criticism of the basic ' deposit ' of the Christian faith as found in the Bible, or even of the Thomist system, which he appears to have accepted without question. It was far otherwise, however, with what he regarded as the western trappings of the Christian faith in India, and to these he devotes many scathing attacks :

> It is the foreign clothes of the Catholic Faith that have chiefly prevented our countrymen from perceiving its universal nature. Catholicism has donned the European garb in India. Our Hindu brethren cannot see the subtlety and sanctity of our divine religion because of its hard coating of Europeanism. . . . They cannot understand how poverty can be compatible with boots, trousers and hats, with spoon and fork, meat and wine. . . . When the Catholic Church in India will be dressed. . . in Hindu garments then will our countrymen perceive that she elevates man to the Universal Kingdom of Truth by stooping down to adapt herself to his racial peculiarities.[1]

He comes to the conclusion that there is no reason why a man should not be a Hindu and a Christian at the same time. We find that more and more he interprets Hinduism in a secularised way, as representing national culture rather than a particular religion. In July 1898, for example, he published in *Sophia* an article entitled *Are we Hindus ?* in which he writes :

> By birth we are Hindus and shall remain *Hindus* till death. But as *dvija* (twice-born) by virtue of our sacramental rebirth, we are *Catholic*, we are members of an indefectible communion embracing all ages and climes. . . Our thought and thinking is emphatically Hindu. We are more speculative than practical, more given to synthesis than analysis, more contemplative than active. It is

[1] Ânimânanda, *op. cit.*, p. 74 ff.

> extremely difficult for us to learn how to think like the Greeks of old or the scholastics of the Middle Ages. Our brains are moulded in the philosophic cast of our ancient country.[1]

This was what led him to the idea of founding his order of 'Hindu-Catholic' *sannyāsis*. He had, of course, the example of De Nobili before him, and he himself set an example which was soon to be followed by Sundar Singh and others. Despite the lack of ecclesiastical support which forced him to abandon the monastery at Jabalpur, he retained the saffron robe to the end, and discarded it only when he had to appear in court on a charge of political treason, and did not wish to defile 'the garb of liberty'. He wrote:

> We can have no rest until we see the religion of Christ lived by Hindu ascetics and preached by Hindu monks; until we behold the beauty of the Catholic Faith set off with oriental vestments.[2]

Brahmabandhab was ahead of his time in these ideas and it is perhaps only today that they are beginning to find support and be put into practice. Both in the practical matter of dress and way of life and more especially in his massive effort to use Hindu ways of thought for the expression of the Christian faith, he was an outstanding pioneer. Ānimānanda has called him 'the greatest Indian that ever found his way to Christ'[3]. Having found his way to Christ he was desperately anxious to show that Christ was the highest: that no follower of the *jñāna mārga* should ever say to him, 'Christianity is all right for you, but my faith in *Brahman* is higher, for it transcends the personal'. And so Christ as *Cit* is seen in *Brahman*, and the ultimate object of human thought, as of human devotion, is the Trinity, *Sat*, *Cit*, *Ānanda*. To have stated this so clearly and to have combined it with such a blazing devotion to Christ the God-Man, the *Nara-Hari*, is a great achievement in the confrontation between Christianity and Hinduism. In the words of an anonymous commentator,

> He attempted the synthesis of philosophy and theology, Eastern and Western, not by evaporating concepts but by crystallising.

[1] Ānimānanda, *op. cit.*, p. 71.
[2] *ibid.*, p. 78.
[3] *ibid.*, p. 196.

the message of the Catholic Church in the Vedanta solution of Sankaracarya.[1]

He did not 'evaporate concepts', but sought to show that, if *Sat*, *Cit*, *Ānanda* is the highest level to which reason or revelation can lead us, then it is there alone, and not at any lower stage, that God is to be seen and worshipped in Christ.

[1] Dust-jacket of *The Blade*. Compare Chenchiah's dictum: 'The negative plate of Jesus developed in a solution of Hinduism brings out hitherto unknown features of the portrait.' v. infra p. 164.

Chapter VI

THE WATER OF LIFE IN AN INDIAN CUP: SUNDAR SINGH

Theological Developments, 1900-1925

The twenty-five years from about 1900 to 1925 marked a distinct change in the theological climate in India. One factor which had a considerable influence on Indian Christian thinkers was the growing national movement, as we have already seen in the work of Brahmabandhab. The foundation of the Indian National Congress in 1885 and the visit of Vivekānanda to the World Parliament of Religions in Chicago in 1893 are two milestones in the growth of national self-consciousness. Towards the end of the century the more liberal and constitutional reformers of the Brahma Saṃāj tradition like Justice Ranade of Bombay found themselves bypassed in popular estimation by the militant attitude of Lokmānya Bāl Gangādhār Tilak, while in Bengal besides the literary and cultural nationalism of Rabindranath Tagore there was the more violent movement centering round people like Bankim Chatterji, Brahmabandhab himself, and later Aurobindo Ghose. For many of these leaders nationalism was closely linked with a reassertion of Hinduism in conscious opposition to Christianity, as for example in the revival of the cult of Krishna which led Brahmabandhab to write as he did on the nature of Krishna's *avatāra*. By the beginning of the twentieth century the stage was set for an unrelenting and continuous national struggle which was to end only with full independence in 1947. The greatest figure of all stepped on the Indian stage in 1915 when, after a long struggle for the rights of Indians in South Africa, Mahatma Gandhi returned to India and gradually established himself at the head of the nationalist movement.

For some years the attitude of most Indian Christians to the national movement was an ambiguous and perhaps embarrassed one. The missionaries, who at least up to 1920 constituted the real leadership in all but the Syrian Churches, were mainly antinationalist, and comparatively few Indian Christians found it possible to throw in their lot whole-heartedly with the nationalist cause. There were of course notable exceptions like the Rev. Kāli Charan Bānerji of Bengal and his famous nephew

Brahmabandhab. Gradually, however, a number of Christians both Indian and missionary—among the latter notably C. F. Andrews—threw in their lot with Gandhi and became openly critical not only of the British *rāj* but of the 'western captivity' of the Indian Church. Gandhi himself was greatly influenced by Christianity, especially by the ethics of Jesus, but strongly objected to 'proselytism' and to what he regarded as the denationalisation of Indian Christians.[1] By the beginning of the 'twenties, then, although most Christians were prepared to continue in a predominantly western tradition of Church organisation, worship and theology, there were already clear voices being heard summoning the Indian Church to be truly Indian, and to accept the Indian national and cultural tradition while still remaining unmoved in their loyalty to Christ.

A second factor which at this time began to influence Christian thought in India was the movement towards Church unity. In the earliest days of missionary work at the beginning of the nineteenth century there had usually been a spirit of co-operation between the various Churches and societies. Later came a less friendly period, not infrequently marked by competition and even 'sheep-stealing'[2]. As time went on, however, cooperation between the non-Roman Churches and societies increased, and from 1872 onwards *Decennial Conferences* of Missions were held, to discuss problems of common interest and publish reports.

There were other, more far-reaching signs of a new spirit of unity. In 1908 the *South India United Church*, a union of Presbyterians and Congregationalists, came into being; and 1910 saw the foundation of the United Theological College in Bangalore and the opening of the Higher Theological Department at Serampore, events which provided India with two fine institutions where future leaders from many different Churches could study and live together. Meanwhile a strong feeling had arisen among Indian Christians that the work of evangelism should not be left only to foreign organisations, with the result that in 1903 the *Indian Missionary Society* of Tinnevelly was founded under the leadership of V. S. Azariah and A. S. Appasamy, while in 1905 came the foundation of the *National Missionary Society*.

[1] For a comprehensive study of Gandhi's relation to Christianity see Otto Wolff, *Mahatma und Christus* (1955).

[2] See K. Baago, '"Sheepstealing" in the 19th Century' in *Bulletin of the Church History Association of India*, No. 10 (1966), pp. 17 ff.

of India, both of them staffed and supported entirely from within India.[1]

The Edinburgh World Missionary Conference of 1910 caught the imagination of the Churches in both East and West and from this event more than any other may be dated the gradual decline of Indian missions and the rise of the Indian Church which slowly but steadily began to assume responsibility for its own support and leadership and, even more important, for its own thought. At Edinburgh the delegation from the younger Churches was numerically small, but men like V. S. Azariah created a deep impression and helped materially to change the relationship between the Churches of the West and the growing Church in India.

An important result of the Edinburgh Conference was the setting up in India in 1914 of the *National Missionary Council*, which in 1923 became the *National Christian Council*.[2] A more indirect result was the intensification of the movement towards Church union in South India which took organised form in 1919. Some of the rising theologians like Chenchiah and Chakkarai felt themselves largely out of sympathy with the aims and methods of the NCC as of the movement towards unity, since for them the prime need of the moment was 'Indianisation' rather than institutional unity. Yet the thinking and writing stimulated by the NCC and by the Church union movement, somewhat western in atmosphere though they may be, are important as providing part of the framework in which the twentieth century Indian Church has sought to express itself.

A third factor influencing Indian Christian thought at this period was the effect of the changing theological climate in the West. During the greater part of the nineteenth century, as we have seen, the theology of most missionaries in India was what might be termed conservative evangelical, while their usual attitude to Hinduism was one of refutation. To say this is by no means to imply that no missionaries were sympathetic to Hinduism; as early as the 18th century Ziegenbalg had made a penetrating study of Tamil religious customs which provoked his home secretary, A. H. Francke of Halle, to write, 'The missionaries were sent out to exterminate Heathenism in India, not to spread heathen nonsense all over Europe'[3]. In general, however, the attitude was that the theology of the sending

[1] D. F. Ebright, *The National Missionary Society of India*, 1905-1942 (1944).
[2] K. Baago, *A History of the National Christian Council of India*, 1914-1964 (1965).
[3] Lehmann, *op. cit.*, p. 32.

Churches in the West ought to be reproduced in India and that those who were won over from Hinduism should sever all connection with their former religion. As the nineteenth century advanced various factors led to a change in this attitude. Missionaries in India were not unaware of higher criticism and of the new trends in theology which accompanied it. In addition, through the work of Oriental scholars like Max Müller there grew up an interest in comparative religion which frequently carried with it a mood of sympathy towards Hinduism, as we have seen in Müller's encounter with Nehemiah Goreh. Among well-known missionaries who reflected the new attitude of sympathy and openness towards Hinduism were William Miller and T. E. Slater of Madras. If we wish, however, to select one figure who more than any other typifies the new approach, we shall turn to *J. N. Farquhar* (1861-1929).[1]

Farquhar felt the crucial need of a workable 'apologetic' approach to the university-educated Indian and as a means to that end sought to find a more satisfactory relationship between Christianity and Hinduism than that of mere mutual exclusion. In a series of writings he gradually worked out his idea of 'fulfilment' which reached classical expression in *The Crown of Hinduism* published in 1913. The kernel of his argument is found in an earlier article (1910), in which he expounds Matt. 5:17:

> Christ's own declaration, 'I came not to destroy but to fulfil', has cleared up for us completely all our difficulties with regard to the Old Testament . . . Can it be that Christ Himself was thinking of pagan faiths as well as Judaism ? . . . If Christ is able to satisfy all the religious needs of the human heart, then all the elements of pagan religions, since they spring from these needs, will be found reproduced in perfect form, completely fulfilled, consummated in Christ.[2]

It was Farquhar's belief that there is an *evolutionary* connection between Hinduism and Christianity, as of lower to higher, so that what is only foreshadowed in Hinduism is fulfilled and perfected in Christianity. Farquhar was not unnaturally attacked by most conservative missionaries. Yet there was an element of misunderstanding in their attack for, as E. J. Sharpe

[1] Eric J. Sharpe, *J. N. Farquhar : A Memoir* (1963).
Eric J. Sharpe, *Not to Destroy but to Fulfil, The Contribution of J. N. Farquhar to Protestant Missionary Thought in India before* 1914 (1965).

[2] Sharpe, *Not to Destroy but to Fulfil*, pp. 311 f.

points out,[1] he never held that the passage from 'lower' to 'higher' was an automatic one, but rather that it depended on individual choice; and he also believed that Christianity must ultimately *replace* Hinduism rather than merely reforming it. In some ways, indeed, his approach foreshadows that recently made by Raymond Panikkar in *The Unknown Christ of Hinduism* with its idea of Christianity as Hinduism which has died and risen again transformed. As long ago as 1909 Farquhar had written, 'Hinduism must die into Christianity, in order that the best her philosophers, saints and ascetics have longed and prayed for may live'[2].

Despite the opposition which Farquhar's book at first aroused, his attitude gradually came to dominate the field and became perhaps the typical missionary theological approach to Hinduism in the 'twenties and 'thirties, right up till 1938 when Kraemer's *The Christian Message in a Non-Christian World* exploded, like Barth's *Römerbrief*, 'on the playground of the theologians'[3].

We have given this account of Farquhar because his views were undoubtedly influential on the coming generation of Indian Christian theologians like Appasamy and Chenchiah. We cannot help noting, however, that Farquhar was not a trained theologian, and the Christianity which was to be the Crown of Hinduism turns out to be merely a version of Harnack's 'religion of Jesus', stressing the 'simple' teaching of Jesus and relying on a moral influence theory of the atonement. In a telling sentence Sharpe sums up some of the things which are lacking in Farquhar's presentation of Christianity:

> There is no treatment of sin and its effect on man's relationship with his Creator; no real treatment of the themes of atonement, forgiveness, reconciliation and salvation; the work of Christ is subordinated to the life and teaching of Christ; there is no eschatology; no mention of the Church as 'the communion of saints'[4].

This is a serious indictment, and makes us realise that some at least of those points which may strike us as weakest in the work of the theologians whom we are about to study stem far less from the Indian modes of thought which they use than from the western theological climate of the India of their day which Farquhar did so much to create.

[1] Sharpe, *op. cit.*, pp. 335 ff.

[2] *ibid.*, p. 360.

[3] The phrase is Karl Adam's.

[4] *ibid.*, p. 345. Sharpe points out the connections with Harnack and with the 'new theology' of R. J. Campbell.

'The Light of the East'

We shall pause here for a moment to refer, all too briefly, to an interesting revival within the Roman Catholic Church of the tradition inaugurated by Brahmabandhab Upādhyāya. We have seen how in his lifetime he was disowned and discouraged by his Church authorities. He died in 1907. By 1920 a number of Roman Catholic thinkers, mainly Belgian Jesuits, were beginning to see his work in a truer perspective and to realise its great and permanent significance. This group of thinkers whose leaders were Fathers G. Dandoy and Pierre Johanns, both Oxford trained orientalists, in 1922 founded a monthly magazine *The Light of the East* which for many years continued Brahmabandhab's work of seeking a positive relationship between Christianity and Hindu philosophy. Over the years a long series of articles by Johanns appeared, entitled *To Christ through the Vedanta*, in which the author, by means of a detailed analysis of the systems of Śankara, Rāmānuja, Vallabha and Caitanya, sought to show how materials from each of them could be used in the task of 'reconstructing' Catholic philosophy.[1] Johanns states his theory explicitly in the first issue of *The Light of The East*:

> If the Vedanta philosophers will only bring their several positive statements into harmony, they will turn disconnected doctrines into a system and that system will be Thomism or something akin to Thomism.[2]

He expresses a deep debt of gratitude to Brahmabandhab, and expounds in a very similar way the doctrine of creation as contingent being, though he insists at the same time on the belief in *creatio ex nihilo* and holds that Śankara's system must be complemented by Rāmānuja's. He compares Śankara's view of the unity of God to a white ray of light, while that of Rāmānuja is like the same ray broken up by a prism into its constituent colours, and comments:

> To know God, we have to learn with Rāmānuja all his infinite qualities but also to remember with Śankara that all these infinite qualities are not inherent in God, but identically the Pure infinite Light of Spirituality.[3]

[1] The articles were later published, in synopsis form, as four pamphlets, entitled *To Christ through the Vedanta* (3rd ed. 1944), and the first two parts, on Śankara and Rāmānuja, were published as a book in French, *Vers le Christ par le Vedanta* (1932).

[2] *The Light of the East*, Oct. 1922.

[3] *ibid.*, Dec. 1924.

Johanns describes the aim of his series as being, 'to show that we can reconstruct our Catholic Philosophy with materials borrowed from the various Vedantic systems'[1]. His Thomistic reconstruction is not one that we should choose to make but his marshalling of the evidence has put all later workers in this field in his debt, and his vision of harmonising the two different 'strands' of Śankara and Rāmānuja into a Christian synthesis has definite possibilities, as we shall see when we come to formulate our conclusions.

Sādhu Sundar Singh (1889-1929)

We come now to one who in many respects stood outside the theological and literary developments of which we have been thinking, though he was contemporary with them: one who is perhaps the most famous Indian Christian who has yet lived, and whose influence has been widespread and prolonged—Sādhu Sundar Singh.[2]

Sundar Singh could not be called a technical theologian. And yet his writings and recorded sayings are full of theology, full of Indian theology, and he must be regarded as one of the greatest of those whose work we are studying. Though he had little formal theological training he was steeped in the teaching of the New Testament and had an instinctive, or perhaps rather inspired, understanding of the nature of theological thinking. His influence on the whole life of Indian Christendom, as well as on leading theologians like A. J. Appasamy, has been so great that we must seek in some detail to find out what he taught.

Sundar Singh was born in the state of Patiala in 1889. Though the family were Sikhs his mother, a woman of outstanding devotion and love, trained her son in the *bhakti*-tradition of Hinduism as well as of the Sikh religion, and as a small boy he learnt the *Bhagavadgita* by heart. His mother's love and example and his early training in devotion were to have a great effect on his life's work, and though she never became a Christian he always acknowledged his debt to her and had no doubt that her *anima naturaliter Christiana* had found its place in heaven.

[1] *To Christ through the Vedanta* (1944 edn.) Part I, Introduction.

[2] Rebecca Parker, *Sādhu Sundar Singh : Called of God* (1918); B. H. Streeter and A. J. Appasamy, *The Sadhu* (1921); F. Heiler, *The Gospel of Sundar Singh* (1927); C. F. Andrews, *Sādhu Sundar Singh : A Personal Memoir* (1934); A. J. Appasamy, *Sundar Singh : A Biography* (1958); T. E. Riddle, *The Vision and the Call : a Life of Sadhu Sundar Singh* (1964).

As a boy at a mission school Sundar Singh came in contact with Christianity but fiercely rejected it. He burnt a copy of the Bible and even his strict Sikh father rebuked him for such an act. But his heart found no peace. Despite his study of the *Gita*, the Upaniṣads and even the Koran, and his practice of the technique of *yoga*, his heart remained restless, and at the age of fifteen he resolved one night that if he did not attain peace he would commit suicide in the morning by lying down on the railway line. Early in the morning, however, and to his complete surprise, he had a vision of Jesus, radiant in his beauty and commanding him to obedience. He obeyed. And immediately there was great peace in his mind, a peace which made him constantly assert that he was living in heaven upon earth.

That was on 18th December 1904, and after further instruction he was baptised in September 1905. His mother had always had the hope that one day he would become a *sādhu* and now, at the age of sixteen, he became one. But it was as a Christian, not as a Sikh, that he donned the ochre robe.

In the course of his early wanderings he met a young American, S. E. Stokes, who was seeking to live in India the life of a St. Francis.[1] They joined forces for a time and from Stokes Sundar Singh learnt much of St. Francis and his life. In 1909, on the advice of his missionary friends, he entered St. John's Divinity College in Lahore, but the academic life did not suit him and he developed a distaste for academic theology. In 1910 he left with a preacher's licence for the Lahore Diocese, which he later surrendered to his bishop as he felt called to exercise his preaching ministry in every Church that would have him, and not merely in the Anglican one.

Now began a period of wandering which took him all over India and especially into Tibet. His spiritual life was nourished by the New Testament, the only book which he constantly carried with him, and he had the frequent mystical experience of communion with Christ. He speaks of many mysterious happenings, such as his deliverance without visible human agency from a dry well full of dead bodies into which he was thrown in Tibet, and his meetings with the aged Christian *rishi* of the Himalayas, who was reputed to be three hundred years old. The reports of these stories led some people to regard Sundar Singh as an impostor, but it is difficult to study his writings and his life with-

[1] Stokes later ceased to be a Christian, joined the Ārya Samāj, and sought to give expression to his faith in a new interpretation of Hinduism based on love.

out coming to the conclusion that he was genuine with the true simplicity of the children of God.[1]

He visited Britain, America and Australia in 1920 and several European countries in 1922 and everywhere created a deep impression. There were still memories of others who had come from India, Keshab Chandra Sen and Swāmi Vivekānanda for example, who had proclaimed what India, through the Vedānta, had to offer to the West. Here was one who was every bit as Indian as his predecessors, who spoke from a profound religious experience in a thoroughly Indian way, and whose message was yet that of the self-revelation of God in Christ. He soon became a world-famous figure, and thousands came to hear him speak in every country he visited. His speaking was effective and there were many conversions, both of non-Christians and of nominal Christians, while many had their faith deepened through hearing him. His impressive appearance, his romantic story, and the simplicity and vividness with which he spoke attracted ordinary people, while theologians were eager to hear an Indian interpretation of the Gospel from one whose spiritual and even psychic experiences seemed so unusual and interesting.

After his return to India he resumed his travels there and in Tibet, and to this period belongs that literary activity which resulted in the production of eight short books, the first of which, *At the Master's Feet*, was published in 1922.[2]

Tibet, which was closed to foreign missionaries, held a fascination for him, and there men of his acquaintance had died as Christian martyrs. The death of a martyr held a strange attraction for him also. We do not know for certain how he died, but it may have been a martyr's death for, in 1929, in failing health, he set out on a journey to Tibet from which he never returned. At the age of thirty-nine Sundar Singh had followed his Master to the end.

The Nature of Sundar Singh's Spiritual Experience

The basis of Sundar Singh's theology is his direct experience of Jesus Christ. For him as for St. Paul the Christian life goes back to a definite, clear-cut experience of the risen Christ, and his spiritual life is, like Paul's, founded on constant communion

[1] For an account of the bitter controversy over Sundar Singh see A. J. Appasamy, *Sundar Singh* (1958), pp. 203 ff., and the Bibliography in Heiler, *op. cit.*, pp. 267 ff.

[2] He wrote his books in Urdu and then, with the help of friends like A. J. Appasamy and T. E. Riddle, worked out an English translation.

with Christ through prayer. And, unlike so many Hindu *bhaktas*—not merely advaitins but even those of the *bhakti* tradition—his prayer is not just a process of self-immersion in the Absolute but rather a continuous dialogue, a 'practice of the presence of Christ', in which the distinction between himself and the personal Christ remains clear. For Sundar the aim of prayer is union with God, but this must be the union of two free personalities rather than of absorption in the divine. He writes:

> If we want to rejoice in God we must be different from Him; the tongue could taste no sweetness if there were no difference between it and that which it tastes.[1]

In common with many Hindu mystics the experience of union was for him frequently an ecstatic one and he has left a description of some of these ecstatic moments in his book *Visions of the Spiritual World*.[2] For much of his life he experienced this ecstatic 'gift from God' as frequently as eight to ten times a month, and it usually lasted an hour or two. These ecstasies were in a waking, not a dream-state. When questioned about their nature the Sādhu replied:

> There are pearls in the sea, but to get to them you have to dive to the bottom. Ecstasy is a dive to the bottom of spiritual things. It is not a trance; but it is like a dive, because, as a diver has to stop breathing, so in ecstasy the outward senses must be stopped.[3]

Suffering held an important place in the Sādhu's religious experience. His life was completely selfless and he frequently underwent severe hardship, but his asceticism was not the rigid asceticism of *haṭha yoga*, which he rejected. His aim was rather to bear witness, through suffering gladly accepted, to Christ's love and grace, and he speaks often of the joy of suffering, of the peace of the Christian way, and of the life of union with Christ as 'Heaven upon Earth'. He vividly illustrates the nature of suffering by telling a story of a doctor striking a weakly new-born baby in order to make it cry and so begin to breathe:

> Through suffering God strikes us in love. The Cross is the key of heaven... The Cross will bear those who bear the Cross,

[1] Quoted in Heiler, *op. cit.*, p. 242. Compare Tagore's lyric, 'What is the use of salvation if it means absorption? I like eating sugar, but I have no wish to become sugar'. (Quoted in Appasamy, *What is Moksa?* p. 91.)

[2] 1926.

[3] Streeter and Appasamy, *op. cit.*, p. 132.

until it bears them up to heaven, into the actual Presence of the glorious Redeemer.[1]

And again, after his miraculous rescue from the well of death at Ilam he writes, 'Christ's Presence has turned my prison into a heaven of blessing'[2].

The background and content of many of Sundar Singh's visions were provided by the Bible. Lest it should be thought that, like Sen and his *adeśa*, he put his visionary experiences, his direct ecstatic intuition or *pratyakṣa*, on the same plane as the Bible, we must consider the testimony of his friend and biographer A. J. Appasamy who affirms that he made it quite clear that even his *pratyakṣa* had to yield to the Bible and that he accepted it only when it was in harmony with the Bible.[3] For him the Bible was the primary standard or *pramāṇa*. And like so many in India he had a preference for St. John's Gospel, though this does not seem to have been caused by any special philosophical affinity. The reason is more simple: 'St. John seems to me to have loved Christ more than the other Apostles'.[4]

Sundar Singh's Method of Teaching

The Sādhu's method of teaching was that of his Master—the use of parables. He draws his examples from scenes of everyday life, from nature, from his own experience, from books he has read including the Upaniṣads, and often from his own rich imagination. Archbishop Söderblom writes:

> To the Sadhu a parable is more than a picture or a sudden flash of inspiration. His parables are not accidental; in his mind they have the stability of articles of faith. Indeed, the pictures which he has discovered in giving rein to his imaginative powers *are* his theology.[5]

Sundar Singh was not interested in producing a logically consistent scheme of theology, and indeed he insisted very strongly on the precedence of 'heart' over 'head'. Yet it is interesting that in fact he is here following a recognised Indian pattern

[1] Heiler, *op. cit.*, p. 117 f. Heiler points out that the phrase is taken from *The Imitation of Christ*, a favourite book of the Sadhu. Compare the title *The Cross is Heaven*, chosen by Appasamy for his anthology of previously unpublished articles by Sundar Singh, (1956).

[2] Heiler, *op. cit.*, p. 119.

[3] In a letter to the author, 11-3-1966.

[4] Heiler, *op. cit.*, p. 200.

[5] *ibid.*, p. 135.

of inference, that of analogy (*upamāna*), which is in some schools[1] held to constitute a separate basis of knowledge. Many religious leaders, such as Rāmakrishna, have used this method widely. When doctrinal questions were put to Sundar Singh he did not reply with a closely-reasoned argument, but instead was often able to give a vivid parable or analogy which threw immediate light on the problem. On the consciousness of sin, for example, he writes :

> It is a healthy sign to feel that we are sinners. It is dangerous when we do not feel it. Once while bathing in the river Sutlej I sank into deep water. Above my head were tons of water and yet I did not feel the burden at all. When I came to the bank, I lifted a pot filled with water and found it very heavy. As long as I was in the water I did not feel the weight. Similarly a sinner does not feel that he is a sinner as long as he lives in sin.[2]

Sometimes his 'analogies' were simple examples from his own experience, like this one. Sometimes they were based on his ecstatic visions. He felt that in some mysterious way the needed answer was given him ; without going through any logical process of reasoning the right analogy seemed to come to his lips and he was able to speak in a way that carried far more conviction to his hearers than a reasoned argument would have done. And yet the teaching of the Sādhu when seen as a whole has a logical coherence, 'not because he aims at system, but because his teaching is the spontaneous expression of prolonged meditation on the New Testament by a man whose own personality has attained to inward unity'.[3]

Despite the fact that most of his teaching is given in this parabolic fashion, despite the fact that he wrote no theological treatises and in fact had an attitude approaching contempt for the systematisation of dogmatic theology, Sundar Singh's teaching deals with a wide range of subjects and it will be illuminating to consider briefly what he says on a number of themes.

A Christocentric Theology

Sundar Singh is always Christocentric in his thought, and his theology begins from his experience of Christ rather than

[1] e.g. the schools of *Mimāṃsa, Advaita, Nyāya.* See N. Smart, *Doctrine and Argument in Indian Philosophy* (1964), pp. 206 f. In India an argument can sometimes be settled by citing a striking analogy or an appropriate proverb.

[2] Streeter and Appasamy, *op. cit.*, p. 166. The story is repeated in *At the Master's Feet*, p. 15.

[3] Streeter and Appasamy, *op. cit.*, p. 53.

from any theistic considerations. Our immediate experience is of Christ and it is only through him, in the power of the Spirit, that we can know the Father. In the description of one of his ecstatic visions we find this point very clearly made. He writes :

> The first time I entered Heaven I looked round about and asked, 'But where is God ?' And they told me, 'God is not to be seen here any more than on earth, for God is Infinite. But there is Christ, He is God, He is the Image of the Invisible God, and it is only in Him that we can see God, in Heaven as on earth.' And streaming out from Christ I saw, as it were, waves shining and peace-giving, and going through and among the Saints and Angels, and everywhere bringing refreshment, just as in hot weather water refreshes trees. And this I understood to be the Holy Spirit.[1]

Christ is fully God, in him alone God is fully revealed, and to know him is to know that he is divine.

Sundar Singh fully accepts the idea of the Incarnation—for which he sometimes uses the term *avatāra*—and vividly illustrates it. Christ is like a king going about *incognito* among his people in order that he may be able to help them ; men saw him, and still see him, but do not recognise his divinity. Another illustration tells of a peasant who saw a red glass bottle which had been filled with milk. Because of the redness of the appearance he could not tell that the bottle contained milk. So men without faith and direct experience cannot accept the divinity of Christ. 'Faith in the Divinity of Christ grows out of the immediate experience of the heart'[2]. A third homely illustration is taken from the practice in parts of northern India of crossing rivers on inflated goat-skins. One crosses 'on air', but the air cannot support one unless it is confined in the skin :

> So God to help man had to become incarnate. The Word of life was made flesh. He will carry those who want to cross the river of this world to heaven. . . We can see the living Father in the Incarnation of Jesus Christ.[3]

The fundamental Christocentricity of his thought can be seen in a very interesting passage in the account of one of his visions, where he describes the relation of the created world to God in a way somewhat reminiscent of Rāmānuja's 'body-soul' analogy, and then describes in his own way the work of Christ and of the Spirit as agents in creation. As the

[1] *ibid.*, p. 54.
[2] Heiler, *op. cit.*, p. 162.
[3] Streeter and Appasamy, *op. cit.*, p. 57.

passage is typical of the Sādhu's visionary insight we shall quote it in full :

> On another occasion I asked, 'Whence is Life ?' I was told that the one source of Life is behind everything. Our clothes are warm, because the body they conceal is warm. There is no heat in the clothes ; that comes from the body within. Just so the Life in all living creatures is derived from the one source of Life behind. Their Life is from the Giver of Life. Again, just as our body is hidden by our clothes, but the shape of the clothes as well as the heat comes from the body inside, so all the vegetables and animals that we see are but the outward forms upheld by the Giver of Life.
>
> I saw waves of Light and Love coming out from Christ, in whom dwelleth the fulness of the Godhead embodied. These give spiritual life. Also in a mysterious way these waves of life and love give life to living creatures of all grades. Matter and motion cannot produce life. The source of life is life.
>
> I was told that the waves of light which I saw were the Holy Spirit. Just as the moon seems to be straight overhead wherever we stand, so the glorious Christ with the waves coming out of Him was seen here, there and everywhere. I saw crowds of people with glorious bodies, all saying, 'He is near me', 'He is near me'.[1]

Taking this positive attitude to the work of creation Sundar Singh naturally regards created matter as something real and good rather than as illusory, and so separates himself clearly from the Hindu view of *māyā*. And so it comes about that, like St. Francis to whom his friend Stokes had introduced him, and whom he often mentions, he has an intense love of nature, not for its own sake, but because it declares the glory of God. Natural theology yields its message only to those who have already received God's revelation through Scripture :

> Those who are born again have the Holy Spirit for their mother. So to them the language of the Bible and of Nature is their mother-tongue, which they easily and naturally understand. [But] the message of the Bible is simple, direct and straightforward, whereas the message of the Book of Nature has to be spelt out carefully letter by letter.[2]

Sin and Karma

Man is God's creature, but he is a sinner, and 'one sin, the smallest sin, even an evil thought' is sufficient to keep us out-

[1] *ibid.*, pp. 131 ff.
[2] *ibid.*, p. 194.

side the Kingdom.[1] Yet sinful as man is, he is made in the image of God, that image which is to be seen perfectly only in Christ. In another of his visions describing his heavenly experiences the Sādhu writes :

> The faces of all the spirits whom I see in heaven look like Christ, but in a lesser degree ; just as the image of the sun is reflected alike in a number of water-pots. Christ is the Image of God—that Image in which God created man—this is the true image, but it is only imperfectly stamped on other men. This explains that feeling of recognition of Christ as one known long ago, which is experienced by all on their first entry to the heavenly state. It shows an original connection between man and Christ, even though one does not know it before. All sinners have within them a battered image of their Divine Creator, and so when converted they recognize and fall down and worship Him.[2]

Before the battered image can be restored, however, man has to allow God to deal with his sin. Sundar Singh's teaching on sin is remarkably interesting and original, because he is able to retain many features of the Hindu doctrine of *karma,* while at the same time rejecting the allied doctrine of *saṃsāra* which says that men must repeatedly be re-incarnated in order to work out the consequences of their deeds in previous existences. Sundar Singh does not underestimate the gravity of sin, but regards sin as the negation of goodness rather than as an active principle of evil :

> Sin has no independent existence : no one can say, therefore, that it is something which has been created. It is only a name for a state of mind, or a disposition... Satan can only injure that which has already been created ; he has no power to create... Sin or evil, therefore, has no independent existence ; it is merely the absence or the negation of good.[3]

This may not strike us as fully adequate, but there is no doubt that Sundar Singh was aware of the power of sin. As to the effect of sin, and its punishment, he holds that sin, like *karma,* brings with it it's own effects :

> God does not judge sinners; it is sin which judges them, and they must die in their sins... God has never sent anyone to hell... It is sin which drives souls into hell.[4]

[1] *The Cross is Heaven,* p. 44. See also *At the Master's Feet,* p. 15.
[2] Streeter and Appasamy, *op. cit.,* p. 124.
[3] Heiler, *op. cit.,* p. 164.
[4] *ibid.,* p. 140. Cf. *At the Master's Feet,* p. 16.

Because man is fallen, he sins ; he is unable in his own power to do what is good. And that sin, in the nature of things, brings with it its own retribution, through the internal change and hardening of a man's character, the degeneration of his whole personality in an inevitable process which might even be called *karma*. This *karma*, the result of our sinful actions, can cast us into hell, unless we avail ourselves of the salvation offered in Christ.

Streeter and Appasamy identify two influences behind this view of sin, one the Sādhu's passionate apprehension of the Love of God, especially as it is portrayed in St. John's Gospel, and the other his familiarity with the Hindu conception of *karma* which he interprets in this new and original way of making the retribution 'the result of an internal change, organic to the personality', whereas *karma* represents it as 'dependent upon circumstances predominantly external'[1]. According to the doctrine of *karma*, there is no possibility of forgiveness, and all suffering is penal, the penalty for sins committed in this or in previous lives. Sundar Singh rejects the view that suffering must be penal, and illustrates the statement with the story of how a little bird was one day driven by a gale of wind into his lap, and so escaped from a pursuing hawk ; in the same way, he says, 'the strong wind of suffering drives us into the lap of God'[2].

In this rejection of the idea of penal suffering and eternal punishment Sundar Singh is far removed from the stern teaching of Nehemiah Goreh. In effect he separates God's love from the *karma*-like, automatic process of retribution. There is indeed suffering in the world, and often it is the penalty for sin, but God is not the author of that penalty and his only desire is to save the sinner. Suffering, then, when recognised as a 'medicine' or an opportunity for learning more of God's love, is to be welcomed, and so Sundar Singh welcomed it in his own life. He gives the illustration of the pearl-oyster which produces a pearl because of irritation and suffering, and explains how the spiritual life—'the Real Pearl'[3]—cannot be attained without suffering and tribulation.

The Work of Christ

Like other Indian Christians, Sundar Singh concentrates more on faith-union with Christ than on the detailed explanation

[1] Streeter and Appasamy, *op. cit.*, p. 159.
[2] *ibid.*, p. 161.
[3] *The Real Pearl* is the title of one of the Sādhu's books, written in Urdu and not published in English till 1966 (tr. M. R. Robinson).

of what took place on the Cross. Yet he constantly dwells on Christ's death and especially on its revelation of the love of God. He writes:

> Christ knew that neither silver nor gold, nor diamonds nor any other jewels, would suffice to procure life to the soul, but that what was needed was the surrender of life for life, the surrender of soul in order to save the souls of men. That is why He gave His life for the redemption of the world.[1]

Here we have something very closely approaching the substitutionary theory of the atonement. And the idea is further elaborated, in terms of self-sacrifice, in a number of parables such as that of a man who gives his life in the act of digging a tunnel under a mountain in order to provide a road between two villages; of a father who for the sake of his badly-injured son gives his blood for a transfusion and so dies; of a mother-bird who, when the tree on which her nest is built is set on fire, stays there and dies with her young rather than trying to escape.[2] For him there appears to be no difficulty in combining a number of 'pictures' of the meaning of the work of Christ, and holding them simultaneously.

There can be no *karma mārga*, no possibility of obtaining salvation by our own works. While other religions say, 'Do good and you will become good', Christianity says, 'Be in Christ and you will do good'. To show the impossibility of our achieving our own salvation Sundar Singh gives the illustration of a man who has fallen into a well, who cannot climb out by his own efforts but must have a rope thrown to him from above. So too the mere moral influence of the death of Christ is not sufficient to help us; Christ's death is rather a 'work' which accomplishes something positive, like digging the tunnel under the mountain; or it provides an active 'power' like the life-giving blood-transfusion. A mother, whose son has been imprisoned until he can pay a large fine, toils all day carrying great stones until she earns enough money for her son's release. From his prison-window the son sees her, toiling with her bruised and bleeding hands. Here we have a combination of moral influence—the sight of the suffering mother—and of positive achievement in the earning of the money to pay the fine. When he is set free the son says, 'I was saved by my mother's hard

[2] Heiler, *op. cit.*, p. 150.
[1] *ibid*, Cf. *At the Master's Feet*, p. 18; *The Real Pearl*, p. 23.

work, by her toil, by the wounds on her body, by her blood'. And so, says the Sādhu,

> Those who realise that God became incarnate and shed his precious blood to save us from our sins, will not like to commit the sin which gives such suffering to their God.[1]

God's love, demonstrated in Christ, is suffering love, self-sacrificing love, a love which has power to achieve the conversion and transformation of a sinner. And when a man has accepted that love he is ready to live the Christian life, and to discover for himself that 'the Cross is Heaven'.

The Life in Christ

Salvation for Sundar Singh is not exhausted by the forgiveness of sins but rather includes all that is known in reformed theology as 'sanctification':

> Many people say that salvation is forgiveness of sins, and of course it is partly that. But complete, perfect salvation is freedom from sin, and not merely forgiveness of sins. Jesus Christ came not only to forgive sin, but to make us free from sin. We receive from Christ a new vital power which releases us from sin. . . To be saved by Christ is to receive new life from Him, to become a new creature.[2]

This statement is, of course, perfectly Pauline (II Cor. 5 : 17), but it is worth noting it specially, as the idea is later taken up in considerable detail in Chenchiah's 'new creation' theology.

Justification and sanctification are closely linked. It is by faith that we are engrafted into Christ and so become new creatures, able to live the 'life in Christ'. Sundar Singh takes an illustration from nature of the camouflage of certain insects which have come to look like the leaves or sticks on which they rest, or the tiger whose striped skin is like the alternating light and shade of the jungle where he lives. In the same way, 'those who live in spiritual communion with God like the saints and angels have a share in Christ's nature, and become transformed into his likeness'[3].

Yet this relationship never becomes one of identity. There is no Vedāntic absorption ; Christ and the believer maintain in union their separate identities :

[1] Streeter and Appasamy, *op. cit.*, p. 62.
[2] Heiler, *op. cit.*, p. 166.
[3] *ibid.*, p. 170. Cf. *At the Master's Feet*, p. 29.

> If Christ lives in us, our whole life will become Christ-like. Salt which has been dissolved in water may disappear, but it does not cease to exist. We know it is there when we taste the water. Even so the indwelling Christ, although He is unseen, will become visible to others through the love which he shares with us.[1]

This illustration is of exceptional interest, taken as it is from the *Chandogya Upaniṣad*, where it is given as a demonstration of the fundamental Vedāntic proposition *tat tvam asi*, 'that art thou'.[2] There the meaning is that Being (*Brahman*) is present everywhere, even though it may not be visible. The seer Uddālaka Āruni says to his son Svetāketu :

> Verily, indeed, my dear, you do not perceive Being here.
> Verily, indeed, it is here.
>
> That which is the finest essence—this whole world has that as its soul.
> That is Reality. That is *Atman*. *That art thou*, Svetaketu.

Sundar Singh's meaning is rather that if Christ dwells in us, then, while unseen to the natural eye, he is yet there in his own identity, changing the quality of our life into conformity with his. For the Christian, faith-union with Christ maintains the personality both of the believer and of Christ. In the Sādhu words, 'through faith we are in God and God is in us. But God remains God, and we remain, His creatures'[3]. As illustrations of this mystical union which involves interpenetration combined with continued self-identity he suggests coal and fire, or a sponge filled with water[4].

As a result of this way of looking at things we do not find in Sundar Singh any systematic exposition of the 'way of salvation' though, as we have seen, his teaching on the death of Christ is thoroughly Scriptural. The dominating feature of his thought is rather the life in Christ, which for him is inevitably a life of Cross-bearing, and that is a life which is to be preferred to all others :

> To follow Him and bear His Cross is so sweet and precious that, if I find no Cross to bear in Heaven, I shall plead before Him

[1] Heiler, *op. cit.*, p. 170.
[2] *Chand. Up.* 6 : 13.
[3] Heiler, *op. cit.*, p. 225.
[4] *At the Master's Feet*, pp. 7f.

to send me as His missionary, if need be to Hell, so that there at least I may have the opportunity to bear His Cross. His presence will change even Hell into Heaven.[1]

The Church and the Sādhu-ideal.

Sundar Singh's relationship with the Church is difficult to define. We have seen how he was baptised an Anglican, but how he later surrendered his preacher's licence when he found that it prevented him from preaching in Churches other than the Anglican. For the rest of his life he preached wherever men would invite him. As occasion offered he partook of communion wherever he happened to be. But he was not really interested in the Church as a visible, organised institution, and preferred to think of it as the whole Body of those who belong to Christ. He writes :

> I belong to the Body of Christ, that is, to the true Church, which is no material building, but the whole corporate body of true Christians, both those who are living here on earth, and those who have gone into 'the world of light'.[2]

When asked to which Church he belonged it was his custom to reply, 'To none. I belong to Christ. That is enough for me'.[3]

His negative judgment on the organised Church applies also to Church dogmatics, and he writes :

> We Indians do not want a doctrine, not even a religious doctrine ; we have enough and more than enough of that kind of thing ; we are tired of doctrines. We need the Living Christ. India wants people who will not only preach and teach, but workers whose whole life and temper is a revelation of Jesus Christ.[4]

There is an obvious danger here. The Sādhu in effect rejects the authority of the Church, and gives first place to the revelations which he himself receives in a state of ecstasy. Yet it is interesting to note how, despite this individualism, his teaching is in fact more Biblical and even 'orthodox' than that of several other Indian theologians, a fact which is no doubt traceable to the way in which all his visions have to submit to the judgment of Scripture.

Sundar Singh was definitely a 'solitary', and we are told that although four hundred young men wished to become his

[1] *The Cross is Heaven*, pp. 39f.
[2] Heiler, *op. cit.*, p. 201.
[3] *ibid.*, p. 210.
[4] *ibid.*, p. 266.

disciples, and a wealthy Christian in South India wished him to set up an *āshram*, he refused both offers. As one would expect, therefore, his attitude towards corporate worship is rather negative. He writes:

> It is quite natural that no form of Church service can ever satisfy deeply spiritual people, because such persons already have direct fellowship with God in meditation, and they are always conscious of His blessed presence in their souls.[1]

This leads us to face the question of the validity for the Indian Church of the *sādhu*-ideal which Sundar Singh adopted for himself and did so much to popularise. Its particular form in his case is closely related to the *sannyāsi*-ideal in Hinduism, and there is no question that he was able to gain great audiences in India and to witness effectively through his familiar appearance and mode of teaching. And of course there are many Christian precedents, in the Desert Fathers, the Vagantes, St. Francis and many others. It is not, however, a way of life that has generally commended itself to Protestant Christians and there have been those, both in India and the West, who have therefore questioned its efficacy, especially in view of the fact that following Sundar Singh there are now many Christian *sādhus* in India, at least some of whom are far from being genuine.

The genuineness and efficacy of Sundar Singh's ministry as a *sādhu* seem clear. As the Indian Church becomes more truly Indian it may be that God will raise up other such men in order to carry out similar special ministries of witness within the Church and to the world outside. As false prophets arise, so false *sādhus* too may arise, but the true Christian *sannyāsis* will be known by their fruits and by their life, and there seems to be no reason why there should not be many such dedicated men. Such a ministry can never be the *normal* one in the Church, which requires the regular ministry of the Word and sacraments; but within the coming Indian Church there must be room for much diversity, and here is a pattern to be followed, if not by many at least by a dedicated few.

Sundar Singh's Attitude to Hinduism

Sundar Singh can never forget the love and devotion of his mother, and his attitude towards the non-Christian saints of India is a positive one, like that of Sen or Upādhyāya. He accepts

[1] *ibid.*, p. 206.

the validity of certain kinds of Hindu religious experience, and believes, that, in so far as the experience is true and valid it is attributable to Christ and the Holy Spirit, even when no such acknowledgement is made or realised. 'The Living Christ reveals Himself to every man according to his need', he writes, and goes on to say that non-Christian thinkers also have been illuminated by the Sun of Righteousness and have received the Holy Ghost. 'Just as every soul that lives breathes in the air, so every soul, whether Christian or non-Christian, breathes in the Holy Spirit, even when he knows it not.'[1] That does not, however, mean that there is no need for the specific Christian revelation of Christ. He alone is the true Light who can fully satisfy. Speaking of the Magi he says :

> In India we have many genuine truth-seekers, who faithfully follow their star ; but it is only starlight which guides them. But you Christians have the glory of the Sun.[2]

He comes close to a position rather like Farquhar's, and it is not unlikely that through his many friends he was kept aware of what Farquhar was saying during these very years. In an expressive picture he writes :

> Christianity is the fulfilment of Hinduism. Hinduism has been digging channels. Christ is the water to flow through these channels.[3]

Thus Sundar Singh's attitude to Hinduism is very different from Goreh's. He seldom criticises even the abuses of popular Hinduism and reserves his criticism rather for its strong points such as the monist view of reality, the *jñāna mārga*, and the practice of asceticism for its own sake.[4] Yet he denies that he has affiliations with any particular school or 'way' of Hinduism. Even *bhakti*, which might seem the closest to his view because of his intense personal devotion to Christ, is rejected, as is the way of *yoga*, while his rejection of *jñāna mārga*, and indeed of all religion which comes from the head rather than the heart, is very outspoken. For him religion means love and commitment, not knowledge, and he reacts against his Hindu environment in much the same way as Paul reacted against the legalistic

[1] *ibid.*, p. 218.
[2] *ibid.*, p. 220.
[3] Streeter and Appasamy, *op. cit.*, p. 232.
[4] *With and Without Christ* (1929), chap. 1.

Judaism of his time. Paul was convinced that men are saved by faith, and not by performing the works of the law. The Sādhu is convinced that men are saved not by the *jñāna* beloved of Hinduism, but by love. The first thing in religion, then, is not ritual or works (*karma*), nor a new philosophy (*jñāna*), but a new heart, and only those who know and love the crucified and risen Christ can understand fully what this means.

Although Sundar Singh rejects the main *mārgas* and *darśanas* of Hinduism—albeit, one feels, with a certain leaning towards *bhakti* and Rāmānuja, a tendency to be worked out later by Appasamy, whom he so deeply influenced—yet he is very Indian in his way of thinking, employs many terms from the vocabulary of Hinduism, and has no hesitation in taking parables and illustrations from the Upaniṣads. He speaks of *tṛṣṇa* (spiritual thirst), of *samādhi* (the state of spiritual ecstasy), of *śānti* (peace), of *maitri* (friendship or *agape*), of *mokṣa* (release or salvation), of God as *Prema-sāgara* (Ocean of Love), as the *Antaryāmin* (Inner Guide), and as *Bhagavān*, of God's Grace as *Iśvara-prasāda*, and—differing here from Brahmabandhab—of Christ's Incarnation as *Avatāra*.

Sundar Singh is a central and crucially important figure in the history of Christianity in India. It is significant of the great and growing interest in him that the standard biography by Appasamy has recently been republished in a paperback edition and that Sundar Singh's own writings are now being re-issued. The acrid mists of controversy seem to have dissolved and recent studies have vindicated the genuineness as well as the greatness and simplicity of the man.

The sources of his theology have been a puzzle to those who have sought to identify him with any single tradition. Heiler places him in the line of the Neo-Platonists, Origen, Dionysius the Areopagite, Augustine, Aquinas, Eckhart, Julian of Norwich, and tries to find also reflections of Luther. Calvinists can find Calvin in him. A Jesuit, de Grandmaison, says that the Sādhu's piety is 'evangelical Christianity which has not developed beyond the Patristic period'.[1] Yet probably all these hypothetical parallels are purely fortuitous. The Sādhu's boyhood background is the *bhakti* tradition in which communion with God, even to ecstasy, is something to be expected and experienced. He was steeped in the New Testament and all his teaching is rooted there. We must not forget either his many friends,

[1] Heiler, *op. cit.*, p. 224.

missionaries and others, who interested him in western books of devotion like the *Imitatio Christi* and the works of St. Francis, and in later years he was to meet and talk with renowned mystical theologians like Von Hügel. He constantly draws on all these sources, though he never strays far from the evangelical tradition in which he was baptised. His mysticism is practical mysticism, not that of the western text-books.

Yet here we have one who is truly Indian in all his ways and thoughts and has yet entered fully, not into the Christian tradition of the West, but into the heart of the Gospel. In his own oft-quoted words, 'Indians greatly need the Water of Life, but they do not want it in European vessels'.[1]

So far other Indian theologians have been slow to follow up Sundar Singh's theological methods, though Appasamy has been greatly influenced by him. Yet it may be that eventually other great saints will arise in the Indian Church, like him in his knowledge of the Bible, experience and intuition, and yet with a deeper technical theological knowledge which will lead to a more comprehensive statement of Christian doctrine. It might even prove ultimately that in the history of the Indian Church and its thought Sundar Singh was actually more important for his theology and its method than for his ascetic way of life and his success as an evangelist.

[1] *ibid.*, p. 232.

Chapter VII

CHRISTIANITY AS *BHAKTI MĀRGA*: A. J. APPASAMY

The Bhakti Tradition

There has been a tendency, in the West no less than the East, to regard the pure monism of Śankara as the typical form of Indian religious philosophy. In our own time Dr. Radhakrishnan has given the weight of his advocacy to an interpretation of religion and philosophy which is ultimately a thorough-going monistic one. And we have seen how Brahmabandhab thought that Christianity could succeed in India only if it could meet the claims of Hinduism at the high level of *advaita* Vedānta.

Yet there is another tradition in Indian religion and philosophy, and one which equally claims to derive from the inspired Vedas. This is the tradition of that *bhakti* religion which Rudolf Otto defined as 'faith in salvation through an eternal God and through a saving fellowship with Him'.[1] This tradition has probably never been absent from Indian religion. Despite the efforts of Swāmi Dayānanda to prove the essential monism of the Vedas, it is clear that they contain the idea of the worship of personal gods. In later times, along with the development towards monism there is also found a tendency to postulate a single *personal* God, *Iśvara*, behind all forms or incarnations, a God who can be loved and worshipped and who remains distinct from the worshipper, a God who can be approached with feelings of deep love and personal devotion.

The earliest extensive teaching of this doctrine is to be found in the *Bhagavadgita*, though indeed many different points of view are represented in this devotional classic, and Dr. Radhakrishnan has given it a monist interpretation.[2] Yet it is clear that the *bhakti* tradition, here seen centred in personal devotion to Krishna as the Incarnation of Viṣṇu, is a dominant one. Later, in about the tenth century A.D. an emotional type of *bhakti* literature developed, in the *Bhāgavata Purāṇas*. Here the theme of personal devotion to the God of one's choice (*iṣṭa deva*) is developed, at times in a sensual and even sexual direction. The reaction from the monism of Śankara is very clear. To this

[1] R. Otto, *Christianity and the Indian Religion of Grace* (1929), p. 13.
[2] S. Radhakrishnan, *The Bhagavadgita*, (1948).

period belongs the great Vaiṣṇava reform movement in the Tamil country, instituted chiefly through inspired singers and poets known as the *Alvars*, who composed devout *bhakti* songs.

But the one who gave solid theological content to this movement, and indeed carried out a reformation in Hinduism, was Rāmānuja, who flourished in the latter half of the eleventh century. Living in his youth at Kanchipuram, he was at first an adherent of Śankara's *advaita*, but under the influence of the Vaiṣṇavism of the Alvars became the leader of a new school which sought to give a theological and philosophical basis to the *bhakti* tradition which was already in flourishing existence. For Rāmānuja the impersonal *nirguṇa Brahman* of Śankara was a useless God. With the *bhakti* poets he longs for salvation through personal fellowship with a personal God, and witheringly attacks Śankara's view that a man in search of salvation must believe that when he is finally saved he will no longer exist as himself. He builds up his own system, centred on a God—*Iśvara*—who *has* attributes. God is related to the world as the soul is to the body, and since this is not a relation of identity, a personal relationship is possible between God and man. The name given to Rāmānuja's system is *Viśiṣṭādvaita*, or *modified* non-dualism.

In answer to the question, 'What must I do to be saved ?' *bhakti* rejects the *jñana mārga* of the advaitins. Similarly *karma mārga* is rejected, for although the *Gita*, for example, recognises that good works must be performed, yet their performance cannot guarantee salvation.

Rāmānuja's tradition was taken by his followers. Fifth in succession to him came Rāmānanda, who in his full and free recognition of the value of human personality broke completely with caste. ' Let no one ask a man's caste or sect ', he said ; ' whoever adores God, he is God's own '.[1] Rāmānanda began his search after God because the worship of the Impersonal laid no hold on his heart. Through his influence theistic thought radiated in all directions and leaders of the *bhakti* tradition arose in many parts of India—Tulsidās for the Hindi speakers, Nāmdev and Tukārām in Maharashtra, Chaitanya in Bengal, Mirābai on the borders of Gujarat and Rajasthan. So it was that when the Christian Church began to take root in many parts of India there was already a strong theistic tradition of *bhakti*, and there

[1] Quoted in C. S. Paul, *The Suffering God* (1932), p. 104.

were those who felt that it had led them towards the Light of Christ.[1]

When we consider the features of *bhakti* thought and of the system of Rāmānuja which supports it, we cannot be surprised at the great attraction which it has held for Indian Christians. Here we are far removed from the cold world of Śankara. Here there is warmth and love and personal devotion; here there is experience of God's grace; here there is that utter self-abandonment to the love and power of God which has distinguished so many Christian saints. Small wonder, then, that to so many, as to Nārāyan Vāman Tilak, there has seemed to be a direct bridge linking the world of *bhakti* with the world of Christian faith, a bridge over which the *bhakta* may cross, and still feel that he has not strayed from home.

Christian Bhakti

For the beginnings of Christian *bhakti* we have to turn back to the early years of the nineteenth century. While Ram Mohan Roy was striving to interpret Christianity through his own brand of 'unitarian' non-dualism, convert Christian poets in Tamilnad, deeply steeped in the *bhakti* tradition of the Hinduism from which they had come, were already writing Christian lyrics which laid the offering of *bhakti* at the feet of Christ.

One of the best known of these Tamil Christian poets, though not the earliest, was *H. A. Krishna Pillai* (1827-1900).[2] He was born in 1827 in a high caste Vaiṣṇavite, non-Brāhman family, and as a young teacher in the CMS College, Tirunelveli, was gripped by the Gospel and embraced the Christian faith through baptism in 1858. His best known works are *Rakshanya Yātrikam*, an epic based on *The Pilgrim's Progress*, and *Rakshanya Manoharam* which describes lyrically the joy of salvation through Jesus Christ.

Krishna Pillai was not a technical theologian and his theology was very much that of the evangelical missionaries with whom he came in contact in his early days as a Christian. He has, for instance, a very strong sense of the power of sin and of Christ's work of sin-bearing on the Cross. At the same time, and in a thoroughly natural, unselfconscious way, his own rich poetic imagination, with its vivid background of Hindu literature both

[1] For English translations of some of the Hindu *bhakti* poets see A. J. Appasamy, *Temple Bells* (1930); Kingsbury and Phillips, *Hymns of the Tamil Saivite Saints* (1921); N. Macnicol, *Psalms of the Maratha Saints* (1919).

[2] See A. J. Appasamy, *Tamil Christian Poet* (1966).

Tamil and Sanskrit, becomes the crucible in which the Christian faith, while remaining essentially the same, is given an attractive Indian form.

In one of his poems, for example, God is spoken of as *King Saccidānanda*, while the *trimurti* of Brahmā, Viṣṇu and Śiva is rejected in favour of the Christian Trinity. And, as so often in *bhakti* poetry, Motherhood is seen as one of the characteristics of God :

He who matched the threefold powers
Of creation, preservation and destruction,
With Trinity of Father, Son and Holy Spirit ;
The God in Whom the Three are One,
And Who is One in Three ;
Holy One in body, speech and mind ;
In form the peerless Mother of all good deeds
And all worthy to be praised—
Himself the precious Medicine for sin—
'Tis He I see upon the Cross.[1]

Many different ' images ' are used to describe Christ. He is the river of life from heaven and the mountain of salvation, the ocean of bliss, the cloud that showers the rain of grace, life-giving medicine, gem of gems.[2] He is the heavenly Gangā (Ganges), which takes away sin :

It washed clear away the slimy sin—Man's heritage !
It became also food and drink for him—pure and satisfying !
Thus nourished the Life of Wisdom ever grew
Yielding the fruit of Salvation true !
Such was the blood of our Saviour—Immanuel—
Shed for all—the Living Gangā ! [3]

A fine passage describes the work of salvation in terms of a swimmer rescuing a drowning man—a figure often used in Indian Christian lyrics :

The cloud of sin, that devoured the world, spread all over and drew the water of suffering. In the river of death, into which it rained its water, the majestic Saviour swam all alone, with countless souls underneath His arms ; was drawn by the floods, laboured without losing the souls, and suffered, being concerned about their salvation.[4]

[1] Quoted in *Tamil Christian Poet*, p. 51. Tr. E. E. White.
[2] D. Rajarigam, ' Theological Content in Tamil Christian Poetical Works ', in *Indian Journal of Theology* (1963), p. 3.
[3] *Tamil Christian Poet*, p. 47. Tr. R. Rangachari.
[4] *Rakshanya Yatrikam*, I, p. 225: 127. Tr. D. Rajarigam.

Krishna Pillai is deeply convinced of the sinfulness of sin, and of the sheer impossibility of trying to overcome it by good works, an effort compared to building a bridge of butter over a river of fire! It is only Christ who can save, and the cost is a terrible one, as he takes our sins on Himself:

> Who crowned thy Head with cruel thorns?
> Put sceptre rough into thy Hand?
> Who spat upon thy lotus-Face,
> And mocked thee with insulting hands?
> Who smote upon thy beauteous Brow,
> And thrust into thy Side the spear?
> Whose the nails which pierced thy Hands and Feet,
> That thy gracious Hands might save mankind?
> Was it not I—ah! wretched me—
> Did not I cause thy agony?
> O Thou that calledst the dying thief,
> And ope'd to him the gate of Heaven!
> O heavenly King, who came to be
> My Guide and Joy eternally![1]

It was men who were within the *bhakti* tradition who were able to make this great step forward in self-expression of Indian Christianity, and practically all of them were themselves converts, who brought with them from Hinduism their lyric ability and vocabulary. Some of them, like Kahānji Mādhavji of Gujarat, came from castes which were traditionally devoted to singing and poetry. Perhaps the most famous of them all was *Nārāyan Vāman Tilak* (1862-1919), the poet of Maharashtra, who came of the same community of Chitpavan Brāhmans which produced Nehemiah Goreh and Paṇḍitā Ramābāi.[2]

Through a chance encounter in the train with a Christian stranger who gave him a New Testament, a conflict began in Tilak's mind which resulted in his becoming convinced of the truth of the Christian faith. He was baptised in 1895, suffering much persecution. His reputation as a poet is by no means limited to Christian circles for he was one of the acknowledged leaders of the 'romantic revival' in Marathi literature at the end of the nineteenth century. Towards the end of a life of faithful service in the Church he began to be attracted towards the *sannyāsi* ideal and, giving up his secure position in the

[1] *Rakshanya Manoharam* III. v. 2. Tr. E. E. White.
[2] J. C. Winslow, *Narayan Vaman Tilak: the Christian Poet of Maharashtra* (1930).

Mission, became a Christian *sannyāsi* in 1917, seeking to gather round himself, in a group called 'God's *Darbār*', a 'brotherhood of the baptised and unbaptised disciples of Christ'.[1] He believed, like Upādhyāya, that

> If Christ could be presented to India in his naked beauty, free from the disguises of western organisation, western doctrines and western forms of worship, India would acknowledge Him as the Supreme Guru, and lay her richest homage at His feet.[2]

Tilak's Christian poems include many lyrics which are used in congregational worship as well as for evangelistic proclamation, and many which are primarily vehicles of intense personal devotion. It was his ambition to write a great verse epic on the life of Christ, but in the end he was able to complete only a small portion of this *Christāyan*, though even this fragment has been described as 'a great *Purāṇa* of the Christian *Avatāra*'. His last collection of poems, *Abhangānjali*[3], is generally regarded as his crowning work.

Tilak's poetry is much more devotional than theological. We shall look at a few examples in translation, which indicate something of his depth of feeling and devotion. The first is one which speaks of Christ as Mother :

Tenderest Mother-Guru mine,
Saviour, Where is love like Thine ?

A cool and never-fading shade
To souls by sin's fierce heat dismayed :

Right swiftly at my earliest cry
He came to save me from the sky :

He made him friends of those that mourn
With hearts by meek contrition torn :

For me, a sinner, yea, for me
He hastened to the bitter Tree :

And still within me living, too,
He fills my being through and through.

My heart is all one melody—
'Hail to Thee, Christ ! all hail to Thee ![4]

[1] Winslow, *op. cit.*, p. 119.
[2] *ibid.*, p. 118.
[3] 'Collection of *abhangas*'. *Abhanga* is the metre in which Tukārām wrote his poetry.
[4] *ibid.*, p. 85. Tr. J. C. Winslow.

Many of the poems illustrate the nature of *bhakti* as the soul's longing for union with God, in the same sort of idiom as is found in the poems of Nāmdev or Tukārām:

The more I win Thee, Lord, the more for Thee I pine;
  Ah, such a heart is mine.
My eyes behold Thee and are filled, and straightway then,
  Their hunger wakes again!
My arms have clasped Thee and should set Thee free, but no,
  I cannot let Thee go!
Thou dwell'st within my heart. Forthwith anew the fire
  Burns of my soul's desire.
Lord Jesus Christ, Beloved, tell, O tell me true,
  What shall Thy servant do?[1]

Tilak's hymns on the atonement are simple expressions of love, and of amazement at God's suffering grace:

Hast thou ever seen the Lord, Christ the Crucified?
Hast thou seen those wounded hands? Hast thou seen His side?

Hast thou seen the cruel thorns woven for His crown?
Hast thou, hast thou seen His blood, dropping, dropping down?

Hast thou seen who that one is who has hurt Him so?
Hast thou seen the sinner, cause of all His woe?

Hast thou seen how He, to save, suffers there and dies?
Hast thou seen on whom He looks with His loving eyes?

Hast thou ever, ever seen love that was like this?
Hast thou given up thy life wholly to be His?[2]

Some of his poems express his longing for India to come to Christ, and for the Church to become truly Indian and so to offer its riches to him:

When shall these longings be sufficed
  That stir my spirit night and day?
  When shall I see my country lay
Her homage at the feet of Christ?

Yea, how behold that blissful day
  When all her prophets' mystic lore
  And all her ancient wisdom's store
Shall own His consummating sway?

[1] *ibid.*, p. 93. Tr. J. C. Winslow.
[2] *ibid.*, p. 98. Tr. N. Macnicol.

Of all I have, O Saviour sweet,—
All gifts, all skill, all thoughts of mine,—
A living garland I entwine,
And offer at Thy lotus feet.[1]

Here are some lines describing the nature of that union with Christ which for the Christian *bhakta* represents at its deepest level the secret of salvation:

As the moon and its beams are one,
So, that I be one with Thee,
This is my prayer to Thee, my Lord,
This is my beggar's plea.

I would snare Thee and hold Thee ever
In loving, wifely ways;
I give Thee a daughter's welcome,
I give Thee a sister's praise.

Take Thou this body, O my Christ,
Dwell as its soul within.
To be an instant separate
I count a deadly sin.[2]

Tilak had been nurtured in the *bhakti* tradition and, as he himself said, had journeyed by the bridge of Tukārām to the feet of Christ. In the words of his friend and translator Nicol Macnicol,

> For Tilak the moon has come down by the stairway of its beams and dwells within his heart. This is the reconciliation of Christianity and Hinduism that this poet has accomplished, and so has claimed for himself and for the Christian Church a rich portion of the Hindu heritage.[3]

The work of Tilak and the many other Christian *bhakti* poets represents a permanent treasury of devotion and theology for the Indian Church, comparable to the Latin hymns of the early Church, or Luther's chorales, or the great German hymnodists Gerhardt, Tersteegen and Neander, or the hymns of Wesley and Watts in England. The work of quarrying out and assessing this wealth has still scarcely begun.[4]

[1] *ibid.*, p. 108. Tr. N. Macnicol.
[2] *ibid.*, p. 101. Tr. N. Macnicol.
[3] N. Macnicol, *India in the Dark Wood* (1930), p. 128.
[4] D. Rajarigam has done pioneering work in this field.

We do not look to the *bhakti* poets for complex theological exposition. But we do find that it is largely through their work that the language of Christian devotion and even to some extent of technical theology has become fixed in the different Indian languages. Some of them had comparatively little knowledge of English and this was perhaps a help rather than a hindrance in enabling them to transform ideas and terms within their minds, speaking in a language familiar to their hearers and from an experience which could be found only in Christ.

The lyrics all reflect a warm, personal approach to God through Christ. Here God is never *nirguṇa Brahman* but rather Lord, King, *Guru*, *Swāmi*, ocean of mercy, Mother and Father. The same terms are applied to Christ. The Holy Spirit is spoken of as a flood of joy, medicine for the heart, the key to heaven, the stream of oil of happiness, sacred milk.[1] The *bhakti* poets are the men who more than any others have made Christianity 'at home' in India; their songs are sung and learnt by heart by thousands who would never read a book of theology and, next to the Bible, their works have probably been the most important in helping the Christian Church to take root in Indian soil and to bear the blossoms which the richness of that soil encourages to grow in such profusion.

A. J. Appasamy (b. 1891)

The Indian theologian who more than any other has identified himself with the *bhakti* tradition is Bishop Aiyadurai Jesudasen Appasamy, who for more than forty years has been a leading figure in the Indian Church to which he has rendered distinguished service as writer, teacher, pastor and bishop.[2] As Brahmabandhab used Śankara as his instrument for elaborating an Indian Christian theology, and as Chenchiah turned towards Sri Aurobindo, so Appasamy has looked to the personalist tradition of *bhakti* and to its philosophical exposition as found in Rāmānuja.

[1] D. Rajarigam, *Indian Journal of Theology*, 1963, pp. 4ff.

[2] Dr. Appasamy has written a brief autobiography, *My Theological Quest* (1964). For critical studies see: *A Christian Theological Approach to Hinduism* (Gurukul Theological Research Group, Madras, 1956). G. C. Oosthuizen, *Theological Discussions and Confessional Developments in Churches of Asia and Africa* (1958). Herwig Wagner, *Erstgestalten einer einheimischen Theologie in Sudindien* (1963).

A larger autobiography, *A Bishop's Story*, was published in 1970.

Bishop Appasamy was brought up in a Christian home, his father, Dewan Bahadur A. S. Appasamy Pillai having been converted from Śaivism to Christianity at the age of twenty-four, partly through the influence of the poet Krishna Pillai, who became a revered friend of the family. After studies in Tirunelveli and Madras, Appasamy left for America in 1915 and spent seven years there and in England, where the subject of his Oxford doctorate thesis was *The Mysticism of the Fourth Gospel in its Relation to Hindu Bhakti Literature.* His studies and his personal contacts with writers like Von Hügel, Heiler and Otto led him deep into the Johannine literature and into Western mysticism, especially people like Eckhart, and this in turn deepened his interest in the work of his own Tamil devotional poets of both the Śaivite and Vaiṣṇavite traditions. He found himself deeply stirred by the firm belief of these poets in a personal God and their intense longing for communion with him. Here, he felt, was an Indian tradition which had close affinities with Christianity and could surely be used as a way leading to the fuller Indian understanding of the faith. Another deep influence on his life which began at this time was that of Sādhu Sundar Singh, who visited Oxford in 1920. Appasamy came to know him well, and collaborated with B. H. Streeter in writing a book on him, *The Sadhu.*

After returning to India in 1922 Appasamy continued his studies, turning now to Sanskrit texts as well as Tamil. His search for a philosophical basis for the *bhakti* tradition which so attracted him led him to a study of Rāmānuja and his system. The fruit of all these years of research was seen in the publication of the two books which are perhaps his best and most original, *Christianity as Bhakti Marga* (1928) and *What is Moksa ?* (1931). These books are an exposition of the Fourth Gospel, illuminated by a wealth of illustration from the Tamil *bhakti* poets. The Christian life is seen as one of loving devotion to God in Christ, and the goal of life—that *mokṣa* or release or salvation for which Hindu and Christian long—is to be found in faith-union with Christ. Not absorption into the divine but a loving personal union with him who said, ' Abide in me '—that is the chief end of man. This is a theme to which Appasamy remains faithful in all his later writings, and it sounds the typical note of his theology.

' *I and the Father are one* '

Many years earlier Keshab Chandra Sen had expressed his belief that Christ's union with the Father is not a material or metaphysical one, but rather one of deep communion, a *unio mystica* rather than a *unio hypostatica*, and had gone on to compare this relationship to that of the believer with Christ.[1] It is in his treatment of this question that we find Appasamy producing some of his most important suggestions, suggestions which are closely linked with his whole understanding of Christianity as a way of *bhakti*. A good point of departure for the discussion is the Johannine text so popular among Indian writers, 'I and my Father are one' (John 10 : 30).

How is Christ related to the Father? Is the relation one of identity of substance? The traditional western solution of the question, that of Chalcedon, is to say that Christ is *homoousios*, of the same substance (*ousia*) as the Father. Thus there is a metaphysical unity between the Father and the Son, Christ is one with the Father *a priori*, as it were, because of the fact that there is a common *ousia* underlying both Persons. Appasamy challenges this view and holds that the union of Father and Son is rather a *moral* unity; the Son, from all eternity, is so conformed to the Father's will, so perfect in his obedience, that the two Persons are one, but in a moral rather than a metaphysical way.

There is good reason behind Appasamy's contention here, and he is not simply attacking the Chalcedonian formula because it is western. Rather he is making a frontal assault on that monist Hindu tendency which we have seen in Ram Mohan Roy and others, the tendency to use the two great Johannine *mahāvākyas* 'I and my Father are one' and 'Abide in me' to prove that God the Father, Christ and the believer are ultimately all one. There are two distinct questions here, that of the nature of the union between the Father and the Son, and that of the union between Christ and the believer. The monist tendency is to say that in each case the union is a metaphysical one. Christ is one with the Father *in substance*; the believer attains or realises complete metaphysical unity with Christ. And so there is ultimately neither believer nor Christ but simply the undifferentiated unity of the Godhead.

Appasamy challenges this view at both levels, holding that the union of the believer with Christ is a moral union, based on love and obedience, and that the union of the Son with the Father is precisely similar. His argument is in large measure based on those passages in the Fourth Gospel which affirm the subordination of the Son to the Father, such as John 14 : 28, 'My

[1] v. supra, p. 30.

Father is greater than I'. Commenting on John 10 : 30, 'I and my Father are one', he writes :

> It may be quite true that on the surface this verse is like the texts in *Upanishads* which set forth *Advaita*. But we must remember that Jesus always thought of God as His Father... This means that the relation between God and Jesus is a personal relation between Father and Son. Jesus also says, 'The Father is greater than I'. This shows that He regards Himself as wholly dependent upon the Father; He is not identical with God . . .[1]

The relationship, then, between Christ and the Father is not one of identity but rather of a 'completeness of harmony in thought and purpose'.[2] We see this illustrated vividly in the story of Gethsemane, with the terrible struggle which terminated in the union of Christ's will with that of the Father. This is not the unity of monothelitism; rather Jesus, as man, has his own will but devotes it entirely to that of the Father. 'The doing of the Father's will was of the essence of His oneness with the Father.'[3]

For Appasamy the question of the relation of Christ to the Father cannot be divorced from that of his relation to the believer. In John 17 : 20 Jesus prays, '. . . that they all may be one; *as* Thou, Father, art in me, and I in Thee, that they also may be one in us.' This '*as*', he says, implies that the two relationships are of the same kind. He writes :

> What this prayer desires is that there should prevail among Christians such a spirit of love and fellowship as exists between Christ and God. This makes it clear that the union between God and Christ which is spoken of in the Fourth Gospel is a union in love and work and not an identity in their essential nature.[4]

This exegesis is intended to show that Christ and the Father are not 'one' in the *advaita* sense. There is a difference of function, and a difference of *person* too, a difference which alone makes possible the moral union of personal love within the Trinity which a purely metaphysical unity seems to exclude. Here we can see Appasamy coming to a solution very different from

[1] A. J. Appasamy, *The Gospel and India's Heritage* (1942), pp. 35-6. (Cited as *Gospel*).

[2] A. J. Appasamy, *What is Moksa?* (1931), p. 59. (Cited as *Moksa*).

[3] *Gospel*, p. 37. Compare J. A. T. Robinson, *Honest to God* (1963), p. 77: 'He is perfect man and perfect God . . . as the embodiment *through obedience* of "the beyond in our midst", of the transcendence of love.' (My italics).

[4] *Gospel*, p. 38.

that of Brahmabandhab, who saw the diversity of *Sat, Cit, Ānanda* as expressions of the underlying unity of *Brahman.*

What is Moksa?

The relationship of Jesus to God, then, is ' not one of identity but of fellowship '.[1] And when we go on to consider the nature of our own relationship to God we find that the *advaita* view of unity is rejected in favour of that of *bhakti.* Appasamy writes:

> There can be no identity between ourselves and God... Fellowship with God does not consist in ... a realization of our ultimate kinship with God, a kinship which always exist though hidden by mists of *illusion* and which has only to be made clear to the soul by some rapturous glimpse of Reality. But it is the harmony of the individual soul with the Divine Soul in thought and imagination, in purpose and will, in humble deed and adoring devotion.[2]

Hinduism uses the words *mokṣa* and *mukti* for the final release of the soul from recurring transmigration, the root meaning of the Sanskrit words being liberation or setting free. In practice, however, the words are frequently used with a content which is positive rather than negative, that is, which implies the joy of union with God rather than the mere negative fact of escape from *karma* and *saṃsāra.* Indian Christians commonly use the words to translate ' salvation '. The theme of Appasamy's book *What is Moksa?* is that Christians should use this popular and ancient Hindu term to indicate the distinctively Christian idea of eternal life, that is, the knowledge of God in Christ and faith-union with him.

Appasamy finds a clear description of the nature of *mokṣa* in the Johannine concept of eternal life. The Christian life, which is the life of *mokṣa* realised here and now, may be described as a life of *bhakti*—as *bhakti mārga.* Of the three traditional Indian ' ways ' of salvation—*jñāna mārga, bhakti mārga* and *karma mārga*—Appasamy of course chooses *bhakti mārga.* In the Fourth Gospel, however, he finds a type of *jñāna mārga* which is quite different from that of the Greek Gnostics or the Indian *jñānis,* and whose use is perfectly reconcilable with the interpretation of Christianity as a form of *bhakti.* Johannine *jñāna,* the ' knowledge ' by which and in which we come to *know*

[1] *Moksa,* p. 68.
[2] *ibid.*

Christ and through him the Father, is no intellectual affair, the mere removal of ignorance or *avidyā*, but is rather the type of knowledge by which we know and love our most intimate friends. Knowledge and love, *jñāna* and *bhakti*, can therefore be united in the Christian understanding of *mokṣa* as eternal life in Christ, and the way of *mokṣa* lies through personal knowledge of and growing love for God in Christ. *Mokṣa*, says Appasamy in an interesting definition,

> is a continuous contact with Reality, personal, conscious and radiant with joy. It is like the life of Jesus with God. It is not the realization of identity but the experience of a moral harmony with the holy and righteous Father. It is a personal experience which, however, in its higher reaches transcends the personal. It is a corporate experience, man mingling with his fellowmen in order to attain the heights of God's love. It begins even in this life and does not wait for an indefinite future.[1]

Like Sundar Singh, and against the *advaita* tradition or the monism of European mystics like Eckhart and Suso, Appasamy insists on the preservation of separate personalities in our experience of union with God, and quotes some words of Tukārām in his support:

> Cursed be that knowledge which makes me one with Thee . . . I am thy servant, Thou art my Lord . . . Water cannot taste itself nor trees taste their own fruit; the worshipper must be separate, thus alone pleasure arise from distinction.[2]

Our union with God in Christ, then, is to take the form of 'deep unselfish love of the whole man for God',[3] for 'love' is perhaps the best translation of *bhakti*.[4] It is to Christ's commandment 'Abide ye in my love' that we must respond, and because *bhakti* is personal this response must engage our whole personality, our will, feeling and thought. 'If ye keep my commandments, ye shall abide in my love,' says Jesus, and so Christian *bhakti*, unlike certain forms of Hindu devotion, demands a response of the will, in ethical living. To show our love to Christ we must

[1] *ibid.*, p. 6.

[2] Quoted in *Mokṣa*, p. 91, from *Poems of Tukaram* I. 76. Compare Tagore's lyric and Sundar Singh's illustration mentioned above, p. 95. The idea is a common one in *bhakti* literature.

[3] A. J. Appasamy, *Christianity as Bhakti Marga* (1928), p. 22. (Cited as *Bhakti*.)

[4] It is usually translated 'devotion' or 'worship'. We shall see how Chakkarai relates it to justifying *faith*. (v. infra p. 178.)

accept and live by his new law of love, by conforming our wills to his. At the same time our emotions also must respond, not in an excess of rapture but rather with that *bhakti* which Rāmānuja compares to 'a stream of steady flowing oil'.[1] And to resolute ethical action and quiet joy must be added also knowledge, *jñāna*, which is not something to be painfully acquired but is rather 'given' to us, as 'the Divine Christ illumines us and pours into our souls floods of light'.[2]

The goal of Hindu *bhakti* is the clear realisation of the presence of God. It is linked with the 'vision' (*darśana*) of God, but is not limited to it, and is far from the *advaita* realisation of the identity of the human soul with God, which Goreh compared to the state of a stone. Followers of *advaita* expect to reach the state of ecstasy, *samādhi*, and such an experience is possible for followers of the *bhakti mārga* also—even for Christian *bhaktas*. For them, however, it is a communion where the sense of the personal is preserved; an apprehension of God which may be described as *pratyakṣa* or immediate perception. Many Indian Christian saints have had this type of experience and some, like Sundar Singh or Appasamy's own father, have left convincing accounts of its reality and its content.

Logos and Antaryāmin

We turn next to another of Appasamy's distinctive ideas, his use of the Hindu idea of the *antaryāmin* or 'indweller'. With his great love of the Fourth Gospel he inevitably turns frequently to the idea of the Logos, and seeks to associate this with the Hindu idea of the immanent God, the one who rules within, the *antaryāmin*.

His argument here hinges on his exegesis of the words 'He was in the world' in John 1:10. Most commentators understand these words to refer to the incarnate Christ, who *came* into the world and so *was* in it, though the world rejecting him 'knew him not'. Appasamy, however, interprets the expression as referring to the immanence of Christ the Logos in the world even before his incarnation, and quotes in support Ranga-Rāmānuja's commentary on a cryptic line of the *Taittiriya Upaniṣad*, 'Having created that, He then entered the same'.[3] The meaning of this verse, he says, is that 'the Supreme One can

[1] *Bhakti*, p. 63.
[2] *ibid.*, p. 67.
[3] *Tait. Up.* 2.6.2.

be known only in the heart of the world'.[1] John, then, is here stating the immanence of God in the world, while at the same time admitting the need of an incarnation in order that men may know him more clearly. Appasamy writes:

> Because men have not understood Him, even though He is immanent in them, He has 'become flesh'. The incarnation is a more effective means of showing God than mere immanence.[2]

The point is continued in the exegesis of the next verse 'He came unto his own' (v. 11). For Appasamy these words imply Christ's coming not merely for the Jews but for all men, for all are 'his own'. Those who are 'born of God' are not those who have experienced a particular 'new birth' but rather all men, as by nature children of God. As the immanent Christ or *antaryāmin*, therefore, God is already present in all men. But men have not yet fully understood him, and so Christ becomes incarnate as a more effective means of God's self-revelation. Though there is light elsewhere in God's world, yet here the light is brightest. Appasamy writes:

> Every man should strive to put himself in the region where the full blaze of the Logos dwells... The path of wisdom lies in choosing the region which is so pervaded by Light. Such a fully flooded region is Jesus... Though the Logos has been quickening men's hearts everywhere in the world He is fully embodied in Jesus.[3]

Here we come close to the heart of Appasamy's teaching. God is immanent in the world and in man. Men of all faiths have seen the Light, in manifestations bright or dim. But we have a duty to come to the fullest Light of all, and that is seen in Jesus, for in him alone the Logos fully dwells.

There is a certain ambiguity about Appasamy's use of the term *antaryāmin*. Here, for example, we have seen it used of the indwelling Logos, but in other contexts it can be used of the work of the Holy Spirit. In his earlier writings Appasamy says little of the *coming* of the Spirit, and speaks rather of the Spirit's indwelling, in terms like those we have already considered in connection with the indwelling Christ. The doctrine of the indwelling God, he feels, is very close to the Christian idea that God is Spirit:

> God is very close to us. He is not an inaccessible, far-off Being, dwelling in remote heavens. His Presence is everywhere; as

[1] *Bhakti*, p. 41.
[2] *ibid.*, p. 43.
[3] *Moksa*, p. 174.

> Spirit He pervades the whole universe . . . Not a moment passes but His presence envelopes us like the air we live in . . . If we go in search of Him, only outside of ourselves, it will be but wasted labour.[1]

In recent years, and as a result of long pastoral experience including a notable revival movement in his diocese of Coimbatore, Bishop Appasamy has written much more positively about the 'newness' of the Spirit, and says, 'The need for the Holy Spirit to change whole communities with His new life has become very clear to me after my pastoral work'.[2] Yet in his major works we miss a treatment of Pentecost and the effect of the advent of the Spirit.

God and the World

We have seen that Appasamy holds that Christ as the immanent, eternal Logos, is present by nature, though perhaps hidden, in all men. Yet it is not only in the hearts of men that he is to be found pre-existing ; he is present in the whole world, for as Logos he is also the Agent of creation. 'All things were made by him.' So we are brought, while still strictly within the confines of Christology, to a consideration of the relation of God to his creation, which, as we know, is always one of the crucial problems of Indian theology, because of the immense pressure exercised by the *advaita* view that ultimately God and the creation are one.

Briefly, Appasamy comes to the conclusion, on the basis of the Johannine text and with help from Rāmānuja's philosophy, that God is not *identical* with the cosmos, but is rather present and active within it as Logos, related to it in somewhat the same way as the human soul is to the body. He gives an interesting quotation from the *Brihad-Aranyaka Upaniṣad* :

> He who, dwelling in the sky, yet is other than the sky, whom the sky does not know, whose body the sky is, who controls the sky from within—He is your Soul, the Inner Controller (*antaryāmin*), the Immortal . . .
>
> He who, dwelling in the mind, yet is other than the mind, whom the mind does not know, whose body the mind is, who controls the mind from within—He is your Soul, the Inner Controller, the Immortal.[3]

[1] *Gospel*, p. 76.

[2] Art. 'Christian Theology in the Indian Church' in *The South India Churchman*, April, 1964.

[3] *Br. Ar. Up.* 3, 7, 8-20. Cited in *Moksa*, pp. 166-7.

Appasamy comments that in this passage God is not identified with the world as in so many other places in the Hindu scriptures but is rather distinctly felt and recognised as different from the world which he animates.[1] As the human spirit is present in the body to animate it, so " there is a Mind or Reason behind the whole world . . . It is not identical with the world ; it is different from the world; but the world lives because of its functioning . . . Underlying all that we see is the operation of this invisible Personal Power '.[2]

This Rāmānujan analogy of body and soul is of great importance in Appasamy's theology, and is used by him in four distinct contexts : first, as here, in describing God's relation to the world ; secondly in dealing with the relation of the divine and the human natures in Christ ; and thirdly and fourthly in discussing the presence of Christ in the eucharist, and in the Church. We shall return later to a consideration of its effectiveness.

Avatāra

Taking his stand in the tradition of *bhakti* and Rāmānuja, it is natural that Appasamy should take a very different view of the use of the term *avatāra* from that of Sen or Upādhyāya. They felt that to call Jesus an *avatāra* was to reduce him to the level of one of the many *avatāras* of popular Hinduism, and would at best make him an *avatāra* of *Iśvara*, the personal God, conceived of as a lower manifestation of the supreme *Brahman*. Appasamy, with his different outlook, finds that the term *avatāra* can helpfully and fruitfully be applied to the incarnation of Christ, provided certain safeguards are observed.

He begins from the well-known verse of the *Gita* which we have already noticed, which clearly states the Hindu understanding of *avatāra* :

> Whenever there is a decline of law, O Arjuna, and an outbreak of lawlessness, I incarnate myself. For the protection of the good, for the destruction of the wicked and for the establishment of the Law I am born from age to age.[3]

Starting from here, Appasamy outlines a Christian doctrine of *avatāra*, noting on the way the undoubted fact that in many Indian languages the word *avatāra* has in fact for generations

[1] *Moksa*, p. 168.
[2] *ibid.*
[3] Gita, IV. 7.8.

been used by Christians to describe the incarnation of Christ. He points out, however, a number of places where a clear distinction must be drawn between Hindu and Christian uses of the word. In Hinduism, for instance, there are many *avatāras* and in most of these God is regarded as being only partially present. The only complete (*purṇa*) *avatāra* usually accepted is that of Viṣṇu incarnate in Krishna. Obviously such a conception is incompatible with the Christian view of the incarnate Christ who is the incarnation of the whole being of God, and in whom the fulness of the Godhead dwells bodily.[1] So too the purpose of the *avatāra* as described in the *Gita* is inadequate, since Christ came not for ' the destruction of the wicked ' but in order to save them. Further, the *Gita* presupposes that God becomes incarnate again and again, as need arises. And indeed classical Hinduism enumerates a whole series of *avatāras*, while it is common to refer to great human leaders and teachers like Sri Rāmakrishna or Mahatma Gandhi as *avatāras* of God. For the Christian the incarnation of Christ is once for all and unique :

> We believe that Jesus was the *Avatāra*. God lived on the earth as a man only once and that was as Jesus . . . It is our firm Christian belief that among all the great religious figures in the world there is no one except Jesus who could be regarded as an Incarnation of God.[2]

The question of the reality and historicity of Christ's incarnation must also be faced, for the *avatāra* of Hinduism is really a theophany rather than an incarnation. There is an old Hindu tradition that when an *avatāra* walks his feet do not touch the ground so that he leaves no footprints. Even the personalist *bhakti* tradition of the *Śaiva Siddhānta* in South India holds that ' God only *appears* is the world to help men. He is not born as a child . . . He does not possess a physical body for a period of years and use it as an instrument for the achievement of His purposes '.[3] Christianity must avoid all such docetism if it chooses to use the concept of *avatāra*. Similarly Hindu thinkers almost invariably hold that the historicity of the incarnation is of little account. Appasamy quotes a saying of Rāmakrishna :

> Whether Christ or Krishna lived or not is immaterial ; the people from whose brain the Christ ideal, or Krishna ideal, has emanated did actually live as Christ or Krishna for the time being.[4]

[1] Colossians 2:9.
[2] *Gospel*, p. 259.
[3] *ibid.*, p. 262.
[4] Quoted in *Gospel*, p. 263.

In rejecting this point of view Appasamy stresses both the reality of the created world and the historicity of the incarnation in Christ. With these qualifications, however, he is prepared to accept the use of the term *avatāra* in connection with Christ. It is, of course, as we have seen, a term which fits into his whole theological structure which, on its philosophical side, is related to the personal theism and *bhakti* of Rāmānuja, not to the rigid monism of Śankara.

Personal or Impersonal?

Yet here we come to another ambiguity in Appasamy's thought. Despite his clear rejection of *advaita* with its impersonal *Brahman* as incapable of becoming the basis of a Christian conception of God, he yet feels that mystical experience—such as that of Eckhart for example—sometimes leads to an understanding of God which requires the use of impersonal terms. Mysticism, including Christian mysticism, has two tendencies, one seeking to describe God as transcending all empirical data, as the absolute ; and the other seeing him as a warm, personal being, full of love, grace and truth.[1] Appasamy finds both these tendencies in the Fourth Gospel. He finds traces of the impersonal in such descriptions of Christ as door, vine, light, way, truth, life, and points out that in the Synoptic Gospels Jesus does not describe himself in these concrete, impersonal terms. His exegesis here seems rather forced, and he is perhaps on surer ground when he speaks of the Logos-conception as being 'semipersonal'.[2] He sums up the Johannine teaching as being 'to emphasize those aspects of Christ which transcend personality as against those aspects which are personal',[3] and finds confirmation of the validity of this in the experience of Christian mystics who, beginning with an experience centred on Christ, are led on 'from divinity realized under human attributes to divinity realized in eternity'.[4]

At this point Appasamy seems to be approaching a synthesis of the views of Rāmānuja and Śankara, perhaps with the uncomfortable feeling, which is so understandable, that for millions in

[1] *Moksa*, p. 101. Recent writers like R. C. Zaehner and Ninian Smart tend to limit the term 'mysticism' to the first of these, while the second is classed as the 'numinous' approach to God.

[2] *ibid.*, p. 99.

[3] *ibid.*, p. 103.

[4] *ibid.*, p. 106. This is virtually a Christian statement of the passage from realisation of *saguṇa* to *nirguṇa Brahman*.

India the conception of God as *nirguṇa Brahman* will always rank as higher than that of any kind of personal revelation. He writes:

> The combination offered by St. John of both these ways of conceiving God is well worth our attention . . . We must not suppose that in the historic Christ we see all there is of God. The Incarnation is but a working hypothesis helping and guiding men to reach a knowledge of the Divine and does not exhaust all the infinite grandeur of God.[1]

In the incarnation, then, Christ points us beyond himself to the infinitude of the God he reveals. He is, says Appasamy, like some high mountain crest which ultimately proves to be but part of the foothills of a great range:

> Such a towering peak is Christ. He is the only point visible to us. But there is around Him stretching to immense distances the glory and the mystery of the Godhead. We may not say with dogmatic positiveness that in Christ we have seen all and remain content, but through Him seek to understand something more of the ineffable God.[2]

For Śankara, men are divided into those who are capable of apprehending the absolute and those who must be content with a personal God. Christianity can tolerate no such dichotomy, and Appasamy feels that even simple believers can, through the Johannine approach, apprehend God as both personal and yet more than personal. He gives the illustration of a telescope which permits us to see stars and worlds which previously were outside our knowledge:

> So through Christ we sweep the heavens and realize the inaccessible depths and distances with all their mystery, stretching to we know not where.[3]

The picture is a vivid one, but one is left wondering if it would not be more appropriate to use it for the written rather than the living Word of God.

Sin and Karma

The average person in India is very clearly aware of his *karma*, but may well have very little feeling of sin. As Appasamy puts

[1] *Moksa*, p. 112.
[2] *ibid.*
[3] *ibid.*, p. 116.

it, 'The problem of getting rid of *karma* is far more pressing than the problem of getting rid of sin'.[1] In *advaita* Hinduism there is very little conception of sin, but the *bhakti* tradition, with which Appasamy has such a close affinity, has produced some moving confessions, such as that of the 17th century Gujarati poet Dādudayāl:

> Before Thee I am guilty in every nerve and vein; a sinner am I every moment; Master, forgive me!
>
> Not a single good deed have I done; no virtue is there in me; no merit is mine.
>
> Yet forsake not Thy sinful child, for without Thee where is my refuge?
>
> Desire, pride, anger and falsehood have misled me since my birth; O miserable man that I am!
>
> Thou only art my help: Father, wash me with the nectar of Thy rich forgiveness and heal the mind that is sore.[2]

Such deep expressions of sin are, however, comparatively rare in Hinduism, and one feels that Appasamy himself is reluctant to commit himself to the kind of positive teaching on the deadly and active power of sin which is so clear in the Bible and in western Christendom. He mentions a missionary friend who had tried repeatedly, but without success, to convince his Hindu hearers of the sinfulness of sins, and suggests a different approach:

> My own conviction is that the more effective way would be to begin with God and not with man. The Hindu has a real passion for God... He should be first helped to understand the wonder and the depth of God's love, particularly as revealed on Calvary.[3]

And yet freedom from the fear of *karma* is something for which every Hindu longs, and Appasamy finds the key to his linking of the doctrines of sin and *karma* in the Johannine text, 'He that believeth on Him is not judged: he that believeth not hath been judged already' (John 3:18). The thought of everlasting punishment repels him and is, he thinks, contrary to the Johannine emphasis on life and love. Those who believe on Jesus, who find union with him, are freed from their *karma*, which he takes on himself. Those who reject Christ, on the

[1] *Gospel*, p. 97. There is an excellent treatment of this question in A. G. Hogg, *The Christian Message to the Hindu* (1947), Chap. V.
[2] Quoted in A. J. Appasamy, *Temple Bells* (1930), p. 62.
[3] *Gospel*, p. 98.

other hand, continue to be subject to the law of *karma* which is all the time judging them and awarding them the consequences of their deeds.

> 'There is a perpetual retributive judgment going on even now. *Men are judging themselves* by their good or bad choices. . . In this sense there is a continual *karma* working itself out in human lives.[1]

In this Christian presentation of the doctrine of *karma* Appasamy acknowledges his debt to Sundar Singh, and like him rejects the idea of transmigration or *saṃsāra*, which for Hindus is invariably a corollary of *karma*. I am responsible only for the sins of this present life and do not suffer for sins which some other person may have committed while my soul was incarnate in his body.

India longs passionately for deliverance from *karma* and Appasamy, accepting what is true and profound in the doctrine, is eager to give the assurance that to those who come to Christ in repentance, trusting only in him, forgiveness is given, and with it freedom from *karma*. He quotes some lines from the 14th century reformer Kabir, in which he speaks of the wearisome transmigration of the soul from one body to another:

> I was in immobile and mobile creatures, in worms and in moths
> I passed through many births of various kinds.
> In this I occupied many bodies;
> But when, O God, I assumed human birth,
> I was a *Jogi*, a *Jāti*, a penitent, a Brāhmachāri;
> Sometimes a king, an emperor, and sometimes a beggar.
> Saith Kabir, 'O God, have mercy on us;
> We have grown weary; make us now whole'[2]

For Appasamy the description of Christianity as *bhakti mārga* is the description of that wholeness.

'*The Uttermost Expression of the Love of God*'

There is a verse of Tukarām's which says:

> I am a mass of sin;
> Thou art all purity;
> Yet Thou must take me as I am
> And bear my load for me.[3]

[1] *Moksa*, pp. 218-20. (My italics.)
[2] Tr. M. A. Macauliffe. Quoted in *Gospel*, p. 119. *Jogi* = *Yogi*; *Jāti* = mendicant; *brahmachāri* = celibate student.
[3] Quoted in *Gospel*, p. 125. Tr. N. Macnicol.

How does God 'bear my load for me'? We have seen how Appasamy concentrates more on the 'positive' side of a life of faith-union with the living Christ rather than on an exposition of the meaning of the death of Christ. Yet his interpretation of the Cross is interesting and typical.

He begins with two Johannine texts, 'Except a grain of wheat fall into the earth and die, it abideth by itself alone; but if it die it beareth much fruit' (John 12: 24), and 'I, if I be lifted up from the earth, will draw all men unto myself' (John 12: 32). The first of these texts is taken to indicate the universal necessity for suffering: in suffering we are more closely united with the suffering Christ. The second forms a basis for a statement of the 'moral influence' theory of the atonement. On the Cross, 'the supreme power of God's love which forgives and redeems, exerts its irresistible influence'.[1] The Cross, Appasamy feels, is not to be thought of in a merely negative way, as the means or occasion of forgiveness of sin. Rather it is the supreme illustration of the love of God, which draws men to him. In an illustration very reminiscent of Sundar Singh's he speaks of a mother whose love to her child never weakens in spite of the child's guilt:

> When the critical hour arrives and a child is guilty of some grave moral lapse, the mother's heart goes out to the child with an agony which passes expression and which sometimes, though not always, works out by sheer force of sacrifice and suffering a great change in character.[2]

Here, however, unlike Sundar Singh's story, 'moral influence' is the only force at work, and there is no hint of an effective 'transaction'. The Cross is a 'manifestation' of God's love which wins our love in return.

The first pole of Appasamy's doctrine of the atonement is, then, the moral effect which the love of God demonstrated on the Cross of Christ has upon the *bhakta*. The second is the self-identification of the *bhakta* with Christ's suffering, in a 'Way of the Cross' like that of which Sundar Singh speaks:

> He who would find life in Christ must follow Him altogether. And as His intensest moments were those spent on the Cross, the Christian must identify himself with the suffering Lord and even share in His agony. Only such entire and willing identity with Jesus can lead to life eternal.[3]

[1] *Bhakti*, p. 112.
[2] *ibid.*, p. 119.
[3] *ibid.*, p. 110.

Appasamy sees two chief obstacles to the acceptance by Hindus of the Christian view of union with God through fellowship in the sufferings of Christ. First of all there is the crucial question, 'Can God suffer?' With few exceptions Hindu teachers have held that God is impassible. According to the *Kāṭha Upaniṣad*,

> As the sun, the eye of the entire world, is not touched by the eternal impurities seen by the eyes, so the one immanent self of all things is not touched by the sorrow of the world, for He is outside it.[1]

For the Hindu, *Brahman* is *Ānanda*, bliss, and so it is impossible to conceive of him as suffering or as sharing in the sufferings of men. The Christian, however, as he sees the Cross of Christ knows that God does suffer. In the words of C. S. Paul, whose interesting book *The Suffering God* (1932) is a study of this theme, 'in the moral world of self-determining personalities the Suffering God is the only Almighty God.'[2] It is a very important point.

Secondly, the Hindu doctrine of *karma* cannot be reconciled with the idea of redemptive suffering, for according to it all suffering is the result of evil deeds, in this life or previous ones, and no place remains for vicarious suffering. Unless the doctrine of *karma* is radically modified—as it was by Sundar Singh—it is a fatal obstacle to the acceptance of any doctrine of atonement involving suffering, either divine or human.

We see then that, while accepting the fact and indeed the necessity of the suffering of Christ, Appasamy finds its application to human need in terms of moral influence rather than of any kind of objective 'sin-bearing'. In some unaccountable way it is revealed to us at the Cross that our sins are forgiven, but *how* this revelation of forgiveness becomes effective is not clearly indicated:

> What is the sacrifice? To whom is it made? For what purpose? These and other questions have been endlessly debated. The sacrifice on Calvary is the uttermost expression of the love of God. . . Through this great sacrifice God has fulfilled Himself and, if we may say so with reverence, has realized to the full the riches of His love.[3]

[1] *Katha Up*. 5. 11. Quoted in *Bhakti*, p. 117.
[2] C. S. Paul, *The Suffering God* (1932), p. 220.
[3] *Bhakti*, p. 125.

That is as far as Appasamy goes in his earlier books, for to him the central fact is not the 'negative' one of sin-bearing but the 'positive' one of faith-union with Christ, a union which is simply strengthened and given added depth by the revelation of suffering love on the Cross, a love in which we join by our own suffering, thereby deepening our union with Christ. In his later book *The Gospel and India's Heritage* (1942), however, Appasamy strikes a more definite note in treating the nature of forgiveness. The law of *karma*, described here as 'the moral law that the wages of sin is death',[1] is upheld by Christ at the cost of his own life. Appasamy writes:

> The Cross is the revelation of the tremendous cost which God has to pay for the redemption of man. It is not as if without any effort on His part He forgives men whatever they may do. The suffering He has borne for us is beyond our reckoning. . . The moral law is not set aside in any sense; where there is sin there *is* suffering. The sin of men has brought about the suffering and death of Jesus on the Cross. If God forgave without the Cross, He would be laying aside His own moral law which He has established among men. . . So the experience of the Cross is absolutely necessary. After the Cross no one can say that God forgives men because it is easy for Him or because He does not care to uphold the law that righteousness should prevail in the world.[2]

This statement is not so very far from penal substitution, though no doubt Appasamy would not accept the term. Men sink under the burden of *karma*, the burden of the fruits of their own sins. But this burden is 'shifted from us to God'[3]. By the law of *karma* we are each responsible for all the fruits of our actions. But if we repent and turn to the one who has been lifted up and who draws all men unto himself we shall share in the fruits of that corn of wheat which is fruitful by dying. He bears our sins, our *karma*, and so we are set free for a life of union with him.

Sources of Authority—the Pramāṇas

Dr. Appasamy has in recent years written on the subject of the sources of authority in the Christian faith, and refers to the possibility of using, in a Christian context, the three traditional standards or *pramāṇas* of Hinduism—*śruti* (Scripture), *yukti*

[1] *Gospel*, p. 122.
[2] *ibid.*, pp. 124-5.
[3] *ibid.*, p. 125.

(reason) and *anubhava* (experience).[1] In Hindu religious discussion on any point it is customary to proceed through these three steps, first of all asking what the inspired Scriptures have to say on the point at issue; then applying to it the canons of reason to see if it will bear rational argument; and finally testing it against one's own experience to ascertain if it has the ring of truth in practice.

The question which gives rise to Appasamy's study is one put by Chenchiah: Can we have direct, unmediated knowledge of Jesus, or must such knowledge always come to us mediated by Scripture and Church tradition? The query is an important one, one which, in a rather different form, was the touchstone of the European Reformation, and it is a vital one today in any kind of dialogue with Hinduism. Appasamy affirms its importance in no uncertain fashion when he writes that 'the primary task of Christian theology in India today is to settle the sources of our authority.'

He himself unhesitatingly gives first place to Scripture or *śruti*. The word *śruti* literally means 'hearing' and in Hindu usage refers to the Vedas, which are supposed to have been 'heard' directly from God by the *rishis* or seers. The word then comes derivatively to mean 'revelation', and so to refer exclusively to those scriptures which are divinely inspired rather than simply 'remembered' by men (*smṛti*). In Appasamy's usage the primary revelation comes in the Gospels; the 'interpretation' offered by Jesus' followers, especially St. Paul and St. John, is also fundamental, though not necessarily of the same importance as the life and teaching of Christ himself. The Old Testament also is of value for us 'as giving us the background in which the historical Incarnation took place.' In an attractive picture he writes:

> Sanskrit books speak of a shining light on the threshold of a house which sheds its rays on either side. The life and death and teaching of Christ is such a light illumining the long historical processes of revelation both before and after Him. In the light which radiates from Him we see what is valuable and worthwhile in the intuitions of sages and prophets both before Him and after Him.

This is a good illustration of the Christocentricity of Appasamy's thought. Christ is the Centre of Scripture and it is in his light that we read both Old and New Testaments, and because all

[1] I have been privileged to read a typescript chapter entitled *What are Pramāṇas?* Quotations in this section are taken from this source.

Scripture bears witness to him the Bible is our primary rule of faith or *pramāṇa*.

The word *yukti* means argument, inference or reason. In the context of the *pramāṇas* Appasamy's meaning is that every theological belief derived from Scripture should be tested by reason. This is not, of course, a plea for natural theology, but rather for the use of scientific method and argument to prove that theological statements are not illogical or contradictory, but are such as can be accepted by honest, modern men. The Christian faith, though grounded in revelation through Scripture—*śruti* in both senses of the word—must be capable of being defended at the bar of logical examination, whether by modern secular men or by traditional Hinduism.

We can accept a belief as our own only when we have proved it true in our own experience. Appasamy, with memories of his own father and of Sundar Singh in his mind, and with his own deep spiritual experience, gladly accepts the third traditional *pramāṇa* of *anubhava* or personal experience as one which must be applied to all theological statements. Only those who know God are qualified to speak of him.

To the three traditional Hindu *pramāṇas* Appasamy adds a fourth—the Church or *sabhā*. By this he means the authoritative teaching of the Church, and in arranging his four Christian *pramāṇas* he would give it second place, following immediately after Scripture, and before reason or experience. In this way he gives a place of decisive importance to 'Church dogmatics', second only to Scripture which controls it, and exercising authority over the tendencies of individuals to follow their own ideas. He writes;

> It is of the essence of the Christian religion that God reveals Himself not merely to individuals but to His Church. The Hindu religion fails disastrously in this respect. It recognizes fully God's dealings with individuals; but it does not make clear God's presence in His believers, as a group or collectively.

Before leaving what Appasamy says about the *pramāṇas*, and more especially about Scripture, we shall look for a moment at his view of the Old Testament and of the Hindu *śāstras*. It is well-known that some Indian Christians, notably Chenchiah, have held that the Old Testament has little significance for the Indian Church, and that to some extent at least its place and function can be taken by Hindu scriptures. Unlike Chenchiah, Appasamy accepts the Old Testament as essential and shows no tendency towards an Indian type of Marcionism which would reject it. The Hindu Scriptures cannot supplant the Old Testament though they may, he feels, supplement it and provide a God-given *praeparatio evangelii* for the people of India. In words reminiscent of Farquhar's *The Crown of Hinduism* approach he writes:

> There are elements in the ancient Scriptures of India which have to be fearlessly given up. But there are also many doctrines and ideals in them which have to be as zealously assimilated and carried on to their natural culmination in Christ. If Jesus blamed his contemporaries for not listening to the voice of Moses, with equal power and vehemence will He condemn us for not listening to Ramanuja, Manikkavacakar, Tukaram, Kabir and Chaitanya who have left behind them teaching of such undying value, pointing the way to Christ.[1]

It is interesting to note that the list of saints and sages he gives contains only those of the *bhakti mārga*, and Śankara is conspicuous by his absence! It was in pursuit of this idea of 'assimilation' that Appasamy published in 1930 *Temple Bells*, a selection of readings from Hindu religious literature, one of the best anthologies of its kind ever published and a real treasury of the best Hindu *bhakti* lyrics in English translation.[2]

'*This is My Body*'

Appasamy's attitude to the organised Church is much more positive than that of many Indian theologians, and his distinguished career has been within the Church as an ordained minister. We find him, therefore, writing interestingly and profoundly about the nature of the eucharist, and we shall examine briefly two of the points where he brings his knowledge of Hinduism to bear on the theology of the Lord's Supper.

In the Fourth Gospel Jesus teaches that he is the Bread of Life and exhorts his followers to feed on him. But how is a Hindu to understand this strange, even revolting conception? Like the Jews, they ask, 'How can this man give us his flesh to eat?' (John 6 : 52), and the eucharist has often been misrepresented as an occasion when Christians are forced to eat meat, an abomination to orthodox Hindus. Is there any way in which

[1] *Bhakti*, p. 166.

[2] Recently some Roman Catholic scholars have been returning to the idea of a 'cosmic covenant', of whose priesthood Melchisedek is the type. Much of Hindu worship can then be regarded as part of a 'cosmic liturgy', whose fulfilment is in Christ. See Bede Griffith, *Christian Ashram* (1966), pp. 194, 219, 247.

the idea of the eucharist can be made meaningful for Hindus? Appasamy turns to a verse of the *Taittiriya Upaniṣad* which says:

> Food is *Brahman*: for from food creatures are born; by food the creatures thus born live; and into food they enter and perish.[1]

This text implies—in a manner not frequent in Hinduism—that matter or the body, here seen as food, may become a vehicle or effective symbol of divine power and grace. Hinduism, not least in its modern Gandhian form, tends to regard the body and its desires as the source of evil. This was the teaching of the early Gnostics, who therefore denied to Jesus the possession of a true human body. The author of the Fourth Gospel is determined to resist such docetism, for the Logos has become flesh and so the body, matter, food are appropriate media for revealing God's grace. Arguing along these lines Appasamy gives a fine statement of the meaning of the sacramental, and more particularly of the Lord's Supper:

> Behold, the living Christ enters into us and forms a part of our inmost self in the same organic way in which food and drink become a part of our being... Christ Himself comes into our souls through the elements and abiding in us endows us with His spiritual energy. Through faith we abide in Him. We turn our thoughts to Him in prayer surrendering all we have into His sacred keeping and He comes unto us and directs us from our inner self.[2]

The Christian faith, then, does not despise the physical. Christ had a fully human body and our own bodies are the temple of the Holy Spirit. And through the chosen physical elements of bread and wine Christ himself comes to us, not corporeally but to faith.

The second point concerns the meaning of the words used by Jesus at the last supper, 'This is my body'. Rather than going into the controversies of western sacramental theology with their discussion of the real presence, transubstantiation, 'in, with and under' and so on, Appasamy turns to Rāmānuja's idea that all created beings are 'the body of God'. He quotes Rāmānuja:

> All sentient and non-sentient beings together constitute the body of the Supreme Person, for they are completely controlled

[1] *Tait. Up.* 3.2. Quoted in *Bhakti*, p. 132.
[2] *Bhakti*, pp. 142, 147.

and supported by him for his own ends, and are absolutely subordinate to him.[1]

So Jesus takes the created elements of bread and wine as the instruments for fulfilling his purpose:

> They were to reveal to men His utter love for them leading to the complete sacrifice of Himself on the Cross... The bread and wine were to become a new body of our Lord. In tasting them we taste His love... Truly the bread and wine become the body and blood of our Lord because through them He fulfils His end of making known His love to men and gathering them into the intimacy and closeness of fellowship with Him.[2]

It is an impressive interpretation. There is no mention of substance and accident, nor even of sign and symbol. Yet God chooses and uses *this* 'body', of bread and wine, and in receiving it we receive the 'Spirit' behind it, Christ himself.

The Rāmānujan Analogy

Appasamy considers that Rāmānuja has expounded three fundamental principles which can be of great help in the philosophical construction of an Indian Christian theology. These are his stress on the *love* of God (reflecting the heart of the *bhakti* literature), and his use of the conceptions of *antaryāmin* and *avatāra*. We have looked at each of these at some length. In addition to these three ideas, however, Appasamy develops, as we have seen, a most interesting use of Rāmānuja's 'soul-body' doctrine of God's relation to the created world, and transforms it into a sort of analogy which he uses in four different contexts. Some western theologians have spoken of 'the Christological analogy' or 'the paradox of Grace',[3] in which the mystery of the union of divine and human in Christ is made a type for the paradox of the divine and human elements in the Bible, the Church and the eucharist. Perhaps in this analogy of Rāmānuja there is a conception which, with proper safeguards, may be more meaningful for the Church in India than the less familiar Chalcedonian formulations.

The first context in which Appasamy expounds the idea is, as we have seen, that of God's relation to the world. We may say, he holds, that God has made the entire universe his body:

[1] Ramanuja, *Śri Bhaṣya* II.2.9. Quoted in *Gospel*, p. 206.

[2] *Gospel*, p. 208.

[3] e.g. T. F. Torrance, *Conflict and Agreement in the Church*, Vol. I, (1959), pp. 230ff. D. M. Baillie, *God was in Christ* (1948), pp. 114ff.

> As a spirit God has no form. . . So He creates the world in order that through it His character may be revealed. The world of physical objects is the instrument by which He makes known His nature and evokes the worship and love of His devotees.[1]

This is the analogy as Rāmānuja himself uses it, in order to avoid Śankara's monism where the creation is regarded as essentially no different from the Creator. In Rāmānuja the creation is regarded as real, and God is immanent within it as the *antaryāmin*. Rāmānuja's analogy certainly gives to the created world a degree of reality which it does not possess in Śankara's *advaita*. It is still, however, very different from the traditional Christian conception of *creatio ex nihilo*.

The second, or truly Christological, use of the analogy is to illuminate the union of the divine and human in Christ. 'God took, as it were, a second body, the fleshly organism of Jesus . . . God revealed Himself to men through the human body of Jesus '.[2] Instead of the time-honoured terms of western Christological controversy which mean little in India, Appasamy here uses the Rāmānujan analogy to show that Christ is a single personality, a union of body and soul, with a fully human, created body, yet within whom God dwells as the Inner Controller or *antaryāmin*.

The analogy is impressive, but might break down if pressed too far in either direction. It could, for instance, be pressed too far in the docetic direction of Apollinaris by saying that the 'soul' of Christ is the Logos, and that therefore he is not fully human. It could also be pressed too far in the opposite or humanist direction by saying that Christ is no different from all men, for all men, as the body of God, are indwelt by the Logos. Appasamy is at pains to deal with the latter difficulty by pointing out the difference between the incarnate Christ and ordinary men. It is true, he holds, that the Logos is immanent in all men, but they have not understood him, and so God has taken the unforeseen step of 'becoming flesh', as 'a more effective means of showing God than mere immanence'.[3] The Logos is immanent in all men; He is *incarnate* only in Christ. And through faith-union Christ comes to dwell in the heart of his *bhakta*. Immanence is not enough, and so incarnation is unique.

We have seen the third use which Appasamy makes of the analogy, to describe the nature of the presence of Christ in the

[1] *Gospel*, p. 206.
[2] *ibid.*, p. 207.
[3] *Bhakti*, pp. 42-3.

eucharist. The fourth shows the relationship of Christ to his Church:

> God took yet another body—His Church. The life of Jesus on earth came to an end. . . So God planted in the world His Church as an instrument by which His rule over men would become real. The Church was to be another medium through which He would make plain His will and render it effective in the world.[1]

The Church is the Body of Christ. It is a human institution and yet it is also divine. God is present within it, despite all its imperfections, as the Inner Controller, the *antaryāmin*. St. Paul speaks of Christ as the *Head* of the Body rather than its scul, yet surely the Head is thought of in the sense of 'Mind' or Controller, that which unites and controls the members and uses them for its own purpose. So here once again the analogy is helpful. God is not simply 'Immanent' in his Church; he is dynamically present, directing and controlling it according to his will and purpose yet acting through the human institution, the human members of whom the Body is composed.

That is as far as Appasamy takes us at this point. Yet seen eschatologically this analogy can perhaps take us further still, and through it we may be able to penetrate to a thoroughly Christian use of the primary Rāmānujan analogy, that of God and the world.

The Church is the Body of Christ; and at the same time it is God's instrument for making his will done in the world, and for bringing every thought into captivity to Christ,[2] through whom 'all things' are to be reconciled to God.[3] In the first chapter of Colossians Paul brings these two ideas into close connection: the Church as the Body of Christ, and the universe 'all things'—as that which is to become the totally dedicated instrument of God's glory. Christ is the Head of the Body, the Church, *in order* that one day he may become the 'first' in all things, in the whole created world. 'He is . . . the head of the body, the church . . . to be in all things alone supreme.'[4]

As he is now the Head, the organising principle of the Church, so at the end he will be the 'first', the Head, the organising principle of 'all things'. We cannot follow Rāmānuja in saying that the world is *now* the body of God. But we do believe that the

[1] *Gospel*, p. 208.
[2] II Corinthians 10 : 5 A.V.
[3] Colossians 1 : 20 A.V.
[4] Colossians 1 : 18 NEB.

Church is the Body of Christ and that ultimately, at the end, the whole creation will be his, will reflect his glory and be the perfect instrument of his will. And so this analogy points beyond itself to the final purpose of God for the world, that of 'summing up' all things in Christ.[1] Christ is *now* the Head of the Church in order that eschatologically He may be acknowledged first in all things.

Thus the Rāmānujan analogy, in the three *derived* meanings which Appasamy gives it—in relation to the Person of Christ, the eucharist and the Church—is capable of immediate and meaningful theological use, while it would seem that in its original application—the description of God's relation to the world as that of soul and body—it becomes significant in a truly Christian way only when viewed eschatologically. The mere fact of so using it, however, gives a sense of purpose and involvement in the world of matter and history, and so this use of the analogy, when so treated, becomes significant and helpful for the Church in India.

In concluding our chapter on Appasamy we should remember that he is in no way bound to Rāmānuja's philosophy and on many points, such as image-worship, transmigration and caste, he totally rejects Rāmānuja's teaching. He is a disciple of Christ, not of Rāmānuja. He has, however, found that for him the *bhakti* tradition and its philosophical expression in Rāmānuja is the best and most helpful available Indian 'instrument' for the proclamation and explanation of the Christian message.

[1] Ephesians 1 : 10 *anakephalaiosasthai.*

Chapter VIII

THE THEOLOGY OF THE NEW CREATION: P. CHENCHIAH

P. Chenchiah (1886-1959)

Pandipeddi Chenchiah is one of the most striking and original figures in the history of Indian Christian theology.[1] A convert from Hinduism, he was baptised along with his father as a small boy, and always retained his interest in the faith of his forebears:

> The convert of today regards Hinduism as his spiritual mother who has nurtured him in a sense of spiritual values in the past... For him, loyalty to Christ does not involve the surrender of a reverential attitude towards the Hindu heritage.[2]

Chenchiah, a layman, became a distinguished lawyer and for a time was Chief Judge of Pudukkottai State. In his youth he, like his friend and brother-in-law, Chakkarai, came under the influence of Dr. William Miller, the outstanding Scottish missionary Principal of the Madras Christian College, whose liberalism in different directions had a great effect on many of his students. In later years Chenchiah was one of the moving spirits in a series of Christian ventures in Madras, and a leading figure in a group of somewhat unorthodox but highly stimulating thinkers who came to be known as 'the Rethinking Group' from the title of their best known publication *Rethinking Christianity in India*. This was the famous book which appeared in 1938 on the eve of the International Missionary Council's World Conference at Tambaram, Madras, as an Indian reply to Hendrik Kraemer's Barthian broadside *The Christian Message in a Non-Christian World*, and in which the Indian Church of 1938 is pilloried because of its subservience to ideas and forms imported wholesale

[1] For studies of Chenchiah see: *A Christian Theological Approach to Hinduism*; C. G. Oosthuizen *op. cit.*; H. Wagner, *op. cit.*, Chenchiah's foremost Indian exponent is Prof. D. A. Thangasamy; see his book *The Theology of Chenchiah* (CISRS, 1967) and also his articles, 'Significance of Chenchiah and his Thought' and 'Chenchiah's Understanding of Jesus Christ' in *Religion* and *Society* X/3 (1963) and XI/3 (1964). See also R.H.S. Boyd, 'Theologie im Kontext Indischen Denkens' in Horst Bürkle (Ed.) *Indische Beiträge zur Theologie der Gegenwart* (1966), pp. 77ff.

[2] *Rethinking Christianity in India* (2nd edn. 1939), p. 49.

from the West. Though Chenchiah was one of the leading contributors to this volume he did not himself publish any books and his theological writings have to be culled mainly from the pages of the Madras *Guardian* and from the two chief books in which he collaborated, *Rethinking Christianity* and *Asramas Past and Present*.[1]

In his theological writing Chenchiah is influenced by a number of distinct and identifiable factors. As a convert from Hinduism and one who had carved out for himself a successful and honourable career in the secular world of twentieth century India he was anxious to retain to the fullest possible extent his Indian, indeed Hindu, cultural heritage, which he felt to be threatened by most organised forms of Christianity. He thus found himself to some extent in conflict with the institutional Church, though in fact he remained a Church member to the end of his life.[2] To him the Church seemed to have become bogged down in institutionalism and to be a slavish copy of Churches in western countries. His antipathy to the organised Church extended also to the Church's formulated doctrines which he felt to be an intolerable burden on the free life of the Spirit. His constant appeal, therefore, was to get away from the doctrinal statements and confessions of the Church to what he called 'the raw fact of Christ'.[3] Christ represented for him a new stage in the evolution of man ; he is the True Man, the New Man. If, by the power of the Spirit, we can become one with him, then we too can become as he is and so become 'new creatures' That is how the 'new creation' begins. And so we find the Kingdom of God coming on earth, a Kingdom whose members are 'Christs', 'new creatures', and who live according to, the *yoga* of the Spirit'. But this is to anticipate.

There are two important influences which must be discussed in more detail as they constitute the philosophical background of his writing and give it many of its characteristic features. These two influences are the 'integral *yoga*' of the famous Sri Aurobindo of Pondicherry and the practical teaching of 'Master CVV' of Kumbakonam. For Chenchiah these two Hindu thinkers were of decisive significance and greatly helped him in

[1] *Asramas Past and Present* (1941), ed. P. Chenchiah, V. Chakkarai, A. N. Sudarisanam. Wagner's book contains a good bibliography of Chenchiah's writings.

[2] The South India United Church (Presbyterian and Congregational), and after 1947 the Church of South India.

[3] The phrase is quoted by Thangasamy in *Religion and Society* X/3 (1963).

his theological quest, just as Plato helped Justin Martyr or as Śankara opened insights for Upādhyāya.

'Master CVV', as he was known to his pupils, was the *guru* of a school of *yoga* at Kumbakonam on the banks of the river Kāveri.[1] His teaching, which was wholly directed to practical living, was a reversal of the major strain of Hinduism which teaches non-attachment as the means of attaining salvation. Master CVV's teaching is world-affirming. The creation is for him not just *māyā*; rather it is precisely through creation that God reveals himself and demonstrates his power (*śakti*). Thus there is meaning and hope and promise in this present life, and the release of divine power brings into being a new quality of life—which Master CVV quaintly calls 'Merry Life'—whose fullest form is to be found not in isolation but in society. This new life is given practical expression in community by means of a special *yoga* or discipline of life, whose main feature is the reception of a new kind of spiritual power.

Chenchiah himself became a pupil of Master CVV and saw this approach as bearing very closely on the Christian understanding of the work of the Holy Spirit and on the nature of the new life in Christ. Here was a way of life which—unlike most kinds of Hinduism—looked to the coming of a force from *outside* man which could enter and change him; which did not shrink from the fact of creation but rejoiced in it and saw God at work in it.

In a similar way Chenchiah found much that appealed to him in the work of Sri Aurobindo, whom he visited at his famous *āshram* at Pondicherry. The aspects of Aurobindo's thought which helped him most were the ideas of a spiritual power which comes *from outside* with a transforming strength, and that of the evolution—empowered by this descent from above—of a new and better type of humanity. The influence of Bergson is to be seen here, both in Aurobindo and in Chenchiah's own thought. Along with these two ideas goes a third, that of 'integral *yoga*', the teaching that this new kind of life can really be put into practice, and that there can in fact grow up a new fellowship, say in an *āshram*, where the new life of integral *yoga*, empowered by a new spiritual force, is a daily reality.

We can see how these two Hindu thinkers acted as catalysts for Chenchiah's theology. He did not wish to express himself in western concepts if this could be avoided. He rejected Śankara's

[1] His full name was Kanchupati Venkata Rao Venkatasami Rao. Chenchiah described his work in *The Guardian*, 1943, pp. 48 ff., 497 ff, 509 ff.

absolute monism with its ambiguous attitude towards the creation and the body and its tendency towards asceticism and non-attachment. Similarly he rejected the *bhakti* approach, which seemed to him too limited and confined. But in the work of Aurobindo and in the practical instruction of Master CVV he found a line of thought which was fully Hindu and yet took into account the findings of modern western thought, especially in the fields of evolution and genetics, in which Chenchiah himself was deeply interested. With these thinkers as his 'instruments' he felt that he was in a position to interpret the Christian faith in a way which would be meaningful to the educated Hindu of the twentieth century.

Chenchiah did not make any attempt to give a full and systematic presentation of his views and in fact was strongly opposed to the idea of the systematic explication of Christian belief. From an examination of his writings, however, it is possible to extract his understanding of the major Christian doctrines, and we shall now look at some of those points where his view represents something different from the work of his predecessors.

'*The Raw Fact of Christ*'

For Chenchiah the central fact of the Christian faith is the direct experience of Christ and so his understanding of Christology must come first in any attempt to penetrate his thought. He writes:

> Let it be clearly understood that we accept nothing as obligatory save Christ. Church doctrine and dogma, whether from the West or from the past, whether from Apostles or from modern critics, are to be tested before they are accepted.[1]

The central fact of Christianity thus consists in the believer coming into direct experiential touch with Christ; we must have the *anubhava* of the living Christ. But who is this Christ who is the centre of our faith, and what is his nature?

Despite his emphasis on the need for experience, Chenchiah explicitly rejects the idea of 'the Christ of experience', as the mere creation of those who find that the Jesus of history does not fit their preconceptions, as he did not fit the Jewish picture of the Messiah.[2] His own emphasis is firmly on the historicity and humanity of Christ—an Antiochian rather than an Alexandrian

[1] *Rethinking*, p. 150.
[2] *ibid.*, p. 54.

approach. It is only *because* Christ is a historic figure that he can be active in our life today:

> The historicity of Jesus will take on a new meaning. God translated the idea of a new man into a fact of history and projected Him into the arena of life.[1]

It is precisely because Christ is a historic, true man that the ideal of what man should be like, and can be like, is no mere abstraction but a concrete possibility. That possibility has been seen in action in the historic Christ, who lives today and is still fully human and yet 'new':

> The fact of Christ is the birth of a new order in creation. It is the emergence of life—not bound by Karma; of man, not tainted by sin, not humbled by death; of man triumphant, glorious, partaking the immortal nature of God; of a new race in creation—sons of God.[2]

Yet in this triumphant, glorious Christ, the human element is not to be regarded as something temporary and evanescent. Rather it is permanent, and indeed Chenchiah feels that Christ's normal and permanent sphere of action is in this world *as man*, rather than as the eternal Second Person of the Trinity. Here he is consciously opposing the Hindu doctrine of the *avatāra*, who assumes a human appearance for a limited period and a specific purpose and afterwards resumes full Godhead. This understanding of the permanence of Christ's humanity leads Chenchiah to emphasise the title 'Son of Man'. He writes:

> Indian Christian Theology regards Jesus essentially as the Son of Man who in the midst of change retains this essential human nature... The classical doctrine which makes incarnation an adventure and episode, a coming into the world for a purpose, necessarily involves that after redemption was achieved Jesus has gone back to his pre-Jesus status in Trinity—does not support the view that Jesus is the unchanging core. Indian Christian Theology interpreting Him as permanently human accepts Him as unchanging to us men, in history.[3]

Jesus as 'permanently human', the 'unchanging core' of the Christian faith, acting in history both during the time of the incarnation and today—these are some of the leading ideas of Chenchiah's Christology.

[1] Quoted in *National Christian Council Review* (1943), p. 362.
[2] *Rethinking*, p. 166.
[3] *The Guardian*, 6.2.47.

When he turns to deal with the relationship of the divine and human in Christ, Chenchiah carefully avoids equating Christ with God. In an interesting passage from *Rethinking Christianity* he writes that Jesus 'is never the absolute—unapproachable, incomprehensible . . . Jesus is not God, the absolute, but God as standing in relation to man—not God who operates vertically and in crisis'.[1] Here Chenchiah is fighting on two fronts—in opposition to Barth, as mediated in Kraemer's *The Christian Message*, and also in opposition to the *advaita* conception of God as *nirguṇa Brahman*. In other words Chenchiah, like Appasamy, is opposed to the classical Christological understanding of Christ as metaphysically one with the Father. 'Of the same substance' is not a category which he would accept. Like Appasamy and Ram Mohan Roy he quotes the text, 'My Father is greater than I' in support of his view :

> Jesus as portrayed in the records is less than God. He says so explicitly (John 14 : 28). We want to make Him the Very God—transcendent and absolute. The Jesus of the Gospels transcends the measure of man : we try to make Him the very man. He presents us a harmonised picture of God man—not merely hyphenated God-Man. But we seek to keep both God and Jesus separate from each other and man from both.[2]

This is a clear attack on the Chalcedonian Christology of 'fully God and fully man'. For Chenchiah Christ is something *new*, something different from either God or man, a new emergence or 'mutation', to use the biological language which he chooses. He even uses the word 'product', a term which would seem to have rather unfortunate Arian overtones :

> Jesus stands to man as man stands to the animal. . .[Man] not only fulfils but also transcends the lower creation. Jesus is not God or man, the 'Son'—Son of God or Son of Man—He is the product of God and man, not God-Man. The Spirit of God overshadowed Mary and Jesus was born. He is a new creation—the Lord and Master of a new creative branch of Cosmos. He is the Son of God because the Spirit of God entered Him. He is the Son of Man because He was born out of the Mother of man—the female. He transcends us as we transcend animals. Reason is our differential, the Holy Spirit is His.[3]

[1] *Rethinking*, p. 158.
[2] *ibid.*, p. 54.
[3] *ibid.*, p. 62.

It is tempting to criticise this statement in a traditional Christological way by saying that it is adoptionist and that the final sentence is a clear enunciation of the heresy of Apollinaris. Chenchiah *appears* to be saying that Jesus was first and foremost a man, into whom God entered through the Spirit, the Spirit taking in him the place of reason in man. Yet Chenchiah's thinking cannot be disposed of so easily. His emphasis is rather on the 'newness' of Christ, who is the firstfruits of the 'new creation':

> He is *adi-purusha* of a new creation... In Jesus, creation mounts a step higher... Jesus is the origin of the species of the Sons of God.[1]

Thus, although Chenchiah frequently uses the titles 'Son of Man' and 'Son of God', he primarily thinks of Christ as a new, living entity, the God Man, the 'bridge' between God and man. The thought of what Christ became through his incarnation interests him far more than speculation about his pre-existence, and he writes:

> If evolution is going to be the crucial concept of Indian Christian theology, it is not pre-existence of Jesus but his entry as a new form and power into the cosmic process that demands attention. Anyhow the Latin isolationism which in its anxiety to present Jesus as unique lifts Him out of all human context, can never take root in the Indian mind which after the ministrations of Upanishads and Sankara, can never reconcile itself to the doctrine of unbridgeable gulf between God and man though it may find considerable difficulty in identifying man with God.[2]

God and man are united in Jesus: the gulf, such as it is, is bridged, and in the word 'Son' we have an indication of the newness of what has emerged in Christ:

> The word 'Son' indicates the measure of unity—something less than complete identity with God but something more than difference in category—between God, Jesus and the Christian. God is God, Man is Man. The twain have met in Jesus: not merely met, but fused and mingled into one. Hinduism always longed for a state in which we could say, as Jesus did, 'I and my Father are one'—which was our Lord's affirmation of the Brahma Vakya *Aham Brahmasmi*... In Jesus it was, for the first time in history, an accomplished reality, not an unrealized aspiration.[3]

[1] Quoted in NCCR (1943), p. 363.
[2] *The Guardian*, 27-2-47.
[3] *Rethinking*, p.168.

Here once again it is easy to apply Christological categories in a western critical manner. The fusion and mingling mentioned by Chenchiah looks like a Eutychian criticism of Chalcedon, while in the application of the *mahāvākya* we find the same confusion between the mystical union of Christ with the believer and the substantial union of the Father with the Son which we have already noticed in the Hindu reformers. And yet Chenchiah's aim is to show the *newness* of Christ, the one totally new factor which has emerged in cosmic history, and the key to the transformation of man and the world. In his view it is wrong to speak of Christ as a metaphysical union of God and man, but right to speak of him as a ' new creation ', a *personality* resulting from the union of God and man. While some of his phrases may seem Eutychian or Apollinarian, his constant stress on the humanity of Christ would seem to clear him from the charge of docetism and indeed the traditional categories of Christological controversy do not seem applicable to his view at all. Although he rejects the application of the *avatāra* conception to Jesus, it is clear that his understanding of the incarnation derives more inspiration from Hinduism than from Judaism or from the philosophical categories of classical Christology.

Sin

Chenchiah has comparatively little to say about the natural man and his state, for his whole theology is orientated towards the *new* creation, towards what man becomes in Christ. He does not share Vivekananda's view that man is not a sinner but feels rather that western theology, in its concentration on sin, has said all that needs to be said and perhaps more. Criticising what he calls the ' radical Biblical realism ' of Barth and Kraemer he writes :

> It describes fairly well the plight of humanity when the drama of redemption began but does not give a faithful picture of the result of the redemptive process.[1]

While thus not denying the fact of sin he feels that it is the fulness of the new life rather than sin which will occupy the central place in Indian theology, and is strongly opposed to the traditional doctrine of the Fall :

> The view of life which would implicate men in tragic fall hardly had they commenced their existence and leave them in the wanderings in the wilderness all through history appalls the imagination.[2]

[1] *ibid.*, p. 178.
[2] *ibid.*, p. 165.

Just as Jesus is True Man, 'man without *karma*', so the sinfulness of the natural man is demonstrated, for Chenchiah, by his bondage to *karma*. Every sin, every evil act brings its fruits and man by himself has no means of escape from this inevitable punishment.

'Reproducing Jesus'

For Chenchiah the work of Christ consists in what he is rather than what he does. He is the New Man, the new stage in the evolution of humanity, the new 'mutation'; and salvation for man consists in being so united to Christ by the power of the Spirit that he too becomes a new creation. Christ is the first fruits of this new type of existence and his work consists in calling men to share this life with him. He, the New Man, is risen and alive and still retains his full humanity, in which he calls us to share. Thus for Chenchiah the 'work of Christ', in so far as the expression is permissible, centres in the resurrection and Pentecost rather than in the Cross.

What sort of union with Christ does Chenchiah envisage? Indian *bhakti* speaks of four distinct types of *mokṣa* or union with God, of which the highest and most complete is *sāyujya*, the state of being fully 'yoked with' or united to God.[1] Chenchiah sees the mystical union of the Christian with Christ as a kind of *sāyujya*, but it is a transforming *sāyujya* in which the believer, though not 'identified' with Christ, becomes as it were 'a Christ' himself. We have already seen a very similar expression in Keshab Chandra Sen.[2] Chenchiah writes:

> I feel the two great urges of the Indian Christians are a desire for direct contact with Jesus (*pratyaksha*) and an aspiration for rebirth—to be born a Son of God in the image of Jesus (*punarjanma*). It is not so much a desire to be a Christian, i.e. a follower of Christ as to be identified with Christ—for *sayujya* with Jesus—a longing that made St. Paul to say 'I no longer live but Christ in me'.[3]

In his description of the relation of the believer to Christ Chenchiah uses that biological language which is so typical of his theology and which shows the influence of Bergson and Aurobindo, and also of the biological studies in which he took such an interest. For here, as so often, Chenchiah tries to carry

[1] The three inferior states are *sālokya*, being in the same sphere with; *sāmipya*, nearness to, intimacy; *sarupya*, conformity, 'being made like to'.

[2] v. supra, p. 32.

[3] *The Guardian*, 6-2-47.

out what a recent critic, H. Wagner, has called a 'double synthesis', the synthesis of his Indian cultural heritage with the Biblical message, and also that of the Biblical message with the neo-naturalistic philosophy of the West of his day, a philosophy by which, in spite of his passionate nationalism, he was so deeply influenced.[1] It is through rebirth that we come to union with Christ, to the state of abiding in him and of being transformed into his likeness. And the process of rebirth is interpreted in the language of biology and genetics:

> If we want to establish the Kingdom of God, we must reproduce Jesus. Christianity is not a juridical or legal problem but a problem in genetics... The unique fact about Jesus is that He was begotten of God. The Christian must be begotten of the Holy Spirit... The future of Christianity lies in the spiritual laboratory. The Indian Christian must concern himself with 'rebirth'. God gave Jesus. True evangelism consists in reproducing Jesus. The Indian Christian should harness the Holy Spirit to the creation of new life.[2]

Chenchiah's thesis is that the destiny of man is to evolve into a higher, spiritual race, and he finds his scriptural basis for his teaching in Romans 8:19: 'For the earnest expectation of the creature waiteth for the manifestation of the sons of God'. Salvation for him is, then, the process of 'reproducing the image of Christ' or even of 'becoming Christ'[3].

Does such a view of salvation leave any room for forgiveness and the removal of sin? As we have seen, Chenchiah thinks that western theology has overemphasised sin and is preoccupied with the negative problem of its removal rather than the positive dynamic of a new life. In an oft-quoted sentence he writes:

> Redemption is effected, not by death but by the larger life... Salvation is not just sinlessness but lifefulness.[4]

We are saved, not by any single act of Christ—much less by our acceptance of a particular interpretation of that act—but rather by the 'fact' of Christ himself, and by the 'transforming adventure of new life' in him.[5] As a result Chenchiah is very critical of all juridical and sacrificial theories of the atonement.

[1] Wagner, *op. cit.*, p. 195.
[2] Quoted by D. A. Thangasamy in *The South India Churchman*, Oct. 1960.
[3] *Asramas*, p. 224; *Rethinking*, p. 63.
[4] Quoted in NCCR (1943), p. 362.
[5] D. A. Thangasamy in *S. I. Churchman*, June, 1960.

He points out how repugnant the sacrificial interpretation of the work of Christ is to Indians with a Hindu background, while the ideas of propitiation and reconciliation by no means exhaust the work of the historical Jesus. He writes:

> The juridical conception of Christianity is an attempt to reduce Jesus to the ideology of Judaism or the political ideology of the State of Rome: in other words to interpret Jesus in terms of sacrifice and propitiation in law, offence and punishment.[1]

Chenchiah carries his *distinguo* right back into the theology of Paul and seeks to separate there two strands of thought, one that of mystical faith-union with Christ, which he accepts, and the other that of a juridical theory of the atonement which he regards as of doubtful value.

> In reaching the kernel of the uniqueness of Jesus, we have to change from one half of Pauline theology which the Western and Eastern Churches have accepted to the other half of his theology which though existing as a doctrine does not function as a live force. St. Paul and St. John both regard Christ as a new creation—the emergence in history of a new chapter in human destiny. . . Christianity is not primarily a doctrine of salvation but the announcement of the advent of a new creative order in Jesus. This is our thrilling discovery imparted to mankind.[2]

Though Chenchiah rejects the juridical theory he believes that our saving relationship with Christ is far deeper than mere moral influence; something objective *does* happen when we are confronted by him, but it is a 'biological' event, a transforming event caused by our union with the risen yet human Christ, which changes us, and not any mere moral influence. And in one particularly moving passage we seem to catch overtones of a deep understanding of the victory of love over evil. He is comparing the battlefield of the Cross with that of Kurukṣetra, described in the *Gita*, where Krishna, disguised as a charioteer, holds converse with Arjuna:

> In the moving tragedy of the Cross, for the first time in history, all power, all might, arrogant aggression of imperialism allying itself with fanaticism, conservatism, obscurantism of the priest, was arrayed against a single man facing life with no other armour than love. Both in the incidents that led to the Cross and the Cross

[1] *Rethinking*, p. 164.
[2] *ibid.*, p. 59.

> itself, we are presented with history in which the powers of the world grappled with the reserves of love and the power of the flesh with the power of the spirit. The Resurrection of Jesus is no happy ending which a sense of justice has invented for a tragedy of woe. It is the triumph of Spirit over flesh, of the new world order over the present, the triumph of *satyagraha* over the passion of the warrior and the ruler.[1]

Here we do sense overtones of the moral influence theory as well as that of 'Christus victor'. Yet even here the stress is on the resurrection rather than the Cross, on the new release of spiritual power rather than on a saving transaction. There is no doubt that ultimately for Chenchiah the work of salvation is to be equated with the saving fact of Christ.

The Yoga of the Spirit and Eschatology

Faith-union with Christ is the essential basis for the Christian life, a life which Chenchiah calls 'the *yoga* of the Spirit'. The believer who is united with Christ becomes himself a new creation, his life becomes the *yoga* of the Spirit, and the sphere of that life is the Kingdom of God. Quoting the opening verses of Romans 12 Chenchiah defines this Christian *yoga* as 'the transformation of oneself into the figure and image of Christ': that, he says—using Moffatt's translation—'is your cult—a spiritual rite'. Our task is 'to realise the Kingdom of God as Christ did'[2], and for this we need to enter deep levels of spiritual experience. It is just here that conventional Christian life and witness so often disappoint and fail the Hindu:

> The Hindu sees only the commonplace Christianity in us. He does not find that there is anything in Christianity corresponding to the deeper levels of Hindu spiritual experience... Of the Holy Spirit, of living with Christ and in Christ, we have not told him.[3]

This Christian *yoga*, which Chenchiah feels should be the normal life of a Christian, must be wholly dependent on the Holy Spirit, who ever since Pentecost abides permanently on earth.[4] *Yoga* is a quite practical operation through which man comes into contact with God as spiritual Person and so receives spiritual power which can be applied to the task of re-creating the

[1] *Asramas*, p. 322.
[2] *ibid.*, p. 287.
[3] *ibid.*, p. 267.
[4] *The Guardian*, 6-2-47.

Christian in the image of God.[1] Summing up his teaching on the work of the Spirit, Chenchiah writes, in his somewhat terse and elliptical style :

> The Holy Spirit is the new cosmic energy ; the Kingdom of God the new order ; the children of God the new type that Christ has inaugurated. The Gospel is that God in Jesus has made a new creation... The children of God are the next step in evolution and the Kingdom of God the next stage in cosmos.[2]

When he speaks of the Spirit as 'the new cosmic energy' Chenchiah uses the word *mahāśakti*, which means literally 'great power'. In Hinduism this word *śakti* is often personified as a goddess of power, though it is also the word for power in ordinary usage. We have seen how Brahmabandhab used it in connection with *māyā* to indicate creative energy.[3] By using the words *śakti* and *mahaśakti* Chenchiah is indicating his belief in both the personality and the cosmic energy of the Holy Spirit, and he feels that India, with its traditional understanding of the meaning of *śakti* as personalised divine energy, is in a good position for developing and deepening the meaning of the Christian life in terms of the *yoga* of the Spirit :

> The 'Holy Spirit'—the doctrine and personality—if my instincts are sound, will play a decisive role in Indian theology. They may receive a new interpretation and become the corner-stone of Indian Christian theology.[4]

Chenchiah's conception of the new creation and the *yoga* of the Spirit is orientated towards the future. Christ *is* already the new creation, and those who are united with him already share in the life of the Kingdom. But the time is coming when, through the power of the Spirit, not only they but the whole cosmos will be incorporated into Christ. Christ has come not merely for the individual nor even for society, but for the whole creation :

> We have exhausted in a way the meaning of Christ to the individual. But we have to discover the purpose and achievement of our Lord in the redemption of the social order or in his relation to the cosmic evolution... Today we have to realize Jesus as the

[1] *The Guardian*, 6-3-47.
[2] *Rethinking*, p. 57.
[3] v. supra p. 76.
[4] *Rethinking*. p. 161.

head of a new world order ; or as the creative expression of God's higher purposes with regard to man.[1]

There is an interesting similarity here between Chenchiah's thought and that of Teilhard de Chardin. Both think in biological terms and both are influenced by Bergson's creative evolution. Chenchiah would probably have given wholehearted approval to de Chardin's conceptions of 'Christification' and the 'Omega-point' at which mankind and the cosmos become conformed to the image of Christ. His interpretation is never purely biological, but is related in a dynamic way to the work of the Spirit. The Christian life for him cannot be the mere passive enjoyment of the immanent presence of God. He consciously rejects *bhakti mārga* as a means of God-realisation, perhaps with Appasamy in mind.[2] For him *bhakti mārga* is a way of retreat while the true way forward is a dynamic one, the way of cosmic redemption, the way of the Kingdom of God. 'The Church', he remarks scathingly, 'has left the Kingdom out of account and has carved out a *bhakti mārga* out of the Christian message.' For him the Christian life to be meaningful must include an active search for the source of God's power, and a conscious submission to and use of that power. And that power is to be found only in and through the Holy Spirit. Hinduism often speaks of the religious life as the flowing of a river into the sea, the sea of unity with God, where all distinctions are obliterated. Chenchiah firmly and strikingly rejects this picture, and then reverses it :

> Eternal life is not a flow back of the river into the sea, but of the sea into the river. It is not the release of the bounded spirit into the expanse of the uncreate absolute. It is the clothing of the absolute in creation.[4]

Eternal life, the life of the Kingdom, comes only when our life is invaded by the mighty power of the Spirit, and it is our task to make sure that we stand at the right place, the place where the power of the Spirit will reach us. Turning from the ideal of the forest hermitage to that of a modern hydro-electric power-house situated where there is a great waterfall he writes :

[1] *ibid.*
[2] He wrote a rather critical review of Appasamy's *Gospel and India's Heritage* in *The Guardian*, 24-7-43.
[3] *Asramas*, p. 283.
[4] *ibid.*, p. 313.

> After Christ we do not abide in the woods of God-realisation: we search for the waterfalls of God, that would release the new energy for the transformation of the world.[1]

For this transformation we do not have to wait till the end, till the coming of the Omega-point, for eschatology is realised and the Kingdom can and does begin now, when any man is in Christ.

Old Testament or Hindu Śāstras?

People who know nothing else about Chenchiah know that he questioned the value for India of the Old Testament. And indeed his views can with some truth be classified as Marcionite for he himself, while criticising the Old Testament conception of God, cites Marcion with approval. Briefly, his view is that the Old Testament is far inferior to the New and in the last resort is scarcely necessary for an understanding of the Christian faith, and definitely unnecessary for salvation. He pays tribute to the ethical teaching of the Old Testament, especially the prophets and some of the psalms, but his final verdict is negative:

> What is there in the teachings and acts of Jesus which a Roman or Greek could not understand? Why should it be necessary to understand the Old Testament to grasp the Sermon on the Mount? ... Why should a Hindu understand the complicated Pauline theology to follow Jesus?[2]

The Old Testament, he suggests, does not in the least help our understanding of the incarnation which can be grasped only through Greek or Hindu thought-forms, since it is a conception wholly alien to Jewish thought, as it is to Islam. He believes that the decision of the Council of Jerusalem against circumcision for Gentile converts implies that Paul decided that the whole Old Testament was unnecessary for Christians who came from a non-Jewish background.

This leads Chenchiah to go on to ask why the Hindu *śāstras* should not be regarded as God's chosen *praeparatio evangelii* for the people of India. He argues that the prophetical references to Jesus given by Matthew and others were selected after the event and claims that similar prophecies of the coming of Christ could be found in the Hindu scriptures:

> I can pick up material for an Old Testament in Hinduism making selections in the light of what Jesus said and did. That was exactly what early Christians did and later Hindu converts ought to do.[3]

[1] *ibid.*
[2] *The Guardian*, 20-2-47.
[3] *ibid.*

It is true that many arresting 'Christian' prophecies have been noted in various forms of Hindu *bhakti* literature, for example among the *Lingāyats* of Mysore and the followers of the *Nakalanka Avatāra* (Spotless Incarnation) in Gujarat,[1] and to some extent Appasamy's anthology *Temple Bells* and other similar books represent a step in the direction here indicated. Yet on the whole Indian theologians have refused to follow Chenchiah's lead here; and it must be admitted that his Biblical scholarship and critical sense were not comparable to his flashes of theological insight. He was a layman who, though deeply versed in the Bible, seems to have been attracted much more towards theological than exegetical work. We can accept the fact that much Hindu literature has a function as *praeparatio*; but India has no more claim to dispense with the Old Testament than has the West.

Why the Church?

Like many Indian Christian theologians, Chenchiah's attitude to the organised Church is very negative. Coming into the Church from a Hindu background he found it oppressively alien and western, introspective and quarrelsome, more interested in administration than in the Christian life.[2] It cannot be denied that there is much in the life of the Indian Church—as of any Church—to justify such criticism. Church administration, the hierarchy, property, ritual, fixed dogmas and doctrines all these were features which he felt should be eliminated in order that men might be able to secure that direct contact with the living Christ which for him was the basis of the faith.

Chenchiah felt that the institutional Church was trying to usurp the place of the Kingdom of God, that Spirit-filled fellowship of 'new creatures' which he believed to be more in accord with the will of Christ than the forms of the visible Church with which he was familiar. He expresses himself very forcibly

> Christianity took the wrong gradient when it left the Kingdom of God for the Church ... Christianity is a failure because we made a new religion of it instead of a new creation ...[3] The

[1] See N. C. Sargant, *The Lingayats* (1963), pp. 22 ff; R. H. S. Boyd, 'An Outline History of Gujarati Theological Literature', in *Indian Journal of Theology* (1963), p. 94. Compare the 'Vedic theology' of K. M. Banerji (v. supra p. 57).

[2] Cf. J. W. Grant, *God's People in India* (1960) for a severely critical portrait of the Indian Church.

[3] Quoted by D. A. Thangasamy in *S. I. Churchman*, Sept. 1960.

Church arrested the Kingdom when Peter added 3000 unto them—a fatal day for the Kingdom and a glorious day for the Church.[1]

This clearly demonstrates his almost totally negative attitude to the organised Church, which he felt to be a hindrance rather than a help to the work of the Spirit. He concluded that it was essential to find new and vital forms of Christian community and turned to the ancient Hindu idea of the *āshram* a small community of faithful people living a life of the greatest simplicity, usually as disciples of a *guru*. This ideal had for centuries ceased to function in Hinduism, but had been successfully revived as a training ground for the national struggle by the Tagores and Gandhi. A number of Christian *āshrams* had been started, and towards these Chenchiah was greatly attracted.[2] The book *Asramas Past and Present* was published in 1941 by Chenchiah and his friends in order to present this living alternative to the institutionalised life of the Church. Like Bonhöffer he was attracted towards a 'religionless' Christianity, and for him religionless Christianity had to be 'Churchless' also. The idea of the Church, he felt, totally fails to appeal to Hindus and so the Church is one of the greatest hindrances to evangelism in India. Christianity ought to give up its large-scale efforts and try instead to meet the spiritual needs of individuals, as Hinduism does, and as Jesus did when he brought in not an organisation but the Kingdom of God.[3] The setting up of the organised Church has been a mistake, he thinks, right from the beginning, as it has largely rendered ineffective the more dynamic idea of the Kingdom of God, and has alienated the Spirit. In a typical sentence he writes:

> When the Holy Spirit became a distant reality and then a dogma, when Jesus went to heaven and did not return, we thought of a Church and built one.[4]

It is clear that Chenchiah regards the Church purely as a historic, ***human*** institution, which is not to be equated with the Body of Christ. At best it is a useful human institution for the

[1] *The Guardian*, 8-2-51.

[2] The first of these was, the Christukula Ashram at Tirupattur, started in 1921 by Dr. S. Jesudason and Dr. E. Forrester-Paton. See *The Christukula Ashram* (1940).

[3] One who has for many years worked in this way is Ācārya R.C. Dās of Benares. See 'My Spiritual Pilgrimage' in *NCC Review*, March 1949, and *Convictions of an Indian Disciple*, CISRS (1966).

[4] *Rethinking*, p. 96.

three-fold purpose of worship, fellowship and propaganda,[1] but it fails at the point where its help is most needed, in assisting the individual to live the life of the Spirit, the life of prayer and meditation. It is then to the Christian *āshram* that we should turn for instruction in the techniques (*sādhana*) of the spiritual life.

Chenchiah's attitude to the Church extends to the sacraments, and he expresses doubt as to whether Jesus in fact instituted any sacraments at all. The thought of having to undergo baptism has kept many a Hindu from open confession of his sincere faith in Christ, and Chenchiah points out how Hindus are often attracted towards Christian *āshrams* partly at least because sacramental observances are not insisted on. What he envisages for India is a 'religionless' Christianity without ritual sacraments:

> There will be no baptisms, no confessions of faith, no credal profession . . . [The Hindu] will slowly and in different degrees come under the influence of the Spirit of Christ, without change of labels or nomenclature . . . The change will be in the realm of spirit—not in the region of *nāma* and *rupa*.[2]

One is reminded here of the attitude of an interesting contemporary of Chenchiah, Manilāl C. Pārekh, a Gujarati Jain who came to baptism in 1918 by way of a spiritual pilgrimage through the Brāhma Samāj. For most of his life he remained apart from the organised Church, feeling that to be a true disciple of Christ meant to be more of a Hindu and not less.[3] He held that Church Christians regard baptism too much as a *social* rite, the act of joining a different community. It is necessary, indeed, because Christ has commanded it, but emphasis should be laid on its spiritual rather than social implications—such as the break with caste—and the 'disciples' (he rejected the word 'convert') should remain as 'Hindu Christians' in their own community, as Pārekh himself did for fifty years. Chenchiah too, writing in 1938, sees baptism as simply part of a *cultus*, parallel to certain ritual acts of Hinduism of a religio-social significance yet seemingly unrelated to real spiritual life.

In a similar way the Lord's Supper seems to him to be unnecessary, and in fact to constitute a barrier to the believer's direct relationship with Christ. The Church appears to be

[1] *ibid.*, p. 95.
[2] *Rethinking*, p. 190. *nāma*=name; *rupa*=form.
[3] Manilal C. Parekh, 'An Autobiographical Sketch' in *Zeitschrift für Religion—und Geistesgeschichte* XI/2 (1959), pp. 157ff. Pārekh died in June 1967.

'mediating' Christ through the Word and sacraments instead of allowing the Christian free access to the 'raw fact', the 'original stimulus' of Christ:

> Why do churches and books intervene and bring Him to us like water from a distant fountainhead? . . . If there could be direct contact with Jesus, why should we seek it through bread and wine? If God speaks to us today, why hear his words through a book written about twenty centuries ago?[1]

Along with the Church and its sacraments Chenchiah attacks its creeds and confessions. For formulated doctrine and for systematic theology in general he had no use, and one of his major series of articles in the Madras *Guardian* is devoted to an onslaught on the view of Church doctrine set forth by Dr. Marcus Ward in his book *Our Theological Task* (1946). This book, which incorporates and comments on the findings of a theological teachers' conference held at Poona in 1942, draws a distinction between 'dogma', the irreducible minimum of Christian belief contained in the Bible and formulated in the creeds, and 'doctrine', the Church's explication of this dogmatic deposit. Ward's finding is that although the Church may interpret its doctrine in various ways, there must be no tampering with the basic 'dogma', which for this purpose includes the Nicene Creed and the Chalcedonian formula. Indian Christian theology for him must therefore be a matter of the interpretation and communication of this basic deposit. Indian terms and modes of thought may be used in the task of interpretation, but the precise meaning of the Church's accepted beliefs must be retained.

Chenchiah entirely rejects this point of view. For him formulated doctrinal statements, especially when couched, as they so often are, in the language of Greek philosophy, are simply barriers to prevent men from having direct access to Christ. Nicaea and Chalcedon are 'not in accordance with Indian or Asiatic genius' and they 'weave a temporary philosophy round the permanent facts of Christianity'[2]. In fact the whole process of formulating theological statements has served only to obscure the essential elements of the Christian faith:

> Every historic religion starts with a historic personality of outstanding significance or power . . . What happens? . . . The fact is interpreted, meaning assigned and its relations to the prevailing

[1] *The Guardian*, 13-2-47.
[2] *ibid.*, 27-2-47.

notions settled. In other words doctrines and dogmas, worship and ritual, mysteries and ceremonies, gather round till at last the bright nucleus gets enveloped by a huge globe of tradition and testimony.[1]

We return here to the starting point of Chenchiah's theology. Christian life must be based on direct experience of Christ. It must be demonstrated as the *yoga* of the Spirit, the life of the Kingdom of God, in living, Spirit-filled fellowship. As far as Chenchiah could see, the visible Church with its sacraments, doctrines and organised life, did not help the realisation of this ideal.

Christianity and Hinduism

Like Brahmabandhab, Chenchiah believes that the Christian faith must be open to receive new insights from Indian culture, and he urges his Christian friends to 'let the sluices of the great Indian culture be opened for the inundation of the Christian mind'.[2] Christians have nothing to fear from such a use of Hinduism, for the *new* creation comes in Christ alone, even though Hinduism in some of its forms may represent a very advanced stage of the old. Christianity, in fact, is not related to Hinduism as one religion to another, but as new creation to old. In words which foreshadow what Raymond Panikkar was to say many years later he writes :

> In Jesus God created the new man : in Hinduism God is sought for perfecting the old man . . . Hinduism makes the perfect man, Christianity the new Man. Hinduism harnesses the *Mahasakti* of nature and man, Christianity brings into evolution the new *Sakti* of the Holy Spirit. Jesus is the first fruits of a new creation, Hinduism the final fruits of the old creation.[3]

Two practical conclusions emerge from this view of the relationship of Hinduism and Christianity. The first is that our understanding of the Christian faith may gain new depth and richness from its contact with Hindu culture, just as it did in the West from contact with Greece, indeed far more so, since Indian religion and philosophy are far richer and more vital than were their Greek counterparts in the early centuries of the

[1] Quoted by D. A. Thangasamy, *S. I. Churchman*, June 1960.
[2] *ibid.*, Oct. 1960.
[3] *Rethinking*, pp. 181, 187.

Church's existence. In a memorable and characteristic sentence Chenchiah writes:

> The negative plate of Jesus, developed in a solution of Hinduism, brings out hitherto unknown features of the portrait and these may prove exactly the 'Gospel' for our time.[1]

The second conclusion is more controversial and relates to Chenchiah's conception of evangelism and the spread of Christianity. He has little or no use for evangelistic preaching and puts forward what would today be called a 'Christian presence' point of view, saying that 'to live Christ is to preach Christ'.[2] He envisages the spread of the Gospel as taking place gradually through the permeation of Hindu culture by the Spirit of Christ and, like Brahmabandhab, believes that Christianity can spread from *within* Hinduism:

> A Christian movement within Hinduism without its umbilical cord being cut is a decided advantage to the Hindu and the Christian . . . There are greater possibilities for the spread of the Gospel if it spreads as life, opinion and inner change than as social groups or spiritual groups outside Hinduism.[3]

It is perhaps still too early to say whether Christianity does in fact spread in this way—though attempts at such an approach are being made—or whether the result of such a process might not be the assimilation of Christianity into Hinduism, as in India Buddhism has been assimilated.

[1] *Rethinking*, p. 162.
[2] *Asramas*, p. 225.
[3] *ibid.*, p. 187.

CHAPTER IX

A CHRISTOLOGY OF THE SPIRIT: V. CHAKKARAI

V. Chakkarai (1880-1958)

Of the well-known trio of South Indian theologians, Appasamy, Chenchiah and Chakkarai, the one whose personal experience of Hinduism was deepest and most prolonged was Chakkarai, who became a Christian in his twenties as the result of much thought and deep study of the Christian faith.

Vengal Chakkarai Chetty was born in 1880 in a well-to-do Madras family of the Chetty caste, the highest non-Brāhman caste in Tamilnad.[1] His father, who died while Chakkarai was still very young, was a follower of the Vedānta while his mother, who greatly influenced him, was a devotee of the Vaiṣṇava *bhakti* tradition.

Chakkarai received his early education in a Scottish Mission School and then went on to the Madras Christian College, where he was deeply influenced by William Miller to whom he, like his brother-in-law Chenchiah, always refers with the greatest respect and affection. Miller understood and appreciated the genuine depths and insights of Hinduism and was able to show his student friends how these might be transformed and perfected in the light of Christ. Through his friendship with Miller and his own study of the Bible he gradually came to a personal experience of Christ, an experience which became the centre and turning point of his whole life. Writing many years later he tells how it was Jesus' cry of dereliction on the Cross which affected him most, leading him to think of Jesus as a mysterious being and ultimately to accept him as his Lord and Redeemer.[2] He made public profession of his faith and was baptised in 1903.

Chakkarai qualified as a lawyer, but later worked for a time with the Danish Missionary Society in Madras, helping with evangelistic work among educated Hindus. As early as 1906 he threw himself into the national struggle, and this remained a

[1] For studies of Chakkarai, see: *A Christian Theological Approach to Hinduism*; C. G. Oosthuizen, *op. cit.*, H. Wagner, *op. cit.*; P. T. Thomas, *The Theology of Chakkarai* (CISRS, 1968). Wagner gives a full bibliography of Chakkarai's writings.

[2] *The Guardian*, 20-4-44.

passionate interest.[1] In 1917 he joined the Home Rule movement and in 1920 Gandhi's Non-Co-operation campaign. In later years he took an active part in the labour movement and became one of the best-known Christian public figures of his time, being elected Mayor of Madras in 1941 and in 1951 serving as chairman of the All India Trade Union Congress. He died in 1958.

Along with Chenchiah he was one of the founders of the Madras group known as the *Christo Samāj*, which worked for the Indianisation of the Church. In 1917 he acquired the ownership of a weekly paper *The Christian Patriot* which he edited and published until its closure in 1926. It was in this paper that he first published those stimulating theological articles which were later expanded and printed in book form as *Jesus the Avatār* (1927) and *The Cross and Indian Thought* (1932). Chakkarai was a prolific writer and contributed frequently to the Madras *Guardian*. He was also one of the chief contributors to *Rethinking Christianity in India*.

Unlike Brahmabandhab, Appasamy and Chenchiah, each of whom attempts to interpret the Christian Gospel in terms of a particular stream of Indian thought—Śankara, Rāmānuja or Aurobindo—Chakkarai has no particular philosophical affiliation. There are, however, certain clearly identifiable features in his approach which give a characteristic colouring to his theology, not the least noticeable being his sheer exuberance, his love of words—both English and Sanskrit—and his addiction to purple patches ! As one reads his work one sometimes has the feeling that it is difficult to see the wood for the trees. We shall attempt, however, to select a few of the issues to which he devotes especial attention, beginning with his Christology, where we shall find him particularly concerned with the *avatāra* conception and with the problem of the relation of the Jesus of history to the Christ of faith. We shall then look at his characteristic treatment of the doctrine of the Holy Spirit, whom he virtually identifies with Christ. Finally we shall see how his understanding of Christian *bhakti* is much more deeply influenced by the death and suffering of Christ than is that of Appasamy, and how of all Indian theologians he makes the most extensive use of Hindu terminology.

[1] His political activities led to a break with the authorities of the DMS but he later joined the small Indo-Danish Mission whose attitude towards nationalism and indigenization was more Gandhian.

Jesus the Avatāra

For Chakkarai as for Chenchiah Christology is the starting point of theology. 'Do we begin our Christian theology with Jesus or God?' he asks,[1] and the answer is that we must take our line of departure from Christ. This leads him to formulate what he calls a 'doctrine of the Christhood of God',[2] for he is convinced that real and valid knowledge of God must begin with personal experience of Christ:

> Our knowledge of God must be founded on the experience and consciousness of Jesus and not on *a priori* speculations like those of Anselm in Europe and Śankara in India . . . If there is a God or if there are elements in Him unrelated to Jesus and existing outside Him, they are simply non-existent to us.[3]

Religion cannot begin with *nirguṇa* or *avyakta* (unmanifested) *Brahman*. The Christian *bhakta* must begin with the *vyakta Iśvara*, God made manifest in Christ, in whom the *Deus absconditus* becomes the *Deus revelatus*. In a characteristic paragraph he expounds this idea of 'the Christhood of God':

> We see God with the face of Jesus. To the ordinary and unsophisticated consciousness there is a black veil God would seem to have cast over His face. But now that Jesus has removed the veil, we behold the face of God Himself . . . We see the face crowned with thorns and the blood trickling down. We see the face looking with tragic grandeur as He sits at the table giving the bread and wine . . . In one word, what is vivid and real to us is the face of Jesus with a shadowy background of unknown and infinite potencies into which we strive to penetrate but catch only stray gleams. Whom we call God stands behind Jesus, and it is Jesus who gives, as it were, colour, light and *rupa* to God. Out of the infinite nebulousness emerges the face of Jesus. God is the unmanifested and Jesus is the manifested. God is the *sat*, or being, and Jesus is the *cit* or intelligence, wisdom and love which indicates the nature of the being of God.[4]

It is only when the unmanifested becomes manifest, when *avyakta* becomes *vyakta*, when *Brahman* becomes *Iśvara*, when God is revealed in the face of Christ, that men can know him as he is. And such knowledge of God is the result, not of *jñāna*

[1] V. Chakkarai, *Jesus the Avatār* (1927), pp. 210 f. (Cited as *Avatār*).
[2] *ibid.*, p. 210
[3] *ibid.*
[4] *ibid.*, pp. 172-3.

mārga, but of the way of *bhakti*, of love for God become man in Christ. 'How do we get our knowledge of God?' Chakkarai asks, and replies that it is only through the experience of Christ that we can attain *paravidyā*, the supreme knowledge of God, for Christ is not just the scaffolding of the building but the corner-stone whom none can reject with impunity.[1]

Chakkarai links the idea of God's self-revelation in Christ with the concept of *immanence* which is so popular in Hindu *bhakti*, but gives to the word a new interpretation of his own, which is very different from that of Hinduism or even from Appasamy's description of the *antaryāmin*. *Bhakti* may indeed describe God as immanent 'in the lotus of the human heart as *antaryāmin*, or as the singing bird within the nest, or as the light within the eye',[2] but for Chakkarai God's immanence takes a special form when Christ becomes incarnate. It is a 'human immanence', when God in Christ comes into the time-order for the redemption of men, the immanence of Immanuel, God with us.

The study of God, then, begins with the study of Christ, and knowledge of Christ must have its start in personal experience, in direct contact with this humanly immanent God, the indwelling Christ. Christ is alive today; it is possible for men to know and love him; and such an encounter is no mere imagination or second-hand speculation:

> Not a mere radiating influence, not the repercussion of His teaching on later *bhaktas* but His very Personality is claimed to be the *antaryāmin*, the inspirer and the *guru* seated in the lotus of the *Bhakta's* heart.[3]

To know this very personality we must know as our living Lord that Jesus of history who lived in Nazareth in great humility, who rose from the dead and ascended to the right hand of the Father. And again it is that risen, transcendent Christ who is immanent in the hearts of those who know and love him. In this one unique personality historicity, transcendence and immanence are all united and all necessary, and we can understand this mystery of Christology only if we have a direct personal experience of him. How immanence, historicity and transcendence can be combined in one Person is interestingly described:

[1] *ibid.*, p. 165.
[2] *ibid.*, p. 196.
[3] V. Chakkarai, *The Cross and Indian Thought* (1932), p. 143. (Cited as *Cross*).

> The immanence of our Lord Jesus Christ, if it has any meaning for men, is the postulation of the immanence of his *ātman* in human lives. That is, as Christian *anubhava* and *sruti* have agreed in emphasising, the Lord Jesus, the Galilean, is still with us ; and His once historical personality, His life and death, have in some unaccountable way established this immanence. Today we speak of Him as the exalted Jesus, but He who ascended is the same as He who once descended. Our contention is that the *avarohana*[1] of Jesus and his *ārohana* are the rhythmic processes of the one indivisible Divine act. The humiliation and exaltation, the death and resurrection, the historical Jesus and the spiritual Jesus constitute the two sides of the one reality.[2]

Writing this in 1926 Chakkarai is well aware of the 'Jesus of History' school, and accepts the importance of the 'quest of the historical Jesus', while remaining convinced that it fails to take us near the heart of the truth. He criticises T. R. Glover's interest in the minutiae of the life of Christ, and says that 'if Dr. Glover had lived in the East with any *guru*, he would have seen more of Jesus than the rustling of his robes and the make of the communion cup.'[3] Yet if we are to understand who this Jesus is who comes to dwell in us as the Christ of faith we must be familiar with the Man of Galilee, for in him alone we see what true humanity is like. He is the True Man (*sat puruṣa*), 'the original pattern in the mind of God Himself after whom all men have been fashioned'.[4] He is not a mere man but the essence of humanity, the *mulapuruṣa* or original man, who is to become 'the spiritual background of all humanity'.[5] Jesus is the place, the person, where alone we can see man as God intends him to be :

> In the picture of Jesus the express image of the Invisible has come out . . . It is a picture in which the Lord of the universe has found His own soul. The Painter and the picture are one.[6]

In his critique of the 'Jesus of History' school Chakkarai emphasises the importance of Jesus' miracles and his sinlessness, not as 'proofs' of his divinity but rather because they show us what sort of person he is. We must not think of Jesus as 'metaphysically' one with the Father in any monist sense, but

[1] *avarohana*=descent ; *ārohana*=ascent.
[2] *Avatār*, p. 196.
[3] *ibid.*, p. 26.
[4] *ibid.*, p. 125.
[5] *ibid.*, p. 154.
[6] *ibid.*, p. 208.

on the other hand we should not look on him as a 'mere' man, for he is the True Man who lives in complete communion with the Father. Chakkarai interprets Jesus' sinlessness in terms of this completely true humanity. Whereas we are dominated by *māyā*, which taints our personality, he is the *sat puruṣa* in whom *māyā* is cast off and transcended so that his full glory and light shine on the world.[1] Satan could not win the victory over him because there was no point at which he could appeal to any selfishness in Jesus:

> The temptations of Jesus could not find any personal and individual points of contact within His Spirit . . . He had no personal life apart from the Kingdom of God in His own heart.[2]

Here Chakkarai comes close to the kind of *kenosis* theory first outlined by Keshab Chandra Sen. Christ's sinlessness consists in complete self-abnegation culminating in his death on the Cross. It is not the sinlessness of a metaphysical divinity but a dynamic sinlessness which is the free choice of his own personality and which works itself out in suffering love:

> His sinlessness is the Cross, and there no self can exist, but is burnt up in the *homa* or sacrificial fire that burns in the deepest heart of God and necessarily of humanity, which is Jesus in history.[3]

Jesus of Nazareth, then, is the True Man who from the beginning has 'perfect unity of mind and heart with God', a unity seen not only in his deep communion with God through the *yoga* of prayer, and in his self-abnegation even to the death of the Cross, but also in his miracles of love and in his sinlessness.

It is through knowledge of this Jesus that we come to know God. And what Chakkarai is here striving to impress on us is that even today, two thousand years after the incarnation, the only satisfying and effective knowledge of God that we can have is the knowledge we gain through the Jesus who was born in Bethlehem and who is *still* 'Jesus the *avatāra*'. The incarnation did not end with the crucifixion but is permanent and is still today advancing to ever new depths of meaning:

> Jesus of history is to us the *Avatār* of God; but the Incarnation, whose real significance we are trying to grasp from the standpoint of Indian thought, was not a static product which admitted of no

[1] *ibid.*, p. 74.
[2] *ibid.*, p. 88.
[3] *ibid.*, p. 89.

growth . . . The Incarnation advanced from stage to stage, from the historical to the spiritual, from the external to the internal, from time to eternity.[1]

This represents an important point in Chakkarai's theology, perhaps the central theme of his book *Jesus the Avatār*; unlike the *avatāras* of Hinduism, the incarnation of Jesus is not temporary and static but is instead permanent and dynamic. The idea requires some elucidation.

The classical Hindu theory of *avatāra*, as we have seen, implies that the *avatāras* come into human history from time to time as need arises, and then disappear, the divine part of their nature being re-absorbed into God. The Christian incarnation, however, occurs once and for all. The Logos, having become man in Christ, remains as God-Man for ever and is not simply absorbed back into the Godhead with the discarding of his human nature. In addition, the incarnation is *dynamic*, and is still at work today through the power of the Spirit. The *avatāra* did not cease with the Cross nor even with the ascension, but God in Christ still continues to be man, living and working in the lives of believers :

> Their Lord never ceased to the disciples to be the man Christ Jesus. What is called the humanity of Jesus was not sublimated into a kind of mystic divinity, and lost in the effulgence thereof. On the contrary, it was because of the consciousness that the Lord whom they had companied with still remained essentially the man Christ Jesus, one who could be touched with the feeling of our infirmities, that He became the Mediator between God and man . . . His humanity was essential, and remained as the abiding consciousness of the Christian Church.[2]

The incarnation or *avatāra* of Christ is thus seen to be no mere theophany but a permanent, mediating union of God and man in him. But besides being permanent it is also dynamic, working in the world today, and this dynamism of the incarnation is found in the fact that God, in Christ, submitted himself to the buffetings of human life and history. The meaning of the incarnation, then, is not to be seem in some metaphysical or substantial union of God and man, but rather in Christ's breaking into the uncertainties of history :

> What a revolution of the ordinary conception of the Incarnation is here ! It is the real operation of contingency and expectancy

[1] *ibid.*, p. 112.
[2] *ibid.*, pp. 138 f.

and uncertainty in the very heart of the Incarnate Lord. Dare we deny this? If we do, then we destroy for the sake of some kind of metaphysics the mystery and reality of the Incarnation. If we may say so, till Jesus appeared, God was in the world, and as the Logos, the Eternal Word, He was in the life of man . . . But in the Incarnation, instead of merely watching, sympathising with and helping man in his struggle, He plunged into the ocean and felt the waves and billows rolling over His head. In other words, not only man entered on a new phase of life but God, too, did so in the Incarnation. Thus . . . the metaphysics of God is not the key to the incarnation, as in Hindu thought, but the life of Jesus is the explanation of the working of the mind of God and his adaptation to the needs of men.[1]

In order to understand how this permanent, dynamic and 'advancing' *avatāra* is at work in the world today we must turn to Chakkarai's treatment of the doctrine of the Holy Spirit.

Christ and the Spirit

Chenchiah once said that the doctrine of the Holy Spirit would play a decisive role in Indian theology,[2] and when we think of the great Indian tradition of spirituality and of the way in which so much Hindu religion is concentrated on the relation of the *ātman* to the *paramātman*, the human spirit to the Supreme Spirit, it would seem that this is a quarter from which we might expect to receive new light. Of all Indian Christian theologians it is probably Chakkarai who has most to say to us here.

To put the matter in its simplest terms, Chakkarai sees the work of the Holy Spirit as a continuing part of the incarnation or *avatāra*, and in effect identifies the Spirit with the risen, living Christ at work in the world today. Jesus had promised the Comforter and had said, 'I will not leave you comfortless: I will come to you' (John 14 : 18)—and at Pentecost this promise was fulfilled. For us today, then, the starting point in our knowledge of Christ, and so of our knowledge of God whom he reveals, is the experience of the power of the Spirit. In India, with its long spiritual tradition, it is natural to begin here rather than in historical enquiry:

The orientation of Indian thought in respect of the Incarnation [is] set on the Holy Spirit and the significance of His indwelling in

[1] *ibid.*, pp. 218 f. Compare the language of the *bhakti* poets, v. supra, p. 113. In Gujarati the regular word for 'Saviour' is *Tāranāra* which means 'rescue from drowning' (lit. 'one who makes to float' from a root *tar* to swim or float). The image is a favourite one in *bhakti*.

[2] v. supra, p. 156.

human lives. The Holy Spirit is the starting point; not that the historical Jesus goes out in the Indian consciousness; He takes His place and functions in the perspective furnished by the Holy Spirit. In other words, while the historical is the primary element in the Western interpretation, the spiritual, is, or will be, the primary element in the Indian conception.[1]

Chakkarai does not intend to underrate the importance of history. He feels, however, that in attempting to understand the significance of the person of Christ and of the incarnation, we *must* begin with the experience of the living Christ. In the early Church that experience, through the power of the Holy Spirit, was vivid and real. Only when with the advance of time it became less real did the necessity arise to reduce the faith to a formulated creed, in which the stress on the historical outweighed that on first-hand experience of the living Christ. Then, in the Church of the Graeco-Roman world, says Chakkarai,

> The Holy Spirit became a distant and mystical something, and the historical Jesus emerged in a strange shape, dimmed by allegory and fantastic interpretation of the ordinary facts narrated in the Gospels.[2]

Today, and especially in India, this order should be reversed, and our consideration of the person of Christ should begin from our direct experience of him through the Spirit, for 'it is from the Holy Spirit our *antaryāmin*, the Indweller, that we start our enquiry concerning the nature of the person of Jesus.'[3]

This brings us face to face with the direct question of the relation between Jesus and the Spirit, and Chakkarai's answer is, quite simply, that 'the Holy Spirit is Jesus Christ at work in the human personality':[4]

> The Holy Spirit is Jesus Christ Himself, taking His abode within us... The starting point in the consciousness of the Christian disciple is that the Holy Spirit is Jesus Himself.[5]

Chakkarai is convinced that western theology has done much to obscure and confuse this truth, whereas Indian Christians, whose minds have not been led astray by western theories but who have

[1] *Avatār*, pp. 114 f.
[2] *ibid.*, p. 116.
[3] *ibid.*
[4] *ibid.*, p. 117.
[5] *ibid.*

had a personal experience of Christ and have submitted themselves to the New Testament, have generally felt that the Holy Spirit is in fact simply Christ at work within us as the *antaryāmin*. Indian theology, he is convinced, does not need to follow western in its precise definitions of the nature and functions of the Persons of the Trinity. After all, the New Testament speaks of the Spirit in many ways, as the Spirit of God, the Spirit of Jesus, or simply as 'Lord'.[1] We have followed Chakkarai's argument as he has said that we can come to know God only through experience of the living Christ, the permanent *avatāra* Jesus, and again as he affirmed that the living Christ can be known only through the Spirit, and that indeed the living Christ at work in our hearts *is* the Spirit. In a brief definition he formulates this understanding of the relations of the Persons in the Trinity:

> Jesus Christ is the Incarnation or *Avatār* of God; the Holy Spirit in human experience is the Incarnation of Jesus Christ.[2]

It is through this inner experience of the Spirit, of Christ-in-us, that we are led to understand the meaning of his person. Chakkarai's Christology is a Christology of the Spirit.

Ātman and Paramātman

Advaita Hinduism often speaks of *Brahman* as *paramātman* or Supreme Spirit, while the human spirit is the *ātman* or *jivātman*; and it is a fundamental Vedāntic belief that when the mists of *māyā* are rolled away, the *ātman* and the *paramātman* are seen to be one. For *advaita*, salvation means the soul's discovery that it is one with *Brahman*. In writing of the work of the Holy Spirit, Chakkarai uses a number of different terms, and we find a certain unwestern ambivalence as the same term may be used at different times for different Persons of the Trinity. Thus God, seen primarily in his spiritual aspect, is the *paramātman*, whom the ancient *rishis* hoped to find, after long searching, dwelling in their inward parts.[3] The Holy Spirit, in contrast, is given as a gift to all who ask, and so lives in them as *antarātman*, the Inner Spirit. And as we try to understand who Jesus is, we must start from our own experience, and that experience is in the first place of the *antarātman*, the *antaryāmin* or Indweller, who is none other than Christ at work within us.

[1] II Corinthians 3:17. Cp. *Avatār*, p. 120.
[2] *Avatār*, p. 121.
[3] *ibid.*, p. 114.

Thus God, as Spirit, constantly and in a variety of ways works on the human spirit, the *ātman*. But how, for the Christian, is the *ātman* to be related to the *paramātman*, for there can be no Vedāntic relation of identity?

The answer to this question is for Chakkarai closely linked with the events of the resurrection, ascension and Pentecost. Because of the resurrection and the presence of the risen Christ through the Spirit, our *ātman* can come into direct contact with the *ātman* of Christ, who 'energizes'[1] within it. The New Testament speaks of those whom God chooses as being conformed into the image of his Son, and we know that 'when he shall appear we shall be like him'.[2] This upward aspiration to be sons of God, says Chakkarai, is really the *jivātman* responding to the *parămātman*,[3] and in the process, he adds, with an adaptation of Paul's words, the *atman* within us bears witness to the *ātman* without.[4]

We can see here that Chakkarai, like Appasamy, refuses to make a 'metaphysical' identification between *ātman* and *paramātman*; rather it is in *bhakti*, in the life of faith-union with Christ, that our soul is united dynamically and spiritually with the Spirit who is Christ at work in us. There is no automatic, metaphysical identity between the *ātman* and the *paramātman*, between man and God. And yet, in Christ this great 'possibility' or *sambhava* is set before us:

> The *mahāvākya* '*tattvamasi*' is a tremendous assertion of possibility. In Christian *anubhava*, it is not a mere metaphysical postulate to start with or to end in. It is an achievement, a *sambhava*. This *advaita* has been wrought on the anvil of the life of Jesus.[5]

Just as Appasamy's Rāmānujan analogy of the world being the body of God has an eschatological possibility and significance, so the *mahāvākya* of *advaita* is given meaning in Christ. Union with God, with the *paramātman*, is not a metaphysical possibility; it is possible for us only in Christ, and only when we, with him, are beaten on the anvil of his suffering and death. The great ideal of the Vedānta becomes effective, though not in the *advaita* way, when through the Spirit we are united with Jesus, the eternal *avatāra*.

[1] *ibid.*, p. 145.
[2] I John 3 : 2.
[3] *Avatār*, p. 205.
[4] *ibid.*, p. 157. Cf. Romans 8 : 16.
[5] *ibid.*, pp. 220 f.

The Bhakti of the Cross

'When we are beaten on the anvil of his suffering and death'.— Some such words are necessary when we follow Chakkarai's description of Christian *bhakti*, for it is a *bhakti* which is firmly centred on the Cross of Christ, and draws its meaning and content from his death and resurrection. Chakkarai is very critical of mystics who try to avoid the particularity of the Cross :

> Certain mystics under the pressure of semi-Hellenistic ideas . . . have even been tempted, and they have fallen a prey to the temptation of substituting dazzling ideas for the rugged edges of the Cross. The circle of their intellectualism, indeed, has never squared with the figure of the Cross . . . In Christian experience no such magical illusion is possible—the habitation of the soul has its foundation in Jesus Christ and His Death.[1]

Christian mysticism, he holds, is significant only when it is firmly linked with the Cross. In language drawn from Shelley's *Adonais* he shows how communion with God is inseparable from the Cross :

> The aspiration towards absolute being, the unconditioned *nirguṇa Brahman*, trembles like the white light of the sun on the extremest edge, but is stained, even at the very centre, like time, by the many-coloured dome of the Cross.[2]

If we want to penetrate to the white light of communion with God the only way is through the many-coloured staining of the Cross. For the Cross marks the place where sinful man meets God ; it stands ' where the turbid flow of human life and the unresting stream of divine grace meet to be transformed by the personality of Jesus '.[3] There, ' under the shadow of the Cross, sin becomes darker and more sinister, and ever more sinful ',[4] but there is a mysterious power at work which removes sin and renews the sinner.

Chakkarai suggests various ways in which the Cross of Christ carries out the work of forgiveness and renewal. They are all connected with the release of *power*, that spiritual *śakti* which is given to those who come into contact with Christ through the Spirit. In some mysterious way the Cross ' opens a channel ' in the heart of man, by which the divine *śakti* flows in a mighty

[1] *Cross*, pp. 229 f. Chakkarai mentions Dean Inge in this connection.
[2] *ibid.*, p. 230. Cf. Shelley, *Adonais* lii.
[3] *ibid.*, p. 14.
[4] *ibid.*, p. 152.

stream into the history of humanity.[1] It is not altogether clear *how* this 'channel' is opened in the heart of man. Christ deals with sin as a disease, for he is the Great Physician, the *parama vaidya* of the soul,[2] and 'from the Cross has descended on men's hearts and minds the healing energy of moral and spiritual restoration'.[3] In a way that we cannot understand, by 'some mystic alchemy', Christ's sufferings are transformed into the radiant *śakti* of his redemptive sacrifice, and so become the active energy or *kriya śakti* of a new world-order.[4]

Chakkarai will not accept the theory of vicarious suffering, and yet is convinced that something more has happened on the Cross than mere moral influence; something definite, effective and 'causal' has taken place:

> We must stress to the full the factual, qualitative, and causal importance of the Cross as something without which man's redemption could not have reached its fruition and assurance.[5]

The Cross is 'causal' in relation to the forgiveness of sin and the bestowing of new life; yet Chakkarai is unwilling to commit himself firmly to any 'How?' beyond the 'mystic alchemy' of suffering turning into active energy. He does, however, glance at some of the other classical theories of the atonement, and finds helpful points in them, while at the same time relating them in an interesting way to Indian experience.

For example, he sees Christ as the Victor who on the battlefield of the Cross fought against the enemies of the world. In the great event of the Cross we can see, he writes,

> . . . the marks of an experience transcending far those of a martyr and sin-bearer . . . Just as the lotus shuts its petals when the sun sets, so the darkness of Death closed upon Him and His mighty *ātman* shrank into the dark and terrible place to struggle alone with its forces, the 'powers and principalities'.[6]

Again, he speaks of Christ's death as a sacrifice, *yajña*, an idea which has parallels in Indian religion, especially the early religion of the Vedas. Here again the dominant idea is that of the release of power, and he describes how Christ, at the Last Supper, sees

1 *Avatār*, p. 71.
2 *Cross*, p. 25.
3 *ibid.*, p. 155.
4 *ibid.*, p. 87.
5 *ibid.*, p. 181.
6 *ibid.*, p. 117. Chakkarai often uses the symbolism of the lotus which in Indian mythology is a sign of divinity.

his death as a sacrifice, the *śakti* of which was to emerge from eating his body and drinking his blood through the symbolism of bread and wine.[1]

Having studied Chakkarai's understanding of the meaning of the Cross of Christ we must now turn to his treatment of the human response to that act. How do men appropriate the salvation which is offered in the death of Christ? Chakkarai replies by giving a most interesting exposition, in terms drawn from Indian *bhakti*, of what is in effect the Pauline doctrine of justification by faith.

Hinduism, like Judaism, has always been a religion of law and works. The Hindu conception of *dharma*, one's duty to God and man, especially as it is portrayed in the legalistic system of the *Purva Mimāṃsa*, is not unlike Jewish legalism. Salvation, according to this *karma mārga*, or way of works, can come only through rigid observance of the laws of *dharma*. And then above this *karma mārga* there is in Hinduism another, higher kind of legalism, the *jñāna mārga* or way of knowledge. Even though its fulfilment lies in cessation from works rather than in their performance, in the overcoming of *karma* rather than in following it out, yet here too man is bound by a rigorous legalism. Where then is freedom to be found? We are held fast in the bonds of *karma-saṃsāra* and the ways of *karma mārga* and *jñāna mārga* both seem to fail to provide *mokṣa*.

This is precisely the problem which is classically faced in the *Bhagavadgita*, and to the *Gita* Chakkarai turns, seeing a clue with Christian implications in the way in which it subordinates *karma mārga* and *jñāna mārga* and subsumes and transforms them into an overriding *bhakti mārga*. Neither works nor knowledge can bridge the gulf which separates us from fellowship with God, yet over this gulf the *Gita*, in a Hindu preparation for Christ, 'threw the bridge of *bhakti*, or, intense and loving attachment to God, as revealed in the incarnation'.[2]

The type of Christian *bhakti* which Chakkarai has in mind comes very close in meaning to the Pauline conception of faith.[3] It is 'intense and loving attachment' to the crucified and risen Christ; and it is no easy method of communion for it has to maintain itself in this world of terrible contradictions 'by bringing together all the energies of the whole personality of man to bear on the Cross'.[4] In *bhakti* so understood Chakkarai finds the

[1] *ibid.*, p. 118.
[2] *ibid.*, p. 216.
[3] *ibid.*, p. 217.
[4] *ibid.*, p. 218.

fulfilment and transcendence of both the Jewish and Greek traditions—a fulfilment which depends on a Christianity interpreted through Hindu categories! The Jews, he feels, followed *karma mārga*, the Law. The Greeks sought wisdom, *jñāna mārga*. Both ways are changed, transformed and fulfilled in the *bhakti mārga* of Christianity, whose centre is the Cross.

We earlier quoted Chakkarai's phrase about union with God being 'wrought on the anvil of the life of Jesus', and linked this with the suffering and death of Christ. Chakkarai develops this thought in connection with the *Gita's* teaching on *niṣkāmya karma*, action done with no thought of personal gain. He sees Christ's death as the supreme *niṣkāmya karma*, the supreme act of self-abnegation. And the *bhakta* who is devoted to Christ, who is justified by his faith in him, must be conformed to Christ's pattern, and wrought on the same anvil:

> The Cross is the true *niṣkāmya karma*, the reconciliation of law and love, *karma* and *jñāna* . . . Being lifted as the Lord of the Cross was, the *bhakta* looks at the world with His eyes, and feels with His heart, and thinks with His mind.[1]

It will be seen that once more Chakkarai does not attempt a description of the 'How?' of justification. He prefers to leave it simply as *bhakti mārga* devoted to the crucified Christ, who lovingly meets with the gift of his transforming power those who share in the fellowship of his sufferings.

Jesus of History and Christ of Experience

Now that we have seen something of Chakkarai's interpretation of the *avatāra* conception, of his understanding of the Holy Spirit as Christ at work in the world, and of the way he makes the Cross central in Christian *bhakti*, we must go back to examine one special aspect of Christology in which we find all these conceptions drawn together in a profound and original way. This problem, to which Chakkarai frequently returns, is that of the relationship between the historical Jesus of Nazareth and the risen Christ whom the apostles proclaimed and whom we know in our own experience. What, he asks, is the 'nexus' between the two?[2] He himself, as we have seen, relies heavily on experience, and is very conscious of the believer's union and communion with the living Christ; yet there must be some valid

[1] *ibid.*, p. 220.
[2] *The Guardian*, 30-3-44.

connection with the Jesus of the synoptic Gospels or Christianity loses all touch with reality. He criticises western theology both for the 'Jesus of History' tendency which exalts the particular and historical but loses the eternal, and also for what he, writing in 1944, took to be the Barthian tendency of neglecting the historical as being evanescent and ephemeral, 'the body of Jesus to be laid aside as the outer man in order that the inner may be revealed'.[1]

The solution cannot lie, he feels, in overstressing either the historical or the spiritual and experiential. Rather there must be some 'nexus', some point at which the historical Jesus passes over into the Christ of experience. There is a vital issue at stake here. If we simply worship the historical Jesus, then he is just a man and we can have no living communion with him today. On the other hand if we say that Jesus has now returned to the *status quo ante* of the Second Person of the Trinity we deny the whole point of the incarnation, and Christianity disappears. For Christians do not worship a man but God, and yet the God we worship is the God who in Christ is incarnate. How does the incarnate, historic Christ, Jesus the *avatāra*, pass over into the one we know in our worship and communion? The answer, says Chakkarai, is to be found in *kenosis*, in the act by which Jesus achieved complete self-abnegation, completely overcame his *ego*, so that he found perfect union with God who himself is completely without selfishness, without even 'personality' in the western sense.

Here we must turn for a moment to look at Chakkarai's rejection of the idea of 'personality' in God. Western theologians, he thinks—and he mentions C. C. J. Webb—are far too preoccupied with the conception of personality in both man and God. The whole idea of personality in the western sense is a development from the Latin term *persona* and is found neither in the Bible, nor in Greek theology—where the meaning of *hypostatis* is quite different—nor in Hindu thought, where *Brahman* is essentially impersonal. Chakkarai mentions with approval the well-known Hindu thought that the human *ego* (*aham*) is a limitation and criticises the assumption of western theistic thought that personality or even individuality is the 'supreme excellence of man' which must be retained to all eternity. He wants to get rid of this 'sickly growth of the *ego*', this overemphasis on self-consciousness, personality and individuality, not simply in our way of looking at God and Christ

[1] *ibid.*

but even in our way of understanding ourselves. 'The Indian theological way,' he writes, 'must be to rid Jesus and the Christ of this over-much consciousness with which his life has been covered by modern theology'.[1] We shall then be able to see a Jesus who, by completely eliminating the *aham*, has become one with God, and with whom, because he is totally self-emptied man and at the same time risen Christ, we can enter into communion.

Here we are coming very close to the type of *kenosis* spoken of long before by Keshab Chandra Sen who wrote:

> Christ ignored and denied his self altogether . . . He destroyed self. And as self ebbed away, Heaven came pouring into the soul. For nature abhors a vacuum, and hence as soon as the soul is emptied of self, Divinity fills the void.[2]

In the same way Chakkarai sees Jesus as being progressively stripped of his *ego* until he is completely emptied and so becomes 'the most egoless person known in history, and therefore the most universal of all'.[3] The *ego* was not, he says, entirely absent in the historical Jesus, but 'it became so thin that only a different kind of experience was required to reduce it to nothing',[4]—and that experience came on the Cross. Jesus did not start off as simply 'egoless' in a metaphysical way; his *kenosis* was 'achieved' by a real process—the learning by obedience through the things he suffered, of which Hebrews speaks, and the self-emptying of Philippians 2, culminating in the degradation and death of the Cross.[5]

In some mysterious way a change took place between the man Jesus who walked the *via dolorosa* and the Christ whom we now worship and who lives in our hearts, who is outside the realm of mere human personality:

> Jesus Christ is worshipped as God; and we cannot meet the difficulty that we are worshipping the creature instead of the Creator unless the Christ is not a human individuality any longer. The historic Jesus was a man with an *ego* . . . When Jesus rose from the dead and entered the inner essence of God, then he ceased to be a

[1] *The Guardian*, 20-4-44. For a positive approach to personality compare P. D. Devanandan, v. infra, p. 188. The subject of personality in its relation to Hinduism is well treated in Stephen Neill's *Christian Faith and Other Faiths* (1961), pp. 90 ff.

[2] v. supra, p. 29.

[3] *The Guardian*, 13-4-44.

[4] *ibid.*, 20-4-44.

[5] *ibid.*

human being,[1] but became the universal spirit, though with the experience of his human history. Unique is such a state—to have the experience of humanity[2] without the possession of an *ego*—which alone can give to us the Christ who while in the Being of God, the ineffable and absolute, is also an indweller—the *antarātman*, of those who are united with him.[3]

Chakkarai now tries to penetrate further, to identify the precise moment at which the historical Jesus passed over into the Christ. And he finds what he is seeking in the cry of dereliction on the Cross, 'My God, my God, why hast Thou forsaken me?'—those terrible words through which he himself had first come to Christ. As Jesus went to the Cross he was stripped of everything that distinguishes a man. Only one thing remained to him on Calvary, one plank on which to sail out over the dark waves of the Cross, and that was his fundamental belief in God as his Father and himself as the Beloved Son. Jesus lived in God, as no one else ever did, but now, at the moment of that dreadful cry, 'the only plank beneath him was carried away, and he plunged into the Nirvana or Suniam where God is not'.[4] Here was the uttermost depth of *kenosis*, the depth than which nothing could be deeper, as Jesus sank into the depth of non-being.

But that non-being was not zero, the nothingness of popular imagination. It was more like the mathematical zero which is the actual beginning of all co-ordinates, or like the Vedāntic *asat* which Brahmabandhab expounded, which is the matrix of being. And so in fact the depth of the process of humiliation becomes the start of glorification, and from the utter *kenosis* of the Jesus of History the Christ of faith arises. Chakkarai explains his argument:

> My meaning is that this was the final phase of the *kenosis*, the self-emptying in Philippians, and after this it was that the glorification of Jesus took place; then he became the divine human indwelling Christ. It is out of this nothingness that remained of the Jesus of history that the Christ arose. Else, He could not dwell in every soul that has united with Him in faith and obedience and love. As the mere human Jesus He could not do it, and as belonging to the Being of God, he could only act as before the earthly life... Between the historical and the spiritual life of Christ in

[1] Contrast Chenchiah's view of the permanent humanity of Christ, v. supra, p. 148.

[2] The text reads 'human', but this is probably a misprint.

[3] *The Guardian*, 6-4-44.

[4] *ibid.*, 20-4-44. *Suniam* = nothing.

man is an unbridgeable gulf that He alone could have spanned and He spanned it in His Death.[1]

This sheds light on what Chakkarai means when he speaks of Jesus as the permanent or 'advancing' *avatāra*. It is different from Chenchiah's idea of the 'permanent humanity' of Jesus. For Chakkarai, the Christ whom we know by faith is neither the pre-existent Son nor the Jesus of history but something new and different. He writes:

> The Jesus plus Christ combination is a new thing in the relations between God and man; not an ego-centric relation but indwelling in God and man . . . an emergence into a more positive being than even the historical.[2]

When we speak of the incarnation—of Jesus the *avatāra*—we do not refer merely to his life on earth but to a long process which includes that life but also his death, resurrection, ascension and *parousia*. And the Jesus whom we know in *bhakti* is *this* Jesus, Jesus the *avatāra*, Jesus whom by the Spirit we know as immanent, as the *antarātman* or *antaryāmin*. Because of the work of the Spirit we men of this age can know Christ in this way, for 'the present is the dispensation of the Spirit and the immanent Christ'.[3]

Chakkarai's exposition of this point is an impressive one, combining as it does insights from several different sources. We see his insistence on a Biblical basis—for his view of Scripture is much more 'orthodox' than that of either Chenchiah or Appasamy—and his interesting development of Sen's view of *kenosis*. At the same time he makes a deeply meaningful use of the *avatāra* conception which Sen rejects. We can see also how he rejects the idea of 'personality' in God, and yet insists that the only true God is the God who suffers. He rejects Chenchiah's idea that the Christ we know *is* the human Christ, yet stresses the fact that the living Christ whom we know as the Spirit at work in us, is the one who

> Still remembers in the skies
> His tears, His agonies and cries.[4]

[1] *The Guardian*, 20-4-44.
[2] *ibid.*
[3] *ibid.*
[4] Scottish Paraphrases, 1781, from Hebrews 4.15.

Hindu Terminology and Christian Theology

Chakkarai, like so many of the men we have been studying, believes that Hinduism has been preparing men's hearts for Christ,[1] and that the God who speaks in the Bible is the same who has revealed himself as *paramātman* in India :

> It is the same *paramātman*, the Supreme, that was in the *rishis* of old and by whom they spoke at different times and degrees, who is the secret of the Christian consciousness. There are aspects of His being that were beyond their dreams as they lived before the Incarnation of the Lord.[2]

He describes Hinduism as one of the great sign-posts of the religious life, which points the way to the deepest longings of the human heart. We are reminded of Sundar Singh's description of the channels dug by Hinduism which Christ is to fill. When Christianity comes to India it cannot be written 'on a clean slate', because the slate of the Indian religious consciousness has been written on over and over again, and so 'Christianity cannot, and nay, Christ himself does not, profess to erase with a magic sponge all this past'.[3] For this reason, it is clear that the Church in India should give primacy to Indian terminology and modes of thought, for Christ 'can admit all truth, transform and purify it in the crucible of His all-comprehending Mind'.[4]

Chakkarai feels that Christians in the period up to his time have tried far too hard—in Bible translation as well as theological writing—to avoid using words with Hindu religious overtones :

> In the first attempts that were made, and are still being repeated, the most important was to translate Christian truth and life from a purely Western vocabulary to an Indian one. The older missionaries and their converts and the Churches set up by them, with meticulous care had avoided words in Sanskrit or the vernacular that would in any way remind us of the fact that in India there are and have been great religious experience and philosophies.[5]

[1] He also grants that salvation may be found *within* Hinduism. Speaking of how it is possible for both Hindus and Christians to be saved he writes: 'The salvation of each, as understood by each, is by the grace of the Lord ; the former by the grace of God without the historic Christ, and the other by the grace of God in Christ.' (*Rethinking*, pp. 76 f.)

[2] *Avatār*, p. 160.

[3] *Cross*, pp. 6 ff.

[4] *The Guardian*, 1-5-47.

[5] *ibid*, 5-11-31. Compare John Wilson's rejection of the word *svarga* mentioned earlier. v. supra, p. 16.

The charge is not entirely true, but it has substance in it and in order to reverse the tendency Chakkarai introduced a large number of Sanskrit terms into his writings, as will have been clear even from the brief extracts we have examined. It has been said—perhaps with reference to Chakkarai and his friends !—that one cannot produce a new theology by substituting Sanskrit words for Greek ones. This may be true, but the whole of Chakkarai's theology demonstrates that this is not in fact what he has been attempting to do. His quest has rather been to abandon Greek and Latin theology, and, starting from Scripture and experience (*śruti* and *anubhava* in Hindu terminology !) to work out a new expression of the Christian faith, using, but at the same time transforming, the available Hindu terms. He and other theologians have been tackling the same problem as was faced in the early Church, that of forging a new vocabulary, different from that of Palestinian Judaism, and yet able to express the deep insights of the Judaic tradition in a way which would make sense in the Hellenistic world and would win men to Christ. Mistakes were then made, some of which have caused trouble ever since,[1] yet the attempt had to be made, and in the end it brought wonderful enrichment and deepening of understanding to the whole Church. The contribution of India to the world Church in the coming years could be no less vital and stimulating, and Chakkarai has played an important part in demonstrating the method.

[1] e.g. the implications of the Latin term *persona*.

CHAPTER X

PREPARATION FOR DIALOGUE: P. D. DEVANANDAN

P. D. Devanandan (1901-1962)

With Dr. P. D. Devanandan we take a step forward into the world of the secular state and contemporary Hinduism. Dr. Devanandan, who died in 1962 while still at the height of his powers, was very much a man of the present day and saw his task as that of understanding the various strands of contemporary Hindu and secular thought in India, and presenting the Christian Gospel in ways that would be meaningful to his Hindu friends and contemporaries. His special interests lay in the fields of sociology and comparative religion rather than in systematic theology, yet his work is of great importance in the development of Indian Christian theology, largely because of his burning concern for contemporary developments in Hinduism and in Indian politics and society.

Paul David Devanandan was born in 1901 in Madras where his father was an ordained minister.[1] He studied in Madras, Trichinopoly and Hyderabad, taught for some time in Jaffna, Ceylon, and then continued his studies at the University of Madras. As a young man he came under the influence of the famous Christian leader K. T. Paul who took him as his secretary on his visit to the United States in 1924-5, after which Devanandan stayed on in America for seven years, studying first in the Pacific School of Religion, California, and later at Yale, where he earned his doctorate with a dissertation which was eventually published in 1950 as *The Concept of Māyā*. K. T. Paul, who took part in the London Round Table Conference of 1930 and was a leader of the nationalist movement and a friend of Gandhi, exercised considerable influence on Devanandan, and it is perhaps to this friendship that we can trace his determination to take a full part, as a Christian, in nation-building activities.[2]

[1] For brief biographical details see: *In Memory of Devanandan* (CISRS, 1962). Also P. D. Devanandan, *I will lift up mine Eyes unto the Hills: Sermons and Bible Studies*, ed. by S. J. Samartha and Nalini Devanandan (1963), which contains a biographical introduction by S. J. Samartha. (Cited as *Sermons*).

[2] H. A. Popley, *K. T. Paul, Christian Leader* (1938).

On his return to India he became a teacher of philosophy and the history of religions at the United Theological College, Bangalore, where he remained for seventeen years. After serving for some time with the YMCA he moved in 1956 to his last and perhaps most influential post as Director of the newly-formed Christian Institute for the Study of Religion and Society (CISRS) in Bangalore, where he remained till his untimely death from a heart-attack in 1962. He was widely known and respected in India and abroad as a Christian thinker and Church leader, and took a leading part in the work of the World Council of Churches, particularly at the meeting in New Delhi in 1961, where he delivered one of the major addresses.[1] His published works, apart from *The Concept of Māyā*, mainly consist of papers and sermons collected and printed, some posthumously, by the CISRS.[2]

As a young man Devanandan revolted against the theological liberalism which was then in vogue, and found in Kraemer and Barth a basis for making a new start. Though he later reacted against Kraemer also, many traces of these theologians are to be found in his writings, especially in his understanding of God as wholly other and yet personal. It might in fact be said that his rejection of Kraemer—the Kraemer of 1938—is limited to Kraemer's negative approach to the 'non-Christian world'. Here indeed he finds himself on the same side as the authors of *Rethinking Christianity* and in total reaction against the Barthian idea that all non-Christian religions are basically human enterprises. Barth and Kraemer, he feels, have stressed the fact that revelation is *from God* at the expense of the fact that it is *to and for the world of men*, and he himself feels called to restore the balance by making a detailed and sympathetic study of man and society in modern India.

The 'newness' of Devanandan's thought, then, is not to be found in any radical reinterpretation of the basic doctrines of the Christian faith, such as we find, for instance, in Brahmabandhab's treatment of the Trinity or Chenchiah's exposition of the 'new creation'. On the contrary, his attitude to the basic affirmations of the Creed is impeccably orthodox, and we find little that is specially 'Indian' in what he says about Scripture, the atonement or the Church. He is not seeking to 'adapt' the Christian message to Hinduism but rather so to

[1] 'Called to Witness', printed in P. D. Devanandan's *Preparation for Dialogue* (1964), pp. 179 ff. (Cited as *Preparation*).

[2] See Bibliography.

understand the inner workings of Hinduism that he may be able to show his Hindu friends the points at which their beliefs can find true meaning only in Christ. Hinduism today is finding it difficult to bridge the gap between its own traditional orthodoxy and the active, developing life of a modern secular state. In this difficulty Hindus find that their theology has to be rethought and reformed and here, strange as it may seem, the Christian may come to the aid of his Hindu brother, in friendly dialogue, helping him to reform his faith *from within*. Devanandan writes:

> One of the functions of the Christian evangelist in India is not so much to counter forces of secularism and irreligion, but to help Hindus, in city or in village, at all levels of culture, to redefine the very nature of what is called religion.[1]

There are certain areas of thought in which it seems specially clear that traditional Hindu theology fails to provide the practical backing which is needed for life in a modern, developing country. These are the understanding of *personality*, where traditional conceptions of the *ātman* work against the ideas of freedom and development; the understanding of the meaning of *creation*, where Hinduism tends to underrate the importance of the material world and so fails to give adequate support to plans for raising the standard of living; the understanding of *history*, where Hinduism fails to provide a basis for the idea of purpose and planning; and *society*, where Hinduism, despite the importance of what Brahmabandhab called *samāj dharma*, thinks mainly in terms of individual salvation and fails to envisage a 'transforming community'. We shall consider briefly what Devanandan has to say on these four topics.

Personality

We have seen how Chakkarai tried to avoid the idea of 'personality' in connection with God, thereby reflecting the Vedāntic teaching that *Brahman* is ultimately *nirguṇa*. Devanandan agrees that God is Ultimate Truth, but maintains that he is also fully personal, and points out that the Biblical phrase, 'The Lord thy God', in effect equates *Īsvara* with *Brahman*.[2] God is hidden yet he reveals himself as personal not simply in Christ but all through the pages of the Old Testament. Writing of the call of Abraham he says:

[1] P. D. Devanandan, *Christian Concern in Hinduism* (1961), p. 91. (Cited as *Concern*).

[2] *Preparation*, p. 153.

> The abiding value of all these encounters is not merely that God called Abraham and the people of Israel, but that God is the Person Who calls, He is the Person Who communicates His will. The Christian faith is based on this discovery. No other Scripture brings this truth so vividly to light as the Old Testament.[1]

God is, however, not personal in a human sense, and Devanandan quotes Barth's view that God's personality is incomprehensible and surpasses all our views of personality.[2] Nevertheless—and granting that he may be spoken of as Ultimate Reality (akin to *Brahman*)—God becomes known only in our personal relationship to him, and never as a series of propositions. 'The cognitive element in the process of understanding is overwhelmed by the existential sense of utter dependence'.[3] This conception of God as personal, speaking to and dealing historically with man as a responsible person, is a fundamental article of faith for Devanandan and is one of the points which he believes to be of basic importance in the Hindu-Christian dialogue.

The idea of personality occupies a vital place in his doctrine of man also, and he interprets the *imago Dei* as implying man's 'kinship' with God, not his substantial identity. The more truly man reflects the nature of God, the more truly is he man as God intended him to be, for it is 'wholeness of personality which is the very image of God',[4] a wholeness which has been shattered by sin and which is restored only when man becomes a new creature in Christ. [We may note in passing that Devanandan takes a very positive view of 'the sinfulness of sin' and does not seek to link it with ignorance (*avidyā*), or *karma*, but rather with *ahaṃkāra*, egotism or selfishness.]

Is there an Indian word which can be used to express what Devanandan understands by 'personality'? He suggests the word *puruṣa* (person), and gives a fascinating outline of its possibilities. He feels that it is a word which could be transformed and filled with new content by some great Indian thinker, just as Gandhi transformed the word *ahiṃsā* from its root meaning of non-violence and gave it a meaning like Christian 'love'.[5] The word *puruṣa* in common usage means 'man' as opposed to woman. In the Sāṁkhya system it signifies the creative principle which operates on passive matter, *prakriti*, in order to

[1] *Sermons*, p. 28.
[2] *Preparation*, p. 166.
[3] *ibid.*, p. 163.
[4] *ibid.*, p. 181.
[5] *Sermons*, p. 60.

produce the created world, while in the *Mundaka Upaniṣad* it describes the Supreme Person, the *antarātman* or *Brahman.*[1] Devanandan lists three essential elements of a true *puruṣa.* First of all, the word implies the ability of persons to stand up to one another in the mutual encounter of I-Thou. Secondly, the two personalities in dialogue penetrate one another; there is an interaction which draws them together as people. And thirdly there is a purposive striving, a reaching out to realise a common end. Persons who truly meet become involved in shared tasks, and to be a true person we must have a *purpose.*

In the Sanskrit-derived languages the word *puruṣa* and the derived abstract noun *puruṣatva* have not yet fully acquired this meaning, and yet the word seems to be the most promising one available, not merely for describing human personality but for defining the Persons of the Godhead. Man's personality derives from God's, and his sense of being an 'I' is the result of his being confronted with the 'Thou' of God and so, when we want to describe man as he ought to be, as God intends him to be, it is perhaps not sufficient to describe him as *puruṣa*; we should go further and describe him as *bhakta,* the worshipper.[2]

Creation Old and New

In dialogue with Hindus it is important to stress not merely the fact that God is personal, but also that it is God himself, the Ultimate Truth (to use again Devanandan's paraphrase of *Brahman*), who is the Creator. Devanandan makes this point very clear, emphasising God's act of creation, his continuous creative activity and providence, and the fact that creation has a purpose, that it is orientated towards the end to which God is directing all things.[3] All men, not merely Christians, are involved in the great redemptive movement in history and have a place in God's concern.[4] The world is real, God created it and still exercises his creative activity on it, and so material things are good and should be used for the work which God intends.

In terminology which recalls Chenchiah, Devanandan holds that God's original purpose in creation, temporarily checked by man's sin, is to be achieved by the *new creation,* which comes to those who are 'in Christ', and in which the whole created universe will participate, as indeed it is already beginning to

[1] *Mund. Up.* 2.1.
[2] *Preparation,* p. 147.
[3] *Sermons,* pp. 67 f.
[4] *ibid.,* p. 115.

participate. Yet unlike Chenchiah, Devanandan here does not imply mere evolution, even spiritual evolution. Christ is the True Man, and man becomes a new creature in him, not by any kind of evolution but in response and commitment:

> In Christ we have a forecast of what God intends man to be from the beginning of creation. And more, of what God is making of man when he totally surrenders himself to the creative purpose in God's design for mankind.[1]

When God's creature, man, the product of the original creation, commits himself to Christ he becomes a new creature, and is able to share with God in the carrying out of God's great purpose for the *whole* of creation. It is the power, the personality, of the living Christ which transforms men and welds them into a new and living community with himself at the centre, and with a purpose to fulfil:

> It is the living Presence which as the living Centre draws each one of us towards it. A magnet may draw bits of iron pieces towards it by a blind force. But the living Christ who draws us towards Him and together to each one of us is a *creative*, healing, *purposive* Reality. Therefore, in the fellowship where the living God is at the Centre, an amazing change takes place in the deep within of the men and women who enter into such a fellowship. He makes over again, makes anew each one of them. 'Therefore, if any one is in Christ, he is a new creation.'[2]

Unlike Chenchiah, Devanandan believes that men can become new creatures only by *conversion*, and he stoutly defends the use of this word, which so often comes under attack in India and is equated with 'proselytism'. Conversion is not a matter of transferring a person from one group to another, but it should be described, as Christ himself described it, in terms of a new birth:

> What is implied is that the new birth begins with a change, a change in the very substance of our being, in the very nature of man. The indwelling Spirit of God, not the sinful nature of man, henceforth becomes the decisive factor in the life of the convert. 'No longer I that live but the Christ in me'—that is being apprehended of God.[3]

[1] *ibid.*, p. 69.
[2] *ibid.*, pp. 100 ff.
[3] *ibid.*, pp. 69 f.

God's purpose in the world can be carried out by people of diverse faiths, and Devanandan is convinced that the Spirit is at work in the selfless lives of his Gandhian friends as well as within the Church. And yet the primary way in which the purpose of the creation is to be fulfilled is through the lives of those who have been made new in Christ:

> It is difficult to see how the realm of God's sovereignty can be extended unless there come into being more and more people who commit themselves to the Lordship of Jesus Christ.[1]

Traditional Hinduism rejects this kind of positive approach to the created world and the possibility of transforming it through purposive activity. Devanandan repeatedly points out, however, that in practice modern Hindus readily accept the value of the material world, the importance of history, and the possibility of transforming both the world and society, even though this clashes with the traditional view of the relation of God and the world. He writes:

> This new conception of history in the making in modern India will have to come to terms with the classical view about God and Reality that had so long held the field . . . The Christian view of man as God's creature and of God as man's Creator, has provided the solution in Christian thought. But in Hindu thinking to accept the doctrine of the creation would be to do violence to the nature of God as Absolute Being, who cannot be in any way involved in world life.[2]

Devanandan sees it as one of the duties of Christian theology to help Hindus towards a reformation in their way of thinking about the created world, in order that their efforts to transform and use that world may find the inner dynamic and undergirding which at present is lacking.

History and 'The Hope of Glory'

This positive view of the created world must extend also to history. Traditionally Hinduism has had little interest in history and has tended to think of events in time as following a cyclic pattern, and being in any case subject to *māyā*. Today—and Devanandan believes that the change is to a considerable extent due to the influence of Christianity—many leaders of

[1] *Preparation*, p. 117.
[2] *Concern*, p. 112.

public life and thought in India take a very different view and look upon history as a process which can be shaped and directed to various ends. The successive Five Year Plans for national development are but one instance of this positive practical thinking in relation to time and history. Devanandan feels that the Christian conception of linear history working towards an ultimate end or purpose is able to provide the new basis for action which traditional Hinduism has so far failed to provide. Once again we find that *purpose*—God's purpose in creation and history—is a dominating element of his thought.

A constantly recurring phrase in Devanandan's writings is 'the Hope of Glory',[1] by which he understands the life in Christ, that unity of our wills with the divine will, of our purposes with God's purpose, which will be ours *in gloria*, but is already ours in so far as we are new creatures in Christ. His understanding of the final outcome of history, that is of eschatology, closely links the individual and the community, the present and the end, and he distinguishes it from the Hindu 'end' of realised identity with *Brahman* :

> Human destiny is conceived not as absorption into the divine but as loving fellowship with God, which in Biblical language is described as 'the hope of glory'. And there can be no 'glory' for the individual until the 'glorified community' comes into being, and the society of the redeemed is complete. That would be the destiny of man, then, in Christian faith—transformed life in the Kingdom of God at the end of time and of creation.[2]

This implies that the end, the 'hope of glory' is already present wherever the new creation is in being, both in individual Christians and in the Church, the reconciling community. We customarily think of the future as being built upon and conditioned by the present, and all secular hopes are built on this assumption. But for the Christian, says Devanandan, the reverse is true ; the present is conditioned by the future since the 'hope of glory', to which all things are moving, is present *now*, changing and transforming men and communities. God's purpose is moving steadily towards fulfilment, and yet in a sense the fulfilment has broken into the present in Christ, in whom eschatology is realised :

> From the standpoint of holy history (that is the theological understanding of history), it is the present that is conditioned by the

[1] Colossians 1 : 27 : 'Christ in you, the hope of glory'. AV.
[2] *Preparation*, p. 161.

> future, the final end. The end is the 'hope of glory', when the whole creation shall have been lifted to loftier planes of undreamt of possibilities. The end is not completion of a process, but consummation of a purpose. Here is fulfilment with a difference—fulfilment of the divine purpose, of God's plan for his creation, the transformation of life.[1]

We may readily accept the idea that God has a purpose in history and is working through it. But a very significant principle is raised when the idea is applied, as Devanandan applies it, to the renaissance and internal reformation which are going on in Hinduism, and to the relation between Hinduism and Christianity. Much of his writing is devoted to a study of reform and development in Hinduism, tracing the movement from Ram Mohan Roy through the Brāhma and Ārya Samāj, Rāmakrishna, Vivekānanda, Tagore, Aurobindo, Gandhi to the Neo-Vedānta of Radhakrishnan, the *Sarvodaya* of Vinobā Bhāve and the secular humanism of Nehru. It is in the context of such modern Hinduism that the Gospel is to be proclaimed. How are Christians to view this development and self-purification of Hinduism? Fifty years ago Farquhar saw it as a sort of evolutionary process whose 'crown' would be Christianity. Twenty-five years later Kraemer, on the other hand, saw little of worth in the non-Christian world. Devanandan's view is different from either. Neither Christians nor Hindus, he feels, are building on the past, in a process of evolution. Rather the future has already broken in on the present, the future which is Christ in us, the hope of glory, the new creation. Christ, through the Spirit, is at work not only within the Church but also *outside* it; he is at work also in the reform of Hinduism, in all those modern developments which go to show the inadequacy of the traditional orthodoxy and the need for a new understanding of God and the world.[2] Over against those who fear 'renascent Hinduism', Devanandan sees in this 'newness' the hand of God, and hears in it a call to dialogue with those outside, so that we and they may stand together in the area of God's new creation. In a penetrating paragraph he writes:

> If all 'New Creation' can only be of God, where else could these 'new' aspects of other beliefs in the thinking and living of people have sprung from? If the whole creation is being directed

[1] *Sermons*, p. 68.

[2] Cf. the thesis of A. T. van Leeuwen, *Christianity in World History* (1964), that the process of secularisation is the present form in which the non-western world is meeting biblical history. See Lesslie Newbigin, *Honest Religion for Secular Man* (1966), pp. 27 ff.

by the redemptive act of God in Jesus Christ towards the final 'hope of glory', a total transformation of present existence, is *fulfilment* in the end the result of the present being fulfilled in the future, or does it consist in the ultimate future being *realized* (and so fulfilled) in the temporal present? If the true reading of salvation-history (Heilsgeschichte) is in terms of eternity flowing into time, the 'coming' of the Eternal Kingdom of God in the temporal order of man, how do we restate the distinctiveness of the Gospel in the context of the religions of the world?[1]

Devanandan draws contrast between the tolerant, Farquhar-type of hope in the 'fulfilment of all religious faith' and the more radical 'Gospel proclamation of the fulfilment of God's promise of the Kingdom', and says of the latter that

> because the promise of the Kingdom is so totally assured, the end is in reality a present fact. It is come! In salvation-history, to the discerning eye of faith, the eternal future is being fulfilled in contemporary present. It is in this sense our Lord declared that He has come not to destroy but to fulfil.[2]

This is something which affects the life and proclamation of the Church, for the new creation is to be proclaimed both within and without the Church as a present reality; *already* we can know in our own experience that 'hope of glory' towards which we are moving in God's purpose. We shall see in more detail later how Devanandan applies this understanding of eschatology to the Mission of the Church.

Māyā

Before leaving Devanandan's treatment of history and eschatology we shall look briefly at an interesting new interpretation which he gives to the concept of *māyā*, not in his book of that name, which is a presentation of the history of the idea from Vedic to modern times, but in some of his later writings where he outlines a possible constructive Christian approach to the idea.

He points out that for modern Hinduism, as distinct from traditional orthodoxy or contemporary village religion, *māyā* is not thought of as mere illusion. Rather there has been, from the time of Vivekānanda right down to Dr. Radhakrishnan in

[1] *Preparation*, p. 177. Compare Chenchiah, 'Eternal life is not a flow back of the river into the sea, but of the sea into the river'. v. supra, p. 157.

[2] *ibid.*, pp. 192 f.

our own time, a persisting claim that Śankara's *māyāvāda* does not deny the reality of life in this world. The phenomenal world *is* real, though not with the same reality as God; it is not nothingness, for it is willed by God and therefore is real. Only *Brahman* has non-created divine reality, but the world does have reality, albeit dependent and created. This is what is implied in Radhakrishnan's view of the world as 'relatively real', and it is very close to that interpretation of *māyā* as 'contingent being' in the Thomist sense which Upādhyāya expounded. The Neo-Vedāntists are anxious to give the maximum 'reality' to the world while still refusing to accept *creatio ex nihilo* or to accord to the creation a reality equal to that of the Creator.

Devanandan gives his own exposition of a possible Christian interpretation of *māyā*, and it is of considerable interest, though quite different from that of Upādhyāya. He finds his two major clues in a comparison of secular history with *Heilsgeschichte*, and in the meaning of the word 'vanity' (Greek *mataiotes*) in Romans 8 : 20, where Paul says that the creation was made 'subject to vanity'. Secular history and *Heilsgeschichte* are not to be regarded as mere parallel processes, for despite the 'vanity' of this world and of so much of its secular history, God's *purpose* is steadily at work in the world, guiding men and events along the line of *Heilsgeschichte* towards the 'end' of the new creation. The two lines of history are closely intertwined :

> Time is, as it were, shot through with eternity. Thus the Christian talks about man as a citizen of two worlds. This is really a way of stating that this is a world of *Māyā*, a world which is both real and unreal, conditioned by time and shot through with eternity, the scene of human endeavour and the plane of Divine Activity. But here the *sat-asat*[1] nature of world-life is not understood in terms of Ultimate Reality but Final Purpose.[2]

In other words secular history moves in a sort of *māyā*-world in so far as it is man-made and has not been brought into line with God's purpose, and it gains reality and ultimate significance as it becomes conformed to that purpose. Devanandan's new contribution here is to transfer *māyā* from the realm of being to that of will or purpose; the unreal passes into the real when man's will and purpose come to coincide with God's. On this interpretation *māyā*, the Biblical 'vanity', is used to describe the state of this world where the vain and self-willed activity of man

[1] reality-unreality.
[2] *Preparation*, p. 155.

in secular history claims for itself a sovereignty which can in truth belong to God alone.[1]

This is an interpretation of *māyā* with definite possibilities, for it affirms that there is no *ontological* barrier between the 'really real' and the realm of *māyā*; the actual world, the world of *māyā* or vanity, can be transformed until it conforms to God's will and purpose. What is evil in the world is not just to be ignored or endured; it can and must be cured.

Devanandan makes a similar point when writing of the nature of ultimate Truth. He understands 'ultimate Truth', of course, as being 'relational' and indeed personal, and yet it is also, he writes, 'ultimate reality in the sense of that which is, in the final analysis, the eternally real, beyond and beneath the temporal actual'.[2] This 'temporal actual', being as it were in the realm of *māyā*, cannot be equated with the real, yet if it is to have any meaning at all it must in some sense reflect the real. The 'actual' can reflect or be shot through with the real, and the more closely our wills conform to the will of God, the more clearly will the actual reflect the real, and *māyā* pass over into reality:

> This world of creation acquires a meaningfulness in that what is regarded as 'natural' is now seen to be shot through with a reality which is 'supernatural'. The phenomenal is conditioned by the noumenal, and what is real in it is real because of the dynamic presence in it of the noumenal.[3]

Thus the doctrine of *māyā*, when brought out of the realm of being and creation into that of will and history, and interpreted in the context of God's purpose for the new creation, acquires a new meaning and new possibilities which it does not possess in any of its current Hindu interpretations. This is perhaps a sample of the kind of reinterpretation which Devanandan hoped would emerge from a Hindu-Christian dialogue, a reinterpretation which could help to bridge the gap between modern Indian 'world-affirmation' and the view of *māyā* found in Śankara.

[1] *ibid.*

[2] *ibid.*, p. 162.

[3] *ibid.*, p. 167. Compare the existentialist distinction of 'authentic' and 'unauthentic' existence, e.g. in Heidegger. See Stephen Neill, *Christian Faith and Other Faiths*, pp. 184 f. The difference between Devanandan's view and that of the traditional three types of existence (v. supra, pp. 47 f.) is that for Devanandan existence itself can be changed from the unreal to the real.

The Transforming Community

Hinduism regards religion as a matter of private religious experience. Devanandan points out how except perhaps in the more recent renascent movements, Hinduism has never thought in terms of congregational worship, where a corporate body of believers approaches God in a sense of togetherness and with the idea of seeking to know and do his will.[1] The conception of the Church is therefore a rock of offence to the Hindu believer :

> The idea of a transforming community is alien to the Hindu genius because of its basic belief about the nature of God as the eternal *Brahma*, and of the nature of man as essentially that of *Brahma* itself. There can, therefore, be no such community as the Church claims itself to be, where there is an inflow and outflow of personal influence which is transforming, because the real bond of fellowship therein is provided by the Holy Spirit which draws the members of the Church together in communion with God as revealed in Christ Jesus.[2]

Christianity on the other hand believes that God has made man not only for fellowship with himself but also for fellowship in community, and that personality implies a relationship of *love*. Jesus said, ' Love God, and your neighbour as yourself,' and this involves us in a three-cornered relationship of love. In Devanandan's words, ' Man is truly man only in so far as he is found in the network of human relations which makes what the Bible calls " people ", and which in modern language we call "society" '. He himself prefers the word *loksangraha* (gathering of the people) or the English word ' community ', both of which suggest a ' holding together of people, in which alone a person finds himself as a person among persons and in relation to *the* Person '.[3] The very nature of man as created in the image of God is bound up with the twin conceptions of personality and community, of man-in-relation-to-God and man-in-community. Man, who is something more than mere *mānava*[4] or even *puruṣa*, should be a *bhakta*, one who lives in communion with God, and should live also in the fellowship of the community of truth, the *satsangha*.[5]

[1] *Concern*, pp. 101 f.
[2] *ibid.*
[3] *Preparation*, p. 149.
[4] *mānava*=man, human being.
[5] *Preparation*, pp. 147, 149.

Before going on to see how Devanandan works out this idea of community in connection with the Church we may pause for a moment to see how it carries with it a rejection of the theory of *karma-saṃsāra*. This theory, as we know, says that each individual must bear the consequences of his own actions, whether good or bad, if not in this life then in future incarnations. Devanandan points out how this principle must be unacceptable to the Christian since it can be applied in fairness only to individuals in severe isolation. For example, according to the principle of *karma-saṃsāra* children should not benefit from their father's good deeds, and a father should not suffer because of the misdeeds of his son. The principle cannot be applied to persons in community without losing its rigorous logic of individual retribution, and in fact Devanandan questions whether it can ever, no matter how interpreted, lend support to what we understand by social justice.[1] Here is another point where traditional Hindu beliefs seem to fail modern Indian social developments and where Christian belief seems to point a way forward. Where the belief in *karma-saṃsāra* has tended to lead to social stagnation and resignation, Christian belief in transforming community and human solidarity can lead to hope and action.

The transforming community is to be found above all in the Church, and, as we might expect from such a well-known Church leader, Devanandan's attitude towards it is positive and dynamic; he is intensely interested in the Church as part of the new creation, as demonstrating the life of the Kingdom of God here and now, as a healing, serving, transforming *koinonia*, the family of God. He is not much interested in narrower ecclesiological matters, nor even in technical discussions on Church unity. For him the overpoweringly important fact is that the Church should be a living, witnessing, serving fellowship, showing to the whole world what the life of the new creation is like. He can be very critical of the organised Church, and says many of the same sort of things as Chenchiah said, though in a more positive way; yet he does not seek the abolition of the visible Church but rather its transformation and revival.

The new creation consists of those who are 'in Christ', and therefore the first essential for the Church's life is that it should be gathered round and vitally related to its Centre, Christ, from whom alone, through the Spirit, it can draw the power it needs in order to be the transforming community:

[1] *Preparation*, p. 149.

> True community is created by the conscious sense which each one in the group has of being vitally connected with a living Centre. And because of this living relationship to the Centre, they are all bound to one another. That is the real difference between the communion of saints and an association of people.[1]

When the whole Church is in this vital relationship to Christ it really becomes the new creation and begins to live the life of the Kingdom. And the mark of this new community is the desire to do God's will, to be used in the world as the instrument of his transforming purpose, in full obedience to him. The Church is therefore 'the fellowship of those who endeavour in community as well as in their own personal lives to "do the will of the Father"'.[2]

For the Church to do the will of the Father necessarily involves it in evangelism, which for Devanandan implies that total 'mission' which includes both *kerygma* and *diakonia*, as well as the spontaneous witness of the living Christian *koinonia*. Christ came proclaiming the arrival of the Kingdom of God, and Devanandan frequently uses this expression in his explanation of the Church's mission; it implies that all people in the world are to be brought to know that this world and everything that happens in it must be brought under the sovereignty of God.[3] When Christ came to earth and identified himself with men it marked a new era in creation and the beginning of a redemptive movement which takes in humanity in its entirety. The Christian cannot keep this good news to himself but 'wants the world of men to share his faith in this all-inclusive cosmic process of new creation'.[4]

When the Church goes out into the world to carry out its mission, there will inevitably be misunderstandings and accusations of 'proselytism' and 'propaganda'. But there is a difference, Devanandan holds, between propaganda and the true 'propagation' of the Gospel:

> The propagation of the Gospel, which is the mission of every Christian believer, is primarily to spread abroad the good news that God has initiated a movement in the history of mankind by Himself entering into this very world of want and violence, of disease and death, of human sin and wilfulness, in order that this whole realm

[1] *Sermons*, p. 99.
[2] *Preparation*, p. 116.
[3] *ibid.*, p. 138.
[4] *ibid.*

of world-life may be transformed into a veritable new creation in which will be acknowledged the sovereignty of God.[1]

The contemporary context in which this Gospel is to be proclaimed and the life of the new creation demonstrated is very different from that of the decaying Hindu orthodoxy of Goreh's day or even of the rationalism of the advanced reform movements of that time. Devanandan is a brilliant exponent of contemporary Hinduism—of the practical, high-souled Gandhian outlook of the *Sarvodaya* movement, the intellectually cohesive and attractive neo-Vedānta of Radhakrishnan, the secular humanism of Nehru, the disillusioned atheism of the Dravida Munnetra Kazhagam (DMK) in South India.[2] This living, renascent and reformed Hinduism has already adopted many new attitudes and practices which go right against traditional orthodoxy—for example in such matters as caste, social justice, the place of women in society, the need for economic and social planning—but has not yet found a firm theological basis for its new *praxis*. Devanandan firmly holds that Christians also are called to share in the great adventure of building the new India, and it is by identifying themselves with their nation and with its cultural traditions that they can best find an opportunity for witnessing to the new life which they possess in Christ and sharing it with others. For the Christian believes that his faith not only allows him to participate in these nation-building activities, but gives him a positive basis and incentive for taking an active part in them. And so the mission of the Church must consist in going into the world of contemporary India and there witnessing by the proclamation of the wholeness of the Gospel, and also by service and by the demonstration of true community in action. In this task there is to be no curtailing of the Gospel, but rather the Christian faith is to be presented in its credal fulness and to be shared with Hindus in such a way that they are encouraged to examine their own fundamental credal basis :

The resurgence of Asian religions is in every case a new evangelistic opportunity for a face-to-face meeting of the credal claims of the Christian Gospel and their [i.e. non-Christians'] foundational doctrines . . . The real task in evangelism is so to declare the Gospel we believe in that its decisive demands on man's total allegiance are made positively clear.[3]

[1] *ibid.*, p. 105.
[2] *ibid.*, pp. 60 ff.
[3] *Concern*, pp. 18 ff.

Devanandan has a passionate devotion to the Christian task of witness, work and reconciliation within modern society. Only those who are themselves reconciled to God and have become new creatures in Christ have the spiritual power to carry out this ministry, but for them the 'end' can be nothing less than the renewal of society and the world in accordance with God's purpose.

Preparation for Dialogue

What many people regard as Devanandan's greatest contribution to the mission of the Church is his interpretation of the task of evangelism—and of the whole relationship between Christianity and Hinduism—in terms of 'dialogue', and to that insight of his we now turn.

His approach to Hinduism is a thoroughly modern and practical one. He looks at the wide variety of modern Indian thought and action and asks, 'What religious assumptions, if any, lie behind current practice?' As a Christian he seeks to share in the rich and varied life of contemporary India and to join his Hindu friends in a 'dialogue', a sharing of experience, in which it may prove possible *together* to arrive at some firm theological basis which will undergird that movement towards God's new creation which he sees at work in the Church and also—though not always so obviously—outside it. He seeks first of all to *understand* his Hindu contemporaries, and makes a penetrating historical and analytical study of the various modern movements, showing clearly how in so many fields Hindu practice has advanced far beyond traditional orthodox theory. The second stage, after the preliminary study, is that of frank interchange in conversation, in which we share with our Hindu friends not only the Christian insights in these different fields and the whole meaning of that new creation which is ours in Christ, but also their understanding of the high values of Hindu culture.

Modern India, as we have seen, clearly demonstrates its concern with the material world, with history, with the value of the individual as a person, and with society. Yet at each of these points Hindu orthodoxy, with its belief in the identity of *ātman* and *paramātman* and its relegation of the world of experience to the sphere of *māyā*, fails to provide the religious basis for practical action. Devanandan comments:

> The real problem in Hindu India is to effect a synthesis between traditional world-view and contemporary secularism. Thoughtful

Hindu leaders are wrestling with this problem and it is in relation to this concern that the good news of God incarnate in Jesus Christ will have to be spelled out.[1]

Many of the new developments in Hinduism owe a direct debt to Christian insight and example, even though the debt may often go unacknowledged. As Christians we must rejoice in this creative activity of the Holy Spirit, and as we enter into dialogue we shall often find that 'the hidden Christ' is there at work before us.[2]

Devanandan envisages three different stages in the 'apologetic' task of the Christian in dialogue. First we must make a detailed study of the different varieties of modern Hinduism—and this is a task to which Devanandan himself has made a noteworthy contribution. Secondly we should go on to a clarification of terminology, of those Indian terms which are used, with differing shades of meaning, by both Christians and Hindus.[3] And thirdly comes what he calls 'the more daring task' of evolving an Indian theological expression of the Christian faith. Devanandan perhaps underestimates what in fact has already been achieved by Indian Christian theologians in this field, and indeed he may have been less familiar than he should have been with the thinkers who are the subject of this book. At all events he expresses very clearly the question which is fundamental to our study:

> Effective communication of the Gospel to the non-Christian man of faith depends on the effective use made of the religious vocabulary with which he is familiar, and of the cultural pattern of life in which he finds self-expression and community being.[4]

It is one of the great merits of Devanandan's approach that he sees Indian Christian theology, not as something academic, but as a living interpretation of the Christian faith which is hammered out on the anvil of dialogue with men of Hindu faith, and which meets their real needs, while remaining true to 'the faith delivered to the saints'

[1] *Preparation*, p. 38.

[2] Cf. Raymond Panikkar, v. infra, pp. 222 ff.

[3] The best study I know in this field is an unpublished dissertation by R. M. Clark, 'A Study of Christological Categories in the Indian Church, as compared with those of the Early Church' (1949). See also R. M. Clark, 'A Study of Theological Categories in the Indian Church' in *International Review of Missions*, 1943, pp. 88 ff.

[4] *Preparation*, p. 191.

One final subject on which Devanandan has an interesting contribution to make is that of *secularism*. There have been secularist tendencies in India ever since the rationalism of Ram Mohan Roy, and there was even an ancient secularist Hindu tradition, the *lokāyata* system, which was both world-affirming and atheistic. With the coming of independence in 1947, however, and the emergence of India as a secular state, secularism assumed a new importance. Devanandan gives a good description of the modern, Nehru-type of Indian secularism:

> It recognizes material values; it gives worth and dignity to the human person; it places importance on all purposive endeavour to realize a just social order; and above all, it points to the need to take this present moment in world-life seriously.[1]

Yet it is widely recognised that modern India, devoted as it so largely is to the pursuit of secular aims of this kind, stands in need of some strong unifying force. The country is formed of many heterogeneous units, and there is a widespread tendency to separatism, on linguistic or religious or cultural grounds. Such separatism needs to be countered by a centripetal force, and the natural tendency is to find this unifying factor in 'Hindu culture'. Modern, 'secular' Hinduism is thus faced with the challenge of preserving the *cultural* aspect of Hinduism while yet ignoring or at least radically transforming 'religious' Hinduism. Devanandan inclines to the view that it is possible, though very difficult, to distinguish between cultural and religious Hinduism. Non-Hindus naturally fear any kind of 'religious synthesis', and yet a 'cultural synthesis' resulting in a common *way* of life rather than in a syncretistic creed might be possible and might provide the unifying force which is needed.

This comes close to the attitude of Upādhyāya, and even to Goreh with his use of the term 'Hindu Christians'. And in support of his conception of a 'secularised Hinduism' Devanandan can quote no less an authority than the late Sardar K. M. Panikkar, a doughty opponent of Christian missions. Panikkar came to the conclusion that Hinduism could be restored to effectiveness only by emphasising the secular character of its social institutions, and demanded 'a re-thinking of social values, a reorganization of institutions and a divorce between law and custom on the one hand and religion on the other'.[2] Devanandan's thesis is that this is the point at which the Christian

[1] *Preparation*, p. 67.

[2] K. M. Panikkar, *Hindu Society at the Cross Roads* (1955), pp. 3 ff. Quoted in P. D. Devanandan, *Our Task Today* (1959), p. 24.

mission should be brought to bear, bringing with it the insights of the Christian faith on creation, history, personality and community—all themes on which secular Hinduism is searching for a deeper vision than traditional orthodoxy can provide. Indian Christians must claim their 'cultural kinship' within Indian society and state their view in dialogue from *within* that society.

That is perhaps as far as Devanandan goes along this road. May it not be, however, that eventually the process of secularisation may go even further than it has already gone, and Hindu society become *completely* secularised, finally becoming Hindu only in a cultural sense, in the way in which Greek religion eventually lost its religious content and became cultural? Then this process—carried a stage further than Devanandan suggests—might combine with another process carried beyond his suggested beginnings, namely the provision of a Christian theological basis to support the structure of modern Indian life in a way which traditional Hinduism can no longer do. Thus 'Hindu culture' would survive, while religious Hinduism would be 'fulfilled' in the Christian faith.

Devanandan nowhere goes so far as this, and might perhaps have felt that to suggest such a possibility goes beyond what is immediately legitimate or charitable in the present stage of dialogue. And yet, when one follows up the various pointers which he has left here and there, this would appear to be the 'end' where they all converge—Indian individuals, the Indian Church, Indian society, all converging in the new creation, fully conformed to the will of God, living in and by the Spirit of Christ, yet still fully Indian; creed, cultus and culture all finally achieving stability and mutual inter-relatedness in a series of concentric circles with Christ, the New Man, at the Centre.[1]

[1] For the symbol of the concentric circles of creed, cultus and culture see *Concern*, pp. 10 ff.

Chapter XI

INDIAN THEOLOGY TODAY

In this final chapter of our historical survey of Indian Christian theology we shall try to give some idea of a number of the various 'fronts' on which theological activity is evident in India today.

Church Union

The Church of South India was inaugurated on 27th September 1947, and the significance of this event and the long theological discussions which led up to it is fully appreciated in ecumenical circles everywhere.[1] November 1970 saw the inauguration of an even more comprehensive union in the Church of North India, while in the South the CSI itself has been carrying on significant conversations with Lutherans and Baptists.

The original CSI negotiators worked on the principle that it was better not to draw up a detailed confessional statement, confining themselves rather to a few important general principles and leaving it to the united Indian Church of the future to draw up, if need be, a more 'Indian' confession. The North India Plan of Union has made similar provision. In Marcus Ward's words, the Church 'sees the danger of tying down the Indian Church at this stage to elaborate statements which would inevitably tend to be framed in Western categories of thought'.[2] This sentence draws one's attention to the fact that the CSI Constitution, the North India Plan and all the publications connected with the Church union movement in India reflect an almost entirely western type of thought and language. One cannot help noticing also that the authors of signed articles are very frequently foreigners. To say this is not to detract from the absolute value of the discussion, and its significance for the Church in India and elsewhere, but simply to note that this is not really Indian theology. The pressures of the Indian situation have forced the Churches to face their divisions, in the realm of theology as well as of organisation, and this is highly significant.

[1] See Bengt Sundkler: *CSI: The Movement towards Union*, 1900-1947 (1954); A. M. Ward: *The Pilgrim Church* (1953); Rajaiah D. Paul, *The First Decade* (1958); and for the theological issues J. E. L. Newbigin, *The Reunion of the Church* (1948).

[2] *The Pilgrim Church*, pp. 69 f.

What has happened so far, however, is that India has acted as the catalyst forcing the western Churches to recognise and resolve their differences of faith and order, rather than that India has in the process evolved her own theological insights. We remember that for this reason men like Chenchiah thought that the unity movement was an irrelevance, and that priority should be given to indigenisation. It might be said with some reason that the Church union movement in India has hitherto been paving the way for an advance in Indian theological thought in the doctrinal field rather than actually making that advance in its official statements.

There are, however, signs of an 'Indian' approach which should not be forgotten. The *Governing Principles* of the CSI, for example, include the statement that the Church desires, 'conserving all that is of spiritual value in its Indian heritage, to express under Indian conditions and in Indian forms the spirit, the thought and the life of the Church Universal'.[1] That is well said, and in matters like this it is probably best to move fairly slowly. It is perhaps in the sphere of worship that we can discern in the CSI a more positively Indian atmosphere. There is, for example, the 'Kiss of Peace' in the Order for the Lord's Supper, taken from the use of the Syrian Churches in Kerala, and the echo of the *Upaniṣads* in the words of the final suffrage of the Order for Baptism, 'From darkness lead them to Light; from death lead them to everlasting Life'.[2] There is also the permitted use of the Indian wedding-necklace or *mangalsutra* in place of a western ring, and the Christian adaptation of the 'seven steps' (*saptapadi*) which is a common feature of Hindu weddings. These, however, are points of detail which affect the 'atmosphere' rather than the theology of worship, and the fact remains that the liturgical forms used in all Indian Churches except the Syrian are still markedly western.[3]

The CSI, and its sister-Church the CNI, are undoubtedly 'great new facts of our time'. While they have not yet produced official doctrinal statements which express the Christian faith in a distinctively Indian way, they are preparing the way for such statements and are moving in the right direction.

Professionals and Periodicals

In contrast to earlier days, when the most important contributions to Indian Christian theology were made by enthusiastic

[1] CSI Constitution, II, 2.
[2] Cf. *Brih. Ar. Up.* 1-3-28.
[3] T. S. Garrett, *Worship in the CSI* (2nd edn. 1965), p. 10.

laymen—one might use the word 'amateurs' in its best sense—like Brahmabandhab, Sundar Singh, Chakkarai and Chenchiah, the tendency today is for most, though not all, theological books and articles to be written by men who are themselves engaged in some form of theological training or in specialised institutions. A corollary of this is the fact that few of those writing today are themselves converts; they have theological training but they do not usually possess first-hand background knowledge of Hinduism.

What sort of teaching is given in the theological schools and colleges of India? Is it still of the kind which earned the wrath of Chenchiah and Chakkarai for its 'westernness' at the time of the publication of Marcus Ward's *Our Theological Task* in 1946? It is hard to deny that the answer is still in the affirmative. Theological education for non-Roman Catholics in India is highly co-ordinated through the work of the Senate of Serampore College, which draws up syllabuses of study and conducts examinations for English and vernacular-medium colleges throughout the country. In addition the Board of Theological Education of the National Christian Council provides a link between the different institutions, promotes conferences and discussions, and acts as a channel for wider contacts with Churches abroad and with the World Council of Churches, especially through the latter's Theological Education Fund. All these ecumenical contacts are useful and necessary, and are of great help in raising the academic standard and the technical excellence of Indian theological education. One might mention for example the excellent series of text-books published since 1951 in the *Christian Students' Library*, a venture sponsored by the Serampore Senate. These books, which are in demand even outside India, are written with the Indian situation in mind, provide good up-to-date scholarship, and are intended for adaptation or translation into regional languages. Yet the great majority of their authors are foreigners and not Indians. A recent project which has stimulated original writing by Indian authors has been the Theological Textbooks programme of the Theological Education Fund of the WCC. This project, designed to encourage the writing of basic theological textbooks in the different languages, has already resulted in the production of a number of good original textbooks and commentaries, especially in Tamil. Yet despite these encouraging features the fact remains that Indian theological education is still on the western model, as can be seen by studying Serampore book-lists or looking at any examination question-paper. Most students come from Christian backgrounds, have little knowledge of Hinduism, go through a westernised college course, and if opportunity offers carry out post-graduate study of a western type or actually go to the West. This situation is an inevitable result of historical developments and leaders in the field of Indian theological education are aware of it and are trying to change it, but the process is a slow one, not least because many of the works of Indian theologians are out of print.[1]

The *Indian Journal of Theology*, founded in 1952 and appearing quarterly from Serampore with which it maintains a close link, provides a valuable forum for the publication of theological writing ; and though the criticism might be made that it carries too many articles by non-Indians and too few with a specific Indian reference, yet it has done much to encourage theological scholarship. Articles which have made a real contribution have not been lacking ; out of many one might select for special mention D. Rajarigam's series on the theology of Tamil hymnology and V. C. Samuel's articles giving a Syrian interpretation of the Alexandrian Christology, Chalcedon and the Monophysites. The *Clergy Monthly*, a Roman Catholic periodical published from Ranchi, frequently contains articles of importance for Indian theology, and carries on the fine tradition of Johanns and the *Light of the East*.

What may in some ways be regarded as a more radical approach to Indian theology, especially in its relation with Hinduism, than the somewhat 'professional' world which we have been considering, is provided by the *Christian Institute for the Study of Religion and Society* (CISRS), founded in 1957 and closely associated with the name of its first Director, Dr. Devanandan. Under him and his successor, Mr. M. M. Thomas, the Institute has done much to stimulate original thinking and research, especially in the fields of sociology and of the relation of Christianity and Hinduism.[2] It publishes a quarterly bulletin, *Religion and Society*, which often carries articles of theological interest and draws upon Hindu as well as Christian contributors. In addition the CISRS has published a number of books, including several of Devanandan's, and also original theological works by Appasamy, Mark Sunder Rao,

[1] The Department of Research and Post-graduate Studies of the United Theological College, Bangalore, has plans for the republication of some of these books, and a comprehensive Bibliography, in preparation for a 'Library of Indian Christian Theology', has been prepared by Dr. K. Baago.

[2] See M. M. Thomas, *The Christian Response to the Asian Revolution* (1966), for an excellent introduction to the point of view of the CISRS.

Dhanjibhai Fakirbhai and others. The Institute carries on in very vigorous fashion the tradition started by Devanandan of constructive and well-informed dialogue with Hinduism, and under its sponsorship many actual 'dialogues' have been held. It provides a useful counterbalance to the more academic theological scholarship represented by the *Indian Journal of Theology*. Both approaches are important.

Some Contemporary Writers

In the years since independence numerous theologians have been at work in India whose writings have dealt with some particular aspect of theology but who have not written extensively enough to merit the attention which we have given to the major figures we have so far studied. The task of selection is an invidious one, but we shall glance briefly at the work of five writers, each of whom represents a different theological 'front'.

Surjit Singh—The Nature of Personality

Dr. Surjit Singh is a professional theologian who now lives in America. His book, *Preface to Personality* (1952) which is perhaps the most thorough-going attempt by an Indian theologian to work out a Christian doctrine of personality, is a study of Radhakrishnan's Neo-Vedāntic view that God is ultimately the impersonal Absolute and that man, though he may have a separate 'individuality', has really no separate 'personality' of ultimate significance, since in the end the *ātman* and the *paramātman* are identical. Radhakrishnan holds that the transcendental self or *ātman* is alone permanent, while the empirical self or personality is simply a limitation and distortion which should be dispensed with as soon as possible. Surjit Singh gives a Christian 'personalist' critique of this view, and his work is clearly influenced more by western thinkers like Kierkegaard, Berdyaev, Buber and Temple than by any Indian school of thought.

In order to understand the meaning of personality in both God and man he turns to 'the fact of Christ', and, like Chakkarai, finds the secret of the person of Christ most clearly demonstrated in the resurrection; for it is there that we see, in the resurrection of the body, the demonstration that the *body* is an essential ingredient in the total personality. It is not merely the incarnate, historic Jesus of Nazareth who has a body; the risen Christ is a psycho-somatic unity also:

> The idea behind resurrection is that soul-body is the complete or whole man. The body in general, representing historical individuality, is not discarded.[1]

In the resurrection we see the positive relationship of God to the world of matter and of man, a relationship which is as distinctive of the Judaeo-Christian doctrine of man as it is repugnant to Greek and Hindu. Surjit Singh points out how the early fathers, in order to win the Greeks, developed the doctrine of the Logos which 'bears witness to the truth of the reciprocal implication of God and the world'[2]. In some such way a doctrine needs to be worked out today which will demonstrate to Hindus that sure 'link' between God and the world which is so fundamental in Christianity. The implication is that when we really understand the meaning of personality as it is seen at its truest in Christ—and so also in God and man—we shall find the needed link. For Christ, the divine-human, soul-body, resurrected Christ, *is* the firm relation, the necessary link between God and man.

Surjit Singh's emphasis on Christ as the 'type' of personality is helpful. His exposition suffers, perhaps, by being too western in terminology; a similar attempt using and developing the term *puruṣa* would be very interesting.

S. Kulandran—The Meaning of Grace

One of the most scholarly studies of a particular doctrine in its Christian and Hindu forms is Bishop S. Kulandran's book on grace.[3] Dr. Kulandran is bishop of the Jaffna Diocese (in Ceylon) of the Church of South India and his book represents the mature reflection of an experienced theologian and church leader. He gives an account of the Christian conception of grace as seen in the New Testament (especially in Paul), and in Augustine and Luther, making it clear that his own position is within the tradition represented by *sola gratia* and *sola fide*. The second section of the book is a detailed exposition of the meaning of grace in the various Hindu theistic traditions, both Vaiṣṇavite and Śaivite. He comes to the conclusion that the Hindu idea of grace, even in such a conception as the *prapatti* or total self-surrender of Southern Vaiṣṇavism, is quite inade-

[1] Surjit Singh, *Preface to Personality : Christology in Relation to Radhakrishnan's Philosophy* (1952), p. 112.

[2] *ibid.*, p. 114.

[3] S. Kulandran, *Grace : a Comparative Study of the Doctrine in Christianity and Hinduism* (1964).

quate for the interpretation of grace in Christianity. So too the Vaiṣṇavite doctrine of *avatāra* fails, through its innate docetism, to help our understanding of Christ's incarnation.

Thus Kulandran's view of the usefulness of the *bhakti* tradition as a *praeparatio* is very different from Appasamy's. He finds the reason for the inadequacy of the Hindu idea of grace in its failure to understand either the utter righteousness of God or the utter sinfulness of man:

> The need for a person to occupy himself intently with the subject of grace in its stark outline arises when he stands before a God, holy and righteous beyond all human imaginings, and feel his achievements and claims crumbling around him and the garment of his saintliness singed into utter nothingness.[1]

The author's examination of Hinduism convinces him that it is lacking in precisely this feeling.

In this connection Kulandran's treatment of the Hindu conception of sin (*pāpa* and *mala*) is illuminating, particularly in his discussion of the difference between the Hindu *ātman* and the Christian idea of personality—a theme which we have just been examining in Surjit Ṣingh. The *ātman* in Hinduism remains fundamentally untouched by sin, and so stays detached from its experience, for although it may take on a succession of personalities as one incarnation succeeds another, these personalities are ultimately alien to it. It is not surprising, therefore, that Hinduism seldom experiences the sense of man's total sinfulness before the holiness of God. According to Christianity it is the integral personality who sins and who stands before the holy God, and that personality, that particular individual person, must be reconciled with God. 'The need for reconciliation does not exist in Hinduism, because the soul is possessed of a worth in its own right.'[2]

Dr. Kulandran is at his best in grappling with some of the issues which Indian theology sometimes seems to avoid, and here his approach reminds one of Goreh. One could mention his exposition of sin, of the meaning of the Cross, and his penetrating attack on the 'moral influence' theory of the atonement, which, as we have seen, is so often accepted by Indian theologians. On all these points his views are Pauline and Lutheran and are stated in uncompromising western terminology. It would seem that, even provided one accepts Kulandran's demon-

[1] *op. cit.*, p. 270.
[2] *ibid.*, p. 239.

stration of the inadequacy of the Hindu as compared with the Christian conception of grace, there is still need for the doctrine of grace to be expressed, with fully Christian content, in terms which are meaningful to Indian—including Hindu—readers.

Dhanjibhai Fakirbhai—The Theology of Love

The writings of Professor Dhanjibhai Fakirbhai, who died in 1967 at the age of seventy-two, are worthy of note as a distinct *genre* in Indian theological literature in that they present profound ideas of Christian doctrine in very clear and concise, almost aphoristic language, with Indian terminology used in a very constructive way.[1] They have the additional merit that they are written primarily for Hindu readers, and that each book has a Gujarati version, so that even in the English editions the underlying Indian language structure is perceptible. Prof. Dhanjibhai was born a Hindu in Baroda and grew up in an atmosphere of devout *bhakti*. He became a Christian as a young man and after retirement from his work as a professor of physics devoted himself to the writing of Christian literature presenting the Christian faith in a way that would appeal to Hindus. His most widely-read book is *Hriday Gitā* (The Song of the Heart), which presents the teaching of Jesus in a dialogue form based on the *Bhagavadgitā*. Two of his books, *Khristopanishad* and *The Philosophy of Love*, have appeared in English.

The dominant note of Dhanjibhai's theology is that God can best be described as Love, *prema*. He can indeed be described as *Saccidānanda*, but we can go even further and say that he is Love, for Love includes and subsumes everything else. Where intellect fails, and can describe God only in negative terms (*neti, neti*), Love goes further, for love transcends all other categories, and to call God Love is to go even higher than *nirguṇa Brahman*. The doctrines of creation and redemption are also seen in terms of Love, and indeed every section of the book *The Philosophy of Love* is a description of some aspect of God's Love in action. Creation, for example, is not the result of illusion, nor did it take place from independently existing elements ;[2] rather

[1] Dhanjibhai Fakirbhai, *Khristopanishad* (1965). This contains a brief critical introduction.

Dhanjibhai Fakirbhai, *The Philosophy of Love* (1966). There is an interesting review of this book. *The Christian Approach to the Hindu through Literature : Problems of Terminology*, by R. M. Clark in *IJT*, XII/4 (1963), (discussing the original Gujarati version).

[2] i.e. the *advaita* and *Sāṃkhya* doctrines are rejected.

> The origin and development of creation took place out of the very nature of God, which is Love. In creation there is nothing like ignorance (*ajñāna*), illusion or fall. Rather it is simply the spontaneous expansion of God's love. Creation is the revelation of Absolute Love (*Parama Prema, Parabrahman*). And so the created universe itself is good, not evil; far from being impure, it is pure and holy.[1]

It is not enough, then, to describe God's relation to man as that of Creator to creature; it is also that of Father to son.[2]

Sin is estrangement from God's Love—'indeed the worst possible evil, the worst possible sin is the destruction of the bond of Love'[3]—and salvation is the restoration of the bond of Love between man and God which sin has broken. It is because of Love that God becomes incarnate in Christ, and the great work of God's Love is Christ's suffering, for 'forgiveness which does not involve suffering is meaningless and worthless'.[4] And to this work we must reply in 'the response to Love'.

Just as Dhanjibhai had interpreted *Saccidānanda* as being subsumed under the more comprehensive category of Love, so he sees the life in Christ—what he calls 'Spiritual Being'—as transcending the three traditional *mārgas* of *karma*, *bhakti* and *jñāna* in an all-inclusive *yoga* of Love. He re-interprets the three *mārgas* and feels that each has its place in the fully-developed Christian life as the *Way of Action through Love* (*karma-mārga*), the *Way of Devotion* (*bhakti*) and the *Way of Loving Knowledge* (*jñāna*) in the sense of personal knowledge of God. It is Love which unites the three ways:

> So it is that the complete *yoga* of Action, Worship and Knowledge, (*karma*, *bhakti* and *jnāna*) is attained through the *Way of Love* (*prema yoga*). To love God with all our hearts, with all our mind, with all our understanding, with all our powers, with all our soul—with our whole personality—*that* is the way of Love.[5]

Mark Sunder Rao—Non-Alterity

An interesting attempt to define the nature of the believer's union with God in a way which combines the different 'strands' of Hindu thought has recently been made by Mark Sunder Rao,

[1] *Phil. of Love*, p. 2.
[2] *ibid.*, p. 3.
[3] *ibid.*
[4] *ibid.*, p. 7.
[5] *ibid.*, p. 12.

a veteran Indian Christian leader who is now on the staff of the CISRS, Bangalore.[1] As the result of an overwhelming yogic experience of union with Christ he came to the conviction that all life is held together in him; 'otherness' is abolished and 'at-one-ness' or *ananyatva* takes its place. Rao translates this term, which literally means 'un-other-ness', as 'Non-Alterity'; it is the union or communion which results when previous alienation is overcome, and because of this dynamic and dialectical character it must be carefully distinguished from the static monism of traditional *advaita*. Rao finds western equivalents in such terms as *perichoresis* and *co-inherence* which signify an interpenetration of the divine and the human, a unity of two elements which are held in a dialectical tension.

He feels that the various Hindu systems are simply different ways of describing the experience of union with God—*advaita* with its stress on identity and on *jñāna mārga*, Rāmānuja with distinctness yet inseparability, the *Śaiva Siddhānta* with *prapatti* or self-surrender, Madhva with his sense of utter dependence on God—and that so the systems are not mutually exclusive, and each has its contribution to make. For him, however, the two most helpful illustrations of *ananyatva*, the overcoming of otherness, are to be found in the Christian doctrines of the Trinity and the Incarnation. Three Persons unite in one Godhead by *perichoresis*; the divine and the human interpenetrate in the unity, the *ananyatva*, of the incarnate Son. Here is a pattern for the union of the *bhakta* with God:

> According to this way of understanding the two doctrines of Trinity and the Incarnation we can, I believe, correctly claim for the Christian believer a non-dualist theology and philosophy. These two doctrines are, I believe, the charter of Christian non-dualism or *Ananyatva*.[2]

This dynamic union of man with God is neither ontological nor 'moral'; it is 'pneumatological', the work of the Spirit. And it is a relationship which is deeper than the mere 'I-Thou' of Buber. Rao characterises it as 'I-in-Thee; Thou-in-me'—a mutual indwelling in which all egocentricity and alienation is overcome by love (*agape*) in a new type of spiritual *yoga*, which is the supreme goal of the spiritual life. This life Rao describes as:

[1] Mark Sunder Rao, *Ananyatva: Realization of Christian Non-Duality* (1964). There is a good review article by James E. Whitehurst, 'Realization of Christian Non-Duality' in *Religion and Society*, XII/1, (1965), pp. 66 ff.

[2] M. S. Rao, *op. cit.*, p. 25.

the consummation of the union, *sāyujya*, of God and man; it consists of an experience of *ananyatva*, non-duality; it has its source in the very nature of the Godhead, in the perichoresis of the Trinity and the Incarnation.[1]

Most of the theologians we have studied have shown themselves to be very largely confined within the 'cluster of ideas' of a single Hindu system, either *advaita* or theism. Rao however steps outside this barrier and makes a deliberate attempt to combine elements from both traditions, subsuming them under his new category of *ananyatva*. Perhaps he underestimates the difficulty of combining these traditions. Yet his attempt to show, in Hindu terminology, that union with God is something more dynamic than mere 'non-dualism', and to combine insights from the Bible, the Fathers, Hinduism and modern personalist philosophy into a new concept of 'Non-Alterity' seems to point the way to a constructive interaction of Hindu and Christian mysticism.

Paul Sudhākar—The Evangelical Tradition

No survey of contemporary Indian Protestant theology would be complete without reference to the strong conservative evangelical tradition which in recent years has crystallised around the Evangelical Fellowship of India. It is probably not unfair to say that in their writings the members of this tradition reflect a type of theology which has little to distinguish it from similar literature in the West, except perhaps for illustrations drawn from Indian life, like those which lend vividness to the writings of the famous Sikh convert evangelist, Brother Bakht Singh.[2] We shall restrict ourselves to a brief glimpse of the work of one who, with a conservative background, has nevertheless sought to use Indian forms of thought and experience—Sri Paul Sudhakar.

Paul Sudhākar is a powerful and effective evangelist and is a Vice-President of the Union of Evangelical Students of India.[3] He grew up as a Hindu, studied philosophy under Dr. Radhakrishnan, and in 1947 at the age of twenty-five, in an experience very similar to that of Sundar Singh, became a Christian. Contrary to what many people imagine to be the attitude of all Indian 'evangelist', Sudhākar did not experience a radical break with

[1] *ibid.*, p. 43.

[2] Cf. Bakht Singh, *The Skill of His Loving Hands* (reprinted 1961), which is autobiographical.

[3] Art. 'Paul Sudhākar' in *Aikya* (SCM of India), Sept. 1964.

his Hindu background, and he holds that the liberal Hindu tradition from which he came was conducive to Christianity. For him, Christ is not to be described as the 'fulfilment' of Hinduism, nor as 'present' or 'hidden' in Hinduism, but rather as 'the Answer':

> Hinduism is a hunger and Christ comes to satisfy it. So I emphasise Christ 'the answer' rather than Christ 'the fulfilment'. God puts the hunger and provides the food for the hunger in Christ.[1]

He feels that much evangelical preaching tends to put too much stress on the Jesus of history and to neglect the Logos, the eternal Christ who rouses so many responsive chords in Hinduism. We must preach the Christ as well as Jesus:

> 'What think ye of Christ?' is the Lord's question which has been only partially answered by the world. India has also the answer to this question . . . Jesus Christ is the Saviour, not Jesus, not Christ. To put it in another way, the Word who became Flesh is the Way, the Truth and the Life, and not the Word only nor the Incarnation only. It is my belief that Hindus have known the Logos. We who have preached so much the Christ of History would do well to see the Christ beyond and behind history in the non-Jewish religions prior to the Christian era.[2]

Sudhākar's theology is thoroughly 'evangelical', and when speaking to Christians he does not hesitate to use western terminology, but when talking to Hindus he avoids words 'like regeneration, redemption, substitution, etc.'[3] and uses such terms as *Iśvara*, *Brahman*, *yoga*, *darśana*, the three *mārgas*, as well as the *bhakti* concept of grace, which Kulandran finds inadequate. These words are not treated as exact equivalents of the Christian terms, but they make preaching possible. In one of his pamphlets, *The Fourfold Ideal*, he gives a very helpful account of the fourfold conception of *mokṣa* as *sālokya*, *sāmipya*, *sārupya* and *sāyojya*.[4] Adam, as original man made in God's image, possessed the fourfold *mokṣa*, being in full fellowship with God and 'in the form' of God (*sārupya*). Fallen man has lost the fourfold ideal, and down the centuries has struggled to regain it. Christ manifests the ideal in his own person, and also makes

[1] *Aikya*, loc. cit.
[2] Letter to the writer, 23-3-66.
[3] *Aikya*, loc. cit.
[4] Undated pamphlet, *The Fourfold Ideal*. For the meanings of the terms v. supra, p. 152, footnote.

it available to man, and it is only in union with Christ that we can regain the ideal, as in *sāmipya* or encounter we come to the Cross which is the meeting place between God and man.

Sudhākar has not written any full-length books. He is significant, however, not merely because of his great gifts as an evangelist, but also because he demonstrates the fact that the search for a meaningful Indian terminology is not just the passing fad of a certain kind of theologian, but is an essential part of the evangelistic task of the Church in India.

Recent Roman Catholic Insights

Within the Roman Catholic Church in India the tradition started by de Nobili, renewed by Upādhyāya and carried on by Johanns continues to have its exponents and in recent years some outstanding scholarly work has appeared, notably in connection with the De Nobili College, Poona, Santi Bhavan, Calcutta, and several other institutions and groups. Like the *Christian Students' Library*, these publications are still largely the work of foreign scholars such as R. V. de Smet, the expert on Śankara, and there have so far been fewer Roman Catholic than Protestant Indian theologians, partly, no doubt, because of a policy of caution which has hesitated to follow up the work of Brahmabandhab. There are today however many signs of increasing Indian participation in the impressive volume of Roman Catholic theological studies in India. We shall select two writers as representative of recent tendencies, Swāmi Parama Arubi Anandam (Fr. Jules Monchanin) and Fr. Raymond Panikkar.

Jules Monchanin

In the case of Fr. Monchanin we must depart from our rule of studying only theologians of Indian birth, for he was a Frenchman who did not come to India till 1939, when he was already forty-four years old.[1] We include him, however, because he so fully identified himself with the Indian tradition, because his work represents an interesting and deliberate development of the theology of Brahmabandhab Upādhyāya, and because his writings and his example have been influential in much recent thought on the question of dialogue with Hinduism.

In 1950 he secured the permission of his superiors to lead the life of an ochre-clad *sannyāsi* in a small *āshram* on the banks

[1] See *Swami Parama Arubi Anandam : Fr. J. Monchanin, A Memorial* (1959). (Cited as *Swami*).

of the river Kaveri in South India. He took the name of *Parama-ārupya-ānanda* ('joy in the Supreme Formless One') in witness of his special devotion to the Holy Spirit, and the *āshram* was called *Saccidānanda Aśrama*, since the purpose of its foundation was that Monchanin and his companion, H. Le Saux, might devote their lives to the adoration and contemplation of God, One in Three, *Saccidānanda.*[1]

It is above all in his understanding of the Trinity as *Saccidānanda* that Monchanin carried forward the work of Upādhyāya, for he saw in the Trinity the solution of some of those antinomies which we have so often noted in Hindu thought:

> Only the mystery of the Trinity is capable of resolving the antinomies which cause Hindu thought to swing endlessly between monism and pluralism, between a personal and an impersonal God. India awaits without knowing it the Revelation of the Trinitarian mystery, a Revelation inaccessible both to metaphysical genius and to holiness.[2]

In *Saccidānanda* monism and pluralism—the one and the three—are reconciled, as are the personal and the impersonal—*Iśvara* and *Brahman*, and so the Christian can fill *Saccidānanda* with a richness of meaning which is lacking in Hinduism:

> More fervently and with greater appreciation than any of his fellow sannyāsins, can the Christian monk utter: *Sat*, when thinking of the Father, the 'Principleless' Principle, the very source and end of the expansion and 're-collection' of the divine life; *Cit*, when remembering the eternal Son, the Logos, the intellectual, consubstantial Image of the Existent; *Ānanda*, when meditating on the Paraclete, unifying together the Father and the Son.[3]

Monchanin's earlier studies in the West had brought him into sympathy with the mystical tradition represented by the pseudo-Dionysius, Eckhart, St. John of the Cross and the modern Bulgakov, and he felt that this Christian monism was very close to Indian spirituality. Unlike the *advaitin* mystics of Hinduism, however, he believed that contemplation cannot be of the *impersonal* Absolute, for even *nirguṇa Brahman*, on the Christian understanding, is personal, since *Brahman* as *Saccidānanda* is

[1] Cf. J. Monchanin and H. le Saux, *A Benedictine Ashram* (revised edn. 1964).

[2] Quoted in J.-A. Cuttat, *The Encounter of Religions* (1960), p. 16.

[3] *Swami*, p. 18. The language recalls that of Keshab Chandra Sen, v. supra, p. 35.

always engaged in the internal colloquy of the Trinity. Christian mysticism, he says, must be Trinitarian or it is nothing.[1] Here, then, in the very heart of the Trinity, is the solution of the antinomy of the one and the many :

> For us God is neither the impersonal nor the unimpersonal. In his intimate life he is Three Persons . . . We believe that it is not despite his Trinity but in very consequence of this Trinity that God is One. He is *Sat*, He is *Cit*, He is *Ānanda*, Being, Consciousness, Bliss—in such a manner that he constitutes three centres of personality, each one polarised by the other two. The Trinity resolves itself in Unity without becoming less and the Unity expands itself in Trinity without becoming more.[2]

The personalism involved in this kind of Trinitarian mysticism is not, however, that of *bhakti*. Monchanin makes a rather sweeping condemnation of all attempts to find a meeting place for Christianity and Hinduism at the level of *bhakti*, even when the object of devotion is Christ.[3] His quest is, like that of Upādhyāya, for union with God at the highest, that is the Trinitarian, level, where there is a different kind of personalism from that of *bhakti*. He writes :

> The divine existence is a personal one, but not a mono-personal one. God is not *it*, is not *he*, is not *I*, but rather is *I* and *I* and *I*. His very existence is identical with tri-personal relationship.[4]

The personal union we seek to find in Christian mysticism is with the highest, with *nirguṇa Brahman*, yet such union must share in the tri-personal inner colloquy of *Saccidānanda*. India, he feels, has been specially prepared by God for this type of mysticism, for where else have men penetrated, by natural theology, to knowledge of the threeness of the One ? In a typical passage, difficult to follow but worth following, Monchanin describes how the worshipper can rise to union with the Trinity, and it is interesting to see how, like Goreh and Chakkarai, he begins with the Spirit, then goes on to Christ, and finally to the Father and the Three-in-One :

> Is not India destined in a very special way to contemplate the mystery of the blessed Trinity ? To begin with, to the contemplation of the Divine Spirit, the 'uncircumscribed' Person, who

[1] *ibid.*, p. 187.
[2] *ibid.*, p. 200.
[3] *ibid.*, p. 221.
[4] *ibid.*, p. 186.

appears only under fluid forms, breath, water . . . fire . ., the Person who is not perceived through the visible like the Word, but through spiritual realities, the charisms, and above all, the *agape*, the charity, the communion of saints, the mysterious immanence of all in every one and of every one in all. He is the very one whom India is awaiting.

From Him, she will pass on to the Word of glory, to the Risen One, clothed with the splendour of the world—then to the Word of sorrow assuming every pain to transmute it into the paschal bliss—finally to the Word in His terrestrial life, not an illusory one as the *avatāra's* but a 'realizing reality' in which every thing, the world itself and our very individualities, have their consistency.

The contemplation of India will end in the abyss of the Father, the Person unmanifest in Himself, whom the two others manifest, in eternity, but the generation of the Word and the procession of the Holy Ghost, and, in time, by the divine missions, the projection of the eternal processions: the Incarnation of the Word and the sending forth of the Paraclete in the incessant Pentecost which is the Church.[1]

In this passage we can catch, behind the Latin and Gallic phraseology which was Monchanin's western heritage, the genuine note—including the rejection of *avatāra* !—of the tradition started by Sen and carried further by Upādhyāya. Here, in a combination of the apophatic mysticism of the West with the *advaita* of Śankara, the atmosphere is rarified indeed, and one wonders to what extent a mystical practice is justified which is so difficult for the ordinary Christian *bhakta* to follow. The attempt is nevertheless a very impressive one.

We have still to examine Monchanin's solution of the other antinomy, that of the personal and the impersonal, *saguṇa* and *nirguṇa*. He finds his key in a sentence from Paul's Epistle to the Colossians: 'For in Him (Christ) dwelleth all the fulness of the Godhead bodily' (Col. 2:9).[2] Stated very briefly, his interpretation is that the word 'Godhead' (Greek *theotes*—a word which occurs only here in the New Testament) describes God *in his essence*, and so corresponds to *nirguṇa Brahman*, while the common word 'God' (*theos*) describes God in his relations to man and so corresponds to *saguṇa Brahman*.[3] But the text does more than this, for it demonstrates God's self-revelation in

[1] *ibid.*, p. 103.
[2] *ibid.*, pp. 177 ff.
[3] Compare Eckhart's distinction of *Gott* and *Gottheit*. For a recent discussion of this whole line of thought, see the chapter 'Beyond the God of Theism' in J. A. T. Robinson, *Exploration into God*, London, 1967, pp. 130 ff.

Christ, in whom the 'fulness' (*pleroma*) of the Godhead dwells in bodily form; that is, Christ, in his incarnate life, reveals in bodily form the fulness of *nirguṇa Brahman*.

Applying this exegesis to the antinomy of *advaita*, we can say that the words God or *Iśvara* or *saguṇa Brahman* point to the divine essence in so far as man is related to it, that is to its aspect of immanence. The words Godhead or *nirguṇa Brahman* point to the same divine essence in its essentiality, unrelated to anything else, that is to its aspect of transcendence. Yet these two words, God and Godhead, *saguṇa* and *nirguṇa Brahman*, do not designate contradictory attributes, but rather complementary aspects of the same Reality. To contemplate Godhead, *nirguṇa Brahman*, means to look at the divine essence as it is in itself—'the unknown and unknowable "Beyond" to which the praise of Silence is the only hymn.'[1] Here, in the breaking off into silence of apophatic mysticism, Monchanin finds *advaita* fulfilled in the contemplation of the divine *Saccidānanda*.

Raymond Panikkar

Fr. Raymond Panikkar was born in Spain in 1918, the son of a Hindu father and a Spanish Roman Catholic mother, and was brought up in an environment of both Christianity and Hinduism, learning the Vedānta with the Bible. He studied in Spain, Germany and Italy, and in recent years has been living in Benares. He has contributed to many learned journals and has become well known in ecumenical circles in India and elsewhere. His best known work so far is his book *The Unknown Christ of Hinduism*, published in 1964.[2]

This is a very interesting and penetrating book. It is also very difficult, for Fr. Panikkar manages to be profoundly technical in both Thomistic and Vedāntic terminology at the same time! Taking his stand on such texts as Acts 14 : 16-17, 'He left not himself without witnesses', and Acts 17 : 23, 'Whom therefore ye ignorantly worship, him declare I unto you', he concludes that Christ is present in Hinduism, and that so Hinduism has for millions of people been an effective means of salvation and union with God, precisely *because* of the hidden presence of Christ within it. It is in Christianity, however, that Christ is *fully* revealed, and so the work of the Christian mission is that of 'unveiling' the hidden Christ of Hinduism, and the relation-

[1] *ibid.*, p. 179.
[2] Other major works by Panikkar, published in German, Spanish and Italian, are not yet available in English.

ship of Hinduism to Christianity can be spoken of as that of seed to fruit, of desire to accomplishment, above all of death to resurrection, for it is in dying with Christ and rising in Him that Hinduism will find its true meaning, since 'risen Hinduism' will in fact be Christianity.[1]

The method which Panikkar adopts in order to demonstrate this conclusion to his Hindu friends is the interesting and promising one of the exegesis of a text from the Hindu Scriptures, the chosen text being an important, if obscure, verse from the beginning of the *Brahma Sutra* (1 : 1.2). This verse reads *Janmadi asya yatah*, which means approximately '*Brahman* is the total ultimate cause of the world'.[2]

This text is a fundamental one for Hinduism and has been interpreted in a variety of ways by interpreters of the different schools, for example those of Śankara and Rāmānuja. For it poses a problem : if *Brahman* is the unconditioned Absolute, as Śankara held, how can the world be said to proceed from him ? This, as we have repeatedly seen, is one of the major problems of Hindu philosophy—the bridging of the gap between *Brahman* and the world. Sankara's later followers were obliged to admit that it is not *Brahman* but *Iśvara* who is the cause of this world, though they of course maintained that *Iśvara*, the personal God, is in fact none other than *Brahman*, but *Brahman* in his aspect of personal God and Creator. Thus *Iśvara* becomes the 'link' between the undifferentiated *Brahman* and the created world, including the world of men.

It is precisely here, says Panikkar—and this is the kernel of what he has to say in this book—that we are to find our point of entry, for the unresolved antinomy of the One and the many in Hinduism can be solved if we realise that *Iśvara* is no other than Christ, the Logos, the Agent of creation, the Mediator between God and man. And so, with a wealth of scholarly detail, Panikkar interprets his text as meaning, '*That from which this world comes forth and to which it returns and by which it is sustained, that "that" is Christ*'.[3] When Hindus think of *Iśvara*—true revealer of *Brahman*, personal aspect of *Brahman*, agent of creation, origin of grace, yet at the same time himself fully *Brahman*—then, says Panikkar, they are in fact, though without realising it, acknowledging the hidden Christ. And the loving task of the Christian mission is to unveil this Christ.

[1] Raymond Panikkar, *The Unknown Christ of Hinduism* (1964), p. 17.
[2] Panikkar, *op. cit.*, pp. 74 ff.
[3] *ibid.*, p. 131.

Here, then, we have a suggested solution to the problem of the 'link' between God and the world of men which is different from the others which have been proposed. It is true that many theologians have seen Christ as the 'link'—Upādhyāya for example as the Logos-*Cit* of *Saccidānanda*, and Surjit Singh as the true 'person' uniting body and soul, humanity and divinity—but this explicit identification of Christ with *Iśvara* is something new, and indeed rather perplexing for Indian Christians who customarily use the word *Iśvara* for 'God', i.e. the Triune God. The validity and usefulness of the identification (which Panikkar does not claim to be absolute but rather to be a 'pointer') depends on the extent to which *Iśvara* can be regarded in Hinduism as not inferior to *Brahman*, and this is a point on which Panikkar by no means proves his case. He relies on the personalist trend which is found in the *Kaṭha*, *Mundaka* and *Svetasvetara Upaniṣads* as against the dominant *advaita*—what he calls their 'counter-offensive in favour of a God superior to *Brahman*'[1]—and tends to neglect the fact that a great many Hindus today think of *Iśvara* as being in fact *ontologically* inferior to *Brahman* because existing only at the *vyavahārika* level of existence and being in fact subject to *māyā*.

Panikkar holds that *Brahman* and *Iśvara*, though undoubtedly different in a sense, both point to the same ultimate reality :

> If we penetrate into the very thing meant—into the *res significata* as Thomas Aquinas would put it — . . . we shall recognise that 'God' and 'Brahman' refer to that Ultimate Mystery, to that attributeless Absolute which is the last and definitive Reality.[2]

And in fact we can only understand that Absolute adequately if we allow the ideas of *Brahman* and *Iśvara* to correct each other and prevent us from swinging too far to one side or the other. These Indian ideas may even help western theology to come to a clearer understanding of the nature of God :

> The personal God without the correction of Brahman may well become an anthropomorphic idol ; the transpersonal Brahman without its complementary vision as God, may well dissolve in the mere abstraction of the *ens commune*. We believe that Indian wisdom offers here immense possibilities of deepening the conception of the Absolute without slipping into the pitfalls in which Indian philosophy has been the first to fall victim.[3]

[1] *ibid.*, p. 107.
[2] *ibid.*, p. 112.
[3] *ibid.*, p. 113.

Panikkar goes on to give a very illuminating picture of *Iśvara*, in which he draws heavily on the *bhakti* tradition. *Iśvara* is the revelation of *Brahman*; he is the personal aspect of *Brahman*; he is that 'aspect' of *Brahman* responsible for the creation of the world; he is the 'Lord', bringer of grace, destroyer of *māyā*; he is conscious, and knows that he is *Brahman*; he is the one through whom souls (*jiva*) realise that they are linked with *Brahman*; it is he who is revealed as *avatāra*; though distinct from *Brahman* he is also identical. In other words, *Iśvara* is the mediator between God and the world of men, and all this impressive evidence points clearly in one direction—to the fulfilment of the concept of *Iśvara* in Christ. And so Panikkar comes to his conclusion, what he calls the Christological *bhāṣya*[1] on the *Brahma Sutra*:

> *That from which all things proceed and to which all things return and by which all things are* (sustained in their own being) that 'that' is God, but *primo et per se* not a silent Godhead, not a kind of inaccessible Brahman, not God the Father and source of the whole Divinity, but the true Isvara, God the Son, the Logos, the Christ.[2]

Panikkar's exegesis of the *Brahma Sutra* has led us to see how under the *Iśvara* of Hinduism the hidden Christ is waiting to be revealed. It is an impressive demonstration.

Panikkar's attitude to Hinduism will have become fairly clear from what we have seen of his method. Like Devanandan and Monchanin he comes in a spirit of loving dialogue, anxious to know and understand Hinduism from within, for 'Christ is already there in Hinduism in so far as Hinduism is a true religion'[3]. But Hinduism does not yet see him clearly:

> Christ has not unveiled his whole face, has not yet completed his mission there. He still has to grow up and to be recognized. Moreover, He still has to be crucified there, dying with Hinduism as He died with Judaism and with the Hellenistic religions in order to rise again, as the same Christ (who is already in Hinduism), but then as a risen Hinduism, as Christianity.[4]

Hinduism with all its incredible variety and inner contradictions is, he holds, simply an '*existential dharma*'; it has no real and defined dogma, no *essential* contents, and Christianity's bold claim is that it provides the true contents for the merely exis-

[1] *bhāṣya*=commentary.
[2] *op. cit.*, p. 126.
[3] *ibid.*, p. 17.
[4] *ibid.*

tential Hindu *dharma*. In other words, Christianity can reveal to Hinduism the *res significata*, the true object of its agelong quest. The relation of Hinduism to Christianity, then, is not one which can be solved by the 'victory' of one over the other, or by any kind of syncretism. It is the relation of seed to fruit, or rather of death to resurrection. Hinduism needs 'conversion' or transformation—

> a passage through death to resurrection . . . a real descent into the living waters of baptism in order to rise again transformed, converted, enlightened, but not as another thing, another religion. . . Hinduism has to be actualized, has to give way to the thing itself towards which, allegorically, it is pointing. Yet this does not represent any *real* loss for Hinduism, but the gaining of its soul. Indeed, Hinduism as a positive religion will suffer a transformation which seen from its present state may appear a radical change. It will be no more what it appears today and yet it will be a better *form* of Hinduism, because of its elevation, its *transformation* into a higher sphere.[1]

The Christian mission, then, is not to eradicate or defeat Hinduism but, through the unveiling of the hidden Christ, to help in its death and resurrection, its transformation into something the same yet new.

A New Moment in Dialogue

Today a certain 'converging' momentum is apparent in the developing dialogue between Christians and Hindus, and it is a rapprochement which brings together Protestant, Roman Catholic and Syrian Christians as well as Hindus. One who has taken a leading part in recent dialogue, Murray Rogers of the Jyotiniketan Ashram, Bareilly, points out that in the past three different attitudes have been typical of the relation between Christians and Hindus: there has been the polemical attitude, seen in the early missionaries and to some extent in Goreh; there has been the neutralist attitude of the great western Indologists like Max Müller; and there has been the syncretistic attitude seen in people like Toynbee or Radhakrishnan. The 'new' attitude of dialogue which is now emerging has several notable features.[2]

[1] *ibid.*, p. 61.
[2] C. Murray Rogers, 'Hindu and Christian—a Moment breaks' in *Religion and Society*, XII/1, (1965), pp. 35 ff. See also Henri Le Saux (Swami Abhishiktānanda), *La Rencontre de l'Hindouisme et du Christianisme* (1966).

As its prerequisite it demands a readiness to listen to what the partner in dialogue has to say, a certain 'putting into brackets' of one's own convictions, an *epoché* or 'suspension of judgment in front of the thing itself, in order to let it speak'.[1] Granted this *epoché* we must then engage in an 'inner' dialogue in which, while retaining a firm grasp of Christ, we 'dive deeply into non-Christian spiritualities', studying the Hindu Scriptures and trying to understand and 'live' the whole Hindu religious experience. As we do this we become more aware than before of the uniqueness and transcendence of Christ and begin to see a coming together in Christ of all that is genuine in non-Christian spirituality and experience. We find that we are at the point where Hindu experience begins to be purified in Christ, and our own Christian faith has been deepened and enriched by what we have learnt.

Then comes the 'external' dialogue, when we actually meet our Hindu friend. We meet him *in Christ*, as one made in the image of God who is already being drawn towards Christ by the Spirit. Remembering that Christ said, 'I have not found such faith in Israel' (Matt. 8 : 10), we acknowledge what we have learnt from our partner, and are prepared to hear God speak through him, just as we believe that God speaks through us. Then for a time in our walk together Christ remains *incognito*, as he did on the Emmaus road, yet our hearts—our Hindu friend's and ours—burn within us as we hear his words and become conscious of his hidden presence with us.[2] And then at last comes the moment of unveiling, when the true Face of the unknown Christ is revealed :

> This is the moment of conversion, a work of the Spirit, when the Risen Christ—in whom the spiritual world of my Hindu, pre-Christian neighbour is gathered up, purified and transformed—is seen, known and worshipped.[3]

In their very different ways the work of all the theologians we have been studying could be said to help in this task of dialogue which culminates in the revealing of the hidden Christ.

[1] J.-A. Cuttat, *op. cit.*, p. 30.
[2] This interpretation of the Emmaus Road is Cuttat's. *Religion and Society*, XII/1, (1965), p. 43.
[3] Rogers, *loc. cit.*

Chapter XII

TYPES AND TERMS OF INDIAN THEOLOGICAL THOUGHT

The Sources of Authority

Our study of a number of Indian theologians has shown a considerable variety of types of theology and we must now attempt to draw together some of the lines of thought which have become visible in the course of our enquiry in order to assess their validity and usefulness in the future development of theology in India. But before doing so we must first turn to what Appasamy has rightly called the primary task of Christian theology in India—the task of settling our sources of authority or *pramāṇas.* This, as the sixteenth century reformers in Europe saw, is a question of fundamental importance, and is especially vital in India where there are so many traditions claiming priority, and where the possibility of syncretism is always present.

Chenchiah would give first place to experience, the personal experience of Christ 'the original stimulus'. Sundar Singh also—who once wrote, 'a revelation which I have received in ecstasy is worth more to me than all the traditional Church teaching'[1]—gives a high place to experience, yet at the same time makes it clear that his experience and visions are always based on Scripture and never contradict it. The brilliant theological insights of Upādhyāya and Panikkar, on the other hand, lead always, as one might expect, to Aquinas and the thirteenth century, and this suggests that for them the teaching of the Church (Appasamy's fourth *pramāṇa*) takes priority over all other sources of authority. Appasamy and Chakkarai, however, agree in assigning first place among the *pramāṇas* to Scripture, and indeed Chakkarai, stressing the fact that this is a distinctively Indian way of looking at things, speaks of Scripture or *śruti* as the *only* authority and the supreme and infallible *pramāṇa.*

If one conclusion of our enquiry may be stressed above all others it is this, that for the Indian Church, as for the Church everywhere, the primary source of authority, the supreme *pramāṇa*, must be the Scriptures, and that no philosophical or ecclesiastical tradition must be allowed to challenge this

[1] Heiler, *op. cit.*, p. 203.

authority.[1] The fact that the Hindu view of the priority of *śruti* among the *pramāṇas* lends support to this assertion makes us realise that the conception of *śruti* itself is a valuable one, which represents a positive contribution of Indian theology to the world Church. The word, as we have seen,[2] has the double meaning of 'Scripture' and 'revelation', both of which, according to the Indian conception, have their origin in hearing, *śruti* being derived from a root *śru* meaning 'to hear'. Indian tradition, including Indian Christian tradition, does indeed give an honoured place to revelation by sight, the unveiling signified by the etymology of the English word (*re-velare*), as for example in Sundar Singh's *darśanas* of the risen Christ, and indeed the word *darśana*, or 'vision' of God, has deep religious significance in India. Yet for Hindus *śruti* is the primary *pramāṇa*, and so too for Christians the *norm* of revelation is by *hearing*, the hearing of the written Word which was originally 'heard' by the writers from the 'speaking' of the Spirit, just as the Hindu *śruti* is supposed to have been heard by the *rishis*. There is much to be said for the view that the word *śruti* is more satisfactory than the Greek *apokalupsis* or the Latin *revelatio* in many contexts, especially in that of revelation through Scripture. It is through the *śruti* of the written Word that the living Word, Christ the Logos-*Cit*, is revealed *ex auditu* in the heard *śruti* of revelation. If with the hearing there is also a vision (*darśana*, *dṛṣṭi*), as happened to Sundar Singh, then the *bhakta* is fortunate indeed. But normally the hearing comes first. Here, then, is a place where the Indian theologian can point to a recognised Hindu tradition and claim it in the service of the Christian faith.

After the *śruti* Hinduism places experience (*anubhava*), and this—though Appasamy accords second place to the Church—would appear to be the right order. The Indian tradition demands direct experience in religion, whether this be the experience of devoted self-surrender to a chosen deity or of calm and blissful absorption in *nirguṇa Brahman*. Hinduism claims to provide here and now the 'realisation' (*sākṣātkāra*, *siddhi*) of union with God, and it was Vivekānanda's question, 'Have you seen God?' which led him to Rāmakrishna, who alone answered him in the affirmative. What has Christianity to offer to the Hindu seeker who comes wanting realisation or immediate experience of God (*pratyakṣa*)? Sundar Singh was able to give one kind of answer

[1] A corollary to this conclusion is the need for a stronger tradition of Biblical exegesis. There are still very few Indian commentaries on the Bible.

[2] v. supra, p. 136.

in his mysticism of the Cross; to him, as to many others in India, realisation came through visions and ecstasies, and this type of religious experience should not be ignored or minimised, for in India it is not uncommon. For most people, however, the answer will be in terms of *śruti* rather than *dṛṣṭi*, in the encounter with Christ through the hearing or reading of the Word. Indian theology points to the fact that we *can* have direct knowledge of Christ, *anubhava* or *pratyakṣa*, but that this experience is normally associated with the *śruti*. Even Sundar Singh, whose frequent and direct experience of Christ is so remarkable and so Indian, was closely bound to the Biblical *śruti* ; his very first vision came to him after burning the Bible, and though he may not have read far he had read enough to know that here was something to reckon with. Few Christians will have Sundar Singh's visions, but all may and should have 'realisation' of Christ, for the *śruti* must result in *anubhava*. Here we see the truth in Chenchiah's stress on experience of ' the raw fact of Christ ', and Chakkarai's Christology of experience.

It is the third *pramāṇa*, inference (*yukti* or *anumāna*), which opens the door for a variety of schools of Indian theology. That faith which is revealed in Scripture and which we have appropriated in our own experience is to be proclaimed, and made intelligible and attractive, to the world around us. India has a rich and diverse tradition of theology and philosophy, notably in the six traditional *darśanas*, in the sub-division of the Vedānta into *advaita* and *viśiṣṭa advaita*, and in the work of the great modern philosophers like Aurobindo and Radhakrishnan. In the West the Platonic and Aristotelian traditions as well as more modern schools like idealism, existentialism and logical positivism have all had their Christian theological exponents, and in India, where so many of the traditional schools still have their enthusiastic adherents, it is important to present the Christian faith in a structure and with a terminology which men can understand and respect. Hitherto the most thorough-going ' systems ' of theology to have appeared have been those of Brahmabandhab, linked with Śankara ; of Appasamy, linked with *bhakti* and Rāmānuja ; and of Chenchiah, linked with Aurobindo. Two other approaches, however, those of Goreh and Sundar Singh, are also of considerable significance because of the principle of inference (*anumāna*) on which they are based, and so before we go on to deal in more detail with some of the types of Indian theology we shall pause for a little to look at the different kinds of reasoning which underlie Indian thought, and which are reflected in Indian Christian theology.

The Logic of Indian Theology

The first tendency to be noted is that of the reconciling of opposites. We have already noticed, for example, how it is possible in Hindu thought to hold simultaneously the belief in such apparently irreconcilable ideas as *nirguṇa* and *saguṇa Brahman*, or in the fact that the soul is subject to illusion and yet is at the same time identical with *Brahman*. This type of reasoning—which Goreh attacked so ruthlessly—represents the conviction of many Hindu thinkers that 'intuition' can reconcile and synthesise opposites ; that so-called 'contradictions' are such only at the mental level but are in truth complementary aspects of reality ; that there is, in Monchanin's words, 'a logic of the infinite' which transcends the logic of the finite,[1] since the higher truth (*paramārtha*) is hidden beyond words and concepts, and cannot be translated into clear-cut ideas. Thus it is easy for Hindu thinkers to say that all religions are true ; what is meant is that on the practical or *vyavahārika* level they are true, but the ultimate Truth which they represent transcends this level, is finally unknowable, and cannot be translated into propositional form. This ultimate Truth is *satya* or *Brahman*, and can in fact be known only through *advaita* Vedānta. The Truth cannot be logically expressed, yet union with the Truth, what Gandhi described as 'insistence on Truth' (*satyāgraha*), brings inner peace.

Western Christian theology has often made use of paradoxes, but not of this type of contradiction whose resolution is as it were lifted into a sphere beyond man's cognition. It would seem that this type of thought, closely related as it is to the theory of different types of existence, can be of little help in Indian Christian theology.

The second type of Indian logic which we have come across is that of analogical thought. We have already discussed Sundar Singh's method of making a vivid parable or analogy serve as a demonstration of a doctrine,[2] and have noted that this is a recognised type of inference in Indian thought. The astonishing thing about Sundar Singh's inferences from his ecstasies is, however, their deep insight and virtually impeccable orthodoxy. The implication would seem to be that the Sadhu was so deeply grounded in the Biblical *śruti* and had such a profound spiritual experience (*anubhava*), that his inference, *yukti*, although it was of the analogical type (*upamāna*) rather than logical in the western

[1] *Swami*, p. 174.
[2] v. supra, p. 97.

sense, yet was controlled as it were from the side of the object in such a way that there was no danger of his being led aside into merely individual paths.

This is an important point, for analogical thinking has been in Sundar Singh and could be in future a profound influence in Indian theology. For it goes back, surely, to the nature of the teaching of Christ himself. His teaching is in parables rather than in logically thought-out propositions. And yet it is controlled from within by the very nature of God himself. In the teaching of Christ who is the Truth, *Satya*, the substance and structure of the ultimate Truth is portrayed, and controls the nature of the teaching. No one can claim to set himself up as an authority in this way, and yet when a Sundar Singh arises, a man of deep Biblical knowledge and with a deep personal experience of Christ, and, from within a living Indian tradition gives teaching of this kind which is verifiable from the *śruti* and even from the teaching of the Church (*sabhā*) such a man should be listened to with deep respect, for God can speak through him and give new insights which a mere formal logic could never deduce.

The third type of logic is that of plain Aristotelian reasoning based on the law of contradiction, the kind of logic used so successfully by Goreh in his 'rational refutation'. Modern India, whose relationship both to western science and sociology and to traditional Hindu orthodoxy has been so skilfully described by Devanandan, uses this western type of logic in all its practical affairs, for there is no lack of distinguished Indian thinkers in such fields as mathematics, atomic science and medical research. As Devanandan has noted, the tendency is for men of this type to forsake orthodox Hinduism and become secularised. The faith of their fathers—or more accurately perhaps their mothers !—will not stand up to the type of logical analysis which they daily apply to the objects of their research.

The Christian faith, if it is to attract such men, must demonstrate that it does not fear the application of this type of logic. The explication of the faith—the explication of the *śruti* and the *anubhava*—must be controlled from the side of the object, that is, by the inner logic of the subject-matter itself. This will involve deep and scholarly study of the Biblical evidence and a refusal to allow any *a priori* mould, however attractive, to shape theology. Even systems like those of Śankara and Rāmānuja should be used only in so far as they serve to illuminate truths which emerge from the 'inner logic' of the object of faith.

* * * *

Having said something about our sources of authority and about the logical processes underlying Indian theology we must now attempt to make some sort of preliminary examination of the terminology which our different theologians have provided for us. We are not here attempting a new presentation of Indian Christian theology, but rather examining some of the 'instruments' which have been put into our hands, in an effort to estimate their effectiveness.

Words for God

What word should we use for God? Christian usage in the Sanskritic languages has tended to settle for either *Deva* or *Iśvara*. *Deva*, though cognate with *theos* and *Deus* and still widely used in many Bible translations and in popular Christian devotion, is manifestly unsatisfactory as it is in Hinduism frequently used in the plural to signify different polytheistic deities. *Iśvara* or *Parameśvara* is more satisfactory as it is seldom used in the plural. However, *Iśvara*, as we have frequently noticed, belongs to the personalist 'strand' of Hindu thought and *advaitins* maintain that beyond *Iśvara* and the personal qualities he represents there is a more ultimate conception of deity, *Brahman*. The question therefore arises, Can Christians use the word *Brahman* for God? Goreh's answer was a clear negative; he had no hesitation in saying that *nirguṅa Brahman* was simply a nullity, and union with such a God the state of 'a stone'. His solution is to say that Hindus—not to say Christians!—must abandon the idea of *Brahman* and recognise that the idea represented by *Iśvara*, as revealed in Christ, is in fact higher and more meaningful than any understanding of *Brahman* could ever be. Yet always one has the uncomfortable feeling that Hindus, hearing the Christian Gospel so proclaimed, will smile and say, 'That is perfectly all right for people at your stage of development; but *our* God is higher, and concern for truth will not allow us to reduce our standards'. And so 'the Christians' God' is dishonoured.

The Fourth Gospel's use of the word Logos shows a different approach to a comparable problem. The pagan world thought of divine action, in creation and providence, in terms of the Logos. The Logos was God at work in the world, and there could be no higher 'name'. So the evangelist in effect said to his Greek readers, 'You say that the Logos created and sustains the world. All right. We say that Christ *is* that Logos'. For him he claimed the highest title known to the non-Christian world, in order that no one could say, 'Our God is higher than yours'. A similar logic would seem to make it plain that Christians—at least in apologetic if not in the language of devotion—should not hesitate to use the word *Brahman* for God. We are not, of course, making a direct comparison of Logos and *Brahman*, but rather pointing to a parallel situation. In order to preserve the uniqueness of Christ the Son the evangelist had to make it clear that the Logos, accepted in much of the contemporary Greek world as the principle of rationality in man and the universe, and as agent of creation, was not superior to Christ, and that indeed it was only in Christ that the Logos-conception could find its full meaning. In a different context—that of the Triune God, not of the Son—Brahmabandhab and others make it clear that *Brahman* can never be regarded as 'higher' than the Christians' God. If Hindus regard *Brahman* as higher than *Iśvara*, then our God cannot be less than *Brahman*, and only in the Trinitarian context can *Brahman* find its full meaning.

No doubt the word Logos sounded Stoic to early Jewish Christians, and certainly the word *Brahman* sounds 'Hindu' to many Christians in India. In the minds of many people the word is linked, as indeed it is etymologically, with the Brahman caste and with the personal god *Brahmā*. Yet originally the word had no such overtones; it is a neuter word, and the fact that it is not a proper name associated with a particular god of the Hindu pantheon is an argument in favour of its use by Christians, freeing it from the objections which would clearly attach to names like *Hari* or *Rāma*.[1]

The very neutrality of *Brahman*, however, raises objections of another type; how can *nirguṇa Brahman*, that abstraction without attributes, possibly be used by Christians to describe the 'God of Abraham, Isaac and Jacob'? Here Brahmabandhab's insight is helped by that traditional understanding of *Brahman* which views It as *saguṇa* as well as *nirguṇa*, simultaneously with and without attributes. The fact that this paradox of *nirguṇa-saguṇa* is found in the *Upaniṣads* and is widely accepted in Indian thought makes the word *Brahman* all the more adaptable for Christian use, for it gives expression, in Hindu terminology, to the fact that God is 'hidden'—the *Deus absconditus* in Luther's phrase—and that yet he can and does reveal himself.

Christians do not claim to know God exhaustively, and the Bible speaks of a God who hides himself and asserts that 'no

[1] The names often used by Gandhi, e.g. 'Harijan', 'people of *Hari*', for 'outcastes'; *Rāmarājya*, 'Kingdom of *Rāma*', for Kingdom of God.

man hath seen God '.[1] It is clear that we cannot ' comprehend ' God, and that so our statement must ultimately be apophatic or ' open-ended ' *towards him.* As Appasamy says, there are ' ranges beyond ' what we can see of him, and we can say only *neti, neti* to any statement which would claim to be exhaustive. Yet God does reveal himself, and in Christ he has done so fully and sufficiently. We cannot see God wholly, but ' we see Jesus ',[2] and that is enough, for the mountain peak which we see in him is the guarantee of those which lie beyond. The limitations of our sight do not permit us now to penetrate further, but we know that the substance and structure of the overwhelmingly great range is that of the Rock we see, which is Christ.[3]

Even more, perhaps, than in the *nirguṇa-saguṇa* polarity, the term *Brahman* becomes meaningful for Christian theology through the famous definition as *Sat, Cit, Ānanda.* Beginning with Sen a succession of thinkers has found this idea suggestive of new and thoroughly Indian ways of expressing what Christians believe about God, and it is worth glancing briefly at some of the advantages in using this concept. First of all, far from contradicting or modifying the Biblical evidence on the nature of God, it provides a useful framework for expounding that evidence in an Indian rather than a western way. *Saccidānanda* is regarded in Hinduism as the highest point reached by natural reason in the search for an understanding of God, and so Hindus are more open to a Christian explanation of God as Triune than would be Muslims or western unitarians. In other words, Hinduism provides a mind prepared for a triune understanding of God as *Sat, Cit* and *Ānanda,* and is in a sense waiting for these terms to be filled with a richer content than they now have. Further, *Saccidānanda* preserves the unity of the Godhead, for nothing is clearer to Indian thought than that *Brahman* is one. Yet while preserving the unity it takes the personal ' colloquy ' right into the very Godhead, so that *Brahman* cannot be reduced to zero, in Goreh's phrase. Christian mysticism thus becomes differentiated, as Monchanin emphasised, from monistic mysticism in which all distinctions are overcome. Rather, in seeking faith-union with *Saccidānanda* men are led into the endless mystery and fellowship and love of the Trinity.

Sat as ' being ' expresses the ' is-ness ' of God, the I AM. *Cit,* ' intelligence ', links up closely with the Biblical conceptions

[1] Isaiah 45 : 15 ; John 1 : 18.
[2] Hebrews 2 : 9. A.V.
[3] Cf. I Corinthians 10 : 4.

of Sophia and Logos, and with the 'Word' of the Old Testament, by which the world was created. And *Ānanda*, joy, emphasises one of the most characteristic aspects of the Spirit, associated as it is with love. Is it mere chance that this correspondence exists? Is not this terminology as well fitted to express the inner nature of the Godhead as are Greek terms like *ousia* and *hypostasis*? It has seemed to some theologians that the correspondence is not fortuitous but is an indication of the way in which God has in India been preparing a people for himself, and giving them instruments of thought by which they might better know and proclaim him.

In certain circumstances, then, we may be prepared to use the word *Brahman* for God, though not unless it is further expounded in terms of *Saccidānanda* or of the *nirguṇa-saguṇa* polarity. A caution must be added, however, in connection with the widely accepted Vedāntic *mahāvākya*, '*I am Brahman*' (*aham Brahma āsmi*), with its postulation of a metaphysical identity between man and *Brahman*. Any such idea of an ontological identity between man and God must be rejected, and with it all such terminology as 'becoming Christ', 'deification' etc. With Appasamy we assert that while the concept of union with Christ, and even with God, may be accepted, it must be accepted in a sense which preserves the separate personality of the individual. It is a union of will, of purpose, of love; the taster and the sugar do not become one. This is the point at which Christian theology, while it may accept the concept of *Brahman* as indicating that nothing can be higher than God, must yet clearly reject pure *advaita* with its monism of the *bhakta* and his Lord, of the creature and the Creator.

This assertion of the preservation of individual personality in our union with God raises the question of the meaning of 'personality' as applied both to man and to God. The western tradition speaks often of a 'personal God', and though the word 'personal' used in this way is not Biblical but rather the product of a long evolution from Greek *hypostasis* and *prosōpon* through the Latin *persona* and modern psychological and personalist 'I-Thou' conceptions, yet there is no doubt that the God of the Old and New Testaments is a God who speaks to and deals with his people. The Neo-Vedāntic view is different:

> Personality is a limitation, and yet only a personal God can be worshipped. Personality implies the distinction of self and not-self, and hence is inapplicable to the Being who includes and embraces all that is. The personal God is a symbol, though the highest symbol of the true living God. . . The moment we reduce

the Absolute to an object of worship, it becomes something less than the Absolute.[1]

We should prefer to say, following Goreh, that *impersonality* is a limitation. Without personality the psycho-somatic unity, man, reduces to an aggregate of chemical particles; why, then, in the highest existence, should impersonality represent a higher reality or a deeper truth? Yet the solution obviously does not lie in ascribing an anthropomorphic personality to God, as is perhaps the tendency in the *bhakti* tradition, which Radhakrishnan is opposing. In maintaining that personality is higher than impersonality we are in effect saying that *nirguṇa Brahman* is not the highest, for ultimately even *nirguṇa Brahman*, the *Deus absconditus*, is revealed as Triune, as *Saccidānanda*, in whom there is indeed no distinction of self and not-self, but rather an endless and loving inner colloquy.

In seeking for a Sanskritic word to convey what we mean by 'person'—a conception notoriously difficult to translate—we would follow Devanandan in drawing attention to the word *puruṣa* and its derivative *puruṣatva* ('personality'). We are not seeking for a single-word equivalent for the word 'person', but rather for a group of Indian terms which will express the deepest Christian insights on the nature of God, of man, and of the God-man Christ, and the word *puruṣa*, which in the Saṁkhya system, in the Upaniṣads, and even in the *Gita*, is used to signify the Supreme Being in a state of action as opposed to rest, would seem to hold considerable possibilities of development.

God and the World

We have seen Indian theologians returning three different answers to the question of God's relation to the created world, answers related to the three different philosophies of Śankara, Rāmānuja and Aurobindo, and all three answers have accepted, though with differing interpretations, the fact that Biblical Christianity postulates *creatio ex nihilo*. Chenchiah, like de Chardin, sees God's power or *śakti* at work in matter as a principle of evolution controlled by his purpose. Christ is at work in the created world, and creation, through him, is being transformed into his image, the new creation. Appasamy uses the Rāmānujan analogy of the world as the Body of God, an analogy which gives reality to matter and to embodied souls even

[1] S. Radhakrishnan, *Indian Philosophy* I, p. 97.

though it may not satisfactorily explain their origin, and may seem to describe creation as a state (*sthiti*) rather than as a creative act (*sṛṣṭi*).

In choosing to link himself with Śankara, Brahmabandhab has set himself a more difficult task. By equating *asat* or non-being with the Thomistic *nihil* he is able to preserve at least a form of the doctrine of *creatio ex nihilo*; in a process of Hegelian dialectic *Brahman*, who is being (*sat*), acts upon *asat*, and so by the power of his *māyā-śakti* the empirical world, or contingent being, comes into existence. Whether in fact this explanation of the origin of matter is satisfactory from a Christian point of view is highly questionable, even though it may approach fairly closely to Aquinas' *creatio passiva*.

To the *advaitin* it is impossible to think of creation except in terms of *māyā*, and Brahmabandhab has made a fascinating attempt to use this concept in his Christian reconstruction. Is *māyā* in fact an idea with constructive possibilities for Christian theology? We must note first of all that *māyā* can be used in two distinct senses: the first as static, contingent being, the empirical world which participates in *vyavahārika* existence; and the second as *māyā-śakti*, the abounding creative energy of God. It seems as though *māyā* can be used constructively only if these two conceptions are separated from each other. *Māyā* may be used, as Devanandan used it, to describe the contingent, transitory world of secular history, the realm of tragedy and comedy which is moving on to the great day of 'the redemption of the body' (Rom. 8 : 23) but still groans and travails. *Māyā*, on this interpretation, is in the realm of the will, not of being. The whole creation is subject to 'vanity' because of man's sin, yet man's return to God, his yielding his will to God's will in conversion, can lead to the end of *māyā* and the entry of the whole of creation into the sphere of the Kingdom of God.

The trouble about the second sense of *māyā*, that of the creative *māyā-śakti*, is that there does not appear to be any scriptural evidence to support an interpretation of this kind, which gives *māyā* as it were an independent existence as agent of creation. The Bible speaks at various times of both the Spirit and the Logos as agents of creation.[1] Yet even if one were to say that *māyā-śakti* could be used as an equivalent of Spirit or Logos or Sophia in this context, one would still be faced with the impossible task of equating the *māyā* of vanity and illusion with that of the creative agent. Brahmabandhab tried to do

[1] Genesis 1 : 2; John 1 : 3.

this and became involved in all sorts of difficulties, especially in the context of the Bengali devotion to the goddess Kāli as a manifestation of *māyā-śakti*. Our conclusion would be that while *māyā* has definite possibilities as a description of the unredeemed, tragic, contingent world of human life, it cannot be used to describe the agent of creation. A more promising line of thought for the theology of creation is to be found in the development of the concept of Logos-*Cit*, as in Sen and Chenchiah.

Words for Christ

Is there any real and firm link between God and the world of men? *Māyā*, which provides a link in *advaita*, gives to the created world only an unreal existence. Where are we to find a link between God and his world which makes creation possible and makes possible also the approach of the creature to his Creator? Dr. R. M. Clark writes:

> India needs a Christian concept of Logos. Over against the capricious play of *māyā* and the uncontrolled dynamisms of *śakti*, India needs the assurance of a steady, dependable relation between God and the phenomenal world, the assurance that God is involved in all nature and all history, and that He acts therein with redemptive purpose and power.[1]

It is just that link which the Christian faith claims to demonstrate in Christ the Logos. In Hinduism the connection between God and the world of matter is always ambiguous and uncertain. But Christ is the God-man who is born of woman and in the precisely defined time and place of first century Palestine becomes the fleshly ladder uniting the creature with the Creator. The Lord of *māyā* enters the world of *māyā* to redeem and transform it.

The different theologians whose work we have studied throw light on different aspects of Christ and his person. He is the Logos, the *Cit* of *Saccidānanda*, as Sen and Brahmabandhab saw, the Word by whose *śakti*—and not that of *māyā*—the world was created from nothing, from *asat*. He is from all eternity one with the Father, with Being, *Sat*, in the eternal colloquy of the Trinity. And yet for the sake of those who had fallen victim to the deceits and temptations of *māyā-śakti* he entered the realm of *māyā*, 'coming down' to earth as the true *avatāra*

[1] R. M. Clark, 'A Study of Christological Categories in the Indian Church' (unpublished dissertation), p. 258.

who is fully man and fully God. With Appasamy and Chakkarai we may accept the Christian use of the term *avatāra*, provided it is used with certain safeguards. He is the *pūrṇa avatāra*, in whom the Godhead dwells in fulness,[1] who comes once and once only to save the world, not merely from a single disaster but from the guilt and power of sin. And in becoming man and taking to himself a single personality, fully divine and fully human, he demonstrates that God is personal and that man too is personal and can enter into living communion with God through him. And, as Chenchiah points out, the union of divine and human is not just temporary but permanent, and is only confirmed and proclaimed by the resurrection and ascension. The link is permanent; Christ *remains* the God-man, and so we are still today able to come to God through him. The Jesus of history, who on the Cross experienced the utmost dereliction and *kenosis*, is the Christ of faith, the risen Lord who today dwells in the hearts of his *bhaktas* as *antaryāmin*. As Logos-*Cit*, as the *śakti* or driving power of creation, He is ever active in the world, and it is through the Spirit, as Chakkarai holds, that we know and experience him in our lives. He is the true Man, the *sat puruṣa*, the real Person, and by the power of his Spirit those who live 'in him' become new creatures and share in the dynamic, evolving, purposeful life of the new creation.

The term *saguṇa* has been applied to Christ, and in some contexts may be helpful, for he indeed has 'qualities'. We must beware only that by using it we do not detract from his oneness with God; as de Smet says:

> Most Vedāntins really think that the Supreme God of Christianity corresponds to *saguṇa Brahman* and that our worship does not reach the real absolute which is *nirguṇa*.[2]

There is a danger here that if Christ is thought of *exclusively* as *saguṇa* his ontological unity with the other persons of the Trinity will disappear. Yet as Logos-*Cit* he participates in *Saccidānanda* which, in the aspect of *Deus absconditus*, may be described as *nirguṇa*. So far as our apprehension is concerned, Christ is *saguṇa*; nevertheless in the inner dialogue of the Trinity the dialectic of *nirguṇa-saguṇa* must be preserved. The confession 'Christ is Lord' must never mean that Christians give up at a stage short of the final one.

[1] Colossians 2: 9.
[2] *Religion and Society*, X/3, (1963), p. 22.

Another aspect of the same dialectical tension may make it possible, as Panikkar suggests, to use the term *Iśvara* in connection with Christology, though there are practical difficulties here as the word is already used so often by Christians as the regular word for 'God'. The term can, however, be meaningfully used of Christ as the Agent of creation, and can also link up in a fruitful way with the whole conception of Christianity as *bhakti mārga* elaborated by Appasamy. In Hinduism the relations between *nirguṇa* and *saguṇa*, *Brahman* and *Iśvara* vary a good deal, and there is a dialectical tension between the members of each pair. The use of such terms in a Christian sense can fill them with new content, while they still remain within the Indian universe of discourse.

The fundamental problem of Christology is that of the relation of the divine and the human in the incarnate Christ; what did Christ mean when he said, 'I and my Father are one'? We have seen how the 'moral union' theory, with its language of *kenosis*, transparency, and 'the Man for others', so strangely modern in atmosphere, has appealed to Indian theologians from Sen to Appasamy and has been given an attractive Indian expression. Yet surely an approach like that of Brahmabāndhab, with his insistence on the ontological unity of the Son with the Father, expressed as the full participation of the Logos-*Cit* in *Saccidānanda*, is closer to the evidence of the Biblical *śruti*. The Nicene and Chalcedonian language of *ousia* and *hypostasis* may well be unsuitable for Indian apologetic or even systematic theology, yet the truth behind the language, the *satya* to which the inadequate language points, is Biblical, and it can be expressed in Indian terms, using some of the 'instruments' which are now at our disposal.

Words for Spirit

India is a country with a very strong tradition of 'spirituality', and Chenchiah seems correct in saying that the doctrine of the Holy Spirit may become the corner-stone of Indian Christian theology.[1] The word *ātman* (spirit, soul) and its cognates *paramātman* (Supreme Spirit) and *antarātman* (Inner Spirit) are obviously capable of use with deep Christian content, and there are other words like *antaryāmin* (Inner Ruler) which are promising, as is the conception of *śakti* when applied—as it frequently is in everyday Christian usage—to the power of the Spirit.

[1] v. supra, p. 156.

Indian Christians find it very natural to think of God as Spirit; besides the evidence of John 4:24, 'God is Spirit', there is the Hindu tradition which regards the *paramātman* as identical with *Brahman*, and in any case the whole of life is thought of as shot through with the spiritual. Thus we find a tendency in Indian theology to blur the distinctions between the Persons of the Trinity, which western theology defines so clearly, and especially to view all of God's dealings with us today as the work of the Spirit. This tendency is clearest in Chakkarai, with his explicit statement that 'the Holy Spirit is Jesus Christ Himself, taking His abode with us[1]', but the same point is illustrated in Appasamy also, when the term *antaryāmin* is used of all the Persons of the Trinity. Indian theology has not as yet worked out the functions of the Spirit in detail, after the manner of western dogmatics, yet throughout these writers the *reality* of the Spirit and his work is apparent, especially in the pages of Chakkarai, but also very clearly in Chenchiah. Chakkarai's explanation of the link between the historic incarnation and the present Christian experience is a case in point; through the Spirit, Christ is present in us today as *antarātman*, and so the incarnation advances from the historical to the spiritual, becoming real in our experience today. Chakkarai was anxious to assert the priority of experience of the living Christ over the liberal historicism of his day; for him as for Chenchiah Christianity begins with 'the raw fact of Christ', and that fact can be mediated to us *only* by the Spirit. Christianity is a 'spiritual' religion not in any vague, disembodied way, but in the sense that it is based on direct contact with the living Christ through the Holy Spirit.

Indian Christian theologians are unanimous in rejecting the Vedāntic identification of the *ātman* with the *paramātman*. Chenchiah sees the *union* of the two—not their identity—as a possibility or *sambhava*, to be achieved through self-commitment to Christ. It might be possible, on this view, for the *ātman-paramātman* conception to be used fruitfully as an illustration of the doctrine of the *imago Dei*; the *jivātman* (embodied soul) is in the image of the *paramātman*, is thus able to enter into relations with him, and is restless till it finds rest in him. But there can be no metaphysical unity of the two, and Appasamy is right in maintaining that the *unio mystica* of the *bhakta* with God is moral and not ontological.

[1] v. supra, p. 173.

Chenchiah's exuberant description of the Spirit as *mahāśakti*, the great power of God whose coming brings us into the new age, and through whom we are united with Christ so that as new creatures we may live according to the '*yoga* of the Spirit', is a powerful and attractive statement, which is echoed in some contemporary western voices like de Chardin and R. C. Zaehner.[1] It is a corrective to Appasamy's somewhat static application of the term *antaryāmin* as the immanent God dwelling by nature in all men. We may accept the fact that in some way God *is* at work in all men, as *antaryāmin* or as that same *paramātman* who dwelt in the *rishis* of old; yet what happened at Pentecost was something *new*, and unless Christianity can point to this newness, to a power which comes from outside us and is not to be found elsewhere, then it has no claim to be able to transform the world, and it is useless to pray *Veni, Creator Spiritus.*

The Indian stress on the *joy* of the Spirit is a very salutary one, 'written in' as it is in the *Ānanda* of *Saccidānanda*. In promising to send the Paraclete Jesus said, 'Let not your hearts be troubled'[2], and it is right that this aspect of the Spirit's work should be stressed in a way which the West neglects.

'Spirituality' (*ādhyātmiktā*) is a word frequently used in modern Hindu circles, especially Gandhian ones, and it is sometimes brought forward as a basis for common ground in dialogue. From the Hindu point of view, however, spirituality is something static; at best it implies the dispelling, through knowledge, of the ignorance which keeps us from realising our oneness with the *paramātman*, and so is linked with the ascetic life and the way of non-attachment. The Christian idea of spirituality, on the other hand, can be defined only in terms of Pentecost, of power and speech and healing and growth. It is something dynamic which involves the *jivātman's* confrontation with Christ in the power of the Spirit. *Śakti* is involved, the power which made the blind to see, the coward to preach, and which turned the world upside down. The doctrine of the Spirit has great possibilities for the transformation of Hinduism from within, and Hindu insights can deepen the Christian understanding of the power of the Spirit.

Man and Sin

The dominant strain in Hinduism thinks of man as a pre-existent and eternal soul, the *ātman*, which has become entangled

[1] R. C. Zaehner, *The Convergent Spirit* (1963), *passim.*
[2] John 14 : 1.

in the world of *māyā* and so is inevitably involved in the round of *karma-saṃsāra* ; it is temporarily united with a body which will be destroyed at death, while the *ātman*, which is identical with *Brahman* or the *paramātman*, continues its eternal existence. In practice this has tended to lead to an undervaluation of the individual—since nothing we do can have any effect on our soul—and a fatalism which attributes all misfortunes to *karma*. As Devanandan has shown, many modern Hindus in practice attribute great worth both to the individual and to society and act on the assumption that man's destiny can be shaped and improved.

The Christian view which seems to emerge from our study is somewhat as follows. Man is not just an *ātman* entangled in *māyā*. God creates men as persons, in whom soul and body are joined in a unity, and the body—made of matter though it is—is not worthless or illusory but good. It is not something to be suppressed or escaped from ; rather we must seek for the redemption of the body which comes about when we live in Christ and so become 'new creatures'. We are by nature 'persons' (*puruṣa*) but are called to become *bhaktas* through self-surrender to Christ, so that in him we may become part of the new creation. The 'personality' is not obliterated at death, nor is the soul then released in order to enter into a new body. Rather the 'person' survives and those who are already 'in Christ' enter fully into his presence. Made in the image of God the *ātman* is not identical with the *paramātman*, yet longs for communion with him. There can be no union in which we lose our identity in God, but rather a loving communion which can be described as *mokṣa* and further defined as *sālokya*, *sāmipya*, *sārupya* and *sāyujya* in which, however, the lover and the Beloved retain their separate identities in the manner described by the *bhakti* poets,

Sin is little stressed in Hinduism, and we agree with Goreh, Sundar Singh and Devanandan that its 'sinfulness' and positive power for evil must be unambiguously emphasised in Indian Christian theology. At the same time the Hindu understanding of *karma* and *māyā* may be used in our description of sin and its removal. For many Hindus *karma* is a terrible burden from which they long to be freed, and to say that there is no such thing or that Christianity has nothing to say about its removal is like telling a patient that he is suffering from the wrong disease.[1] We can indeed go to the Hindu with a message of *mokṣa*, of release from the bonds of *karma* for those who by faith are united with Christ, the one who is free from *karma*.

[1] Cf. A. G. Hogg, *The Christian Message to the Hindu*, pp. 13 ff., 73 ff.

Sundar Singh stresses the gravity of sin, and links it in a meaningful way with *karma*, which he interprets as automatic retribution for our sins. God is a God of love who does not wish any to perish,[1] but yet our sins are terrible and bring their own fruits with them. God sends no one to hell, but our sins, by a process of *karma*, can take us there unless we turn to Christ in repentance and self-surrender.

Devanandan shows how the concept of *māyā* can be used not merely for the illusoriness of the world, but also to describe the positive force of evil, the perverse *māyā-śakti* which leads us astray into false paths of sin. He also makes good use of the term *ahaṃkāra*, egoism or selfishness, to show how sin is rooted in the pride and selfishness which makes us try to take God's place and to lord it over our neighbour. Though some Indian theologians think of sin as merely the deprivation or negation of virtue, as darkness is the negation of light,[2] yet when it is seen as an evil *śakti* and as *ahaṃkāra* a deeper understanding of man's nature results.

Hindus like Vivekānanda and even Christians like Chenchiah have charged western theology with a morbid interest in sin, and most Indian theologians are more interested in the positive fact of God's glory and love than in the negative one of man's sin. Yet surely this is a case where the Biblical tradition, confirmed as it is by the insights of Sundar Singh and the experience of people like Goreh and Devanandan, must receive more emphasis than it has in the past.

The Work of Christ

To anyone trained in the western tradition the soteriology of many Indian theologians seems somehow unsatisfactory; it is not that the Cross is neglected but rather that there is a reluctance to define closely the 'How' of Christ's work there. It is widely assumed that Christ's work of salvation is carried out just as much by his incarnation, life and resurrection and by his Person as by his death on the Cross. On the whole it would be true to say that for many Indian theologians Christ saves by what he *is* rather than by what he does. This tendency is very like that of the eastern Church of the early centuries, and indeed of the eastern Churches today; interest centres much more on cosmology and the incarnation than on soteriology. In both cases

[1] 2 Peter 3 : 9.
[2] e.g. Dhanjibhai Fakirbhai, *Khristopanishad*, p. 36.

the reason is probably to be found in the cultural surroundings in which the Church is called to witness. Greek and Hindu thought is interested in the problems of creation and of the One and the many, and developing Christian thought has to grapple with these issues. In India also the popular belief in *avatāras* forces attention on the question of the nature of Christ's incarnation. Indian thought, like Greek, is unfamiliar with the Hebrew sacrificial tradition and the Roman juridical conception and so has tended to turn to those aspects of the life and work of Christ which seemed more familiar.

Starting from the time of Sen, then, the Cross is regarded as 'a beautiful emblem of self-sacrifice unto the glory of God'[1], whose 'vast moral influence' affects the life of individuals and society. Chenchiah turns more to the 'newness' of Christ himself, by union with whom men are made new and take a step forward in spiritual evolution. The leading themes here are those of moral influence and of faith-union with Christ. The Johannine *mahāvākya* 'Abide in me' predominates, and perhaps also the apodeictic 'Behold the Lamb of God', and yet comparatively little is said about the taking away of the sin of the world, which is equally Johannine.[2] It is not unusual in these writers to find references to the blood of Christ, 'overflowing to drown and annihilate our sins'[3], but a full statement of the western doctrine of penal substitution is not found. The fact is that Indian theologians find this conception difficult to accept. As C. S. Paul has pointed out, such suffering seems to contradict the idea of justice implicit in *karma*, where everyone must suffer for his own sins alone, and also to offend against the prevalent belief in God's impassibility.

Perhaps there is a corrective here for certain types of western theology. Sundar Singh's teaching, for example, clearly states the *effectiveness* of Christ's work on the Cross; the desired end was achieved, as it was by the mother who with bleeding hands earned the money for her son's release. This 'work' can be described in many ways—a blood-transfusion, victory in battle, rescue from drowning (the image beloved of the *bhakti* poets)—and penal substitution is only one such picture. The great fact is the truth that through the life and death and resurrection of Christ men are pardoned, healed and restored, and that by union with him in faith they find salvation and new life.

[1] v. supra, p. 31.
[2] John 1 : 29.
[3] Cf. passage cited above, p. 33.

In Chakkarai's ' mysticism of the Cross ' with its idea that the death of Christ has in some mysterious way opened a channel in the heart of man for the inflowing of the divine *śakti* we find a distinctive insight, and one which firmly links the Cross with the resurrection and Pentecost. The Cross is ' causal ' in salvation yet the ' cause ' is not to be seen in the vicariousness of the suffering but rather in the release of spiritual energy there achieved. Devanandan echoes the same thought when he writes :

> Out of the agony of the Cross is released saving power by which the world is being recreated from century to century. . . . In me a new creation is wrought into being because He died and rose again.[1]

Chenchiah too lays emphasis on this *śakti*, though for him its *locus* is not so much in the death of Christ as in his very existence as the *ādi-puruṣa* of the new creation. It is clear from all these writers that the conception of spiritual power is a very real one for Indian theology ; the Hindu idea of *śakti*, perverted as it has sometimes been into the more ghastly aspects of *Kāli*-worship, has been a *praeparatio evangelii*, and has made men ready, in William Carey's words, to expect great things from God.

Chakkarai's exposition of Pauline justification by faith in terms of *bhakti* is interesting, for indeed the meaning of *bhakti*, so often translated as ' love ' or ' devotion ', does come close to the idea of loving, reckless self-commitment which is far closer to the Pauline *pistis* than is any kind of assent to credal propositions. It is in the *bhakti mārga* of love for the crucified Christ that there takes place that great release of spiritual energy which alone can transform our lives. This emphasis on the release of power is by no means absent in western theology, and one may think of William Cowper's words :

> Dear dying Lamb, thy precious blood
> Shall never lose its power
> Till all the ransomed Church of God
> Be saved to sin no more.[2]

Yet Indian theology seems to lean in the direction of a specially close link between the work of Christ and the release of the power of the Spirit.

The Church and Sacraments

Many of the theologians we have studied are highly critical of the organised Church as it is found in India, chiefly on account

[1] *Sermons*, p. 16.
[2] William Cowper, 1731-1800.

of its 'foreign-ness'. This anti-western critique may be accepted in its general implications, for the Indian Church does still retain far too many of its western trappings, not least in its way of thinking. Experiments along the lines of Christian *āshrams*, indigenous forms of worship, architecture and organisation are therefore of very considerable value. But enthusiasm must be tempered with realism, for it is a sobering fact that many of those most enthusiastic for 'Indianisation' are now middle-aged and elderly, and not a few of them are foreigners! The Church must take care that the advancing mood of secularisation and modernisation, particularly among young people, does not result in the marooning of a small island of 'Indian Christianity' using excellent indigenous patterns of behaviour which have long since ceased to be current in Indian society at large! The fact remains, however, that sixty years after Brahmabandhab's strictures on the westernness of the Church, the Churches—with the partial exception of the Syrian—remain distressingly western, as may be seen not only from the obvious monolithic character of Indian Roman Catholicism, but also from the constitution of any Protestant Church, or even from a study of such a recent and enlightened document as the *Plan of Church Union in North India*.

Mere 'Indianisation' inspired by nationalism is of course not the answer. In the time of Upādhyāya or Chenchiah, when India was under a foreign power, it was both understandable and natural. Yet there is great danger in any Church movement which sets out to be purely 'national', the danger into which the 'German Christians' of Hitler's day fell, when the state, or even national culture is put at the centre instead of Christ. Now that India is independent, the Church need no longer seek to prove itself 'national' in that way, though of course any direct foreign control which remains should be removed. The Church should simply be itself, living in 'cultural kinship' with its non-Christian neighbours and drawing the dynamic of its development not from a superimposed nationalism but from the Spirit of Christ working within it, from the natural growth of the tree now firmly rooted in Indian soil. Such 'indigenisation' need not conflict with openness in fellowship and sharing with the universal Church of Christ which knows no boundaries of nation, race or culture.[1]

Chenchiah's critique of the Church was almost entirely negative, and he felt that the life of the Kingdom of God and of

[1] The point is well made in D. T. Niles, *Upon the Earth* (1962), pp. 170 ff.

the new creation which for him was the true *yoga* of the Spirit could be found only in fellowship-groups such as *āshrams* outside the Church. The kind of criticism which he made is today again being made by many in both West and East who advocate 'religionless Christianity'. A more constructive and positive approach to the Church is found in Devanandan's idea of the 'transforming community'. Why should not Chenchiah's conception of a dynamic, Spirit-filled new society find its fulfilment within the visible Church? The Church, on Devanandan's view, should not be written off because of its obvious defects; it owes its existence to Christ and the Holy Spirit and can still be transformed, and used for the transformation of society and the world. Yet it is true that for those who look forward, as Monchanin did, to seeing a new and transformed 'Indian eschatological Church', the pace of change must seem unbearably slow. The western Church in India must die, in order that the Indian Church may arise. But it is uncommonly long in dying!

The question-mark set against the sacraments by Chenchiah and even to some extent by Sundar Singh, represents chiefly resentment against the Church's supposed claim to control the 'means of Grace' and thereby to discourage the direct access of the believer to his Lord. It is, indeed, very important in India that the eucharist should never become a mere ritual, part of a sort of *purva mimāṃsa* or *karma mārga* where it is thought that Christ is received *ex opere operato.* The priority of the *śruti*, of conscious confrontation with the living Christ through the hearing of the Word, must be maintained or Indian Christianity can easily relapse into a form of idolatry such as Ram Mohan Roy would vehemently have rejected. Indian theology needs to give more attention to the meaning of the eucharist. Goreh's eucharistic teaching is very valuable, and Appasamy's attempt to work out a theology of the eucharist in terms of Rāmānuja's soul-body analogy is very interesting and helpful. But much remains to be done, and it can be done only within the context of a deeper relationship with the Church than some of our theologians have had.

The objections against baptism raised by Parekh and others need to be faced. There are in India many 'lovers of the Lord' who refrain from baptism because of its social implications, involving their banishment from their social and family milieu. Baptism as practised in India is not just a 'religious' sacrament; it involves entry not merely into the Christian Church but also into the Christian community, which in many places constitutes virtually an independent caste group. And the separation of the new Christian from his own background makes any prospect of approach to his caste-fellows through him almost impossible. If we believe that Hindu society is becoming more and more secularised, the time may soon come when it will be possible to receive baptism without having to sever all one's connections with one's community. 'Conversion' must be seen to be something inner and personal, and not merely an outward 'change of religion' (*dharmāntara*). There is need here for a new and careful study of the evidence of the New Testament and the early Church, and need also for new attitudes on the part of both Christian and non-Christian communities.

History and Fulfilment

Gandhi once said, 'I have never been interested in a historical Jesus. I should not care if it was proved by someone that the man called Jesus never lived . . . For the Sermon on the Mount would still be true for me.[1]' This rather Bultmannian lack of interest in the particularity of history is fairly representative of Indian thought. Goreh saw the problem and tackled it in his examination of the veracity of the Gospel narratives; Chakkarai has given his interesting solution to the question of the relation of the Jesus of history to the Christ of faith; while Devanandan has pointed out that the political and social life of modern India depends on holding the realistic view that human activity and plans can and do influence history and that history itself is significant. It is, however, worth reminding ourselves that few Hindus are impressed by the argument that Jesus was a historic Person; such particularity reduces rather than increases their regard for him, and they are more interested in knowing what the effect of the indwelling Christ is in the heart of a *bhakta* than on the proof of his historicity. We must be ready to meet their 'felt need', while still maintaining the fact that without the historic incarnation there would have been no Sermon on the Mount and no life in Christ.

We have seen how Sen and Chenchiah have spoken of a creative purpose at work in the world, the power of the Spirit. This view, with its implication of the reality of creation and the worth of matter, is not typical of classical Hinduism, but Aurobindo's stature gives it weight among present-day Hindus, and it constitutes a valuable stream of Indian Christian thought.

[1] Gandhi's Christmas sermon, 1931, delivered on board ship while returning from the Round Table Conference. Quoted in *The Guardian* 7.1.32.

Devanandan's contribution in this field is significant, combining as it does the ideas of new creation and the Kingdom of God into a special kind of 'fulfilment'—the realisation here and now, by union with Christ in the new creation, of that 'hope of glory' to which we and the whole world are called. Instead of there being only an automatic process of evolution towards a better world, we find that the pattern of the Kingdom of God, the hope of glory which is identical with the living presence of Christ, is here and now present in the world, transforming it. And the mission of the Church is to demonstrate in its own self that Christ-filled life, while proclaiming to the world that the 'glory' is for all.

Christ is *already* present in the history and events of the world, and in the religious strivings of Hinduism, and it is our task to reveal how he is even now 'summing up' all things. A Roman Catholic writer who recently made a pilgrimage to the source of the Ganges, there to celebrate the eucharist, expresses a similar thought:

> Priests make their offerings in the temples, sadhus meditate and fast in their caves, pilgrims strive and pray and chant on their way to the source. All this is the mystery of Christ who is still hidden, of Christ who is already present though still invisible. Everything is in fact announcing and foretelling His coming in glory. The Spirit Himself is already present in all this, bringing everything back to the Father, 'converting' everything that happens in time and is done by men, into the mystery of Christ. The role of the Christian priest is to bring all this to its eschatological completion.[1]

For him that eschatological completion is the eucharist. For others it is rather the act of meeting with the living Christ in that personal communion of the Word and prayer which can transform men and societies. But however we may put it, this linking up of 'realised eschatology' with the mission of the Church, with our attitude to our Hindu neighbours, and with the idea of the Kingdom of God as extending to all mankind and already proleptically present, represents a valuable new insight in which Indian theology is brought into 'engagement' with the non-Christian world.

'Strands' of Theological Thought

This survey and summary of some of the terms and trends of Indian theological writing is of course very selective and in-

[1] *The Mountain of the Lord*, by Two Pilgrims of the Way. (CISRS, 1966), pp. 32-3.

complete, and it has been our purpose to present the material, along with some comment, rather than to pass definitive judgment on the various terms examined. One fact, however, has emerged very clearly from our survey, and that is the existence, within Christian theology no less than in Hindu philosophy, of two main 'strands' of thought, the *advaita* strand represented especially by Upādhyāya, and the personalist or theistic strand seen in Appasamy, with the two strands tending to have mutually exclusive 'clusters' of ideas.[1] Thus Upādhyāya's outlook inclines towards monism—relieved, of course, by his exposition of *Saccidānanda*—in which the transcendent unity of God is not impaired. He rejects the idea of *avatāra*, which comes from the theistic strand, favours mysticism of the 'monistic Trinitarian' pattern rather than simple *bhakti*, and finds the distinction between God and the world in a version of *māyā* rather than in a firm doctrine of creation. Appasamy on the other hand thinks of God primarily in personal terms, encourages Christian *bhakti*, welcomes the *avatāra* idea as applied to Christ, and see the world as real, through the Rāmānujan analogy of soul and body.

Both these thinkers accept the authority of Scripture, and both speak from a living experience of Christ. How is it, then, that they have taken such divergent ways? Is there an ongoing dialectical process at work, like that which in the West swings theological opinion from liberalism to Barth and then back to Bultmann. Are different types of inference at work? Or is it simply that in India certain psychological, sociological and historical circumstances tend to lead men to accept certain clusters of ideas and reject others? Within Hinduism it has certainly been true that certain families and groups belong to a particular tradition; though Goreh, to give but one example, before becoming a Christian changed from the Śaivite to the Vaiṣṇavite tradition from which, perhaps, his transition to belief in the Christian incarnation was easier.

Historically the strand of Rāmānuja arose in opposition to the monism of Śankara, with the purpose of allowing a place to devotion to a personal God, and the two traditions have for centuries maintained their separate existence. Must this distinction be reflected and perpetuated in Christian theology in India? There are already signs that the edges of the two positions are not altogether clear-cut; the monist Upādhyāya worships the God-man *Narahari*, while the *bhakta* Appasamy

[1] The terminology is R. N. Smart's. See *Reasons and Faiths* (1958), Introduction.

points to the ranges of God's being beyond the personalist 'summit' which we see in Christ. But in any case, would it not be easiest and best simply to abandon the Śankarite position as hopelessly incompatible with the Christian faith? Goreh advised this. Rudolf Otto felt that only *bhakti*, 'India's Religion of Grace', could be regarded as a *praeparatio* for Christianity. And Ninian Smart has recently pointed out that though a place for mysticism can always be retained in Christian theism, pure monistic mysticism ultimately leaves no room for theism, except at the illusory (*vyavahārika*) level.[1] Why, then, should we not write off Brahmabandhab's attempt as a gallant fiasco?

The answer is that from the point of view of the Christian mission we dare not do so, any more than the author of the Fourth Gospel would have dared to say that Christ was not the Logos. If we adhere only to the terminology of *Iśvara*, Creator, and *avatāra*, we shall never convince the *advaitin* that our faith is more than a second best to Hinduism. Brahmabandhab saw this clearly, and so asserted with magnificent boldness that the God of the Christians *is Brahman*, and proceeded to give to that term a fulness and depth which it never possessed in Hinduism. We cannot therefore neglect Śankara without thereby admitting defeat in the face of an all-absorbing *advaita*.

On the other hand—and this is the issue seen so clearly by Appasamy—it is only in the vocabulary of the theistic tradition that we find that personal conception of God without which Christianity ceases to exist. What we must at all costs maintain, then, is that the God whom we worship is greater than anything that can be conceived, and that yet he is at the same time fully personal, knows us, and can be known by us. As Chakkarai said, in him *śakti* and *bhakti*, power and love, must be united.

It seems then that Indian theology is being driven to an intertwining of the two strands, a synthesis of *jñāna mārga* and *bhakti mārga*, and indeed in their different ways Upādhyāya and Appasamy both seem to admit this possibility. For this reason, in our assessment of the different terms which we have considered, we have not allowed ourselves to be persuaded into the uniform acceptance or rejection of items from one strand or the other, but have felt rather that 'a comprehensive faith will be one which mingles together the two great strands'.[2] Signs of this mingling can be seen in the interpretation of *Saccidānanda-Brahman* as Trinity, leading to a development of the Logos-*Cit*

[1] R. N. Smart, *Philosophers and Religious Truth* (1964), p. 158.
[2] *ibid.*, p. 156.

idea ; in the dialectical treatment of the *nirguṇa-saguṇa* polarity ; and in maintaining the equality of *Brahman* and *Iśvara* while at the same time identifying *Iśvara* with Christ.

In Hinduism, a great gap exists between God and the world of men. It seems to be essential in Indian Christian theology that in one of the ways we have outlined, or in some such way, the gap between *Brahman* and *Iśvara*, between *Brahman* and the world, between God and man, should be bridged. And only one Bridge, only one Link, is possible. Whatever term we use—*Narahari*, *Iśvara*, *saguṇa Brahman*, *Cit*—points only to Christ. He alone is that sure Link between God and the creation which Indian philosophy and Indian religion so deeply need.

Chapter XIII

AN ASSESSMENT AND A PROSPECT

The Emergence of Indian Theology

Indian Christian theology has arrived ! It is far from negligible in volume, it is marked by a lively concern to grapple with the problems of witnessing to the Gospel in the Indian cultural environment, and it represents a wide variety of traditions and viewpoints. We have attempted to trace its growth, and have seen how certain distinctive ideas have emerged and been gradually developed. For various reasons there has been little attempt to write complete *Summae* of theology. The early Church, after all, was more concerned with forging single doctrines in order to meet controversial situations, and the great *Summae* had to wait for a later age. Nevertheless we have been able to gain a reasonably comprehensive picture which shows the mind of the Indian Church grappling with theological formulation over the whole range of the doctrinal spectrum. The jibe that the Indian Church has so far failed to produce even a heresy is patently misleading. Traces of 'heresy' there are, perhaps, but far more important, the Indian Church has demonstrated many new insights into the fundamental truths of the faith, aided—as the Church has never been aided since its earliest days—by a rich and flexible terminology whose resources have not hitherto been brought into the treasury of Christian theology.

Christianity began in a Jewish cultural environment, with a Hebrew or Aramaic vocabulary and a background of Semitic hopes and longings, and the Gospel's first great confrontation was with Judaism, to which it came as fulfilment to promise. Christ's own announcement of the meaning of his coming was couched in such terms : 'The time is fulfilled, and the Kingdom of God is at hand : repent ye, and believe the gospel.'[1] When the first Christian laymen and missionaries began their proclamation to people of Greek cultural background in Antioch and later in Europe they had to use a different vocabulary and even to refer to the fulfilment of different promises, as Paul did when he quoted Aratus on a famous day in Athens. When writing for people who believed that the Logos was God's highest revelation,

[1] Mark 1 : 15.

the author of the Fourth Gospel claimed that word and its content for Christ. The author of Hebrews uses Platonic phraseology in speaking of Christ as 'the very image of God's substance '[1]. And gradually the language of Christian theology changes, with many Greek words and ideas being added to the Jewish ones already in use. In order to win the Graeco-Roman world in this second great cultural confrontation, the Gospel laid Greek philosophy and Roman juridical concepts heavily under contribution. And the Gentile converts of the early Church did not accept Jewish Christianity without change. Even in the New Testament period there were radical changes in ceremony, such as the rejection of circumcision which had seemed essential to the 'Mother-Church' of Jerusalem; and in Church-structure, like the development of the office of the *episkopos*, which gradually diverged from the functions of the Jewish *presbuteros*. At first, no doubt, the efforts of the Jewish apostles and missionaries were halting, and expressed largely in the Jewish imagery of Messiah and prophecy and sacrifice, and in the organisation of the synagogue and the upper room. But gradually the 'indigenous' leaders arose, the Apologists and their successors, who in the work of evangelism used the ideas and vocabulary of Greek philosophy. The time for systematic statement came later, through heresy and controversy.

For many centuries the Church has continued to live in that same Graeco-Roman world, changing its theological expression from time to time to fit the changing moods and the changing history of that world. Barbarian Europe was evangelised and gradually assimilated to the culture of Christian civilisation. Islam arose from within the Judaeo-Christian tradition, and the confrontation between Christianity and Islam has remained mainly hostile. Since the modern missionary movement began there have been encounters with tribal cultures, where the tendency has been for the Christian pattern to submerge what was there before. The confrontation with Chinese culture, where along with the dominant Confucianism and Taoism there was also the Indian-derived Buddhist tradition, has now been virtually broken off, with the irruption there of communism, itself a product of the Judaeo-Christian line. There can be no question, then, that Christianity's third and last great culture-confrontation is that with Hinduism. As Zaehner says, 'We are faced with two chosen people, not one; for, whereas Europe and the Near East owe their religion directly or indirectly to the Jews, further

[1] Hebrews 1 : 3. RV.

Asia owes hers directly or indirectly to the Indians.'[1] The task of presenting the Gospel in India is, then, of quite exceptional importance.

For many years there has been a continuous debate in missionary and ecumenical circles about 'presenting Christ to India,'[2] a debate in which a distinguished succession of western thinkers has taken part—T. E. Slater, J. N. Farquhar, A. G. Hogg, W. E. Hocking, Hendrik Kraemar and others. The time has now come, however, when we should listen rather to the voice of the Indian Church, not merely when that voice speaks, as it so eloquently can,[3] of the methods of evangelism and Christian strategy, but above all when it expresses the Christian faith in new terms, for a new cultural situation.

For this is not just a question of an 'approach', of a new evangelistic technique. It is a question of the theology of the Church. The Church must carry through this third great confrontation, and as it does so the marks of a new terminology, of new insights and visions, will be left not only on the language of Indian Christians, but on the Christian tradition of the whole world. Chenchiah wrote of India: 'Even if a common faith could be evolved without her, it cannot be complete without her contribution'.[4] This does not, of course, mean that the Christian faith is not 'complete' without an alliance with Indian thought-forms; the faith of the apostles, after all, was 'complete' even before the Gospel adopted Greek philosophy as its instrument. But that Greek instrument was necessary for the winning of the Graeco-Roman world, and the theological structure in which that instrument played a vital rôle has remained a part of the heritage of ecumenical Christendom. The materials for the erection of a comprehensive theological structure for the world Church will not be completely assembled until Indian thought-forms take their place among them.

What is Indian Theology?

Dr. Radhakrishnan has often complained that Christianity is a dogmatic religion which requires the assent of its adherents to propositional statements; he feels that the absolute character of theological doctrine is incompatible with the mysterious character

[1] R. C. Zaehner, *At Sundry Times* (1958), pp. 165 ff.
[2] Cf. *Presenting Christ to India Today* (1965), by P. D. Devanandan, A. E. Inbanathan, A. J. Appasamy, J. E. L. Newbigin.
[3] e.g. in the writing of D. T. Niles.
[4] *The Guardian*, 30.1.47.

of religious truth.[1] Chenchiah too objected strongly to 'dogmatics', in the sense of a body of doctrine officially promulgated by the Church for the acceptance of its members. We must therefore ask ourselves what we have in mind when we speak of 'Indian Christian theology' or even of 'Indian dogmatic theology'. Are we referring to the confessional statements which are printed in the constitutions of the various Indian Churches, or to the chapters on doctrine in the Plans of Union? Do we go further back to the classical confessions of the reformation as they were brought to India by western missionaries, or to the theology of Aquinas? Or going still further back, do we say with Dr. Marcus Ward that the Indian Church must accept the 'dogma' of the early and undivided Church, including the formulae of Nicaea and Chalcedon? Obviously we must allow to the Indian Church freedom to interpret the Christian faith in its own way; but what is the Christian faith which it is to be free to interpret?

The term 'dogmatics' was historically first applied not to theology but to physics, as a science in which we understand and interpret the fact in accordance with its own inner principles and not in terms of external authorities. From physics it came to be applied to Christian theology, first by Reformed and later by Lutheran theologians, and was intended to signify a scientific, objective approach to the Christian revelation, in conscious rejection of the authoritarian Roman Catholic tradition. Dogmatic theology is thus not an exercise in reproducing the official teaching of the Church but rather an attempt to expound the meaning of the Christian faith in terms of its own inner structure, with no external control by any imposed system, philosophy or thought-pattern.[2] Scripture is treated as its own interpreter, and the 'shape' of dogmatics develops according to the interior logic of the faith which is being expounded, or rather of the Truth underlying that faith. The Truth, the *Satya* which is revealed in Christ the living *Satya*, imposes an inner pattern upon all true human formulations of truth. The truth may become distorted as men seek to make it conform to their own patterns and schools of thought, and yet the living Truth uses the instruments of thought which are in men's hands, and the greatest theologians of all ages and countries have used, while at the same time transforming, the thought-forms of their day. True theology is firmly anchored in the Bible and in knowledge

[1] S. Radhakrishnan, *The Bhagavadgitā*, p. 142.
[2] I am indebted here to Prof. T. F. Torrance.

of the historic tradition of the Church, and it cannot be written without direct experience of Christ on the part of the theologian, yet its structure is not derived from any official pattern—not even that of the ancient creeds—but rather from the very nature of the subject with which it deals. It is not an exposition of the Church's official beliefs, much less can it be mere speculation; rather it is an enquiry, in the context of the surrounding culture and on the basis of Scripture, into the Truth which underlies all formulated 'dogmas', the *Satya* which is in Christ. And each doctrine as it is examined and formulated in words however inadequate is not regarded as a 'dogma' to be accepted or rejected, but rather as a signpost, or as a finger pointing—like the finger of John the Baptist pointing to the crucified Christ in Barth's favourite picture by Grünewald—to the Truth which shines through all true formulations but can never be exhaustively defined, the Truth which is Christ.

When Indian thinkers, whether Hindus like Dr. Radhakrishnan or Christians like Chenchiah, criticise Christianity for its 'dogmatism', they tend to stop short at the idea of dogmatics as a compendium of beliefs which must be subscribed, and do not appreciate the deeper and more dynamic meaning which dogmatic theology may bear, but which has so often been absent in the types of western theology which have been seen in India. Yet the profound grappling with Truth which true dogmatic theology demands is surely not alien to the Indian tradition.

Does the Church in India today provide the kind of framework in which theology of this kind can flourish? The answer must be a reluctant negative, though there are signs that the atmosphere is changing. Even today in many Indian theological colleges the names and ideas of Barth and Brünner, Tillich and Bultmann are more familiar than Brahmabandhab or Chenchiah. The time is ripe for a new liberty, the liberty to discard, if so desired, the western modes of thought which have for so long been obligatory, and to move freely in the Indian universe of discourse, both classical and contemporary, building on the work of the pioneer theologians we have studied, and forging ahead into new realms of enquiry.

To use a familiar simile, the Church in many parts of India has been like a pot-plant transplanted into a garden. At first it grew in its imported soil, and perhaps the assistant gardener who accompanied it forgot to break the pot! The time has come, however, when the plant has taken root in the new environment; the pot has been shattered from within and the imported soil has been absorbed and replaced. No longer does the gardener have to bring the water of the Word from a distant source, for the plant has struck its own deep tap-root to the perennial springs. It grows larger and more luxuriant than it ever did in its bleak northern home. And the time for fruit-bearing has come. The western confessions have indeed been channels for bringing the Water of Life, but they are not the only ones and the Indian Church must in time develop its own confessions, a development to which many official statements and publications already look forward.

Summae are perhaps written only in so-called 'Christian' countries, lands with a long and dominant Christian tradition. India's immediate need is not so much for an Aquinas, a Calvin or a Barth as for men like Clement and Origen, men of adventurous mind and vivid imagination, men like Sundar Singh who can convince people's minds in their own language and win their hearts. It is a working, witnessing, convincing theology that is needed and that is in fact being forged today. It would seem that before a *Summa* or *Church Dogmatics* or even an Indian confessional statement is formulated, there is need for much grappling with the very heart of the Christian revelation and of the Biblical witness, in order to undertand its inner meaning and inner structure, and to expound that meaning through Indian terms and thought-forms both old and new. The need is not for speculation, or 'adaptation' of Hinduism, or mere 'translation' of western theology. It is rather for the understanding of the deepest Christian insights into the very nature and being of God, Christ, man and the world, and their expression in Indian language which can be understood and so accepted.

What Indian theology is attempting to do should be sharply distinguished from the work of western theologians like Bultmann, Tillich and Bishop Robinson in reformulating Christian doctrines in modern 'demythologised' terminology. It is a disturbing but demonstrable fact that Christian theological statements when demythologised according to the Bultmann pattern become virtually indistinguishable from the 'demythologised Hinduism' of Dr. Radhakrishnan.[1] Some people may feel that this indicates a deep underlying unity between Christianity and *advaita*, but surely the more convincing explanation is simply that the process of demythologising applied to Christian statements denudes them of their true content as well as of their 'mythological' form. Bultmann and Robinson

[1] e.g. Bultmann's letter to the Sheffield Industrial Mission quoted in *The Honest to God Debate* (1963), p. 138.

are operating within the western tradition where Greek and Latin terminology is still that used and understood, albeit in a developed context, and where the need is rather for explanation of the so-called mythology than for its removal. But the whole Indian cultural background is different and what is needed for effective Christian witness is not demythologising but rather the re-clothing of the underlying Truth in another set of terms and thought-forms, which is already in existence and is as rich and vivid as the original Graeco-Roman context. If it was legitimate for the Church to use western language at Chalcedon, and indeed ever since, it must be legitimate for the Indian Church to use Sanskritic language now and for ever! Indian and western theology begin with the same *śruti*, while the *anubhava* of the Damascus road, or of Augustine's garden at Ostia, is fundamentally no different from that of Sundar Singh in the Punjab. Only the *yukti* is different, the inference from the facts, and the systematic statement in terms taken from the surrounding cultural environment.

The task of Indian theology which we have in mind should also be distinguished from that attempted by Fr. Johanns in *To Christ through the Vedānta.* His idea was to assemble from the different Indian schools the building materials which would enable him to 'reconstruct' the Thomist system, using only Indian components. To a considerable extent the work of Roman Catholic theologians in India—De Nobili, Brahmabandhab, Monchanin, le Saux, Panikkar—suffers from the same defect, both in regard to the general Thomist approach and also with particular reference to the eucharist as the 'normal' means of encounter with the living Christ. The work of the non-Roman Catholic writers we have studied is different; it is a testing out of various Indian interpretations of the *śruti* with a view to the construction of a *new* theology which yet witnesses to the same *Satya*, Christ himself. The Indian theologian must not keep looking over his shoulder to see if he is in step with Aquinas or Calvin or Barth; rather he must 'look unto Jesus', the hope of glory who is present in his Church and in his *bhaktas*. As he does so, basing himself firmly in the Christian *śruti* and using all the resources of thought and terminology which are available to him, the inner, underlying Truth of the Christian faith will make itself plain.

Christian Theology and Hinduism

When Christianity entered the Graeco-Roman world and initiated that great confrontation with an alien socio-religious culture, what was the eventual result? It was, surely, twofold. Greek and Roman religion which with its rich mythology and varied cultus had long been in decline, eventually, though slowly, disappeared. Much of the mythology, however, survived as part of secular culture, in epic, dramatic and lyric poetry, in painting, sculpture and music. It was the Church itself which preserved his heritage through the dark ages, and with the Renaissance that Greek spirit was once more set free in the World, where to this day it continues to exercise a profound influence on almost every side of the western cultural environment. Greek philosophy, on the other hand, began to be brought into alliance with Christian theology, first Stoicism and Plato, and later Aristotle. It was used by Christian theologians as an instrument for carrying the Gospel to the Graeco-Roman world and the alliance thus formed between theology and western philosophy has never been totally abrogated and in many generations if not in all has been a source of strength to the Church.

Are there any indications that something similar could or should happen in India? The relationship between religion and philosophy is much closer in India than it was in Greece where, with the growth of scientific and sceptical traditions, philosophy was to a considerable extent independent of any very profound religious feeling. In India, on the contrary, the greatest philosophers have always been regarded as religious leaders also. And yet it is clear that India is moving—and has been for more than a hundred years—in a secular direction, despite renascent popular Hinduism and despite the religious aura surrounding the Gandhian and *Sarvodaya* movements. As Devanandan has pointed out, traditional Hinduism simply cannot provide the religious undergirding needed by an India which is making rapid strides in politics, social development, industry and science.

Despite the brilliant efforts of men like Aurobindo and Radhākrishnan, *religious* Hinduism is playing less and less part in men's lives, and many of those who find most help from the writings of these two great men regard them as secular philosophers rather than as religious leaders. For the modern educated man in India religion is philosophy or it is nothing. Hindu *culture*, on the other hand, as seen in music, art, dance, drama, literature—and the cinema!—is highly popular. The situation is, indeed, not unlike that of the Graeco-Roman world of the first three centuries.

As long ago as the beginning of the century Bankim Chatterji and Brahmabandhab were talking about 'secularism' in this way.

For Bankim, Hinduism was a purely rational 'spirituality' rather than a religion, while Brahmabandhab sought to separate religious from cultural Hinduism, rejecting the former, the *sādhana dharma*, and replacing it with Christianity, while enthusiastically retaining the *samāj dharma* or social and cultural aspect of Hinduism. This corresponds closely with Devanandan's more recent statement with its encouragement to Christians to claim " cultural kinship' with their Hindu neighbours, while at the same time seeking to share with those neighbours the theological basis which alone will enable them to stand the strains caused by the collapse of traditional orthodoxy.

The carrying out of this process involves, as did the similar process in the first centuries, an alliance between Christian theology and different types of non-Christian philosophical thought, in order that the Hindu tradition may be transformed—not into a new syncretistic religion but into a Christianity which is simultaneously faithful to the *śruti* and yet culturally 'at home' in India.[1] Brahmabandhab himself took a great step in that direction and others, as we have seen, have followed. The process still goes on. It is not a process comparable to Farquhar's 'Crown of Hinduism' approach. It is closer to what Devanandan describes as 'fulfilment', not in the sense of a historical process culminating in the establishment of Christianity but rather as the breaking in here and now of 'the End' that is of the Christ on whom the whole movement of history, both sacred and secular, is converging. It can also be described in Panikkar's terms as fulfilment related to promise, as fruit to seed, as resurrection to death. For in this process *religious* Hinduism must die and all its finest insights be taken up and given their fulfilment, their true and full meaning, in Christ.

When Paul preached at Athens he spoke of 'the unknown God', whom men worshipped without knowing who he was. Their Scriptures told them they were his offspring and they daily received blessings from him—but they did not know his Name.[2] The age-long quest of Hinduism is similar; it has produced deeply moving Scriptures, and those engaged in it have not been without the signs and gifts of God's love. But he has remained unknown; even at the summit of human thought he has been *Brahman*, which is no name.

As India has wrestled with God, seeking to know who he is, so Jacob wrestled at Peniel and said, 'I will not let the ego except

[1] Cf. W. A. Visser 't Hooft, *No other Name*, London, 1963, p. 123.
[2] Acts 17 : 22-31.

thou bless me ', and then, ' Tell me I pray thee, thy Name'[1]. In the words of Charles Wesley's hymn, India, locked in the struggle, says,

> Speak, or Thou never hence shalt move,
> And tell me if Thy Name is Love.

Christians know the answer to this cry from the heart, and it is their task to make it known :

> 'Tis Love! 'Tis Love! Thou diedst for me!
> I hear Thy whisper in my heart ;
> The morning breaks, the shadows flee ;
> Pure universal Love Thou art ;
> To me, to all, Thy mercies move ;
> Thy nature and Thy Name is Love.

The 'unknown Christ ' is there within Hinduism. He has given many blessings, but still his Name is not known, and his face has not been revealed. In many aspects of Hinduism he is there, waiting to show the full significance of teachings which without knowledge of him are but hints of the reality. The mission of the Church in India is to proclaim the Name that is Love, and to demonstrate the Love which is his nature, so that the veil may be taken away, and God's true Name and nature be revealed in the face of Christ Jesus.

Genesis 32 : 26, 19.

Chapter XIV

HINDU CHRISTIANITY?

In our final chapters we shall take up the work of a number of theologians who received comparatively little notice in the first edition of this book (1969), but whose writing demands our attention. Some of them, like K. M. Banerjea, A. G. Hogg and Manilal C. Parekh, are linked with earlier parts of our story; others are contemporary.

Manilal C. Parekh (1885-1967)

In a previous chapter brief mention was made of Manilal C. Parekh and his views on baptism.[1] Although Parekh died in 1967, his writings have recently been attracting considerable attention, partly because many of his pungent criticisms of the organised Church anticipated those which have recently become familiar in the West through the writing of Charles Davis and others, partly because his views have been given considerable publicity in India by M. M. Thomas and Kaj Baago, and partly because of the fascination of his own spiritual pilgrimage, which led him from Jainism to Vaiṣṇavism, then to the New Dispensation of Keshab Chandra Sen, thence to Christianity, and finally to a personal theistic synthesis which he called the *Bhāgavata dharma*. We shall look especially at this interesting experiment in the evolution of a Christocentric religion of *bhakti*.[2]

Born in 1885 in a Jain family in Rajkot, Parekh as a young man became an ardent follower of Keshab Chandra Sen. Sen had died a year before Parekh's birth, yet Parekh always regarded him as his spiritual father (*dharmapitā*), and followed him in everything, including his devotion to Christ. At a time when the Bengali leaders of the New Dispensation were forsaking Sen's Christocentricity, this young enthusiast from Gujarat steadfastly maintained it, and this ultimately led him to baptism in 1918. Earlier, however, his study of the Swami Narayana tradition of Gujarat had taken him beyond the rationalism of the Brahma Samaj to a belief in the necessity of divine incarnation.

[1] v. supra p. 161.

[2] For biographical detail see 'An Autobiographical Sketch' (v. supra p. 161). There is a much fuller autobiography in Gujarati, *Autobiography of a Bhagavata*, Rajkot, 1963. See also R. H. S. Boyd (ed.) *Manilal Parekh: Dhanjibhai Fakirbhai—a Selection.* (CLS, Madras)

His spiritual journey, however, did not end with baptism. He was soon disillusioned by the Christian community, which he felt to be westernised, mercenary, quarrelsome, and depressingly permeated by people of low-caste origins. Under the influence of Sen's New Dispensation—of which he was for a time a missionary or *pracārak*—and of the efforts of men like Kali Charan Banerji and Palni Andi[1] to found a purely national Christian Church, he began dreaming of a future 'Hindu Church of Christ', and—following the title of P. C. Mozoomdar's well-known book—he gave to his home in Rajkot the name 'Oriental Christ House'. In this, as in so many aspects of his life, he was following in the steps of Sen, of whom he wrote:

> If the affiliation of the mystic consciousness of the Hindu race to the Spirit of Christ through the establishment of the Hindu Church of Christ were the only work that he did, his contribution to the world as a religious teacher and an apostle of Christ would be unique.[2]

From the time of his baptism, Parekh thought of himself as a 'Hindu' Christian, though he interpreted the word 'Hindu'—derived as it is simply from the name of the river Indus—in a national and cultural rather than a religious context.[3] His relations with organised Christianity, never very close, became increasingly strained and bitter, especially after the publication in 1933 of Bishop Pickett's well-known book *Christian Mass-Movements in India*, in reply to which he eventually wrote a very biting attack on missionary methods and mass-evangelism with the title *Christian Proselytism in India: a Great and Growing Menace* (1947), a book which some years later was to earn him a place on the Niyogi Commission of 1956.

Meantime, Parekh had been demonstrating his ability as a clear thinker and fluent author with a series of biographical studies—first on the Brahma Samaj and its founders Ram Mohan Roy and Keshab Chandra Sen, and later on the 19th century Gujarati reformer Swami Narayana, on the religion of the Parsis, and on Sri Vallabhacharya.[4] For many years he had been

[1] For K. C. Banerji and Palni Andi see K. Baago, *Pioneers of Indigenous Christianity*, (1969), pp. 1-17.

[2] Art. 'Keshub Chunder Sen: his Relation to Christianity' in *IRM*, Jan. 1928, pp. 145-154.

[3] Guj. *Autobiog.*, pp. 246 ff.

[4] *Brahmarshi Keshub Chunder Sen*, 1926; *Rajarshi Ram Mohan Roy*, 1927; *The Brahma Samaj*, 1929; *Sri Swami Narayan*, 1936; *The Gospel of Zoroaster*, 1939; *Sri Vallabhacharya*, 1943.

contemplating writing a life of Christ, and this—his largest book—was eventually published in 1953 as *A Hindu's Portrait of Jesus Christ*. This book, interesting as it is in many ways, is disappointing in that much of it is taken up with critical material reflecting the liberal studies of the 1920s in the West, and there is in it little of the author's own religious experience. One misses the penetrating insight into and sympathy with the object of the biography which are so striking in the books on Sen, Swami Narayana and Sri Vallabhacharya, and it is hard to avoid the impression that despite his baptism he feels a closer affinity with these three than with the Christ towards whom he was earlier so strongly attracted. It is sad to reflect that the lack of sympathy towards him on the part of the Church played a considerable role in his change of attitude.

In the final stage of his long pilgrimage, Parekh had ceased to think of Christianity as a separate religion, and indeed had come to the conclusion that if it were to spread any more widely in India as a separate religion it would constitute a great peril for the country. He began to think of it rather as 'an essential part of a harmony of all religions',[1] and so the home in Rajkot was given a new name—'Harmony House'. Unlike Vivekananda, Parekh does not advocate the equality of all religions, nor does he accept the Gandhian term *samabhava*, or equal respect for all faiths. The term he prefers is *samanvaya* or harmony, and he has a clear idea of what this harmony ought to be like; it is to be a type of personal theism, and its manifestation can already be seen wherever there is a religion of personal *bhakti*, whether in Christianity, Hinduism, Islam or Zoroastrianism. To this type of faith, Parekh applied the name *Bhāgavata dharma*, and its propagation became the aim of the closing years of his life. His later books were published over the imprint 'Sri Bhāgavata Dharma Mission'.

Hindu Christianity and Beyond

As the title of his biography of Jesus shows us, Parekh delighted to call himself a Hindu Christian. 'To me', he wrote, 'to be a true Hindu was to be a true disciple of Christ, and to be a true disciple of Christ meant to be more a Hindu and not less'.[2] At the same time he is bitterly critical of the westernness of Christianity in India, repeating many of the charges which we have already seen in Brahmabandhab. We find in

[1] Guj. *Autobiog.*, p. 302.
[2] Autobiographical sketch.

his writings attacks on baptism as a ceremony of admission into what he sees as virtually a Christian caste-group ; attacks on Christian communalism and on the institutionalising of the Christian faith ; attacks on mass-movement evangelism ; attacks on the failure of Christianity in India to face the challenge of vegetarianism ; attacks on 'the Christian monopoly of Jesus' ; attacks on what he regards as the excessive secularism of Protestantism. His criticism, however—and it is criticism which deserves to be read and pondered by all who are interested in the Church in India—does not lead on, like that of Brahmabandhab, to a positive stage of Indian theological construction ; instead he moves gradually away from his earlier Christocentric position, first to 'Hindu Christianity' and then to the syncretistic *Bhāgavata dharma*. An interesting term which he coins to express his Hindu view of religion in general and Christianity in particular is *swadharmāgraha* or 'enthusiasm for one's own religion'.[1] Every disciple (he much prefers the word disciple to 'convert') should, he feels, remain within the framework of the *dharma* in which he has grown up, and he makes it clear that within his own particular framework of Jainism and Hinduism he is ready to give a large place to Christ. Yet he envisages his own personal faith as part of an encompassing Indian, or rather Hindu environment which includes the Brahma Samaj and also the *sampradāyas* of Vallabhacharya and Swami Narayana. It is interesting to note that this idea of Hindu *swadharmāgraha* was worked out in a book—that on the Brahma Samaj—which was originally commissioned by J. N. Farquhar. Parekh's treatment, however, did not appeal to Farquhar, who rejected the manuscript. When the book was eventually published privately it bore a dedication which is a clear criticism of Farquhar's 'Crown of Hinduism' approach : 'To that Inter-communal and Inter-religious Fellowship which is the Proper Crown of New Hindustan'. For Parekh the Crown of Hinduism was no longer Christianity, not even Hindu Christianity. It was the *Bhāgavata-dharma*.

The Meaning of Bhāgavata Dharma

Parekh tells us that when he began to study the life of Swami Narayana (1781-1830) he experienced a definite feeling that in this great reformer God had in some sense become incarnate.[2] At the same time he came to the conclusion that it is undesi-

[1] Guj. *Autobiog*. p. 201.
[2] *ibid*., p. 442.

rable to change one's religion or to encourage others to do so.[1] As he searched for the right term to describe his new position, the word *Bhāgavata* came to his mind—a term much used by Mahadeva Govind Ranade, the Bombay social reformer and leader of the Prarthna Samaj. Parekh writes,

> As I see it, all religions which believe in God can be counted as Bhāgavata Dharma. For if we believe that whoever believes in Bhagavan and worships him is a Bhagavat, we can surely say with conviction that all religions which believe in God are merely different forms of the one Bhagavata Dharma. In this way I include in it Christianity, Judaism, Islam, Zoroastrianism and all the religions which believe in God.[2]

Many ingredients go to make up this faith, though its personal theism makes it quite different from the kind of advaitic idealism envisaged by Dr Radhakrishnan. Parekh writes with deep appreciation of the medieval European mystics like Eckhart and Tauler (whose sermons he translated into Gujarati). He is attracted to the idea of God's 'friendship' with man, and compares Jesus' saying, 'I have called you friends' (John 15 : 15) with Sri Krishna's friendship with Arjuna in the Bhagavadgita.[3] He finds much of positive worth in the often criticised *puṣṭi mārga* of Vallabhacharya, and accepts a spiritual interpretation of the erotic imagery used in this tradition, which he compares with the Song of Solomon.[4] Like Narayan Vaman Tilak he feels that Christianity, especially in its Protestant form, has thought and said too little about God as Mother.[5] He finds a pure form of *Bhāgavata dharma* in the singing of negro spirituals, which impressed him so much on his visits to America.[6] For Parekh, true religion is a religion in which the human heart responds in love and total self-surrender to the grace of God; it should be a religion which 'ushers the soul into the immediate presence of God, a fact which is well signified by the term *Brahma-Sambandha*, relationship with God'[7]. Here is a term, drawn from the Vallabhacharya tradition, which would appear to have definite possibilities for use in a Christian sense. Parekh, however, is not really interested in using Hindu terminology to express Christian ideas; he prefers to immerse himself successively

[1] Guj. *Autobiog.*, p. 442.
[2] *ibid.*, p. 443.
[3] *Vallabhacharya*, pp. 80, 81.
[4] *ibid.*, pp. 195, 6 and 259, 60.
[5] *Portrait*, pp. 146-50.
[6] *Vallabh.*, pp. 116, 7.
[7] *Vallabh.*, pp. 195, 6.

in one *bhakti* tradition after another, and the earlier Christocentricity, inherited from Sen, has largely evaporated in his later writings.

The Spiritual and the Secular

Much of Parekh's criticism of institutional Christianity has a contemporary ring, and, as we have seen, this side of his writing has had considerable influence on recent Indian writers like M. M. Thomas. Yet there is another aspect to his thought which immediately seems to relegate it to a world very different from that of the modern secular theologian, for Parekh regards his *Bhāgavata dharma* as something which is very definitely spiritual, and is highly critical of 'secularism'. Indeed he has little use for involvement in the world of politics and social action—the sphere of *samāj dharma*—which, in a Pauline phrase, he scathingly characterises as 'carnal'. Much modern writing on secularism, involvement, and the importance of the material creation and the body would have left him profoundly unimpressed, for his emphasis, like that of most Hindu traditions except that of Aurobindo, is on the primacy of the spiritual. 'The Jews', he writes, 'unfortunately had no clear conception of soul as an entity apart from and transcending the body'; and many Christians, he implies, still hold this view.[1] Jesus, on the other hand, did distinguish between soul and body, and this, for him, is the importance of the story of the temptation. The words, 'Man does not live by bread alone', says Parekh, 'mean that man is primarily an *ātman*, a spirit, and though the body is integral to man as man, it is altogether secondary'. The passage shows, he says, that Jesus had attained *ātmaniṣṭha*, faith in his being a spirit.[2] So too the kingdom of God is thought of as a spiritual kingdom, and contrasted with the kingdom of this world.[3] Parekh writes with approval of the complete severance of spirit from matter in the Hindu mind, and contrasts the Jewish and Christian tendency to think of man as a psychosomatic unit in which spirit and flesh are both essential. The whole western world, he feels, has become secularised and 'carnal' —Luther's own attitude to life had much to do with the development[4]—and as a result it is now 'intoxicated with pride of race, culture, creed and empire'[5].

[1] *Portrait*, pp. 134 ff.
[2] *ibid.*, pp. 215, 6.
[3] *ibid.*
[4] *Vallabh.*, p. 58.
[5] *Portrait*, p. 331.

Parekh's position here, with its rejection of the body, and of involvement in secular life, is very different from that of M.M. Thomas or Kaj Baago, who in other ways have drawn considerrable inspiration from him. It is interesting to remember that although some of Parekh's friends—notably Mahatma Gandhi and Indulal Yagnik, both men of great personal asceticism—were deeply involved in the national movement and in party politics, he himself on the whole remained politically aloof. He felt—as indeed did Gandhi and his closest followers—that asceticism and renunciation were essential components of the highest form of religion, and was attracted not only by Hindu asceticism but by the Roman Catholic monastic tradition. He felt that classical Protestantism, in its virtual rejection of asceticism and its full-blooded acceptance of involvement in the world, had been reduced to a purely 'secular' faith with little in it to attract Hindus.[1]

The Church, Baptism and Caste

Although Parekh was baptised in the Anglican Church he never took an active part in the life of the Christian community, and in fact became increasingly critical of organised Christianity. His earlier desire was to form a 'Hindu Church of Christ' along the lines of Sen's New Dispensation, but later even this Christocentricity was abandoned, and Christianity was reduced to a single component part of the theistic *Bhāgavata dharma*. Unlike Subba Rao, whose teaching we shall shortly be considering, Parekh did not attack the sacrament of baptism as such, but he refused to regard it as a rite of admission into the visible Christian Church, and held that it should not be treated as signifying a break with the new disciple's caste-group.[2] He regarded it as a purely spiritual sacrament, signifying the dedication of the disciple to Christ, and demonstrated his conviction not only by his own baptism but by administering baptism to others.[3] Many Christians today would agree with his view that a new Christian should remain in close contact with his caste-group—as Parekh himself did.

Yet when we examine his views on the institution of caste we find that they are very conservative, and are rightly criticised by

[1] *Portrait*, p. 285.
[2] 'The Spiritual Significance and Value of Baptism', Art. in *NCC Review*, Sept. 1924, pp. 324-9.
[3] Guj. *Autobiog.*, p. 293.

M. M. Thomas.[1] He felt, for example, that it was pointless to insist on table-fellowship between Christians of different caste or racial backgrounds: it is better, he said, to let them have a purely spiritual fellowship like that of the Swami Narayana *satsangha.* Caste Hindus, for example, can enjoy the emotional singing of Harijan *bhajan maṇḍalas* without having to share table-fellowship with them. Or again—and here his argument sounds very strange after Martin Luther King—he expresses his delight, during a visit to America, at listening to the profound *bhakti* of negro spirituals, while at the same time indicating his approval of the segregation of blacks and whites into separate congregations.[2]

Briefly, then, his ideas on the Church, baptism and caste are that individual 'disciples' should express their devotion to Christ by baptism, but should remain as members of their caste-group, and should refrain from any act which would lead them to change their *samāj dharma*, so setting up a new and heterogeneous community—a process of the confusion of castes which Parekh, like the *Bhagavadgita*, rejects in no uncertain terms.[3]

* * *

It is interesting to compare Parekh with Upādhyāya. Both sought to carry on the tradition of Keshab Chandra Sen, and this brought both of them to baptism. Both were harsh critics of the organised Christianity of their day, and both sought to perpetuate the Christocentricity of Sen. But whereas Upādhyaya laid the basis of an impressive Christian *advaita*, Parekh's study and experience in the field of *bhakti* led him eventually to a *Bhāgavata dharma* in which Christ was no longer at the centre, and for which the Bible was not the primary *pramāṇa*, but only one among other scriptures. As a result, one feels that the *Bhāgavata dharma* which he envisaged—and indeed practised—was a synthesis based primarily on his own emotional commitment to Indian culture and to the idea of fellowship with God. He never makes clear what the object of *bhakti* is. Is it the God who is the Father of Jesus Christ? It is hard to say. It is difficult to avoid the conclusion that Parekh's *Bhāgavata dharma*, though it may be faithful to the spirit of Hinduism, has in fact moved away from the historic Christian faith as it has been accepted down the ages.

[1] M. M. Thomas, *The Acknowledged Christ of the Indian Renaissance*, pp. 264-6.

[2] Guj. *Autobiog.*, pp. 393-5.

[3] *Gita*, I. 41-43.

M. M. Thomas writes sympathetically[1] of Parekh's conception of the Church taking a new form as 'a Christ-centred fellowship of faith and ethics in the Hindu religious community', and goes on, 'I cannot see any difference between the accepted missionary goal of a Christian Church expressing Christ in terms of contemporary Hindu thought and life patterns and a Christ-centred Hindu Church of Christ which transforms Hindu thought and life patterns from within.' Ideally this may be true, but one cannot help noticing that in the two examples quoted by Thomas—K. C. Sen and Parekh—the 'Hindu Christian Church' did not in fact achieve stability on its Christ-centre, and in both cases the movement advanced a stage further to a new form of Hinduism. It would seem that in order to *remain* centred on Christ a group must be related in a living way to the living tradition of the historic Church of Jesus and the apostles.

K. Subba Rao (b. 1912)

An interesting contemporary leader of a 'Hindu-Christian Movement' is K. Subba Rao of Munipalle in Andhra Pradesh,[2] who has become well-known for his devotional meetings and his work as a divine healer, no less than for his outspokenly critical views on the institutional Church.

Subba Rao's devotion to Christ goes back to a vision of Christ which he had in 1942, at a time when he was virtually an atheist, and completely sceptical about all religions—as indeed he still is today. Along with the vision came the gift of spiritual healing, which he has exercised with great effectiveness ever since. Subba Rao had previously had little if any contact with Christians, and he has never felt any need for baptism or for the fellowship of the visible Church, and in fact is implacably hostile to both of them, regarding them as impediments which prevent many people from coming to know Christ and surrender themselves to him.

Subba Rao has not written any comprehensive works, but some of the Telugu lyrics which he sings to the accompaniment of the *tamburā* at his devotional meetings have been translated and published, as well as some of his letters, while a biography by C. D. Airan and a brief study by Kaj Baago have made his work known to the public.

[1] M. M. Thomas, *Salvation and Humanisation*, p. 40.

[2] K. Baago, *The Movement around Subba Rao*, Madras, 1968; C. D. Airan, *K. Subba Rao, the Mystic of Munipalle*, Secunderabad, n.d.; K. Subba Rao, *The Outpourings of my Heart*, Guntur, n.d.; K. Subba Rao, *Translations of the New Songs*, Vijayawada, n.d.

Retreat, Padri!

We need not spend long on his vehement criticism of the Church, of baptism, of ministers and organised religion in general, since they are not essentially different from what we have already seen in the writing of Brahmabandhab and Manilal Parekh. One example of his biting sarcasm will suffice:

> When the Lord asked John to follow Him, why did he not say, 'Wait, Lord, first of all let me go to a Padri and get myself plunged in water'?... Straight away he followed the Lord, leaving on the spot every worldly thing, but he did not go to you, Padri, as you say, to be baptised. Why don't you search for John, ... catch him by his neck, dip him in your bucket and throw him headlong in your deep pit of religion?[1]

Subba Rao feels that for those who have been baptised by the Spirit, water-baptism is a meaningless and even harmful ceremonial. He has no wish whatever to be associated with the visible organisation of the Church, feeling that it is enough to be one with Christ, and to live out that unity in service of others.

Even Subba Rao's admirers admit that the language he uses about the organised Church is 'harsh'[2] and certainly a reading of his published work suggests a lack of understanding of and sympathy for what the Church seeks to do. Yet there is also a genuine note of prophecy here, to which the Church would do well to pay attention—a note not unlike that heard in Amos or Isaiah or Luther. One is reminded of Jesus' rebuke to his disciples when they tried to stop one who, though not a member of their group, was casting out devils in Christ's name: 'He who is not against you is on your side' (Luke 9:50). In his Preface to Baago's study of Subba Rao, M. M. Thomas quotes some wise words of the NCC Consultation on the Mission of the Church in Contemporary India, which he applies to Subba Rao's movement:[3] 'We rejoice in every such evidence of the work of Christ and seek the fellowship of such persons while continuing to testify to the meaning of full discipleship as we believe our Lord intends it.'[4]

A Christo-centric Mysticism

The outstanding feature of Subba Rao's faith is his complete dedication to Christ, which contrasts very noticeably with Manilal

[1] *Retreat, Padri!*, pp. 13 ff, quoted in Baago, *op. cit.*, p. 10.
[2] Quoted in Airan, *op. cit.*, p. 146.
[3] Nasrapur, 1966.
[4] Quoted in Baago, *op. cit.*, p.v.

Parekh's later tendency to accept a variety of *avatāras* and to allow considerable variation in the object of his *bhakti.* Ever since his vision in 1942, Christ has been the centre of Subba Rao's life, and it is in his name alone that the works of spiritual healing are performed. He writes:

> The very name JESUS inspires me. The moment I hear that Name, the moment I see Jesus on the Cross, I am overwhelmed with something I can't describe.... He is everything to me. I need nothing more.... I am mad in love for Him. My madness for Him won't allow anything else into my head. For Him I live, and for Him I die. That is my religion. That is my baptism—That is my philosophy—That is my heaven—That is my everything. I need nothing more.[1]

For him, the meaning of faith is to become one with Jesus, and therefore to follow his example in everything, especially in loving service, including the ministry of healing. Too many Christians, he feels, make even their inner life a matter of self-centred petition and Bible-reading:

> I shall no more beg you and call it prayer.
> I shall no more bore you in reading and reading what you said
> and did.
> *I shall live as you lived.*[2]

Like Keshab Chandra Sen, Vivekananda and others, he believes that we are called not merely to be Christians, but to *become* Christ. One of his verses, addressed to a Christian friend, runs

> By religion and baptism you became a Christian.
> Don't you know that you too must become Christ
> by living like Jesus?[3]

There is no doubt, then, about Subba Rao's Christo-centricity. But what about his Christology? Does he regard Jesus as God? Kaj Baago concludes that he does not, and that Jesus is rather for him the Gurudev or Sadguru,[4] who brings salvation. Yet surely his own experience of unity with Christ, and his stress on the necessity of such unity indicates that he does in fact regard Christ as God, as the one in whom alone God is fully manifested. A poem which includes the lines, 'And now I

[1] C. D. Airan, *op. cit.*, p. 159.
[2] *New Songs*, Song 10, p. 36.
[3] *New Songs*, Song 6, p. 20.
[4] Baago, *op. cit.*, p. 17.

know that I am that Eternal Spirit (Paramatman)', and 'I have become You' begins with the words 'O my dear Jesus!'. It would seem that here we have a genuine experience of the indwelling Christ which is almost totally unaffected by the traditional Christian way of describing such experiences, and so represents a genuine Indian, or rather Hindu, approach to a genuine encounter with Jesus.

Renunciation

Union with Christ, then, is the goal of our faith. The means of achieving it, Subba Rao holds, is renunciation and the conquest of self. His view of the superiority of spirit over flesh, and of the need to suppress the body and its desires, is very like that of Manilal Parekh, or indeed of Gandhiji, and is in line with the great ascetic tradition of Hinduism. 'Realisation' is to be achieved by detachment from the things of the flesh and the attainment of a state of God-consciousness in which we experience our unity with Christ.[1] Subba Rao writes:

> My Eternal Guru summoned me to follow Him and become a 'Premayogi'. He warned me that wife and children were obstacles and counselled me to overcome the bodily desires and renounce everything; and thus acquire the only qualification to become a disciple.[2]

And again:

> Denying self is the only condition to follow the Brother.
> Whatever you do without denying self will never bear any fruit.[3]

In a letter to his friend and biographer C. D. Airan, Subba Rao writes,

> How to renounce—how to deny—self; how to hate the world—is the only problem for a seeker after Truth. And if you can solve the problem you too will become Christ. For this you have to learn and imitate and live just as He lived. Renounce like Him, annihilate the self like Him, live and die for others like Him. That is the WAY; that is the only WAY. That is TRUTH. That is LIFE everlasting. Mind nothing else. Religion, baptism and all the rest do not come into the picture.[4]

[1] Cp. Airan, *op. cit.*, p. 97.
[2] *Outpourings*, Song 2, p.3.
[3] *New Songs*, Song 6, p. 17.
[4] Quoted in Baago, *op. cit.*, p.30.

We are here facing yet again a question which has concerned us repeatedly in this book—the dualism of body and spirit, and the traditional Hindu, or at least Gandhian, view that the seeds of sin are in the flesh, which must therefore be suppressed. In a letter to Baago, who had questioned the dichotomy of body and spirit on the ground that it does not help in the great contemporary task of building a new Society, Subba Rao expresses a somewhat modified form of this teaching; it is really *selfishness* rather than the flesh as such which is the source of evil and of bondage. 'Bondage makes us live for ourselves and freedom makes us live for others,' he writes.[1] 'Freedom from "Self"—from bondage of the body—alone creates good things. . . . It is exactly annihilation of Self—living for others—which enables us to create a new society.'[2]

The Real and the Unreal

Subba Rao accepts the Vedantic idea of the unreality of the created world, including the human self; all is *māyā*, and salvation means the realisation that we are one with Reality, that is with Christ, and that all distinctions of 'mine' and 'thine' are blotted out. This is really a Christo-centric exposition of *tat tvam asi*:

> Forgetfulness has now vanished,
> I now see myself in you.
> And now I know that I am that Eternal Spirit (Paramatman)
> I have become You, and You have become I.
> How then can I worship You?
> How can You worship me?
> Can You and I be torn asunder?[3]

And again:

> It's enough if I can be free from the delusion that this body is 'I'.
> Better still it is to know that 'I' in this body is 'You', (Christ).[4]

Salvation then consists in 'realising' that the world is unreal, *māyā*, and that we are in fact one with Christ, in an *advaita* which spells the end of all dualism. We have seen, however, that this 'Christian Vedanta', as we may call it, is balanced for

[1] Quoted in Baago, *op. cit.*, p. 28.
[2] See the further treatment of this subject below, pp. 46-48.
[3] *New Songs*, Song 1, pp. 4, 5.
[4] *ibid.*, Song 2, p.6.

Subba Rao—as Vivekananda balanced his Vedanta—by a whole-hearted commitment to unselfish service of others. Unity with Christ, the Truth, is to be found by overcoming the selfishness of the body, and in this way we receive 'release'—a release which sends us out into the world to serve those in need. In Subba Rao's own life this service takes the very effective form of a ministry of spiritual healing in the name of Jesus, and there are thousands of people to attest the reality of this ministry.

• • •

It is not difficult to find fault with Subba Rao's theology. One of his most vulnerable points is certainly his attitude to the Bible, of which he claims to have only a limited knowledge.[1] Occasionally he even enjoys shocking his hearers by telling them that he does not read the Bible, since, in the words of his biographer, 'the wisdom of the Scriptures seems to be stored in his mind and flows freely whenever needed.'[2] His prayer-meetings include reading and exposition of passages from the New Testament, but never from the Old.[3] Subba Rao presumably claims that he has direct realisation of and unity with Jesus, so that the witness of the written record is unnecessary, but clearly this is a highly subjective and questionable position, and one which the Church could never accept. Subba Rao would set the *pramāṇa* of *anubhava* above that of *śruti* and far above that of *anumāna*. Yet in this he is really going against not only Christian but also Hindu tradition.

On the credit side, however, we must set Subba Rao's single-minded devotion to Christ; in him, perhaps, much more than in the later K. C. Sen or Manilal Parekh we find 'a Christ-centred Hindu Church of Christ which transforms Hindu thought and life from within'[4]; and the secret of his strength lies in his Christo-centricity.

Kaj Baago—who views Subba Rao with much sympathy—has criticised his negative and ascetic view of creation and the body, and feels, like Devanandan and M. M. Thomas, that such asceticism, Gandhian though it may be, has little to contribute to an India which is trying to provide basic living standards to a vast and underprivileged population. This is a criticism which applies to most schools of Hinduism, and it is obviously a ques-

[1] Airan, *op. cit.*, p. 40.
[2] *ibid.*, pp. 50-57.
[3] Baago, *op. cit.*, p. 11.
[4] M. M. Thomas, *Salvation and Humanisation*, p. 40. *v. supra*, p. 9.

tion which will be debated for years, for the ascetic point of view still has many champions, among Christians as well as Hindus, and among evangelicals as well as catholics. It may well be that at a time when a full-blooded Chestertonian anti-asceticism has so largely captured the Christian West there is a need for voices like those of Parekh and Subba Rao who plead a Gandhian renunciation. But a fuller and more careful evaluation of the biblical evidence is needed than either of these thinkers provides.

Chapter XV

FULFILMENT—IN THE CAVE OF THE HEART

We have already discussed J. N. Farquhar's idea of Christianity as the fulfilment or crown of all that is best in Hinduism.[1] Farquhar's approach was pushed into the background by Kraemer in 1938, but in recent years a not dissimilar attitude to Hinduism has again become popular, largely through the writings of Roman Catholic authors like Raymond Panikkar and Swami Abhishiktananda (Henri Le Saux), and through the support given to this approach by Vatican II. For an earlier expression of the idea that Christianity is the fulfilment of Hinduism, however, we have to go back into the mid-nineteenth century.

The 'Vedic Theology' of K. M. Banerjea (1813-1885)[2]

The Indian theological tradition whose long course we have been tracing in this book received some of its early stimulation from the leaders of the Brahma Samaj, especially Keshab Chandra Sen. Strangely enough, the highly anti-Christian Arya Samaj,[3] founded by Swami Dayananda Saraswati in 1875, was also responsible for provoking the emergence of a distinctive type of Christian theology. The Arya Samaj called upon Hindus to forsake the various later traditions and return to the pure original religion of the Aryan people, as seen in the Vedas. Among those who were thus stimulated to a study of the Vedas was a Bengali Christian, who had in 1867 retired from being a theological professor at Bishop's College, Calcutta. He was Krishna Mohan Banerjea, and many years earlier he had become a Christian through Alexander Duff. Until the time of his retirement his theological position had been similar to that of Nehemiah Goreh, and indeed his earlier book *Dialogues* had been written as an essay in the same literary competition which produced Goreh's *Rational Refutation*, and reflects a similar approach to Hinduism.

[1] *v. supra* p. 89.

[2] For an account of Banerjea's theology see K. Baago, *Pioneers of Indigenous Theology*, Madras, 1969, pp. 12-17 and 89-103; also R. D. Paul, *Chosen Vessels*, Madras, 1961, pp. 138-167. Banerjea's own main works are: *Dialogues on Hindu Philosophy*, Calcutta, 1861; *The Arian Witness Or Testimony of Arian Scriptures in Corroboration of Biblical History and the Rudiments of Christian Doctrine, including Dissertations on the Original Home and Early Adventures of Indo-Arians*, Calcutta, 1875.

[3] *v. supra* p. 58.

After his retirement, however, and no doubt as a result of the interest in the Vedic religion aroused by the emergent Arya Samaj, his views changed considerably. He was deeply impressed by the high-mindedness of the Vedas, and especially by certain features of them which appeared to be prophetic of the Christian faith. Here, he felt, was the pure religion of the Indian people, a religion which had become muddied and perverted by later developments. It was, moreover, a religion which pointed beyond itself to its fulfilment in Christianity; the ancient Aryans, indeed, if they were to return to the world, would find themselves much more at home in Christianity, than in any of the modern Hindu traditions. Christianity was, in fact, the logical conclusion of original Hinduism.[1]

In 1875 Banerjea published *The Arian Witness*, whose subtitle reads, 'Testimony of Arian (sic) Scriptures in Corroboration of Biblical History and the Rudiments of Christian Doctrine, including Dissertations on the original Home and early Adventures of Indo-Arians.' In this book Banerjea seeks to prove that the origins of both the Aryan and the Jewish race are to be found in Media, and he supports his argument with etymological parallels between the Hebrew and Sanskrit languages.[2] This common background, he holds, explains the parallels to be found in the Vedas to such biblical passages as the narratives of the Creation, fall and deluge in Genesis. It is, however, above all in the institution of sacrifice that the Vedas foreshadow and are fulfilled by the Christian faith, and this is seen especially in the self-sacrifice of *Prajāpati*, the Lord or supporter of the Creation, who is both the *Puruṣa* begotten before the world and the *Viśvakarma*, or author of the universe.[3]

In the course of time, Banerjea affirms, Hindus have forgotten the true meaning of sacrifice, but the testimony of the Vedas remains, to remind them of the faith they once held, a faith which had 'the stamp of universal truth' at its commencement.[4] This precious truth, though temporarily lost to India, is not, however, lost to the world:

> It was in fact a fragment of a great scheme of salvation, which was at first partially revealed and has since appeared in its integrity in the Person of *Jesus Christ*—the true *Prajāpati* of the world, and

[1] Baago, *op. cit.*, p. 14.

[2] This was a fairly common approach at the time. Cp. James Glasgow's foreword to Shapurji Edalji's English-Gujarati dictionary, c. 1864.

[3] *Arian Witness*, Introd. pp. 11 ff., quoted in Baago, *op. cit.*, p. 98.

[4] *ibid.*, p. 102.

in His Church—the true Ark of Salvation, by which we may escape from the waves of this sinful world.[1]

A favourite image of the Rig Veda is that of the 'good navigating vessel' of salvation, on which one embarks through the performance of sacrifice, and Banerjea continues,

> Do you wish to embark on that 'good navigating vessel'—sacrifice, the image of *Prajāpati* the self-sacrificing deliverer of the world? And if *Prajāpati* be found only in the Person of the historical Christ, it will follow that the good navigating vessel or ark is no other than the Church of Christ.[2]

What Banerjea is here asserting is the existence, from the time of Adam, of a 'cosmic religion', one of whose basic principles is that without shedding of blood there is no remission of sin. The sacrifices practised by Abel, Noah and others were prefigurative of the great Sacrifice of 'the Lamb slain from the foundation of the world'[3] and therefore, typical of the sacrifice of Christ on Calvary which they foreshadowed. But it is not alone the Old Testament which prefigures the sacrifice of Christ; Banerjea holds that the fundamental principles of the Gospel were recognised, and acknowledged, both in theory and practice, by the Brahmans of Aryan India.[4] He writes:

> Christian evangelists, when they draw our attention to the claims of Gospel truth, do not utter things which can be called strange to Indian ears. Salvation from sin by the death of a Saviour, who was God and man himself was a conception which had administered consolation to our ancient *Rishis*, and may yet, in a higher form, and to a greater degree, do the same to all India.[5]

At the risk of over-simplification we could perhaps summarize Banarjea's teaching in three propositions. First, that sacrifice is an essential part of religion, and that in the Vedas this great truth is illustrated in the self-sacrifice of *Prajāpati*, who is both the *Puruṣa* begotten before the world, and also the *Viśvakarma*, or Author of the universe, and who is at the same time both priest and victim. Secondly, this prophetic foreshadowing of a great Redeemer has been fulfilled in one historical person only—Jesus of Nazareth. Thirdly, this strange pattern of pro-

[1] *ibid.*, p. 103.
[2] *ibid.*
[3] *ibid.*, p. 90.
[4] *ibid.*, p. 95.
[5] *ibid.*, p. 101.

phecy and fulfilment points to a primeval cosmic religion or cosmic covenant, so that the Vedic writings on sacrifice 'may be viewed as fragments of diamonds sparkling amid mud and dust, testifying to some invisible fabric of which they were component parts, and bearing witness like planets over a dark horizon to the absent sun of whom their refulgence was but a feeble reflection.'[1]

Banerjea's 'Vedic Theology' was, as an apologetic approach, in some ways parallel to Goreh's appeal to the Brahmos. To them, Goreh said in effect, 'By accepting the reformed Hinduism of the Brahma Samaj you have made a good start in your search for truth: accept Christ, and you will have the Truth itself.' To the Arya Samajists Banerjea is saying, 'You are right to have forsaken popular Hinduism and returned to the pure Aryan faith of the Vedas. Now you must realize that the pure faith to which the Vedas testify is found in its fulness in Christ, the true Person, the Agent of Creation, the true Self-sacrificing *Prajāpati*.'

K. M. Banerjea was not the only writer of his time to adopt this approach to Hinduism, and his method is seen in some of the popular apologetic and evangelistic literature of the period. In Gujarat, for example, we find the publication of evangelistic tracts with titles like *The Way of the Vedic Religion* (1863), *and What is in the Veda?* (1883).[2] Other writers, both Indian and missionary, find similar prophecies of the Christian faith in the literatures of many of the Hindu traditions and sects. The Kabir sect, for example, in its description of Kabir Saheb, seems to give strangely accurate prophecies of Christ, and we find these prophecies collected and expounded in 1881 in a book entitled *Sources of Kabir's Religion* by the Gujarati writer Vahalji Bechar.[3] Other groups whose literature has been similarly interpreted are the followers of the Nakalanka Avatara in Gujarat and the Lingayats of Mysore.[4]

The classical exposition of the idea of 'fulfilment' comes, as we have seen,[5] in the work of J. N. Farquhar. In view of the fact that the outlook symbolised by the title of his best-known book, *The Crown of Hinduism*, has been given a renewed lease of life in recent Roman Catholic writing on this subject, it will perhaps be helpful if we look briefly at one of the most penetrating

[1] *ibid.*, p. 103.
[2] See R. H. S. Boyd, 'Outline History of Gujarati Theological Literature', pp. 7-8.
[3] Boyd, *op. cit.*, p. 8. Baago, *A Bibliography*, p. 14.
[4] *v. supra*, p. 159.
[5] *v. supra*, pp. 89 ff.

criticisms of Farquhar, that made by his own Scottish missionary contemporary, A. G. Hogg.[1] First of all, however, we should note that Farquhar's conception of fulfilment, is considerably more conservative than one might expect from the title of his book.[2] The major part of *The Crown of Hinduism* is devoted to a straight, and very illuminating, exposition of religious Hinduism ; when he comes, from time to time, to a direct comparison of Christianity and Hinduism, Farquhar is surprisingly unsympathetic to Hinduism. He does not, for example, attempt to show how a Hindu conception like *avatāra* can be of use in an Indian exposition of the Christian faith ; rather he points out how inferior the Hindu *avatāra* is to the Christian understanding of Christ's incarnation[3]. Similarly for many other Hindu beliefs and practices ; world-surrender must be replaced by self-surrender, indifference by love, inaction by service, self-torture by self-sacrifice.[4] The 'fulfilment' of idol-worship he sees in Christ the image of God, and writes, 'Jesus actually takes in the Christian life, the place which is held by idols in idolatrous systems. He is effectively the image of God.'[5] There is, Farquhar believes, a basic truth behind all idolatry, the truth that man needs, and can have, access to the heart of God ; yet this truth has been 'pitiably distorted' in idolatry, and can be 'crowned' in Christianity only in the sense that Christ *replaces* it. Farquhar writes, 'Christ passes everything through His refiner's fire, in order that the dross, which Hindus know so well, may pass away ; but the gold will then shine all the brighter.... He is not the Destroyer but the Restorer of the national heritage.'[6]

Not unnaturally Hogg, who had a much more acute theological understanding than Farquhar, found the idea of fulfilment unsatisfactory, and criticised it in reviews of Farquhar's book, and also in an earlier paper which he wrote as part of the preparatory material for the Edinburgh Conference of 1910. When Hogg writes that 'what Christ directly fulfils is not Hinduism but the need of which India has begun to be conscious'[7],

[1] See Eric J. Sharpe, *The Theology of A. G. Hogg* (Madras, 1971), especially pp. 47-59.

[2] *v. supra.*, p. 90.

[3] We have already noted (v. *supra*, p. 81) that Farquhar's views on Krishna involved him in a controversy with Upadhyaya in 1904. It is doubtful if he had much sympathy with Upadhyaya's approach, even though he recognized Vedanta as the 'summit of Indian Thought'. (*Crown*, pp. 219 ff.)

[4] *Crown*,, p. 293.

[5] *ibid.*, p. 350.

[6] *ibid.*, p. 54.

[7] Quoted in Sharpe, *op. cit.*, p. 50.

he is perhaps expressing what Farquhar really meant, despite the evolutionary implications of the word 'crown'. Hogg's own view is, I believe, more profound than Farquhar's, though at first glance it seems to be rather negative. Instead of searching out points of similarity between Christianity and Hinduism, as Farquhar does, we ought, he feels, to seek to identify those points where Christian and Hindu conceptions are most radically opposed; and then try to formulate Christian doctrine in a way which speaks clearly to the actual need of our Hindu partners in dialogue. Hogg follows this pattern in his own approach and, as a result we find him giving a deeply relevant exposition of the atonement in the context of the Hindu belief in *karma*, and of the question of unmerited suffering. Again, against the background of the dominant Hindu idea of asceticism and renunciation he works out an interesting exposition of Christianity as redemption *from* the world: as offering 'to save the world from itself —to save all that is precious in our world-order from all in it that makes for decay and corruption.'[1] Hogg never takes a Hindu belief simply in order to say facilely, 'this is fulfilled in Christ.' Rather he selects a basic Hindu belief like the doctrine of *karma*, studies it deeply, seeks to find to what profound and anguished need of the human soul it is the answer, and then gives his own exposition of the corresponding Christian doctrine, speaking to the condition of his Hindu partner in dialogue. Christianity, in this view, is not the 'fulfilment' of Hinduism; yet the encounter with Christ may bring a Hindu to the point where he realizes his own need—a need of which he was previously unaware—and then sees that this need is fulfilled in Christ. 'Christian influence can somehow make Hinduism cease to be a gospel to the Hindu. Christianity is the solution of a religious problem; which the typical Hindu does not feel but which, under favourable conditions, he can be made to feel.'[2] The task of the Christian, then, is to introduce his Hindu friend to Jesus, 'the great Awakener of new deeps of soul-hunger.'[3]

At this point Hogg appears to be more critical of Hinduism than does Farquhar; certainly his critique of Hinduism—for example of *karma* and of the doctrine of *avatāra*—is deeper and more sensitive than Farquhar's. In another direction, however, he goes just as far as Farquhar in his sympathetic appreciation of the depth and genuineness of Hindu religious experience. Farquhar acknowledges that 'a man may be acceptable to God in

[1] Quoted, *ibid.*, p. 121.
[2] Quoted, *ibid.*, p. 52.
[3] Sharpe, *op. cit.*, p. 108.

any religion '[1], and that multitudes of men and women have found God through the great non-Christian religions,[2] since ' the condition under which a man reaches God is utter sincerity.[3] Hogg agrees, and affirms that 'the history of religion in India cannot be described as the pursuit of a vain quest ; it has been a finding as well as a seeking.' There are Hindus who have had genuine religious experience, and this experience ' includes fruition as well as yearning.'[4]

Hogg was unsympathetic to the idea of reformulating Christian thought in terms of Indian philosophy, ' since Indian philosophy is full of non-Christian implications '[5]. Yet it is an interesting tribute to his integrity and insight that a number of Indian theologians, notably Chenchiah, Chakkarai and C. S. Paul, were influenced by him, as we can see for example in Chakkarai's treatment of the *avatara* conception, and C. S. Paul's book *The Suffering God.*

The Revival of the Conception of Fulfilment

As we have already seen, in the period between Edinburgh 1910 and Tambaram 1938, the idea of Christianity as the fulfilment of the non-Christian faiths became widely accepted. Thereafter for about twenty years, from the publication of Kraemer's *The Christian Message in a Non-Christian World* in 1938 until about the end of the 1950s, it dropped out of favour. In the past ten years, however, under the influence of the ' dialogue ' approach, and with the blessing of Vatican II, it has once again become popular, especially in the writings of a number of Roman Catholic theologians, some of whom, like Panikkar, we have already mentioned. Most of these writers are indebted in various ways to Fr. Jules Monchanin, who in turn, as we have seen, regarded himself as heir to the De Nobili, Brahmabandhab, Johanns tradition. Swami Abhishiktananda, for example, a Frenchman by birth, was Monchanin's friend and colleague, joined him in 1950 in the foundation of the Saccidananda Ashram at Tiruchirapalli in South India, and after Monchanin's death in 1957 continued and developed his work. Raymond Panikkar and Klaus Klostermaier have both participated in some of the dialogue meetings on Hindu and Christian spirituality

[1] *Crown*, p. 27.
[2] *ibid.*, p. 28.
[3] *ibid.*, p. 27.
[4] Quoted in Sharpe, *op. cit.*, p. 106.
[5] Sharpe, *op. cit.*, p. 57.

which began in 1957, and whose insights are described in Abhishiktananda's *Hindu-Christian Meeting Point*[1]. We have already, in Chapter XI, given some attention to the work of this group, but we shall now examine some writings which were not available when the first edition of this book was written.

Swami Abhishiktananda (1910-1973)

Fulfilment

We shall look first at Abhishiktananda's understanding of 'fulfilment', which in some important ways is different from that of Farquhar. Following the lead of Upadhyaya and Monchanin, he regards Vedanta, especially as seen in Saccidananda-Brahman, as the highest form of Hinduism. He also accords to the Hindu religious experience a deeper and more permanent value than does Farquhar. Farquhar describes the details of Hindu belief and practice only to pass a sweeping judgment on the whole 'system', as he calls it. Abhishiktananda on the other hand lovingly examines each detail in order to see how it can be fulfilled in the Christian experience. Our study of Hinduism is to be in the context of its 'eschatological fulfilment in the very heart of the *Pleroma*',[2] he writes, for he holds that it is the Christian experience which brings the advaitin experience to its full fruition.[3] God, he believes, has planted the seeds of true faith in Hindu hearts, and it is the task of the Christian mission to help that holy seed to germinate, since 'in the designs of God, Hinduism tends of its very nature towards Christianity as its eschatological fulfilment.'[4] This is very like the 'prophetic fulfilment' approach of K. M. Banerjea. The Scriptures of India, says Abhishiktananda, and especially the Upanishads, 'will find their full and definitive meaning in Christ the Lord and the Pleroma.' The Upanishadic revelation will one day unfold its eschatological meaning through the work of some future Indian theologian, who has been to the depths of the Vedantic experience and there encountered the glory of Christ, and who, in his Christian exposition of the Hindu Scriptures, will set the seal upon all that God has predestined for

[1] Swami Abhishiktananda: *Hindu-Christian Meeting Point within the Cave of the Heart*, Bombay, 1969. (Cited as *Cave*). Abhishiktananda died on December 3, 1973, after the following section had already gone to press.

[2] *Cave*, p. 3.

[3] *ibid.*, p. 15.

[4] *ibid.*, pp. 23-25.

Hinduism.'[1] For, 'all that was said in the Upanishads was in reality said of Christ.'[2] In a phrase strongly reminiscent of Farquhar, he writes, 'The Bible appears to the Christian in his faith as the crown and completion of the Upanishads.'[3] Fulfilment in this context means 'transposition and sublimation'—the 'passage' from the Vedantic to the evangelical experience, and it is not possible without a leap of faith. Fulfilment is not a continuous glide towards Christ; there is here a break in continuity, and grace alone enables a man to reach 'the other bank'.[4]

As we shall see in a moment, Abhishiktananda regards fulfilment as a matter of deep spiritual experience, rather than as a theological exercise. And so he sees the deepest and best Hindu experience as being fulfilled and completed in Christ: 'a living synthesis—rather an osmosis—will result only from the achievement and completion in Christ of the Hindu Vedantic spiritual experience, within the heart of the elect.'[5] For, 'it is at its very source that the Hindu dharma must pass through the mystery of death and resurrection which alone leads to the full glory of Christ right in heaven—in the bosom of the heart—at the right hand of the Father.'[6]

'*In the Cave of the Heart*'

It is important to remember that Abhishiktananda's theology is the product of actual dialogue with Hindu friends, in which spiritual experience at the deepest level is shared in a spirit of love and fellowship. Using a Hindu phrase, he describes this meeting of Hindu and Christian as taking place 'in the cave of the heart', by which is meant the secret and deep place where each individual meets God—'the place of ultimate encounter, where the spirit of man becomes one with the Spirit of God'.[7] Here we come to what is perhaps the major difference between Abhishiktananda's idea of fulfilment and that of Farquhar: Farquhar on the whole deals with doctrines, ideas and practices, while Abhishiktananda is interested in 'spirituality'—the deep experience where a man, whether Hindu or Christian, meets with God and gives his response in love and obedience. There is here no place for intellectual argument; what is needed is

[1] *ibid.*, pp. 44-5.
[2] *ibid.*, p. 89.
[3] *ibid.*, p. 92.
[4] *ibid.*, p. 49.
[5] *The Church in India* (CLS, 1969), p. 37.
[6] *ibid.*, pp. 68-9.
[7] *Cave*, p. xvi.

rather a loving sharing of experience, an attempt to penetrate into the depths of one another's heritage.

According to Vedanta, the deepest spiritual experience is that of the unity of the *ātman* with *Brahman*. Abhishiktananda follows Upādhyaya and Monchanin in believing that the fullest meaning of Brahman is realized only when it is seen as Saccidananda, and when Saccidananda is experienced, not at the paracosmic or metacosmic, but at the interpersonal level, as the Christian Trinity. What happens then, when Christian and Hindu meet in deepest sincerity in the cave of the heart is that, first, there is a profound 'immediate experience of the ultimate non-duality of existence'—an experience in which Christian and Hindu both participate fully; and secondly, as the true meaning of Saccidananda is revealed, there comes 'the experience of divine Sonship in the unity of the Spirit',[1] when it is realized—as Monchanin held—that mystic unity must be Trinitarian or it is nothing. Abhishiktananda believes that the first of these experiences is 'ordained' by God to pass over into the second, showing that 'the Christian experience is not inferior to that of the Vedanta, but that without destroying or diminishing any of the essential values of that experience it opens as it were, from within, into new depths of the unfathomable mystery of God.'[2]

This experience involves the Christian in 'non-duality' or *advaïta*, but it is a Christian, inter-personal *advaita*, not unlike the *Kristādvaita* of Dhanjibai Fakirbhai, which we shall be considering later. There is, for example, the non-duality of the believer with God, but this can be experienced only as the believer enters into the non-duality of the Father with the Son, for 'the ultimate experience of God must be an experience of the mystery of the eternal generation of the Son in the depths of the Godhead, and of the inexpressible "non-duality" of the Father and Son'.[3]

What Abhishiktananda is saying here is that it is essential for union to pass over into communion—the *ekatvam* of *advaita* into the *koinonia* of 'As thou, Father, art in me, and I in thee, that they also may be one in us' (John 17 : 21). And he sees the *advaitin* experience as a profound preparation, a valid path, to the Christian realization of union with the triune God. He writes :

In the depths of the Upanishadic identities, faith makes us

[1] *ibid*, p. 19.
[2] *ibid*.
[3] *ibid*, p. 18.

discover the reciprocity and communion of love which, far from contradicting the *ekatvam*, the unity and non-duality of being, is its very foundation and *raison d'etre*. Yet what surer path can there be into the unity of the Spirit than the Advaitic experience of the *ekatvam* of being.[1]

True dialogue for Abhishiktananda comes when there is a meeting of hearts—Hindu and Christian—in the very depth of this mystical experience of unity. The Vedantic experience of Saccidananda is a 'natural' experience, the very summit of natural theology indeed, as we have already seen,[2] and no philosophy or religion in the world can give a man a better preparation for the deepest experience of all. 'The penetration of man into the ontological depths of his own being in the Vedantic experience certainly seems to be the final preparation possible to the human spirit on the natural level for entry into the depths of God, and the revelation of the ultimate secret of its existence.'[3] It is, however, only in the Trinitarian experience that Saccidananda is seen in its real meaning—'the Christian Saccidananda, which is no longer a closing in upon itself but an awareness, no longer monad but communion.'[4]

The Trinity

Abhishiktananda follows the line of Keshab Chandra Sen, Upādhyaya and Monchanin in his understanding of the Trinity as Saccidananda, but as his exposition is considerably more detailed than any of theirs we must attempt to grasp at least some of its features. Like so many Indian theologians, he finds a major source of inspiration for what he has to say in what he calls 'The Johannine Upanishad', which he describes as the completion and crown of the Upanishads and the Bible.[5]

We have referred to the combination of union and communion, of *ekatvam* and *koinonia* which Abhishiktananda sees in the Trinity. The centre of this mystery is in the relationship of Father and Son, 'the "face-to-face" of Father and Son in the essential *ekatvam*',[6] to describe which—following Sen's use of *Cit*—Abhishiktananda uses the terminology of *Logos*, of *Vac* and of *OM*. He writes of 'the silence from which the Word

[1] *ibid*, p. 92.
[2] *v. supra*, p. 82.
[3] *Cave*, p. 129.
[4] *ibid*, p. 85.
[5] *ibid*, p. 51.
[6] *ibid*, p. 62. *v. supra*, p. 28, for a comparable passage from Sen.

is uttered in the bosom of the Father . . . . the very Word in which all things originate, the Vedic OM, the primordial utterance . . . . the Word, the Logos.'[1] In this 'procession' of the Son, God makes himself known; the Father speaks to the Son as 'Thou', and the Son replies with 'Abba, Father'. But then there is the second 'procession', that of the Spirit, which brings into unity (*ekatvam*) the communion of 'the One' with 'the Other', of Father with Son; in this procession it is the unknowableness of God which is revealed. 'The first procession is the existential foundation of everything that appears manifold here below. The second reveals in all things the mystery of *ekatvam*, unity, non-duality.'[2] And as the word 'Abba'—in which the believer too is invited to join in the power of the Spirit (Rom. 8 : 15-16)—is symbolic of the personal relationship of communion, so for the ineffable mystery of unity, *ekatvam*, there is the word OM :

> OM introduces man into the mystery of the Holy Spirit, the Unspoken and Unbegotten Person, who will reveal to the elect the mystery of the Son, and whispers in the sanctuary of the heart the eternal ABBA. ABBA then is the last word uttered by the creature, for it leads directly to the unfathomable mystery of the Father. Abba is the mystery of the Son, OM the mystery of the Spirit.

Creation and the Problem of Duality

We have already noticed on several occasions the difficulty of interpreting the Christian doctrine of creation in conjunction with the Vedantic conception of non-duality, and Abhishiktananda does not evade the issue, though in its solution he would appear to be combining certain elements from Rāmānuja with his natural preference for Śankara, and it is significant that part of his exposition occurs in the context of a study of the Isha-Upanishad,[3] which is generally recognized as tending towards personalism rather than monism.

Two things, says Abhishiktananda, must be affirmed: first, the unity, the *ekatvam*—in the Spirit—of all things in heaven and on earth, and secondly the 'utter irreducibility of the creature to the absolute being of God.' There is indeed unity, a unity between God and the creature which both Hindu and Christian can experience 'in the cave of the heart', but this is

[1] *ibid*, p. 97.
[2] *Prayer*, p. 63.
[3] *Cave*, pp. 65 ff.

not an 'ontological identification of God and the creature.'[1] Yet the world has no separate existence without God; it 'exists only in God, in the Word, by whom it was made....in the most secret and profound abyss of the Love of the Father of which it is the unutterable expression and manifestation'.[2] 'Creation adds nothing to God, to Being. Nothing that is can ever be anything but a manifestation of God, in the very depth of God.'[3] The world for Abhishiktananda is real—real as the manifestation of God. He does not attempt to follow Brahmabandhab's exposition of *māyā*, but comes closer to Devanandan's view that *māyā* signifies the sin and anguish of separation from God. 'The world is not denuded of truth, of reality', he writes; 'it is not *māyā* or illusion, unless it is thought of as separated from Him who reveals Himself in it, because its whole function as a sign, its whole reason for existing, is precisely to manifest Him.'[4] Though Abhishiktananda seldom mentions Rāmānuja, it would seem that here he comes close to the idea of the world as the body of God, in the sense that it is an instrument for God's self-manifestation :

> Creation is simply the communication of [God's] presence, this mysterious life of God in himself. Everything that exists, every being that lives and thinks, does so by sharing in his being, his divine life and self-awareness. It is from and through this very presence of God to himself that all creatures exist.[5]

For Abhishiktananda, it is the Christian faith alone which is capable of resolving the paradox of created being, the paradox of duality and non-duality[6]. and this resolution can come only through an experiential understanding of the Trinity, of the incarnation and passion of Christ, of creation and new creation. We must not posit two separate types of existence—for example the true and illusory types of the Vedanta—since everything is in God, who at the first brought creation into existence by his Word, in a 'passage from nothingness to being'. And it is Christ, and Christ alone, who holds everything together in this unity, for he is the one who, in his incarnation, realized the presence and *pleroma* of God *bodily*, at the heart of space-time; and it is he who now, returning from the heart of time to

[1] *ibid*, pp. 72-3.
[2] *ibid*, p. 74.
[3] *ibid*, p. 95.
[4] *ibid*, p. 74.
[5] *Prayer*, p. 3.
[6] *ibid*, p. 82

the Father, still remains present to all times in his meta-temporal resurrected existence.[1] The Hindu in the cave of the heart seeks authentic existence by overcoming *māyā* and finding unity with Brahman. For the Christian the true meaning of such unity is realized only in the 'Pasch'—the sacrificial death and resurrection of Christ. 'The passage from nothingness to being' occurs in me only at the moment when the Spirit inspires me to murmur 'Abba' in my heart, so accepting Christ and what he has done for me, in an 'act of faith which justifies man.'[2] 'In the last resort the Pasch is the awakening of my awareness of being, at the very well-spring of being. I am so wholly plunged in the depths of the mystery of God that it is in the very act by which God calls Himself into being that I too am.'[3]

For the Christian then—and this is a deep insight of that Indian Christianity which has learnt from Hindu spirituality—the most profound thing in life is to share in the inner communion of the Trinity, to become one with God in the sense of penetrating into and sharing that deep mystery. 'In reality the *Advaita* lies at the root of the Christian experience. It is simply the mystery that God and the world are not two. It is this mystery of unity, *ekatvam*, that characterizes the Spirit in God, and in the whole work of God.'[4] The fathers of Chalcedon were grasping for this truth when they said that in the one person of the incarnate Christ two natures were united without separation and without confusion : here the idea is extended to God's self-revelation in the whole created world. 'Advaita means precisely this : neither God alone, nor the creature alone, nor God plus the creature, but an indefinable non-duality which transcends at once all separation and all confusion.'[5]

Abhishiktananda's portrayal of Christian *advaita* goes beyond that of Brahmabandhab, through his more detailed penetration into the mystery of the Trinity. Only in the inner relations of the Trinity can we know what 'being' is, and those relations are entirely informed by love and communion, so that Abhishiktananda can say, 'being is love'.[6] *Māyā* then becomes the sin which separates us from sharing in God's love, and authentic existence means our sharing—by the power of the unifying Spirit—in the love of Christ's incarnation and death, the eternal,

[1] *ibid*, p. 99
[2] *ibid*, p. 101
[3] *ibid*, p. 100
[4] *ibid*, p. 109
[5] *ibid*, p. 107, cp. Mark Sunder Rao's exposition of ananyatva, v. *supra* pp. 214-6.
[6] *ibid*, p. 90

reciprocal love of Father and Son. And the incarnate Christ is the one who overcomes all non-duality, bringing man and his world into unity with God.

> Christ is the one who . . . gives to the universe as well as to the individual man reality and consistency, who raises man from the *asat*, that is the non-being of the creature and of the sinner, up to the Being, the Awareness, the Bliss, the *Saccidananda* of the Father.[1]

The Father utters his 'Thou' to the Son, and the Son responds with 'Abba'. We too can join in the dialogue:

> Here there is certainly an ineffable 'I' and 'Thou'. But there is also, and inseparably, a no less ineffable *ekatvam*. Only awareness of this *ekatvam*, the unity of the Spirit, gives entry into the mystery of the communion of Love at the heart of that unity, and it is the Spirit of wisdom, the divine *Pneuma* in the very depths of our own *pneuma*, who makes us experimentally aware of this. . . . This indivisible mystery of *koinonia* and *ekatvam*, of simultaneous communion and non-duality, is found everywhere in being: between the divine Persons, between men, between men and God. It is in Jesus, the man-God, that it is most fully revealed.[2]

The Cosmic Covenant and the Pleroma

Earlier in this chapter when discussing the Vedic theology of K. M. Banerjea, we referred to the idea of a primal 'cosmic religion'—a sort of fundamental underlying religion of humanity, thought of as having been implanted by God in all men, but today obscured except for fitful gleams here and there. Abhishiktananda finds this idea a useful one in his effort to define the relationship of Christianity and Hinduism, and indeed it is one which has become widely current recently through its use by the Panikkar group, and its reflection in some of the literature arising out of Vatican II.[3]

Abhishiktananda gives a very helpful review of the biblical evidence, paying special attention to Melchizedek, whom he calls 'a priest of the cosmic testament', and also to Isaiah 60, and Malachi 1 : 11 ('My name is great among the nations; everywhere fragrant sacrifice and pure gifts are offered in my name'). The worship of such ethnic sacrifices is seen as a foreshadowing of the

[1] *Church*, p. 36
[2] *ibid*, pp. 130-1
[3] See, e.g. Hans Küng in *Christian Revelation and World Religions* (ed. J. Neuner, 1967), pp. 37-47.

sacrificial death of Christ, and so it may be seen as an example of a 'cosmic liturgy', to be completed eschatologically in the Christian Church, but meantime to be seen not only in these Old Testament instances but also in the worship of the great non-Christian faiths.[1]

This brings us to a concept of 'fulfilment' perhaps closer to that of Banerjea than that of Farquhar. The Vedas and Upanishads find their completion—their *sensus plenior*—in Christ, who is really 'the end of the Vedanta, since He is the Beginning and the End, the Lord of everything.... Hindus have nothing to lose of their own spiritual riches in recognizing Christ as the real and definitive *Purusha*'.[2] This gives Christians a clue as to how they should react when invited to witness Hindu religious ceremonies; it is an invitation 'to open wide our minds and hearts to discern, beyond the vivid sights and sounds which meet our senses—the perhaps outdated symbols, the formalism, even the superstition—the very reality which these liturgies in a mysterious way foreshadow'.[3] Acting on this insight, Abhishiktananda, Panikkar and others have attempted the gathering of material for a 'cosmic liturgy,' a task not unlike that attempted earlier by Appasamy in *Temple Bells*.

For Abhishiktananda the idea of a cosmic covenant is closely bound up with that of its fulfilment in the *pleroma*—the 'plenitude' of Christ and his Church. In a phrase reminiscent of de Chardin and Zaehner, he speaks of Christ as 'the End on whom all things converge'—since all the fulness of the Godhead dwells in his theandric being[4] (Col. 2:9)—and goes on to describe the Church as the gathering together of all men and all other creatures, the realization or 'recovery' on earth and in time of that plenitude which is the very mystery of God and of eternity.[5] Abhishiktananda insists very strongly, however, on the Christo-centricity of this plenitude, and the fact that it can be experienced only when sin is effectively dealt with. He rightly criticizes Teilhard for his blindness to the strength of sin, and says bluntly, 'the Cross is at the centre of history, and nothing can come to God save through the Cross of the Lord.'[6] It is not possible for man to share in the *pleroma*, in the 'Paschal order of things' where all is 'theandric' (at the same time wholly

[1] *ibid*, pp. 38-41.
[2] *Church*, p. 35.
[3] *Cave*, p. 39.
[4] For a discussion of the term 'theandric' v. *infra* p. 24
[5] *Cave*, p. 47
[6] *ibid*, p. 48

of God and wholly of man) without a break in continuity, a leap of faith,[1] and faith comes only in encounter; it is 'the coming face to face of man with God, the awareness of the divine Presence'.[2] The wonderful thing about the Christian faith is its affirmation, seen, for example in I Cor. 15:28—that 'the unique and infinite Plenitude is present also here below'—in Christ—and that men are therefore able to share in it. Abhishiktananda turns from prose to poetry in his effort to describe the indescribable:

> Plenitude is the Lord,
> Plenitude is His Church
> His very Body and the Plenitude
> Of Him, who, being All in all things,
> Is Himself Plenitude![3]

Abhishiktananda's writing is very attractive—even intoxicating! In addition to *Hindu-Christian Meeting Point* he has published a book entitled *Prayer* (1967), and a critique of the Westernism of the Church called *The Church in India* (1969) besides being co-author, along with Panikkar, of the anonymously-published booklet *The Mountain of the Lord* (1966).[4] Underlying all his writings are certain presuppositions. One is that western theology is too concerned with intellectual formulations, while the insistence on realisation and experience—characteristic of Greek theology as well as of Hindu spirituality—has been neglected in the West and needs to be recovered. The aim of the Upanishads is not to impart conceptual knowledge, but to help the disciple himself to reach the fundamental experience[5] whereas western Christian theology has too often been marred by a dualism which misleads the Hindu as to the true essence of the Christian faith, giving him to understand that Christian experience is at a hopelessly superficial level.[6] Aided by Indian spirituality, Christian theology must now recover the experiential wholeness which it has lost. Later there will be another task—and it is a task to which all the Indian theologians whose work we are studying have contributed—when we must use our intellect to forge out our thoughts 'until the foundations of our

[1] *ibid*, p. 49
[2] *Prayer*, p. 10
[3] *Cave*, p. 66
[4] *v. supra*, p. 251.
[5] *Cave*, p. 53.
[6] *ibid*, p. 105.

conceptual thinking correspond at last to the mystery which is dawning in our inmost being '[1]—the mystery of God the Truth.

A second presupposition of Abhishiktananda's is that the spiritual life is the most important issue for Christians, at least in India. It is a natural assumption for a monk to make, trained as he is in the western ascetic tradition, and now for years steeped in that of India. But there are many Christians, among them M. M. Thomas, who would criticise his statement that contemplative prayer is the most urgent need of the Church in India,[2] or that 'the whole of the Christian life is prayer and contemplation in faith'.[3] The road ahead for Indian theology and spirituality does not lie only in a 'return to the sources', but also in effective proclamation of the Gospel, and effective encounter with the secular world. The kind of Christian spirituality which Abhishiktananda outlines is both profound and fascinating, but it is hard to see that it could ever be a practical faith for more than a select few; could it ever become what Bishop Newbigin calls 'honest religion for secular man'? Nevertheless, this writer's work is full of interest, and many of the latent thoughts of Brahmabandhab and Monchanin find an explicit and attractive outworking in his writings.

Panikkar on the Trinity

We have already examined Raymond Panikkar's book *The Unknown Christ of Hinduism.*[4] Other books of his deal with the meaning of 'religion' and its relation to actual religions; with the eucharist in its relation to Hindu sacramental religion; with the encounter of Hinduism and Christianity; and with the nature of faith.[5] These works are not as yet available in English, however, so here in continuation of what has been said earlier about Panikkar we shall limit ourselves to his second major work to appear in English, *The Trinity and World Religions.*[6]

This book, Panikkar tells us in the Introduction, is 'far more of a meditation than an erudite study, far more a mystical and

[1] *ibid*, p. 19. Compare what is said on the 'shape' of dogmatics above, pp. 258-9.

[2] *Cave*, p. 20.

[3] *Prayer*, p. 15. For M. M. Thomas' critique of this approach see *Salvation and Humanisation* (1971), p. 35.

[4] *v. supra* pp. 222 ff.

[5] *Religion und die Religionen*, Munchen, 1965; *Kultmysterium in Hinduismus und Christatum*, Feeiburg, 1964; *Maya e Apocalisse; l'incontro del induismo et del Cristianismo*, Roma, 1966; *L'homme qui devient Dieu; la foi dimension constitutive de l'homme*, Aubier, 1969.

[6] Raymond Panikkar, *The Trinity and World Religions*, CLS, Madras, 1970

"praying" theology than an analytical and cogitative philosophy'. We are living, he feels, in a time of crisis or '*kairos*', in which there seems to be a converging movement among the great world religions towards a centre whose still point is Christ, and against that background, Panikkar sets out to link the Christian doctrine of the Trinity with the deep inner spiritual experience of Hinduism. The doctrine of the Trinity has, as we have seen, had a fascination for many theologians in India, particularly for the line represented by Sen, Brahmabandhab, Monchanin and Abhishiktananda, who have all interpreted it in terms of *Saccidananda*. This is a tradition which is closely linked with some of the Trinitarian analogies of early Christian Fathers like Tertullian and Augustine, especially the psychological analogy of *being*, *knowledge* and *love*. Panikkar explicitly rejects this analogy, on the grounds of its anthropo-centricity[1]. Nowhere in the book does he refer to the *Saccidananda* interpretation, and in a work on the Trinity such a remarkable omission leads us to suppose that he rejects it also, or at least does not find it particularly helpful.

He finds his clue rather in the three traditional types of 'spirituality' or *mārgas* of Hinduism—*karma*, *bhakti* and *jñāna*—which he builds into a triple *schema*, relating them to the special 'spiritualities' of the Father, the Son and the Holy Spirit respectively. This arrangement allows him to bring together a number of concepts, in three parallel columns as it were. At the risk of over-simplification, these could perhaps be summarized as follows:

(i) *Karma mārga* is described as the 'spirituality' of the Father, the transcendent, the Other, the Creator, the Master, who is present in the Old Testament; the One whom no man can see, whose commands must be obeyed and before whom man's only response is obedience and the breaking off into silence of *apophatism*. Because man cannot see the Absolute, he tends to make images or icons of him, as do the followers of the *karma marga* of Hinduism. Such icons are not necessarily visible images; they may be mental, and Panikkar does not reject them, provided only that they point beyond themselves.

(ii) *Bhakti mārga*, which he describes as 'personalism', is linked with the Son, who is properly called 'Son of God' rather than 'God'. As Panikkar has explained in *The Unknown Christ of Hinduism*, the Son is the Divine Person, the Lord (*Iśvara*), and indeed we ought properly to use the word 'person'

[1] *op. cit.*, pp. 66-7

only of the Son, and not of the Father or the Spirit.[1] As 'Lord' he is the one who is described as Principle, Being or Logos in many different religious traditions, and whether manifest or hidden he is the mediator, the link, the priestly bridge-builder or *pontifex*, the only way to God ; and he is fully revealed in the Christian Church.[2] In a phrase of Irenaeus, the Son is the 'visibility of the invisible';[3] He is the Father's 'Self', his THOU, the Being who is derived from the Father's Source of Being.[4] In this sphere of the Son's 'spirituality', man is faced with the choice of accepting or rejecting the person of the Lord, and the appropriate response is love, prayer and praise.[5]

(iii) *Jñāna mārga*, the way of non-dualism (*advaita*) is linked with the Holy Spirit, the Spirit of God, 'God beyond person'. Panikkar regards the Spirit as immanent, not transcendent, the immanent Absolute which we cannot prove but can only discover by realisation : 'at the deepest level of Divinity what there is is the Spirit'.[6] The Spirit is God immanent, the *ātman*, the Ultimate Ground, who is *Brahman* itself.[7] So far as man's response is concerned, the basic categories here are knowledge and ignorance,[8] and the 'spirituality' is silence, detachment, abandonment—not dialogue but union, where there is no place for the subject 'I'.[9]

These three *mārgas* of Hinduism are, Panikkar feels, typical of man's many and varied approaches to Reality, and each is found in some shape or form not only in Hinduism, but in all the world religions, and even in modern secularism. Sometimes, indeed, the *mārga* may take a perverted form. *Karma mārga*, for instance, may be perverted into atheism, with its concomitant 'spirituality' of nihilism whenever men, in their genuine thirst for the Absolute are driven to reject the traditional religious solutions.[10] (The political nihilism of violence and the barricades he would view as ultimately valuable, an inverted form of *karma mārga* to be incorporated into the final synthesis). In a similar way, he asserts, *bhakti mārga* can lead to a purely humanist personalism, while the way of the Spirit can be over-

[1] *ibid*, p. 50
[2] *ibid*, pp. 52-3
[3] *ibid*, p. 48
[4] *ibid*, pp. 59 and 46
[5] *ibid*, p. 29
[6] *ibid*, p. 58
[7] *ibid*, p. 32
[8] *ibid*, p. 29
[9] *ibid*, p. 38
[10] *ibid*, p. 76

stressed to the point where it becomes a disembodied 'angelism'. (One feels that here Panikkar—who lists montanism, jansenism and puritanism among the so-called perversions—shows little knowledge of or sympathy for the pentecostal tendency in the Church).

In today's *kairos*—the new situation of crisis and opportunity which has arisen through the meeting of different faiths—the time has come for a synthesis of these three spiritualities, a synthesis which Panikkar believes will derive its 'shape' from that of the Trinity. In the structure of the Trinity with its mutual relations of Father, Son and Spirit, he sees the pattern of all true religious thought and devotion, something answering to the inner structure of Reality. For the Christian, Christ is the Person, the Lord, the one in meeting whom we come into touch with God, with ultimate Reality. Yet there is an openness in Christ, and open-endedness in two directions—to the Father, the Source of Being, and also to the Spirit, the atmosphere, or medium or 'Ocean' in which we experience or realize God. Only when these three unite together can we be sure that we are in touch with Reality. In other words, when a Hindu most fully experiences and understands Reality, he finds that he is close to the Christian Trinitarian experience, while the Christian's understanding of his own faith and experience can be greatly deepened by entering into the three *mārgas* of Hinduism. This gives us what Panikkar, in a favourite phrase, describes as the 'mutual fecundation' of the different spiritual attitudes which comprise religions.[1]

How does Panikkar describe the inner relations of the Trinity? He is anxious to avoid using the Western terminology of the early Councils, such as nature and person, and indeed his aim in this book is not an exposition of the Trinity but rather an inter-religious reconciliation of the three *mārgas* in the light of the Trinity.[2] Nevertheless, his theological suggestions are interesting. Ignoring *Saccidananda*, he quotes with approval the Greek Fathers' image of the source, the river, and the ocean,[3] and goes on to give his own adaptation of it: the Father is the Source of Being; the Son is Being; and the Spirit the 'Return of Being' or Ocean of Being. He finds a Scriptural basis for this in Ephesians 4:6, where Paul speaks of God as '*above* all, *through* all, and *in all*'. The Father, 'above all', is the

[1] *ibid*, p. 43
[2] *ibid*, p. 41
[3] *ibid*, p. 61

Source of Being; the Son is Being itself, the one through whom and for whom everything was made; and the Spirit, 'within all', is the divine immanence.[1] (One wonders if his exegesis of 'through all' is legitimate in the context). Of even greater interest, perhaps, is his Trinitarian exegesis of the *mahāvākya* 'I am *Brahman*', so widely regarded as the cornerstone of *advaita*, which, as we know, has usually been rejected by Christian theologians. To explain his interpretation Panikkar uses the illustration of an arc stretching like a bridge between the transcendent God (*Brahman*, but also in Panikkar's exegesis, Father) and the immanent Divinity (*ātman*, and so Holy Spirit). This arc or bridge is none other than the supreme Bridge-builder, the *pontifex maximus*, the Logos, the Son. He is the Word of the Father, but in a strange way he here becomes the Word of the Spirit also. No mere man can say 'I am *Brahman*', but here it is the Spirit, the *ātman*, who speaks, and the Spirit *does* have the right to say 'I am *Brahman*'. 'The one who can speak thus is the Spirit and the word who is thus spoken is the Logos'.[2] The mahavakya *aham Brahmaāsmi* thus finds its Christian meaning as an utterance of the inner colloquy of the Trinity.

As we have seen, Panikkar's aim is to encourage the development of a universal synthesis of the three *mārgas*. In describing this synthesis he rejects the adjective 'Trinitarian', choosing instead the Greek word 'theandric' (divine-human), as 'the classical and traditional term for that intimate and complete unity which is realized paradigmatically in Christ between the divine and the human and which is the goal towards which everything here below tends—in Christ and the Spirit'.[3] The 'theandric synthesis' which he seeks will be one which 'permits each religion and each believer to come . . . to the plenitude and perfection of faith and mystical experience',[4] and in it will be found—though perhaps by other names and forms—'the apophatism and transcendence of the mystery of the Father, the immanence and fulness of the mystery of the Spirit, and the homogeneity to man of the personal mystery of Christ'.[5]

Can one risk putting the message of this book in a nutshell? It is really a continuation of *The Unknown Christ of Hinduism*, whose thesis was that when Hindus think of *Iśvara*—true revealer of *Brahman*, agent of creation, origin of grace—they are

[1] *ibid*, p. 67
[2] *ibid*, p. 62
[3] *ibid*, p. 69
[4] *ibid*, p. 74
[5] *ibid*, p. 70

in fact, though without realizing it, acknowledging the hidden Christ. In this book Panikkar is saying that the deepest experience or realization to be found in all of the great world religions is in fact Trinitarian, so that it is possible for members of every faith to come—even without their explicitly knowing it—' to the plenitude and perfection of faith and mystical experience '.[1] In other words, we might, as it were, speak of ' The Unknown Trinity of the Great Faiths ', and Panikkar would hold that it is in the Christian understanding of the Trinity that its inner meaning is most fully revealed, as we meet with Christ, the true Person, the one who is open both to the transcendence of the Father and to the immanence of the Spirit.

The synthesis which Panikkar is here seeking is not a synthesis of doctrines, a syncretism of Hinduism and Christianity, but rather a synthesis of ' spiritualities ', of ' the different spiritual attitudes which comprise religions ',[2] and in seeking this combination of the three great Indian *mārgas* he is surely right, for each needs to be complemented by the other two, and taken together they have much to contribute to an Indian theology, as Fr. Johanns saw long ago. One wonders, however, if it is not imperative that a deeper and more searching biblical exegesis should be brought to bear on the task: the argument does not indeed rest on Panikkar's somewhat dubious exegesis of Ephesians 4 : 6, but it could be greatly strengthened by a more thorough-going grappling with the Christian *śruti*.

Klaus Klostermaier

One of the most readable and attractive books to have emerged from the ' dialogue ' circle is *Hindu and Christian in Vrindaban* (1969) by Klaus Klostermaier, a young German theologian who as a member of the Order of the Divine Word lived for two years in Vrindaban, birth-place of Krishna, and entered deeply into the spiritual experience of his many Hindu friends. He also took part in some of the meetings for dialogue described by Abhishiktananda in *Hindu-Christian Meeting Point*.[3] *Hindu and Christian in Vrindaban* is a moving and beautifully-written book, describing the author's experiences in Vrindaban, and incidentally leading the reader into many of the basic questions of the relationship between Hinduism and Christianity. Some

[1] *ibid*, p. 74.
[2] *ibid*, p. 43.
[3] K. Klostermaier, *Hindu and Christian in Vrindaban*, S. C. M., London, 1969. (Cited as *Vrindaban*)

of the material in the book, especially the chapter entitled *What do men say about the Son of Man?* had already appeared earlier in more condensed and academic form in the author's booklet *Kristvidya: A Sketch of an Indian Christology* (1967)[1]

Klostermaier's experience in Vrindaban prompts him to ask the question, 'What is the meaning of Christ in the terms and categories of Hindu religions?'[2], for it has become obvious to him that the terms of western theology, and even the terms used in Indian translations of the Bible, are misleading and ineffective. The aim of an Indian Christology he sees as being 'to express in Hindu terms Christ as the living relationship of everybody with the Ultimate'.[3] But first of all this living relationship with the Ultimate must be realized in experience, for India does not require new dogmas on the nature of Christ, but needs rather the Christ-experience in depth, the experience of reality.[4]

There can, however, be many depths to this experience, some of them unplumbed by western Christians. Like Panikkar and Abhishiktananda, Klostermaier examines in turn the three great *mārgas* of Hinduism, and finds helpful features in each of them. His exposition of *Brahmavidyā*, which we shall look at presently, would seem to indicate that his own preference is for *jñāna mārga*, and this is confirmed by his blunt rejection of Christian attempts to use the *avatāra* conception, yet he makes it clear that Christology should not limit itself to the experience and terminology of *advaita*, and that Sankara cannot be taken as speaking for Hinduism in general, just as Aquinas cannot be taken as normative for Christianity. 'If we would content ourselves with a "*Christian Advaita*" it would cripple our *Kristvidya* and make it inaccessible for many.'[5] We shall look at some of the ideas—taken from all three *mārgas*—which he uses in his sketch of an Indian Christology.

Śabda-Brahman. From *karma mārga*, particularly as seen in the Purva Mimamsa's exposition of the Vedas, he takes the conception of *śabda*, the Word, and examines it as a means of expressing the truth behind the Logos of the fourth Gospel.[6]

1 K. Klostermaier, *Kristvidya: A Sketch of an Indian Christology* CISRS, Bangalore, 1967. Klostermaier was perhaps not aware that in many Indian languages, e.g. Gujarati, *Khristvidya* (spelt thus) is the usual term used in Christian circles to translate the word 'Christology'.

2 *Kristvidya*, p. 40.

3 *Ibid.*

4 *Vrindaban*, p. 108.

5 *Kristvidya*, p. 34.

6 It is worth noting that *sabda* is in fact the word used to translate *Logos* in various translations of the Bible, e.g. Gujarati.

He points out that in its technical sense in the *karma mārga*, *śabda* is the Vedic *mantra*, a group of letters whose enunciation conveys a certain meaning and has a certain effect; and its meaningfulness is caused by its connection with *akṛti*, the 'uncreated idea', which in itself is incomprehensible and is never exhausted by the individual word.[1] The Upanishads speak of a *Śabda-Brahman*—Brahman in the form of Word,[2] and this opens up the possibility of speaking of Christ as the *Logos*, the *Śabda*, the one who reveals the hidden, eternal, formless Word which is God Himself. As in Greek and English, the use of *Śabda* establishes a clear connection between Christ the Logos, the *Śabda-Brahman*, and the written word, *Śabda*, of Scripture. Further, it places Christ firmly on the highest level of existence —'the sphere of *Logos*, *Śabda-Brahman* and *Akrti*', taking him away from the lower level of existence, the level of *māyā*, which for a Hindu is implied by phrases like the Hindi *Iśvar ke putra* (Son of God)'.[3] This illustrates how Klostermaier shares Brahmabandhab's conviction that 'nothing but the highest' is worthy of Christ: *Khristvidyā* must be at the level of *Brahmavidyā*, because 'Christ is unique in the sense in which *Brahman* is unique, not in the sense in which one among many sons of God could claim uniqueness'.[4]

This leads Klostermaier to an interesting reference to the *pramāṇas* or standards of authority in religion. He feels that *pratyakṣa* (face to face encounter), *anumāna* (inference) and *upamāna* (analogy) cannot be the ultimate *pramāṇa* for Khristvidya but only *Śabda*, the Word, which is identical with *Brahman*. This insight is close to Appasamy's interpretation of *śruti*, but has the added effectiveness that the word of Scripture, by which our theology must be judged, is seen in its vital relationship to Christ the living Word.

The Five-fold Procession of Iśvara

Turning to *bhakti mārga*, Klostermaier is almost as outspoken as Brahmabandhab in his rejection of the use of the term *avatāra* for Christ. He insists, as a matter of principle, that Christians when they use Hindu terms should use them in the same way as Hindus do; it is an axiom for Hinduism, however, that there must be many *avatāras*, and so if Christ is called

[1] *Kristvidya*, p. 21.
[2] Klostermaier quotes *Mund. Up.* II. 2, 4; *Mand Up.* I. 1 f.
[3] *Kristvidya*, p. 22.
[4] *ibid*, p. 38

an *avatāra* he cannot at the same time be called the *only* one. Therefore, ' even an elementary knowledge of bhakti theology will show at once that the Church's understanding of Christ would exclude the use of a term like *avatāra* '.[1]

However, the word *avatāra* does not exhaust the Christological possibilities of the *bhakti* tradition, and Klostermaier finds an interesting suggestion in the *Pāṇcarātra* theology of the five-fold manifestation of God. According to this tradition *Iśvara* is manifested in five-fold form as *Para, Vyuha, Vibhava, Antaryāmin* and *Arcāvatāra*. We have already seen how Appasamy and others have used two of these terms—*antaryāmin* and *avatāra*. Klostermaier, however, suggests a different interpretation, and gives a five-fold Christian exposition :

> *Para* is the procession of the Son from the Father, *Vyuha* is the proceeding of the Spirit (*ex Patre Filioque,*) *Vibhava* is the divine mission of the Word into the world, *Antaryamin* is the real presence of God in man through faith and sacrament, *Arcāvatāra* is the Eucharistic presence.[2]

We are concerned here only with the first of these manifestations, *Para*, which is used in the *Pāṇcarātra tradition*, to signify Narayana, but appears notably in the compound word *Parabrahman*, signifying that the one who issues from God is himself *Brahman*—God in the highest.

Klostermaier merely suggests this as a possible terminology which could 'help to point out the "Unknown Christ of Hinduism" and to deepen our understanding of Christ.' He is aware of the dangers of misinterpretation, and that the use of such terminology in an Indian Christology would mean a re-interpretation of *bhakti* theology; but it does raise certain issues in connection with incarnation and ' procession ' which need to be faced.

Viveka and the Problem of Dualism

When he turns to *jñāna mārga* Klostermaier leads us straight into a discussion of the great recurring issue of Indian theology, that of dualism—the relation between God and the things of the Spirit on the one hand and the work-a-day world of men and created things on the other.[3] Sankara's *advaita* makes absolute the distinction between *Brahman* and *non-Brahman*: there is absolutely no communication between the created world

[1] *Vrindaban*, p. 115
[2] *Krstvidya*, pp. 31-2.
[3] *v. supra*, pp. 237-9.

and the Absolute, as there is no communication between non-being and being, between *māyā* and *satya*. We can never come to know *Brahman* by perception (e.g. of the physical world) nor even by analogy (as in the Thomastic *analogia entis*) but only by 'realisation', which requires our complete separation from matter. *Brahman* therefore can be known only by the realization of identity—the realization in experience that the *ātman* is *Brahman*.[1]

One of the many sets of terms used to describe this dichotomy of two spheres of existence is *karma* and *ādhyātma*. The sphere of *karma* is the ordinary world of cause and effect, the world of *saṃsāra*, but also the world of science and human enterprise, and of personal relationships, including that with the Lord, *Iśvara*.—Over against this is the world of *Brahman*—the realm of *Adhyātma*, of the Self, of the Spirit, of Reality, which can be described only by the negation of *neti, neti*.[2] The question arises—as it arose for Goreh and Brahmabandhab—What does the Christian faith say to this dichotomy? And beyond that there is another—In which of these spheres of existence does Christ belong?

Klostermaier rightly rejects the idea of an 'esoteric' Christian teaching, like that of the Gnostic-influenced apocryphal gospels of the early centuries.[3] Yet the Hindu follower of *jñāna mārga* will be unwilling to accept a Christ who belongs merely to the sphere of *karma*. There *is* an '*adhyatmic* Christ', Klostermaier holds, and we have a duty to point him out to the *jnānis*. 'The New Testament knows the basic discrimination between the realm of change and the realm of changelessness, of appearance and reality, of flesh and spirit, of sense-perception and seeing in faith.'[4] In some sentences which recall Manilal Parekh's constantly reiterated attack on 'secular' Christianity and his insistence on its fundamental 'spirituality'[5] he writes:

> The *Karma* reality of whatever can be seen and heard by means of the senses is a 'veiling' of reality, illusion, *maya*. . . . Paul constantly stresses the reality of Christ as being a spiritual reality—Kyrios is pneuma! . . . The centre of the Christian message is a reality of the spirit. The radical character of the Christian detachment from the world is as total as the detachment of an *advaitin* from *karma*.[6]

[1] *Kristvidya*, pp. 34-5.
[2] Compare Goreh's discussion of the types of existence, *v. supra* pp. 47 ff.
[3] *Kristvidya*, p. 36.
[4] *ibid.*
[5] Cp. M. C. Parekh . . .
[6] *Vrindaban*, p. 117.

Klostermaier is writing of Christology at this point, and so, quoting Paul, he asserts that 'the true Christ is a spiritual reality'[1] 'Christ is unique in the same sense as *Brahman* is unique—has to be unique, not in the sense of one among the *avataras* who may claim pre-eminence. . . . Christ is not outside *Brahman* in the province of *karma*, but in the very 'heart of *Brahman*', 'in the cavity of the heart'.[2] And the way to salvation is the way of union with this '*adhyatmic*' Christ, a way which demands 'a complete losing of the "Ego", a *kenosis* —an emptiness which alone can keep Him'.[3] This experience, the realization of our oneness with Christ, is parallel to the *Brahmavidyā* of the *jnānis*, for *Brahmavidya* implies identity and realization, never just intellectual understanding. *Khristvidyā*, therefore, is of the nature of *Brahmavidyā*, and demands the same kind of 'interiority'—as Abhishiktananda has said so clearly, and Christ is not 'outside' but 'inside' *Brahman*. *Khristvidyā* is not an intellectual discipline, but a matter of the inner life of realization and unity. 'We are not concerned with the *concept* of Christ (or Brahman) but with the *reality* of Christ. And existential reality can only be grasped in existential experience.'[4]

Klostermaier's 'Indian Christology', then, is based on the fact of realization. It is only those who have experienced union with Christ who are qualified to speak of *Khristvidyā*. But when some one who is steeped in the *advaita* tradition does in fact have this experience, he is entitled to use the vocabulary of *Brahmavidyā* to describe what he has realized of the *adhyatmic* Christ.

Klostermaier has raised the problem of *viveka*—the distinction between the realm of *karma* and the realm of *Brahman* but he has not in fact advanced a thorough-going solution to the problem. This is a question to which have alluded many times in this book, for example as we considered Brahmabandhab's doctrine of *māyā*, Appasamy's interpretation of Ramanuja's soul-body analogy, and Devanandan's insistence on the reality and crucial importance of the created world and human history. Klostermaier has been ready to adopt insights from *karma mārga* and *bhakti* as well as from *advaita*, yet his understanding of the value of the created world is far from clear. Is a solution possible?

[1] *Kristvidya*, p. 37, quoting Rom. 8: 4-13; Gal. 5:16; II Cor. 3:17.
[2] *Vrindaban*, p. 117.
[3] *Kristvidya*, p. 37.
[4] *ibid*, p. 38.

Before attempting an outline of a possible solution we should do well to heed Klostermaier's warning about the danger of mixing up terminology from the different 'strands' of Indian spirituality—a danger from which some of the theologians we have studied have certainly not been immune. For example, if we attempt to convince an advaitin of the importance of turning from 'the world' (*saṃsāra*) to God (*Iśvara*), he will not at all be impressed, since for him *saṃsāra* and *Iśvara* already belong to the same sphere of existence. Only a 'call' to pass over from the realm of *karma* to that of *Brahman* will convince him that he ought to respond. An appeal to stop being 'bad' and become 'good' will have the same disappointing effect, for good and bad, like hot-cold, dark-light, etc.—are simply *dvandvas* or pairs of opposites on the lower, 'karmic' level of existence. For an *advaitin*, nothing on the lower level is of any use; in order to find *mokṣa*, we have to transcend the lower level completely. It is highly unlikely, therefore, that a theology which mixes up terminology from the various 'strands' will carry conviction to a Hindu, and the Christian theologian is left with a great difficulty: how is he to substantiate his claim that Christ is God at the *highest* level—the level of *Brahman-Paramātman*—and at the same time demonstrate the reality and goodness of the created world, including the human personality, the human body, and human history?

* * *

We have already hinted at one aspect of a possible solution in what was said earlier about interpreting *māyā* in the realm of the will rather than in that of being.[1] The argument there was that it is sin which keeps us from union with God, and following Devanandan we looked at Romans 8:18-25, interpreting the word *mataiotes* vanity, (frustration) of 8:20 as *māyā*. It is not only mankind which suffers from this *māyā*; the whole created universe 'groans as if in the pangs of child-birth' (NEB), waiting for God to 'set our whole body free' (vv. 22, 23). Paul goes on, in vv. 26 ff. to say that it is the Spirit who comes to our aid in this impasse, in order that we may be 'shaped to the likeness of the Son' so that finally we may reach the stage of union with 'the love of God in Christ Jesus our Lord', from which nothing can separate us (v. 39).

[1] *v. supra* p. 238, and earlier on Devanandan's understanding of *māyā*, pp. 195-7.

Can this insight of Paul's be given an interpretation which will be convincing to an *advaitin* ? It is important to realize that although there is this 'dichotomy' in *advaita* between the realms of *karma* and of *Brahman*, there is no 'dualism' : it is only an apparent dualism which is overcome when *māyā* is dispersed, and when it is realised that all is *Brahman*. What we are looking for, then, is not something which will effect a compromise between the two levels of existence, but rather something which will give to the realm of man, creation and history that reality, that supreme quality of being which God has.

In order to reach a solution of the problem it would seem that one further axiom must be added to those of the *advaitin*, and that is the basic Christian assertion that God is Love (I John 4 : 16). It might seem at first sight that this was an impossible assumption for an *advaitin*, since God is pure being, yet surely it is implied in the *ānanda* of *Saccidānanda*. We have seen how Dhanjibhai regards Love as the best of all descriptions of God, the description in which all others are subsumed. Love plays a dominant part, of course, in the *bhakti* tradition of Vaisnavism, especially in 'the highest step of *Prema-bhakti*, where all opposites disappear'[1], symbolised by the love of Radha and Krishna. And in the *karma yoga* of Gandhi, with its emphasis on an *ahiṃsā* which goes far beyond mere non-violence we see an interpretation of life which virtually equates *satya* with *ahiṃsā*, so coming close to 'God is love', for with Gandhi *satya* and God were identical. We are not far from the mark if we say that, for Gandhi, reality is truth in action as love.

Now let us go back to Romans 8 : 20 ff. Paul is saying that there are two 'spheres of existence'—that of the flesh (*sarx*) and that of the Spirit (*pneuma*), by which he means not the human but the Holy Spirit. Man himself, in his state of sin—in all his violence and hatred and greed and lack of love—is in the realm of flesh, of sin, of *māyā*. Yet it is possible for him to pass over into the realm of the Spirit, the *paramātman*, the realm of truth (*satya*) and love (*prema*). This happens when his sin is removed and he is united with God, so coming to live 'in the Spirit'.

It is not man alone who can make this passage ; the whole created universe also is waiting for its 'salvation'—waiting to be brought into the sphere of the Spirit, to find there its true use and meaning. The sphere of the Spirit is the sphere of truth and of love, where every created thing finds its true and rightful use—

[1] *Vrindaban*, p. 36

without exploitation or pollution—and where every relationship is characterized by love, not selfishness nor violence.

Mere good works are insufficient to bring man or the universe into the realm of the Spirit; they still belong to the realm of *karma*, to the 'pairs of opposites' (*dvandvas*). What is needed is transformation, 'conversion' into the realm of love and of the Spirit. And this is the point at which man by his own *jñāna* or his own works can accomplish nothing. He depends entirely on the grace of the One who comes from the realm of Reality, as the *Śabda*, the Word of God, and entering the world of *karma* and *māyā* carries through in love the great action which is necessary for the abolition of the *māyā* of sin. And those who commit themselves to him in faith find that they are new creatures, that they have entered into the realm of the Spirit, and that the created world around them has found its true meaning and use, in response to love.

CHAPTER XVI

THE WAY OF ACTION: M. M. THOMAS.

M. M. Thomas (b.1916)

Abhishiktananda, Panikkar and Klostermaier all represent a return to the sources of traditional Hindu spirituality, especially of the *jñāna mārga.* It would be wrong to assume, however, that this is an approach which commands universal acceptance among present-day Indian theologians. Dr. M. M. Thomas is the leading representative of those who advocate a theology much more closely related to modern, secular India, and to the world of the Asian revolution.[1] As we have seen, Dr. Thomas succeeded Devanandan as Director of the Christian Institute for the Study of Religion and Society, and he has carried on, developed and deepened the work of Devanandan, just as Abhishiktananda has explored and continued the tradition of Brahmabandhab and Monchanin.

Dr. Thomas is a layman, who as a student, and later on the staff of the World's Student Christian Federation, became deeply involved in social and political questions, his theological apprenticeship taking him into close contact with Marxism, the national struggle and Barthian theology. His wide-ranging study and his many international contacts have made him familiar with modern theological thought both in Asia and the West, and for many years now he has played a leading and creative role in the ecumenical movement, both in the World Council of Churches and also in the East Asia Christian Conference. At the same time he has remained a loyal, though by no means uncritical, member of his own Mar Thoma Church, and has collaborated in writing the history of the Syrian Churches of South India.[2]

Christianity as Karma Marga

In carrying forward Devanandan's experiments in dialogue, Thomas speaks of three different levels at which dialogue with

[1] M. M. Thomas, *Christians in the World Struggle* (with J. D. McCaughey), London, 1951; *The Christian Response to the Asian Revolution*, SCM, London, 1966; *The Acknowledged Christ of the Indian Renaissance*, SCM, London, 1969; *Salvation and Humanisation*, Bangalore, 1971; *Joyful and Triumphant*, Madras, 1970; *The Realization of the Cross*, Madras 1972.

[2] C. P. Matthew and M. M. Thomas, *The Indian Churches of St. Thomas*, ISPCK, 1967.

Hinduism must be carried on.[1] First, there is the dialogue which studies the contribution of each faith to man and society—a secular conversation which should, he believes, lead on to the possibility of a common culture—not a 'Christian' culture, but an 'open' culture based on a common humanity. Secondly there is the type of dialogue which seeks to come to grips with the central theological issues of each faith. And thirdly there is dialogue at the level of interiority—the dialogue 'in the cave of the heart' of which Abhishiktananda writes. All of these are necessary, but Thomas' own special interest is in the first type, where Christian and Hindu meet together in the context of modern, secular India in order to find common fields of action and service for the good of the nation as a whole and of individual 'persons'.

In *The Christian Response to the Asian Revolution* (1966) Thomas gives a clear account of the impact of the West on Asia, and of the resultant political and social turmoil as western ideas and technology, as well as the Christian faith, have produced a variety of reactions, challenging and disturbing the traditional patterns of life. He agrees with writers like van Leeuwen and Newbigin in regarding the present state of dynamic confusion as part of the way in which the Gospel is at work in the world, and encourages Christians to see that this is so, and to join in the task of nation building, as part of their response to God's action in Christ.

His major work so far—*The Acknowledged Christ of the Indian Renaissance* (1969)—is a fascinating study of the interaction of the Christian Gospel with the Indian reforming tradition, showing how from the time of Ram Mohan Roy the Christian faith has been responsible for introducing new elements into the Indian situation which—even when there has been no large-scale acceptance of Christianity—have resulted in changes at the very heart of Hindu society and thought. The title of the book is a conscious comment on Panikkar's *The Unknown Christ of Hinduism*; Thomas' attention is fixed, not on the static systems of traditional Hinduism, but on the dynamic world of the Indian renaissance, where he sees Christ at work and already acknowledged, albeit partially: 'the Christ in the Western Culture awakening the Christ in the Indian Culture and preparing India for the new life and the Gospel of Christ'[2]. This large volume, which carries a stage further Devanandan's researches into the historical roots of the modern Indian outlook, is a study of the great reform-

[1] *Response*, pp. 115 ff.
[2] *Acknowledged Christ*, p. 251.

ing figures of the past century and a half—Ram Mohan Roy, Keshab Chandra Sen, P. C. Mozoomdar, Vivekananda, Radhakrishnan and Gandhi—who are examined as it were in dialogue with the Christian thinkers who were their contemporaries—Joshua Marshman of Serampore, Lal Behari Day and Nehemiah Goreh, Brahmabandhab Upadhyaya, Manilal Parekh, S.K. Rudra, C.F. Andrews, S. K. George and others. It is a book which, like Barth's *Protestant Theology in the 19th Century*, enables the author to work out his own position on a variety of subjects as he discusses the great figures of the past.

We gradually come to see how Thomas, like Devanandan, is constantly on the look-out for the emergence of a theology which will prove an effective spring for action—action in the four spheres of the created world, the person, the community, and history.[1] Thus he admires Ram Mohan Roy's passionate concern for social righteousness and his 'secular' approach to religion, critical as it was both of the way of mystic spirituality and of that of *bhakti*.[2] We see here how Thomas himself is attracted to a faith which issues in constructive social action—perhaps indeed a form of *karma mārga*. 'Is there not a path', he asks, 'to understand and encounter Jesus Christ as the ground and salvation of reason and morality within a secular framework without a return to traditional religiosity?'.[3] It is a question which in various forms is heard repeatedly in all Thomas' writing.

Despite Ram Mohan Roy's social passion, however, Thomas feels that he was lacking in his understanding of the meaning of love, and here his partner in controversy, Joshua Marshman, was unable to help him; rationalistic Hindu reformer and evangelical Baptist missionary both failed to appreciate the centrality for faith of the self-emptying and self-sacrificing love of Christ which discloses 'the nature of divinity as love.'[4] Thomas finds more to attract him in 'Sen's idea of Christ emptying himself of self and demonstrating his oneness with God through 'an active unity of will and communion through obedience to God and his righteousness.'[5] He links Sen's conception of Christ's 'divine humanity' with the idea of Christ's 'inhumanisation' of divinity, found in Russian orthodox theologians,[6] and this in

[1] For Devanandan's treatment of these four spheres, *v. supra*, pp. 188 ff.

[2] Thomas' own rejection of both monistic mysticism and *bhakti* is seen in *Salvation and Humanisation*, pp. 35, 6.

[3] *Acknowledged Christ*, p. 30.

[4] *ibid*, p. 33.

[5] *ibid*, p. 60.

[6] *ibid*, p. 68.

turn leads on to his own term 'humanisation'[1]; Christ in his incarnation, passion and resurrection comes to share man's lot, to show what it is to be a real 'person', and to help all men everywhere in their 'struggle for a new humanism'[2]. Speaking of Sen's follower P. C. Mozoomdar, Thomas points out how for him, as for so many leaders of the Indian Renaissance, there was 'a conflict of two loves—between love as spiritual union and love as doing the will of God on earth.'[3] It is an acute comment, and Thomas later develops it into the theme of his book *Salvation and Humanisation* (1971). He repeatedly makes his own position clear: the love of God which finds its goal in mystic union is important and valid, but only if it finds its outlet in love for man, and in the doing of God's will on earth. 'Our concern should be that spirituality and metaphysics serve moral regeneration of life[4], for 'humanisation is inherent in the message of salvation in Christ.'[5]

The conflict between these two loves is seen very clearly in Vivekananda, who tried to bridge the gulf between the two by synthesising advaita with what was virtually Christian philanthropy.[6] Thomas notes with approval K. T. Paul's description of this attempted synthesis as 'enriching the content of *karma yoga* by reading into it, in addition to selfless *dharma*, unselfish service in the most human sense of the term, what indeed we cherish as the distinctive message of Jesus Christ.'[7] Perhaps we should not go far wrong if we were to describe Thomas' own approach to theology as an 'enriched *karma mārga*'—not of course in the sense of *karma* as a way of ritual, or of mere 'good works', but as the way of loving, self-sacrificing service. Mere spirituality or mere ethics are of no use to him, for he holds that the vital criterion of truth in religion is 'relevance to the moral regeneration of individual and corporate life in contemporary India.'[8]

It is in his discussion of Gandhi that Thomas' interpretation of Christianity as *karma mārga* in the light of suffering love can be seen most clearly. Despite Gandhi's upbringing in the

[1] cp. *Salvation and Humanisation*, 1971.
[2] *Acknowledged Christ*, p. 72.
[3] *ibid*, p. 97.
[4] *ibid*, p. 145.
[5] *Salvation and Humanisation*, p. 10.
[6] *ibid*, p. 143 and 147-8.
[7] *ibid*, p. 144.
[8] *ibid*, p. 146.

bhakti mārga of Vaisnavism[1] he was in later years happy to describe himself as a follower of the *karma mārga*.[2] In his hands, of course, *karma mārga* was transformed ; the action was action without desire for enjoyment of the fruit of action (*niṣkāmya karma*) ; the inspiration of action was a non-violence (*ahimsā*) akin to Christian love, and its goal was truth (*satya*). Thomas is critical of certain aspects of Gandhi's thought—his view of the body as the source of sin, with its corollaries of celibacy and asceticism ; his blindness to the spiritual sin of pride and self-righteousness ; his rejection of modern technology ; above all, his failure to see Christianity as anything more than the ethics of the Sermon on the Mount—the failure, as Stanley Jones put it, to pass beyond the principles of Christian ethics to the Person of Christ.[3] Yet he feels that Gandhi, more than any other leader of the Indian renaissance, has grasped and acted out the fundamental truth of Christian action. 'Because of his life and death', he writes, 'the meaning of suffering love has been deepened and its larger application to the struggles for political and social justice opened up for the whole world.'[4] Thomas realises that this interpretation of suffering represents a real break from Indian tradition ; it is a classic example of how the 'challenging relevancy' (to use Hogg's phrase) of Christian love has acted as the catalyst to produce a new attitude within Hindu society. 'Gandhi has made intelligible to India the idea of vicarious suffering, in a way which makes it impossible for India to return to the doctrine of karma in its old individual form.'[5] And it is a contribution which has had its effect in the West as well as in India, for example in Martin Luther King, whose application of 'the technique of *satyāgraha* for the humanization of the structures of collective life cannot be understood apart from Gandhi.'[6]

Despite his great admiration for Gandhi's achievement, however, Thomas is far from accepting the Gandhian *karma mārga* without qualification as one that could become the model for a type of Indian Christian theology. Take the question of sin, for example. Unlike Ramakrishna and Vivekananda,

[1] For a good account of Gandhi's religious and cultural background see Chandran S. Devanesen, *The Making of the Mahatma*, Orient Longmans, Madras, 1969, pp. 25-37.

[2] cp. Nirmal Minz, *Mahatma Gandhi and Hindu-Christian Dialogue*, Madras, 1969, pp. 29 and 143.

[3] *Ackn. Christ*, p. 226.

[4] *ibid*, p. 234.

[5] *ibid*, p. 235.

[6] *ibid* p. 234.

Gandhi was deeply conscious of sin, and indeed the tradition of Vaisnava *bhakti* literature abounds in examples of the confession of sin.[1] Yet for him the essence of sin lay in the body and its passions, and the way to victory was through non-attachment (*anāsakti yoga*); he could not comprehend 'the Christian idea that the spirituality of the moral man seeking his own righteousness in works is the essence of sin, and that not more moral principles but divine forgiveness is the only answer to it.'[2] Thomas admires Gandhi's social passion and his political involvement, but he knows, that the asceticism of *anāsakti yoga* can never be the answer to the problems of the modern world. Something is needed, which will really go to the root of the tragedy of man's existence, and deal with the sin of man's pride and selfishness and rebellion against God. Against sin of that kind asceticism is of no avail: all that can avail is the grace of God, and forgiveness, working through the Person of Christ the Mediator. Gandhi's conception of the meaning of personality in man and in God is too limited to be effective in dealing with the real problems of human existence. Thomas writes:

> Lacking the awareness of this dimension of sin and the need of divine forgiveness, Gandhi does not move through the principles to the Person. Probably the basic theological issue in the debate between Gandhism and Christianity lies precisely in the concept of human selfhood. The Christian message of the centrality of the divine act in the Person of Christ for reconciliation stands or falls with its view of the tragedy inherent in man's pursuit of a righteousness of the law, and of the need of divine initiative from beyond the tragedy.[3]

Thomas believes in social and political action just as much as Gandhi did, and to that extent we may call him a follower of *karma mārga*; certainly he has little sympathy for a thoroughgoing theology based on *bhakti* or *jñāna*. He looks rather for a new type of *karma mārga* which will take full account of the power of sin, of the tragic aspect of life (in the Niebuhrian sense), and of man's need for forgiveness if his true humanity is to be restored in Christ. 'One of the most important tasks of the Church', he writes, 'is to reconstruct the Gandhian insights about the ethics of Christ within the framework of its doctrine

[1] cp. the quotation from Dadu Dayal, *v. supra* p. 131.
[2] *Acknowledged Christ*, pp. 235-6.
[3] *ibid*, *p.* 236.

of redemption in Christ.'[1] Thomas' own work may be regarded as a major contribution to this reconstruction.[2]

Secularisation and Humanisation

We have already noted Devanandan's view that God's work in the world is not limited to the Christian Church, but is to be seen also in the reform of Hinduism, and in the great secular and revolutionary upheavals of our time.[3] Since Devanandan's time—and partly no doubt as a result of his work, especially at the New Delhi meeting of the W.C.C. in 1961—this point of view has become widely prevalent among Western theologians, particularly through the writings of Harvey Cox and A. J. van Leeuwen.[4] The conception that God works through secular history is of course not a new one, as the references to Cyrus the Persian in Deutero-Isaiah make clear. Thomas points out how early missionaries like Alexander Duff, and even national leaders like G. K. Gokhale, believed in the providential character of British rule in India.[5] At the time of the national struggle comparatively few Christians threw in their lot with Gandhi, and today there are many—perhaps the majority—who prefer to keep out of political involvement ; many also who prefer to think of Christians as standing up in witness *against* such non-Christian institutions as the secular state, and who look with something like nostalgia to the persecutions of the early Church, the sufferings of the confessing church under the Nazis, or the persecuted Christian minority in Communist states. In a discussion of the famous Barmen Declaration of the Confessing Church in Germany, Thomas rejects such a view, and comments that the Declaration while it was a heroic confession against the 'institutionalised idolatry' of the Nazis, cannot be considered as 'the normal form of Christian witness in secular or Church history.'[6] Christians should not seek for persecution, but should witness in the complex situations of the secular world, and see its great events as part of God's purpose. 'This can

[1] *ibid*.

[2] There were, of course, a number of well-known Christian Gandhians like S. K. George and J. C. Kumarappa, who followed Gandhian teaching in a much more uncritical way than M. M. Thomas, holding that his *satyāgraha* illustrated Christianity in action, and that his own life was a vivid illustration of the way of the Cross. Thomas (*op. cit*. pp. 215 ff.) is critical of S. K. George's 'conformity to Gandhian theology.' (*ibid*, p. 236)

[3] *v. supra*, p. 194.

[4] Harvey Cox, *The Secular City* (1965); A. J. van Leeuwen, *Christianity in World History* (1964).

[5] *Acknowledged Christ*, p. 240.

[6] *Response*, p. 23.

be done only through a continuous confession of responsible participation in secular history, with discrimination between the creaturely and the idolatrous, affirming the creaturely and resisting the idolatrous in the power of the Holy Spirit.'[1] The Church must endeavour to discern how Christ is at work in the revolution of contemporary Asia, and must share that work with him, declaring his presence and his Lordship.[2] In particular, Thomas feels that the Indian national struggle,—'nationalism as a legitimate expression of faith'—was one of the ways, and one of the most significant ways, in which India has responded to the Gospel.[3]

We must be clear, however, about the reason why we participate in the secular revolution, and about the goal which that revolution should serve; and here again Thomas speaks very clearly, affirming that the goal of the revolution must be increased human dignity, the fuller development of the human personality. 'Through the revolution, God in his providence is creating in Asia the basic conditions of greater human dignity, enhanced human creativity and maturer human living.'[4]

Here we see the great emphasis which Thomas, like Devanandan, places on the importance of the personal, and on the dimension of love, both in God and in man; and perhaps we can infer the influence on him of the thought prevalent in Student Christian Movement circles in the period during and just after the Second World War—the influence of Buber and Barth and Reinhold Niebuhr, for example—combined with the political humanism of the national movement of pre-1947 days. These, rather than the *bhakti* tradition which we see in Appasamy, are—with the existentialist Bible study which accompanied them—the basis of Thomas' personalism. It is a biblical, existentialist, socially and politically conditioned personalism; and it is poised to fight against all those factors—political, social, racial, technological or religious—which prevent man made in the image of God from reaching the fulness of humanity which God created him to enjoy. It is a 'battle for a true anthropology', and Thomas' vision for the future is of 'spiritually purposeful persons realizing themselves in an ultimately meaningful history' within the context of God's purpose for the world.[5]

[1] *ibid.*

[2] *ibid*, p. 28, quoting the inaugural Assembly of the East Asian Christian Conference, Kuala Lumpur, 1959.

[3] *Acknowledged Christ*, p. 109.

[4] *Response*, p. 29.

[5] *Acknowledged Christ*, pp. 147 and 300.

So far as Thomas himself is concerned, the secret of true humanism is to be found in the divine humanity of Christ—'the Gospel of Jesus Christ and his New Creation', as he describes it, in terms recalling Chenchiah[1]; and he approvingly quotes Chenchiah's rejection of the conception of God as the Absolute—whether in Sankara or Kraemer!—and his demand that God shall be Emmanuel, the one who becomes man and continues to remain man with man.[2] Yet in the task of freeing man so that he may enjoy his humanity to the full, Christians can gladly join with secular humanists 'within the context of a common concern for the moral regeneration of human society', for in their work and service too we may discern 'the pressure of a living God and his Christ on India', as Christian and non-Christian together seek 'to realize the dignity of the human person and the fellowship of persons as the fundamental values of our society.'[3]

On this point Thomas finds himself involved in the controversy which arose after the Uppsala meeting of the World Council of Churches in 1968 over what Dr. Peter Beyerhaus has characterised as 'a radical shift of the centre from God to man, and accordingly the replacement of theology by anthropology.'[4] Thomas, following Barth's insight on 'the humanity of God', feels that this is a false antithesis : Christians are not called upon to choose between an abstract theology and a mere anthropology, but are summoned rather to a living encounter with Christology, for Christ is the true man, 'God-for-man.'[5] In a sense, then, wherever Thomas uses the term 'humanisation', we should think of it, not in terms of a mere anthropology, but in relation to Christ the true man; the kind of humanity which he wants to see established on earth is the pattern of real life established by the one whom Chenchiah called the *ādi-puruṣa* of the new creation.

Thomas rejects the conservative evangelical tendency to limit the work of the Christian mission to preaching and Church-growth; the Gospel of salvation must work itself out also in the realm of history and politics, and in the campaign to provide conditions where men can live as real men. 'The mission of salvation and the task of humanisation are integrally related to

[1] *ibid*, p. 146.
[2] *ibid*, p. 162. cp. *Salv. and Hum.*, p. 37.
[3] *ibid.*
[4] *Salvation and Humanisation*, p. 6.
[5] *ibid*, p. 7.

each other, even if they cannot be considered identical.'[1] And he is able to strengthen his case by pointing out how the great evangelical missionaries of the past, notably William Carey, carried out their mission in precisely this comprehensive way.[2]

The Prophetic Core of the Christian Faith

In establishing the principle that Christians in India should join with their Hindu fellow-citizens in working for a new and better framework for the full development of human personality, Thomas makes it clear, that this does not involve any surrender of the distinctive Christian witness. On the contrary, Christians are called to a full exercise of their 'prophetic' ministry as a contribution to the development of a truer humanism, and indeed it may be argued that the process of secularization which is already at work in the world, and the secular patterns of understanding human existence which have already emerged, are themselves the product of the ferment of the Gospel working in traditional societies.[3] Indian Christianity, Thomas holds, 'can best make its contribution to the development of the indigenous foundations of the new humanism in India by its insisting on its own fundamental prophetic core.'[4] What is this 'prophetic core'.?

In answering this question Thomas reveals his conviction that the difference between Christianity and Hinduism is a radical one, and that Christianity, in its message of the Cross and Resurrection, brings to the world something totally new. The core of the Christian faith is 'the message that God has acted in a unique way in a secular historic event, namely the incarnation, life, death and resurrection of Jesus Christ, to inaugurate his kingdom.'[5] There can be no reduction of this core, which must be maintained against those who would—in a Gandhian direction—reduce it to a mere system of ethics, or those who—following Radhakrishnan—would seek to turn it into a 'naturalistic mysticism'; and indeed any such reduction would betray not only the Christian faith but the secular renaissance of the Asian people, to which the Christian prophetic message has contributed so much, awakening them to the per-

[1] *ibid*, p. 8.
[2] *ibid*, p. 12.
[3] *Acknowledged Christ*, p. 306, quoting Cox and van Leeuwen.
[4] *ibid*, p. 187.
[5] *ibid*, p. 117.

sonal dimension of human existence.[1] Speaking of the mission of the Church, Thomas defines it very positively as 'communicating the gospel of the crucified and risen Jesus Christ to all men, to the end that they may accept him as Lord and Saviour, and enter into the fellowship of his Body the Church which is the bearer of witness to him.'[2] The core of the faith is, then, a definite act of God, and without that central act of the Cross there can be no 'realisation' of salvation.[3] He criticises Sen, for example, for his lack of emphasis on the Cross[4] Mozoomdar for his failure to understand the seriousness of sin[5], and makes the telling comment on Brahmabandhab's *Cit*-Christology that it does not distinguish clearly between the eternal Logos and the incarnate Logos, and therefore lacks the basis of concrete human individuality in Jesus Christ.[6]

Two recently published booklets give us an interesting and moving insight into Thomas' personal understanding of the Cross and of suffering. One, *Joyful and Triumphant* (1970), is an account of his wife's last illness and death, and besides giving us a series of meditations by her, it also records a number of conversations dealing with the deep issues of suffering and death, doubt and certainty, resurrection and hope. The whole book is an illustration of the fact that 'personal relationships are of the essence of Christian spirituality'[7], and that at their deepest level, such relationships depend on the risen and living Christ who makes his presence certain.[8] The other booklet, *The Realisation of the Cross* (1972) is a series of meditations and prayers dating from 1937. It is significant that the author has published them now, for they are, in the words of the preface, 'a personal affirmation of the centrality of Christ and his Cross', and they point to 'the new world-order which, amidst the pain and joy of the world and man, will transform and transmute creation itself.' Thomas sees the Cross always in the context of the resurrection—the bodily resurrection—of Christ, which is the guarantee of true manhood, since 'his humanity is the goal set for all men.'[9] He sees Christ's death as the power of creative love : 'It is in communion with the risen Lord that we

[1] *ibid*, p. 119.
[2] *Response*, p. 93. cp. *Salvation and Humanisation*, p. 2.
[3] *Acknowledged Christ*, p. 53.
[4] *ibid*, p. 66.
[5] *ibid*, p. 96.
[6] *ibid*, p. 108.
[7] *Joyful and Triumphant*, p. 11.
[8] *ibid*, pp. 12 and 23.
[9] *Realization of the Cross*, p. 28.

realise that love is at the heart of the universe, that it is the one creative force in the world. The vision of the power of the Cross is also the vision of love eternally creative.'[1]

Concerned as he is for the world of politics and revolution, of violence and hunger, M. M. Thomas has no doubts about the reality, the danger and the tragedy of sin. This makes him very critical of the *advaitin* tendency—seen for example in Vivekananda—to regard evil as metaphysical rather than moral, as the spirit's involvement in matter and plurality.[2] He himself takes the biblical view of sin, and knows that its removal requires the action in judgment and redemption of the living God—the God of Abraham, Isaac and Jacob, the Father of Jesus Christ.[3] And, as we have already seen, sin is not merely a matter of the body and its passions, to be overcome by asceticism, but of the corrupt will, and of man's selfish urge for power. God takes the initiative to deal with sin—and with man's alienation which has led to the loss of his true humanity—for God is the great 'hound of heaven' (in Francis Thompson's phrase) who relentlessly pursues those who flee from him.[4] And man's response to God's initiative must be *faith*—a response of the heart, 'the engagement of the total man in acknowledging God as revealed in Christ.'[5] When man thus responds to the love of God, his whole outlook towards his fellow-men will be transformed by that love.

Despite his great sympathy for, and understanding of secularism, Thomas feels that the followers of a secular philosophy fail to understand the tragic element in human life, and he cites the examples of Achyut Patwardhan and Jayaprakash Narain who both eventually found that socialist secularism was inadequate to 'grapple adequately with the dimension of tragedy'[6], and so gave up politics for theosophy and *advaita*. Here is where the Christian Church should be able to help, through its deeper understanding of the meaning of life: 'the Church has to affirm the Easter faith, which knows the tragedy of the Cross but goes on to affirm the resurrection beyond tragedy and, on that basis, sees history and the whole universe moving towards a consummation in the kingdom of God and his Christ.'[7]

1 *ibid*, p. 48.
2 *Acknowledged Christ*, p. 126.
3 *ibid*, p. 145.
4 *ibid*, p. 285.
5 *ibid*.
6 *Response*, p. 122. cp. *Salv. and Hum.*, p. 45.
7 *ibid*, p. 123.

Way of Unity or Way of Love ?

In Brahmabandhab, Monchanin and Abhishiktananda, we have seen a form of Christian Vedanta, a spirituality whose ultimate goal is the unity of the soul with God, of the *ātman* with the *Paramātman.* In Appasamy's Christian *bhakti* we have seen the way of love, a love whose dominant motif is the intimate personal relationship of the *bhakta* to his God. If we allow ourselves to describe the theology of M. M. Thomas as *karma mārga* we must make it clear that the ' action ' involved is chiefly action ' in the world ', the action of loving *diakonia.* We have seen his appreciation of the social passion of Ram Mohan Roy, Vivekananda and Gandhi, and at the same time his feeling that all of them fall short in their understanding of man in his created, human situation, in his sin, his suffering, his need. It is the prophetic strain in the Christian faith, seen in the Old Testament prophets[1], but above all in its Cross-centred ' core ', which alone can effectively deal with man in his tragedy. And that means *love*, the ' starting point and key ' of all theology. As Manilal Parekh pointed out in his study of Ram Mohan Roy, ' Love is the last term in the moral and religious vocabulary of man, and all true love logically ends [in] or is synonymous with sacrifice... The vicarious death of Jesus is a new category in the religious thinking of the world'[2].

We are brought back once more to the great question which repeatedly confronts anyone standing within the Indian cultural tradition, especially now that that tradition has been deeply marked by the Christian faith and by secular humanism : ' Which way am I to take ? The way of unity or the way of action ? The way of mystical identity with God, or the way of obedience to God and loving service of mankind ?' Thomas agrees with Bishop Newbigin's blunt answer that the idea that mysticism is the clue to ultimate reality is ' a flat denial of the central truth of biblical religion.' [3] It is a statement which is perhaps rather hard to reconcile with the type of theology advocated by Abhishiktananda ! Standing as he does within the tradition of personalism, Thomas expresses grave doubts about the validity of a world-view based, like that of Radhakrishnan, on *advaitic* mysticism ;

[1] *Salv. and Hum.*, p. 33. Thomas stresses the importance of the O. T. prophetic interpretation of history, carried over into Marxism as well as Christianity.

[2] M. C. Parekh, *Rajarshi Ram Mohan Roy* (1927), pp. 89 ff., quoted in *Acknowledged Christ*, p. 31.

[3] J. E. L. Newbigin, *A Faith for this One World* (1961), p. 39, quoted in *Acknowledged Christ*, p. 180.

he questions whether Radhakrishnan has really succeeded in the task of giving ultimate reality to the personal God who is 'the Absolute humanized', or ultimate spiritual significance to 'the human world and its values'[1]. It is a question, as Devanandan saw, of bridging the gulf between the 'classical theology' of *advaita* and the 'new anthropology' of modern, secular India. Vivekananda faced the problem in what Thomas calls his 'struggles to bridge the discontinuity between *paramārthika* and *vyavahārika* levels of reality as a basis for his concern for man's dignity and for justice for men in society, and for historical action to realise it'[2]; but his solution, though it represents a real change of direction in Hinduism, fails to take full account of sin and tragedy. It is here that the Christian faith can help towards a deeper solution of the problem. The prophetic Christian faith affirms a definite series of distinctions: of becoming as distinct from being; of human nature distinct from the divine in its finiteness and freedom; of 'the two natures in the unity of Jesus Christ which makes him other than all men as the mediator between God and man and the fulfilment of the purpose of becoming'[3].

'Becoming not being'; 'action not passivity'; 'love not mere unity'—these are some of the emphases which we find in Thomas, for example in his appreciation of Ram Mohan Roy's social passion, and in his critique of both Roy and Marshman's failure to realise the implications of love, especially suffering love.[4] We cannot help noticing that of all the Christian writers whom he discusses, the two whom he commends with least reservation are S. K. Rudra and C. F. Andrews, and the reason for this probably lies in their commitment to active love and service and suffering, as followers and 'members' of the suffering Christ. Andrews, in fact, seems to fulfil Thomas' criteria for a Christian Gandhism, a Gandhism reinforced by a more positive approach to creation, the body and human freedom. For Andrews 'the one supreme test' of all action and thought was 'love of God and love to man'[5]—the love of Christ working through his followers to transform the world. Thomas notes how Andrews' own witness was related to his experience and understanding of Christ, and writes, 'The whole life and theology

[1] *Acknowledged Christ*, p. 187 (51a), *ibid*, pp. 147-8.
[2] *ibid*, p. 188.
[3] Thomas does, however, note with approval Marshman's interpretation of the 'omni-attributes' in terms of love. *ibid*, p. 34.
[4] *ibid*, p. 271.
[5] *ibid*, p. 269.

of Andrews was an exploration of the universality of Christ as the Eternal Word, the Son of Man, the Source of life and the Divine Head of humanity'[1] and he goes on to say that there is no doubt that Andrews 'has carried the idea of the Divine Humanity of Christ as centre and goal of universal religions and social history, to a new stage of development.'[2]

This conviction of the priority of the way of action as loving service, and of Christ as the source of that action, does not, however, mean that Thomas takes a wholly negative view of *advaita* ; he is too deeply steeped in the Indian tradition for that, and is familiar with the approach of Panikkar and Abhishiktananda, having taken part, in fact, in many of their meetings for dialogue. Vedanta is far too important a tradition in India for it ever to be ignored in the formulation of Christian theology, and the reformulated Vedanta of Vivekananda is chiefly remarkable for its attempt to retain the structure and terminology of *advaita* while making room within it for a form of Christian ethics and 'philanthropy'.[3] In a sense the theology of Brahmabandhab, Monchanin and Abhishiktananda follows the same principles. Thomas' own approach to Vedanta is different. He is conscious that the Indian Church, although it has done valuable work in the fields of service, and of social and political thought, has largely failed, hitherto, in meeting the challenge of Neo-Vedanta at the philosophical level ; and he is anxious that this challenge should now be met. He approves, for example, of Mark Sunder Rao's *ananyatva*, with its effort to bring the insights of Vedanta into a comprehensive Christian *darśana.*[4] His own attitude to Vedanta can perhaps be best described in connection with the term 'pre-understanding', which he has taken from John Macquarrie.[5] If the fact of Christ and the 'core-faith' which interprets him as God's supreme act in relation to man are to be presented effectively to those who have grown up in the world of Vedanta, it is essential to take into account their previous 'patterns of understanding'. The 'new' fact of Christ must be presented in terms which are familiar and meaningful. The Christian witness, then, must use terms and thought-forms derived from the Vedanta 'pre-understanding'. It is a point which has already been made more than once in this book. Thomas goes on to emphasise—

[1] *ibid*, p. 274.
[2] *ibid*, p. 143.
[3] *ibid*, pp. 181 ff.
[4] *ibid*, pp. 301 ff.
[5] *v. supra*, p. 143, in connection with Appasamy's use of Ramanuja.

as does Appasamy[1]—that the function of pre-understanding must always be ancillary rather than normative ; certain patterns of Vedantic thought will be helpful, while others will not, and we should hope for a wide variety of theological terms and models, rather than for rigid standardisation along the lines of a particular *darśana*. 'Faith must find ways of speaking of Jesus Christ and his salvation in metaphysical fashion', he writes,[2] but we must beware of making the philosophical patterns normative, and shaping the 'core-faith' to conform with them. The way to proceed is by learning to speak of Christ in terms of Vedantic pre-understanding, and then, through the 'challenging relevance' of dialogue with the Christian Gospel in its biblical fulness, the Vedantic patterns will be transformed and developed, so becoming clear and satisfactory media for the expression of the Christian faith.[3]

Thomas' answer, then, to the question of the relative importance of seeking to understand the truth of God's being on the one hand (the metaphysical quest), and finding out and performing God's purpose for human existence on the other (the way of ethics and action) would be to say that we cannot neglect either ; 'we can never reduce theology to ethics or dispense with metaphysics in theology.'[4] His criticism of the 'Christian *advaita*' tradition (as seen for example in Abhishiktananda) would, however, be that it takes too little account of the world in which we live—the world of revolution and industrialisation, of war and racialism—and gives us too little guidance as to how we should act in such a world, how we should show in practice the love, power and justice of God in Christ. 'The emphasis on the vision of God as the end of man weakens the emphasis on the will of God and ethics,' he writes[5], and again 'the Church should be concerned with defining the positive meaning of mysticism and metaphysics within the context of the Christian faith and of its concern for spiritual and moral purposes in society and history.'[6] Mysticism and metaphysics have their place, and we must study and re-interpret them. But we must never do so at the expense of the prophetic core of the Christian faith ; the way of unity should serve and promote the way of love.

[1] *Acknowledged Christ*, p. 303.
[2] *ibid*, pp. 303-5.
[3] *ibid*, p. 288.
[4] *ibid*, p. 109.
[5] *ibid*, p. 145.
[6] *Response*, pp. 96 ff. See also the Preface to Eric Sharpe, *The Theology of A. G. Hogg*, p. iv.

Christianity and Hinduism: A Challenging Relevance

In seeking to define the relation of Christianity and Hinduism Thomas frequently quotes the phrase of A. G. Hogg, which we have already studied—'a challenging relevance'. In fact he finds in Hogg's conception a theological 'model' which transcends not only Farquhar's 'crown of Hinduism' idea (and possibly also 'the unknown Christ of Hinduism' conception, which, as we have seen, is in some respects similar to it), but also Kraemer's negative approach.[1] The 'challenge' for Thomas means the disturbance of the Hindu consciousness which has resulted from the Christian mission, and also the social implications of the Gospel to which, from the time of Ram Mohan Roy, the world of reformed Hinduism has felt obliged to respond. But what Hogg wrote of as a possibility for the future apologetic of the Church, Thomas sees as a challenge which has already produced a remarkable effect, both in renascent Hinduism and also in the great secular and revolutionary movements of our time.

He gives several interesting examples of ways in which the challenging relevance of the Christian faith has in fact stimulated changes in the Hindu way of looking at things. There is, for example, Radhakrishnan's interpretation of *māyā* in terms similar to the Thomist doctrine of contingent being, which we have already noticed in our discussion of Brahmabandhab.[2] There is the changed attitude to suffering found in Tagore, who acknowledges that the doctrine of vicarious suffering is 'a spiritual seed from the tree of Christ's life'[3]. There is the whole new attitude, for example in the Sarvodaya movement, towards the individual personality—what Thomas calls the 'new anthropology'; it is an attitude which Hindus must now try to relate to their 'classical theology'[4]. All these, he feels, are simply examples of a very important development, a radical break with the authority of the spiritual core of Hinduism.[5] This shift away from the traditional authority (*pramāṇa*) of the Hindu Scriptures can be clearly seen in Gandhi, who always estimated the value of Scriptures on the basis of their ethical teaching and

[1] *Response*, p. 82. *supra*, pp. 74 ff.

[2] Rabindranath Tagore, *Towards Universal Man*, New Delhi, 1961, p. 167, quoted in *Response*, p. 87.

[3] *Response*, p. 90.

[4] *ibid*, p. 78.

[5] *Harijan*, 18 April, 1931 and 5 Dec., 1936, quoted in *Response*, p. 81.

said that he could not let a scriptural text supersede his reason.[1] Or again one can think of Vivekananda, who despite his rejection of the 'core' of the Christian faith was challenged by that very faith to redefine the 'core' of *advaita* so as 'to make room for personality and history, and make Hinduism relevant to the human issues raised in contemporary India through the impact of Western culture and Christianity.'[2]

Thomas agrees with Van Leeuwen in seeing this Hindu response to the Gospel as part of God's way of working in the world today. As we have already seen, he is not prepared to accept any reduction in the 'prophetic core' of Christianity, and he admits that there is 'mutual exclusiveness' at the core of Hinduism and Christianity.[3] But he does believe in the possibility of a common ethics, philosophy and culture, in which Christian and Hindu can share fully—'not a religious syncretism, but a cultural synthesis . . . secular in its framework and personal in its orientation'[4].

Thomas' attitude to Hinduism, then, is a rather 'tougher one than that of Abhishiktananda', in that, following Hogg, he insists on facing honestly and squarely the basic differences between the two faiths, and holds that the encounter forces Hinduism to change its 'core' in various ways. At the same time he finds a vast common ground—largely ignored by Abhishiktananda—in the shared struggle of Christian and Hindu for a true humanity and a common culture.

Criteria of a Living Theology

M. M. Thomas is not particularly interested in the detailed outworking of the terminology of Indian Christian theology, though he is convinced that its formulation is a work of importance. His special gift, rather, is to see the task of theology against a very broad and challenging background, a background which includes the tensions and excitements of the revolutionary third world, the traditions and insights of ancient as well as reformed Hinduism, and also the fluctuations of western theological thought. For him the only valid and living theology is one which is hammered out in dialogue with these different viewpoints, a theology arising from what he calls a 'dialogical situation'[5]. Indian theology must do its work 'not in isolation

[1] *Acknowledged Christ*, pp. 143-4. cp. *Salv. and Hum.*, p. 22.
[2] *ibid*, pp. 189-90.
[3] *Response*, p. 92.
[4] Preface to Sharpe, *op. cit.*, p. iii.
[5] *Acknowledged Christ*, pp. 187-8.

from but in dialogue with the new Hindu philosophy and theology; that is, by restating the fundamentals of the Christian faith positively within these terms.'[1]

The word 'restating' here implies a recognition of the problem of demythologization, and in fact Thomas shows that this is a question of great relevance in Indian as well as in western theology. He reviews five different types of western theology—orthodoxy (Protestant and Roman Catholic); the 'biblical realism' of Kraemer and Barth; Bultmann's demythologization; the 'dekerygmatization' of Fritz Buri, which in effect reduces Christianity to an ethic of love, of which Christ is the mere symbol; and monistic mysticism which concentrates on the mystic union of the soul with the Ultimate and which does away with the need of a historic Christ.[2] Of these views the last exercises no attraction on him; in each of the others, however, he can see valuable elements. Orthodoxy and the credal tradition of the Church is important, though it must always be checked against the Bible, and allowance should be made for the expression of individual opinions, for often heretics have been the Church's most original theologians, and heresy becomes dangerous only when it makes itself absolute and so steps outside the 'great tradition' of the Church.[3] As for 'biblical realism', it will be clear from all that has been said that Thomas insists that all Christian doctrine should be firmly grounded in the Bible. Yet a theology which is *merely* biblical cannot undertake 'the new creative re-engagement with new situations' which is essential if Christianity is to be challengingly relevant in India.[4] Bultmann's concern for evangelism and his presentation of the living Christ in new categories of thought is important, as is Barth's insistence on the importance of love in action; yet the danger here is the weakening of the link with the historical, and for Thomas that is a fatal defect.

Thomas holds that there is a place for much variety in theological presentation, and that there is no harm in such variety provided that 'dialogue' is maintained with four essential factors: first, Scripture; then Church tradition; then the *koinonia*

[1] *ibid*, pp. 291 ff.

[2] *ibid*, pp. 310 ff.. In speaking of Sen, Thomas recognizes that the '*adesh* of the Holy Spirit must be anchored in the Scriptures, and work within the.. living tradition of the continuity of faith, the historic Church of Christ' (ibid, p.73). His attitude to the organized Church is positive, though he holds that its sacramental and social realization of the fellowship of *agape* is only partial, and that the true realization is eschatological, (*ibid*, p. 80).

[3] *ibid*, p. 299.

[4] *ibid*, p. 300.

of the Church; and finally its mission in the contemporary world.[1] The task of the theologian, he says, involves his 'walking the razor's edge between the biblical *kerygmà* and the process of its demythologization with a view to remythologizing its truth and meaning for men in different climates of thought and cultural milieux.'[2]

* * *

All this adds up to a massive and consistent theological statement. Thomas begins with the 'prophetic core' of the Christian faith—the incarnation, death and resurrection of Christ—and refuses to allow it to be reduced' into either an ethic of love or a mystic experience—as various thinkers, Indian and Western, would reduce it.[3] The theologian must be fully committed to this core of faith, and must also be so thoroughly steeped in the 'pre-understanding' of his own culture and philosophy that he can bring his compatriots to share in his own experience. But the context of theology is not merely a religious and philosophical one; it is above all the context of a revolutionary, modern world. And the response to the Gospel cannot be mere passive understanding or acceptance or mystical experience; it means sharing in the love of Christ, and passing on that love to the world, in active, loving service and suffering.

This, I believe, comes close to the view, and the practice, of C. F. Andrews. Thomas has drawn together many different strands, from East and West, from past and present, and woven them into an attractive and convincing way of action—a Christian *karma mārga*. One feels that if Gandhi *had* become a Christian, and had lived through the turmoil of the quarter century since his death, his theology might have been something like this.

[1] *ibid.*
[2] *ibid*, p. 301.
[3] *ibid.*

CHAPTER XVII

KHRISTĀDVAITA: DHANJIBHAI FAKIRBHAI

(1895-1967)

The Shape of Theology

To end this postscript on some recent developments in Indian theology we shall take a second look at one whom we have mentioned earlier, Dhanjibhai Fakirbhai.[1] At the time of his death in 1967 he left an unpublished manuscript with the title *Ādhyātma Darśana*', 'A vision of Spirituality',[2] in which he brings together passages on various topics from the Bible and the Upanishads, and links them together through a brief commentary of his own. The title and composition of the book, taken along with some of Dhanjibhai's other publications like *Śri Khrista Gitā*, *Khristopanishad* and *Prema Tattva Darśana*, indicate his great interest in the question of the 'shape' of Christian teaching. He felt that it was not enough that Christian theology should use an Indian vocabulary; the structure should be Indian too, and on a small scale he illustrated his own theory, for example in *Khrista Gita*, which reproduces the dialogue structure of the *Bhagavadgita*. This is an important issue for the future of Indian Christian theology. Western dogmatic theology has tended usually to follow the Trinitarian structure of the Apostles' Creed, and this organising principle should not be lightly discarded, especially in view of the importance of the Trinity in relation to Indian spirituality. On the other hand it may prove that the form of the *bhāṣya*, or commentary on Scripture, is ultimately that best suited to an Indian systematic theology. That, after all, is the method which Barth used when the *Commentary on Romans* foreshadowed the *Church Dogmatics*, and it is the method adopted by Panikkar in *The Unknown Christ of Hinduism*, which is a commentary on a few lines of the *Brahma Sutra*. We noted at the beginning of this book Bishop Westcott's hope that some day an Indian theologian would write a really Indian commentary on the Fourth Gospel. Yet perhaps a profound Indian *bhāsya* on the Epistle to the

[1] *v. supra*, pp. 213-6.

[2] The MS will be published in part in a forthcoming volume in the Library of Indian Christian Theology. *Manilal Parekh; Dhanjibhai Fakirbhai—a Selection*, ed. R. H. S. Boyd.

Romans might in the end give an even more comprehensive expression to Indian systematic theology. Dhanjibhai attempted nothing so ambitious ; his works are all very brief, but his choice of titles and his arrangement of material in a number of different ways has effectively drawn our attention to the importance of the question of the shape of Indian dogmatic theology.

We shall select two of the leading ideas of *Ādhyātma Darśana* for brief examination : first, Dhanjibhai's use of the term *prajñāna*, or primeval intelligence, for Logos ; and secondly the word *Khristādvaita*, the term on which he ultimately settled as descriptive of his own theological position.

Prajñāna

In an interesting Christological section of *Ādhyātma Darśana* Dhanjibhai gives a terse but illuminating account of how Christ the Logos originates from the Father and becomes incarnate. He uses the ' model ' of the sun and its ray, an illustration which goes right back to the Apologists and Tertullian, but which Dhanjibhai apparently draws, quite independently, from the *Brahma Sutra* (3.2.18). Dhanjibhai, unlike Sen, does not describe the Logos as *Cit*, but instead mentions two other Upanishadic terms, *Śabda-Brahman* and *prajñāna*. We have already discussed the term *Śabda-Brahman* in our treatment of Klostermaier.[1] *Prajñāna* is clearly a useful term in this context, not only because of its literal meaning of ' pre-knowledge ', but also because the Upanishads equate it with *Brahman*. The Upanishadic passage which Dhanjibhai quotes (Ait. Up. 3.1.2-4) is as follows :

> That which is heart, mind, consciousness, perception, discrimination, intelligence, wisdom, insight....all these, indeed, are appellations of *Prajñāna*. He is *Brahman*....All this is guided by *Prajñāna*, is based on *Prajñāna*. The world is guided by *Prajñāna*....*Brahman* is *Prajñāna*.

At this point in *Ādhyātma Darśana* Dhanjibhai's text is very compressed, and interlaced with quotations from the Upanishads and the Brahma Sutra, so we shall attempt simply to give the gist of his argument in a few sentences :

> *Prajñāna*, primeval intelligence, is the power which creates, maintains and inspires the world and human beings. *Prajñāna* is power and wisdom, is the Word of God (*Śabda-Brahman*), is

[1] *v. supra*, p. 27.

God himself—*Brahman.* This Word of God, *Prajñāna*, took a body in the man Jesus. As the heat of the sun's light, according to the Brahma Sutra, is no different from the heat of the disc of the sun itself, so this incarnate *Prajñāna*, the *Avatara*, is fully God.

This is Christological language which a Hindu can understand, and which—if he does understand it—takes him very close to the orthodox Christian doctrine of the incarnation of the Logos, yet in an idiom quite different from that of the Christological controversies of the first five centuries.

Khristādvaita

Dhanjibhai's term *Khristādvaita* is likely to cause misgivings to some who will think that it suggests merely a Christian form of monistic mysticism. In its intention, however, it is not unlike Sunder Rao's term *ananyatva*, yet it has a more positive and Christo-centric ring about it. We should remember that although Sankara's *advaita* is undoubtedly monistic, the term which Ramanuja used to describe his personalist *bhakti* was *viśiṣṭādvaita*, or modified non-dualism, while Vallabhacharya's equally personalist system is described as *śuddhādvaita*, or 'pure' non-dualism. For Dhanjibhai the meaning of *Khristādvaita* is primarily faith-union with Christ, in the Johannine or Pauline sense, a word which describes what Paul means when he says, 'Who shall separate us from the love of Christ?' (Rom. 8 : 35). Dhanjibhai's coining of the term illustrates his conviction that the Christian life is essentially one lived in constant faith-union with Christ—the union of love, not absorption.

In his description of *Khristādvaita*, Dhanjibhai is very conscious of the fact that Christ is, as it were, the nucleus of unity for the whole cosmos, and he enumerates six different kinds of unity, in all of which he is the controlling power: (i) the unity of the Son with the Father; (ii) Christ's unity with the created world, in the Ramanujan sense that he controls it, and that it is the instrument of his purpose; (iii) the more obvious meaning of the faith-union of the disciple with his Lord; (iv) the mutual unity of the disciples with one another; (v) the coming unity of all men of all nations in Christ; and (vi) man's unity with nature, in the sense that physically we are part of the created world, and should therefore use it to God's glory, not exploiting it by pollution, erosion and so on. Obviously this very wide understanding of the principle of unity gives scope for an interesting view of man, society and nature, and the controlling factor is that Dhanjibhai sees it all as being centred in Christ; it is in relation to Christ—in his incarnation, life, death and resurrection —that we are to approach all our problems of alienation and brokenness.

We should not be tempted to imagine that this is a sort of veiled pantheism. It is perhaps more like Teilhard's idea of everything moving towards the eschatological omega-point of Christ, or Zaehner's conception of the 'converging spirit', drawing all things to himself. For Dhanjibhai this 'Christification'—to use Teilhard's term—is never a matter of natural or automatic evolution; rather, every individual must make his own decision for or against Christ, and only when the individual himself lives 'in Christ', himself shares in *Khristādvaita* can he join in God's great movement towards the day when 'the creation itself will be set free from its bondage to decay and obtain the glorious liberty of the children of God' (Romans 8 : 21), and when, according to God's promise, we shall see 'new heavens, and a new earth in which righteousness dwells' (II Peter 3 : 13). The quotations are those given by Dhanjibhai himself.

The understanding of faith-union with Christ as *Khristādvaita* is closely linked with the Church. Dhanjibhai writes, 'When individuals have really become one with the Lord Jesus their relation to one another is that of the members of a body. They all form a body for the Spirit of the Lord.' That, I think, is a typical piece of Dhanjibhai's writing. It is thoroughly Biblical, thoroughly evangelical, and at the same time it subtly hints at a Hindu idea with which Hindu readers are familiar—Ramanuja's conception of the world as the body of God. And so Dhanjibhai is able to convey to his Hindu friends something of the true nature of the Christian Church as a community of those who are united to their Lord and to one another, and are his body in the sense that they are the totally surrendered instrument of his will, ready to do his work of love in the world. It is a conception of the Church which, unfortunately, the actual Church too frequently obscures by its lack of love and concern, and its appearance as an institution rather than as the body of Christ.

* * *

Dhanjibhai is not one of the more widely known Indian theologians. Yet there is a reality and a sincerity about his writing which carries conviction. Much of what he says has been said in far more detail by others—by Chenchiah, by Abhishiktananda, by Panikkar, by Sunder Rao. Yet while their writing is in a sense speculative, his is evangelistic; he is, as it were, practising what others preach, writing not for brother theologians, but for brother Hindus. Here is an Indian disciple of Christ seeking to express the truth which has gripped him in a way which his Hindu friends may find intelligible and convincing.

We find in him, as in Chenchiah, a number of syntheses. There is first of all the synthesis between the modern scientific outlook and traditional Hindu culture. But there is also a conscious synthesis of the three *mārgas* of *karma*, *bhakti* and *jñāna*, all of which are carried up into and transformed by the way of Love. His own background is that of *bhakti*, but he appreciates and seeks to appropriate the insights of Vedanta, as we see in his use of the Upanishads and his interest in terms like *Śabda-Brahman*, *prajñāna* and *Khristādvaita*. He also appreciates the need to be involved in the world of science and politics and sociology : *karma mārga* in the Gandhian sense of the way of service is never far from his thought, as we can see in *Prema Tattva Darśana*, where the whole scope of Christian belief and practice is related to the concept of love in action. Where Abhishiktananda, Panikkar and Klostermaier advance theories—attractive and stimulating indeed, but still theoretical —on the possibility of a synthesis of the three *mārgas*, Dhanjibhai, with a simplicity that is deceptive, brings them all together in a series of short books which are an actual and positive Indian presentation of the Christian faith.

Dhanjibhai's work is very fragmentary and brief, yet in this series of miniature studies he has, one feels, demonstrated something of what the shape of Indian theology might be, and something also of its richness when these three great *mārgas* are brought together into a way of Love which transcends them all.

* * *

The European reformers of the sixteenth century delighted to speak of Christ as Prophet, Priest and King. These were the three great anointed 'offices' of the Old Testament, and in him they were fulfilled and transformed, both in his life on earth and in his continuing work as Mediator. In a strange way, the three great *mārgas* of India seem to correspond to these offices. *Jñāna mārga* is the way of *prajñāna* of the Word, of the *Śabda* who became flesh, and who still today reveals himself to us by his Word. *Bhakti mārga* is the way of the one who comes in love to meet sinners and forgive them; the way of the great High Priest who is also the victim, and who continually makes intercession for those who love him and are by faith united with him. And *karma mārga* is the way of action, the way of the King who is also the Servant, who establishes the reign of justice in the world through his own self-giving humility. And beside these three traditional ways of older India we have seen also the dynamic way of the new creation, of the power from beyond, the power of the Resurrection and the life-giving Spirit of Pentecost. These four traditions have already provided a rich and varied pattern of Indian theology, though they have not as yet assumed any definitive form. Today Indian Christian theology is a recognised part of the theology of the world Church. And as Christians witness to their faith—in proclamation, in loving service, in the pursuit of justice, and in the deep sharing with their neighbours of their experience of God in Christ—new and liberating chapters of theology are in the making.

GLOSSARY

Note.—In the past there has been great variety in the conventions adopted in transliterating words from Indian languages into English. In all quotations in the text of this book the original author's spelling has been retained. In addition, for some well known names such as Krishna, and certain words which are familiar in English usage, such as *ashram*, *rishi*, *swami* etc., the traditional anglicised spelling has been retained in the text. In the Glossary which follows, variations on the standard transliteration are given in brackets.

ācārya	Leader, spiritual guide.
ādeśa (adesh)	Command, 'inspiration'.
ādhyātmiktā	Spirituality.
ādi	Original (prefix).
ādi-puruṣa	Original man, person.
advaita	Non-dualism, monism.
aham	I, ego, self.
ahaṃkāra	Egoism, self.
aham-pratyayi	The organising principle of the ego (aham): personality.
ahiṃsā	Non-violence.
ajñāna (agnana)	Ignorance.
ānanda	Joy, bliss.
ananya	What is not-other.
ananya-bhakti	Worship of what is not-other, i.e. undivided attention to God.
ananyatva	Non-other-ness, 'Non-alterity'.
antarātman	Inner spirit.
antaryāmin	The one who 'rules within'. The inner guide, ruler.
aṇu	Atom.
anubhava	Experience.
anumāna	Inference.
ārohaṇa	Ascent.
artha	Meaning, purpose, wealth.
asat	Not-being.
āśrama (ashram)	A place of religious retreat and instruction where a *guru* lives and teaches his disciples.
ātman (atma)	The soul.
avarohaṇa	Descent.
avatāra (avatar)	'Descent', used of the coming to earth of a god, especially Viṣṇu, in human or other form.
avidyā	Ignorance.
avyakta	Unexpressed, unmanifested.

Bhagavān	The Lord, the One who is worshipped in *bhakti*.
bhakta	A worshipper, devotee.
bhakti	Loving devotion to God.
bhakti mārga	The way of attaining salvation through devotion.
bhāṣya	Commentary.
Brahman (Brahma)	The Supreme Being of the Vedānta philosophy.
Brāhma (Brahmo)	An adjective derived from Brahman, e.g., 'Brāhma Samāj'.
Brahmā	The god Brahmā, one of the triad Brahmā, Viṣṇu, Śiva.
Brāhmaṇ (Brahmin)	A member of the 'Brahmin' caste.
brahmācāri	Celibate student, in the first stage of a Brahman's life.
cit (chit)	Intelligence.
darbār	Royal court, kingdom.
darśana (darshan)	A vision. A vision of reality, thus a 'system' of philosophy.
dās	Servant.
deva	God (cognate with *theos*, *deus*).
dharma	Religion, duty.
dharmāntara	Change of religion.
dṛṣṭi	Sight, vision.
dvija	Twice-born.
guṇa	Quality, attribute.
guru	A religious teacher.
Hari	A name of Viṣṇu or Krishna, popularly interpreted to mean 'vanquisher of sin'.
Harijan	'People of God'; the name given by Gandhiji to the so-called 'untouchables'.
haṭha (hath) yoga	That form of yoga which demands severe bodily discipline.
homa	Fire-sacrifice, burnt-offering.
iṣṭa	Desired, chosen.
Iśvara	Lord, God (personal).
jay (jai)	Victory.
jiva	Life, soul.
jivātman (jivatma)	The human soul.
jñāna (gnana)	Knowledge, *gnosis*.
jñāna mārga	The way of attaining salvation through knowledge.
jñāni (gnani)	A follower of the way of *jñāna*, knowledge.

Kāḷi	The Mother Goddess, Śakti, in terrifying form.
karma	Action, fruit of action, retribution.
karma mārga	The way of attaining salvation through (ritual) deeds.
koṣa (kosha)	A sheath.
kriya	Action, act.
kṣamā	Pardon, forgiveness, forbearance.
loka	World, region, people.
loksangraha	Community, gathering of people.
mahārṣi (maharishi)	A great *rishi*, seer.
mahāśakti	Great power.
mahāvākya	Great saying, key-text.
maitri	Friendship, fellowship.
mala	Filth, sin.
mānava	Human.
mārga	Way, path.
maṭha (math)	Monastery.
māyā	Illusion, creative power etc.
māyāvāda	The 'ism' of *māyā*.
Mimāṃsā	One of the six Hindu philosophical systems, emphasising scriptural exegesis and detailed ritual.
mokṣa	Release, salvation.
mukti	-do- -do-
muḷa puruṣa	Original (root) person.
nakalanka	Without spot, immaculate.
nāma	Name.
namratā	Humility.
nara	Man.
nara-Hari	One who is man and God; the God-man.
neti	'Not thus!'
nirguṇa	Without attributes (*guṇa*).
nirvikalpa	Without conceptual qualifications.
nirvikalpa samādhi	Union with *nirguṇa Brahman*.
niṣkāma (nishkam)	Free from desire (kāma), detached.
niṣkāmya	-do- -do-
Nyāya	One of the six Indian philosophical systems, specially devoted to logic.
pāpa	Sin.
para	Beyond, distant, transcendent (prefix).
parabrahman	The transcendent *Brahman*.
parama (param)	Best, first, supreme.
paramārtha	Highest, supreme meaning.

paramārthika	Adjective describing *true* existence as opposed to (1) practical and (2) apparent (in Vedānta).
paramātman (paramatma)	The Supreme Soul.
Parameśvara	Supreme Iśvara, God.
pariṇāma	Result, evolved product.
prjāpati	Lord of creatures.
prakṛti (prakriti)	The underlying stuff of the material world.
pramāṇa	The rule or standard of authority.
prapatti	Devoted self-surrender.
prārthnā	Prayer.
prasāda	Grace.
pratibhāśika	Adjective describing *apparent* existence as opposed to (1) true and (2) practical (in Vedānta).
pratyakṣa	Immediate perception.
prāyaścitta	Ritual atonement.
prema (prem)	Love.
prema-sāgara	Ocean of love.
punarjanma	Rebirth.
Purāṇa	A class of Hindu Mythological literature.
purṇa	Full, complete.
puruṣa	Person, man.
puruṣatva	'Personhood', personality.
purva	Original, prior, Eastern.
rāj	Rule, government.
ṛṣi (rishi)	Seer.
rupa	Form.
śakti	Power.
Śānti	Peace.
Śāstra	Scripture.
ṣiṣya (shishya)	Disciple.
śloka	A Sanskrit verse.
śruti	Scripture, revelation. (literally, 'thing heard').
sabhā	Meeting, association.
Saccidānanda	i.e. *sat* (being), *cit* (intelligence), *ānanda* (bliss). The highest description of *Brahman*.
sādhana (sadhan)	Practice, performance, means, devotion.
sādhanā	Religious exercise, means of attainment.
sādhu	A holy man devoted to a life of simplicity.
saguna	With attributes (*guṇa*).

sākṣātkāra	That which makes (God) immediately present : 'realisation'.
sālokya	Being in the same sphere (*loka*) as God : the lowest of the four types of *mokṣa*.
samādhi	Absorbed contemplation of God, usually involving a trance-like state.
samāj (somaj)	A society.
sambhava	Possibility.
sāmipya	Being near to God : the second of the four types of *mokṣa*.
Sāṃkhya (Sankhya)	One of the six Indian philosophical systems, which posits a dualism of *puruṣa* and *prakṛti*.
saṃsāra	Entanglement in the world, the round of successive births.
sandhyā	Evening.
saṇnyāsi	One who has given up the world and adopted the life of a religious mendicant, in the fourth and final stage of a Brahman's life.
sārupya	Being made like in form (*rupa*) to God : the third type of *mokṣa*.
Sarvodaya	'Uplift of all'. The rural reconstruction movement associated with Acharya Vinoba Bhave.
sat	Being. (*adj.*) true.
sati	(lit. a true woman). The custom whereby a widow burnt herself to death on her husband's pyre.
satsangha	True community, community of truth.
satya	Truth.
satyāgraha	'Grasp of Truth' (of Gandhiji's passive resistance).
savikalpa	With conceptual qualifications.
savikalpa samādhi	Union with *saguṇa Brahman*.
sāyujya	Complete union with God : the highest of the four types of *mokṣa*.
siddhānta	Principle, system of thought.
siddhi	Fulfilment, realisation.
smṛti (smriti)	The thing 'remembered', of Scriptures whose authority is secondary to the *Śruti* (thing 'heard').

sṛṣṭi (sristi)	'Creation', the act of giving form to a material cause.
sthiti	A settled state of existence.
sunya (suniam)	Nothing, zero.
svarga	(Indra's) heaven.
svāmi (swami)	Lord, master, religious leader.
trimurti	Triple image: the Hindu triad of Brahmā, Viṣṇu and Śiva.
tṛṣṇā (trisna)	Thirst.
upamāna	Analogy, comparison.
Upaniṣad	A class of literature included, along with the *Vedas*, in the *Śruti*, and expounding the philosophical significance of the Vedas.
vāda	Way, system, 'ism'.
vairāgya	Giving up the world, asceticism.
Vaiśeṣika	One of the six Indian philosophical systems, which holds that the world consists of eternal atoms.
Veda	'The Vedas', i.e. the earliest Hindu Scriptures, the *Śruti*.
Vedānta	The best known of the six Indian philosophical systems, centred on the relation of the soul (*ātman*) to *Brahman*.
viśiṣṭa	Modified, special.
Viśiṣṭādvaita	'Modified Non-dualism', the system of Rāmānuja.
Viṣṇu	The god Visnu, who takes many incarnations (*avatāras*).
vivarta	Illusory effect, illusory self-modification.
vyakta	Expressed, manifested.
vyakti	An individual.
vyavahār ika	Adjective describing *practical* existence as opposed to (1) true, and (2) apparent (in Vedānta).
yajña (yagna)	Sacrifice.
yoga	Union: a way of achieving union with God.
yogi (jogi, yogin)	One who follows a way of union with God.
yukti	Reason, inference, stratagem.

BIBLIOGRAPHY

of works cited in the Text

ANDREWS, C. F. *The Renaissance in India.* London, 1912.
——— *Sadhu Sundar Singh : a Personal Memoir.* London, 1934.
ANIMANANDA, B. *The Blade* : Life and Work of Brahmabandhab Upadhyaya. Roy and Son, Calcutta, n.d. but probably c. 1947.
APPASAMY, A. J. *Christianity as Bhakti Marga* : a Study of the Johannine Doctrine of Love. CLS, Madras, 1928.
——— *Temple Bells* : Readings from Hindu Religious Literature. YMCA, Calcutta, 1930.
——— *What is Moksa?* a Study in the Johannine Doctrine of Life. CLS, Madras, 1931.
——— *The Gospel and India's Heritage.* SPCK, London and Madras, 1942.
——— *The Cross is Heaven* : The Life and Writings of Sadhu Sundar Singh. London, 1956.
——— *Sundar Singh : a Biography.* London, 1958.
——— 'Christian Theology in the Indian Church', in *S. India Churchman*, April, 1964.
——— *My Theological Quest.* CISRS, Bangalore, 1964.
——— *Tamil Christian Poet.* London, 1966.
——— *What are Pramanas?* (unpublished).
ASIRVATHAM, EDDY. *Christianity in the Indian Crucible*, 2nd edn., YMCA, Calcutta, 1957.

BAAGO, K. *A History of the National Christian Council of India*, 1914-1964. Nagpur, 1965.
———' "Sheepstealing" in the 19th Century', in *Bulletin of the Church History Association of India*, Nov. 1966, pp. 17 ff.
——— 'The First Independence Movement among Indian Christians' in *Indian Church History Review*, June 1967, pp. 65-78.
BAILLIE, D. M. *God was in Christ.* London, 1948.
BANERJI, K. M. *Dialogues on Hindu Philosophy.* Calcutta, 1861.
——— *The Arian Witness* : or Testimony of Arian Scriptures in Corroboration of Biblical History and the Rudiments of Christian Doctrine, including Dissertations on the original Home and early Adventures of Indo-Arians. Calcutta, 1875.
BIRNEY, W. S. 'Early Anglican Worship in Hindustan, 1658-1672', in *Bulletin of the Church History Association of India*, Nov. 1966, p. 3.
BOYD, R. H. S. 'An Outline History of Gujarati Theological Literature' in *Indian Journal of Theology* XII/2 and 3 (1963).
——— 'Theologie im Kontext Indischen Denkens' in Horst Bürkle (Ed.) *Indische Beiträge zur Theologie der Gegenwart*, Stuttgart, 1966, pp. 77 ff.
BRAHMABANDHAB UPADHYAYA. '*Vande Saccidanandam*', in *Sophia*, Oct. 1898.
——— 'The Incarnate Logos', in *The Twentieth Century*, Jan. 1901, pp. 6 ff.
——— 'Christ's Claim to Attention', in *The Twentieth Century*, May 1901, pp. 115 ff.
——— 'Christianity in India', in *The Tablet*, 3-1-1903 and 31-1-1903.
BROWN, L. W. *The Indian Christians of St. Thomas.* Cambridge, 1956.
BURKLE, H. (Ed.) *Indische Beiträge zur Theologie der Gegenwart.* Stuttgart, 1966.
BUTLER, J. F. 'The Theology of Church Building in India' in *Indian Journal of Theology*, Oct. 1956 and Oct. 1959.

CHAKKARAI, V. *Jesus the Avatar.* CLS, Madras, 1932.
——— 'What is to Indianize Christianity?' in *The Guardian*, 1-10-1931 and 14-1-1932.
——— *The Cross and Indian Thought.* CLS, Madras, 1932.

CHAKKARAI, V. (with P. Chenchiah and A. N. Sudarisanam) *Asramas Past and Present*. Indian Christian Book Club, Madras, 1941.
——— 'Indian Christianity and its Critics', in *The Guardian*, 9-3-1944 to 20-4-44.
——— 'Rethinking Christianity Continued' (a critique of A. M. Ward's *Our Theological Task*) in *The Guardian*, 17-4-1947 to 17-7-47.
CHANDRAN, J. R. 'A Comparison of the pagan Apologetic of Celsus against Christianity as contained in Origen's *Contra Celsum* and the neo-Hindu Attitude towards Christianity as represented in the works of Vivekananda'. (unpublished dissertation).
CHENCHIAH, P. 'Master C.V.V. of Kumbakonam and Briktha Rahitha Tharaka Yoga. A study of a recent religious development in India', in *The Guardian*, 1943, pp. 48 ff, 497 ff, 509 ff.
——— (with V. Chakkarai and A. N. Sudarisanam) *Asramas Past and Present*. Indian Christian Book Club, Madras, 1941.
——— Review of A. J. Appasamy, *The Gospel and India's Heritage* in *The Guardian*, 24-7-1943.
——— 'Who is Jesus ?' A Study of Jesus in Terms of the Creative Process, in *The Guardian*, 29-7-1943 to 19-8-43.
——— 'Indian Christian Theological Task' (a critique of A. M. Ward's *Our Theological Task*), *The Guardian*, 2-1-1947 to 6-3-47.
——— 'My Search for the Kingdom', *The Guardian*, 8-2-1951.
CLARK, R. M. 'A Study of Theological Categories in the Indian Church', in *International Review of Missions*, 1943, pp. 88 ff.
——— 'A Study of Christological Categories in the Indian Church, as compared with those of the Early Church.' (unpublished dissertation).
——— 'The Christian Approach to the Hindu through Literature ; Problems of Terminology,' in *Indian Journal of Theology* XII/4 (1963).
CRONIN, V. *A Pearl to India* : the Life of Robert De Nobili. London, 1959.
CUTTAT, J. A. *The Encounter of Religions*. Desclee Co., 1960.

DANIEL, K. N. *A Critical Study of Early Liturgies*, especially that of St. James. 2nd edn., Tiruvalla, 1949.
DAS, R. C. 'My Spiritual Pilgrimage', in *National Christian Council Review*, March, 1949.
——— *Conviction of an Indian Disciple*. CISRS, 1966.
DE SMET, R. V. 'Categories of Indian Philosophy and Communication of the Gospel', in *Religion and Society*, 1963, pp. 20 ff.
DEVADUTT, V. E. 'What is an Indigenous Theology ?' in *Ecumenical Review*, Autumn 1949.
DEVANANDAN, P. D. *The Concept of Maya*. London, 1950.
——— *Our Task Today* : Revision of Evangelistic Concern. CISRS, 1959.
——— *Christian Concern in Hinduism*. CISRS, 1961.
——— *I Will Lift up mine Eyes unto the Hills* : Sermons and Bible Studies, ed. S. J. Samartha and Nalini Devanandan. CISRS, 1963.
——— *Preparation for Dialogue*. CISRS, 1964.
[DEVANANDAN, P. D.] *In Memory of Devanandan*. CISRS, 1962.
DEVDAS, NALINI. *Svami Vivekananda*. CISRS, 1968.

EBRIGHT, D. F. *The National Missionary Society of India*, 1905-1942. Chicago, 1944.
ESTBORN, S. *Gripped by Christ*. A study in Records of Individual Conversions in India. London, 1965.

FAKIRBHAI, DHANJIBHAI. *Khristopanishad*. CISRS, 1965.
——— *The Philosophy of Love*. ISPCK, Delhi, 1966.
FARQUHAR, J. N. *Gita and Gospel*. 1904.
——— *The Crown of Hinduism*. Oxford, 1913.
——— *Modern Religious Movements in Hinduism*. London, 1918.

GANGULY, NALIN, C. *Raja Ram Mohun Roy.* YMCA, Calcutta, 1934.
GARDNER, C. E. *Life of Father Goreh.* London, 1900.
GARRETT, T. S. *Worship in the Church of South India.* 2nd edn., London, 1965.
GIBBS, M. E. 'The Anglican Church in India and Independence' in *Bulletin of the Church History Association of India*, Feb. 1967.
GOREH, NEHEMIAH. *A Rational Refutation of the Hindu Philosophical Systems.* (Eng. transl. by Fitz-Edward Hall). Calcutta, 1862.
——— *A Letter to the Brahmos from a Converted Brahman of Benares*, 2nd edn., Allahabad, 1868.
——— *On Objections against the Catholic Doctrine of Eternal Punishment.* Calcutta, 1868.
——— *Proofs of the Divinity of Our Lord*, stated in a Letter to a Friend, 1887.
——— *Christianity not of Man but of God.* Calcutta, 1888.
GRANT, J. W. *God's People in India.* CLS, 1960.
GRIFFITH, BEDE. *Christian Ashram.* London, 1966.
GURUKUL THEOLOGICAL RESEARCH GROUP. *A Christian Theological Approach to Hinduism.* CLS, Madras, 1956.

HEILER, F. *Christliche Glaube und Indisches Geistesleben.* München, 1926.
——— *The Gospel of Sundar Singh.* (abridged Engl. tr. by Olive Wyon), London, 1927.
HOGG, A. G. *The Christian Message to the Hindu.* London, 1947.
HEWAT, E. G. K. *Christ in Western India.* Bombay, 1950.
——— *Vision and Achievement, 1796-1956*: A History of the Foreign Missions of the Churches united in the Church of Scotland. Edinburgh, 1960.
HUME, R. E. *The Thirteen Principal Upanishads*, 2nd edn., Oxford, Bombay. 1962.

INGHAM, K. *Reformers in India, 1793-1833*: An Account of the Work of Christian Missionaries on behalf of social Reform. Cambridge, 1956.

JOHANNS, P. *Vers le Christ par le Vedanta.* Louvain, 1932.
——— *To Christ through the Vedanta*: A Synopsis. Part I, Saṃkara; Part II, Ramanuja; Part III, Vallabha; Part IV, Chaitanya. 3rd ed., Ranchi, 1944.

KINGSBURY, F. AND PHILLPS, G. E. *Hymns of the Tamil Saivite Saints.* YMCA, Calcutta, 1921.
KRAEMER, H. *The Christian Message in a Non-Christian World.* London, 1938.
KULANDRAN, S. *Grace: a comparative Study of the Doctrine in Christianity and Hinduism.* London, 1964.

LEHMANN, E. A. *It Began at Tranquebar.* CLS, Madras, 1956.
LE SAUX, H. *La Rencontre de l'Hindouisme et du Christianisme.* Paris, 1966.

MACNICOL, N. *Psalms of Marātha Saints.* YMCA, Calcutta, 1919.
——— *Pandita Ramabai.* London, 1926.
——— *India in the Dark Wood.* London, 1930.
MIRANDA, J. L. *The Introduction of Christianity into the Heart of India, or Father Robert De Nobili's Mission.* Trichinopoly, 1923.
MONCHANIN, J. AND LE SAUX, H. *A Benedictine Ashram.* Revised edn., Douglas, Isle of Man, 1964.
[MONCHANIN, J.] *Swami Parama Arubi Anandam* (Fr. J. Monchanin): A Memorial. Tiruchirapalli, 1959.
MOZOOMDAR, P. C. *The Life and Teachings of Keshub Chunder Sen.* Calcutta, 1887.
——— *The Oriental Christ.* Boston, 1898.

MULIYIL, F. 'An Examination in the Light of N.T. Doctrines of the Treatment of Christian Theology in Modern Reformed Hinduism, as illustrated by the Brahma Samaj.' (unpublished dissertation).

NEILL, S. C. *Christian Faith and Other Faiths*. Oxford, 1961.
NEWBIGIN, J. E. L. *The Reunion of the Church*. Revised edn., London, 1960.
——— *Honest Religion for Secular Man*. London, 1966.
NILES, D. T. *Upon the Earth* : the Mission of God and the Missionary Enterprise of the Churches. CLS, Madras, 1962.
DE NOBILI, ROBERTO. *Gnanopadesa, Kandam* I-IV. Tuticorin, 1963-68 (Tamil).
——— *Gnanopadesa 26 Pirasangangal*. Tuticorin, 1963. (Tamil).
——— *Punar Janma Akshepam*. Tuticorin, 1963. (Tamil).
——— *Gnana Sanjeevi*. Tuticorin, 1965. (Tamil).
——— *Gnanopadesam Kurippidam*. Tuticorin, 1955. (Tamil).
——— *Devamatha Sarithiram* (Life of Our Lady). Tuticorin, 1964. (Tamil).

OOSTHUIZEN, G. C. *Theological Discussions and Confessional Developments in the Churches of Asia and Africa*. Franeker, Holland, 1958.
OTTO, RUDOLF. *Christianity and the Indian Religion of Grace*. CLS, Madras, 1929.

PANIKKAR, K. M. *Hindu Society at the Cross Roads*. Asia Publ. House, Bombay, 1955.
PANIKKAR, RAYMOND, G. *The Unknown Christ of Hinduism*. London, 1964.
PARADKAR, BALWANT, A. M. *The Theology of Goreh*. CISRS, 1969.
PARANANDA, SRI. *The Gospel of Jesus according to St. Matthew* : as interpreted to R. L. Harrison by the Light of the Godly Experience of Sri Parananda. London, 1898.
——— *An Eastern Exposition of St. John*. London, 1902.
PAREKH, MANILAL, C. *Brahmarshi Keshub Chunder Sen*. Rajkot, 1926.
——— *Rajarshi Ram Mohan Roy*. Rajkot, 1927.
——— 'An Autobiographical Sketch' in *Zeitschrift für Religions—und Geistes-Geschichte*, Köln, XI/2 (1959), pp. 157 ff.
PARKER, REBECCA. *Sadhu Sundar Singh : Called of God*. 1918.
PAUL, C. S. *The Suffering God*. CLS, Madras, 1932.
PAUL, RAJAIAH, D. *The First Decade : an Account of the Church of South India*. CLS, Madras, 1958.
——— *Chosen Vessels*. CLS, Madras, 1961.
PHILIP, E. M. *The Indian Church of St. Thomas*. Nagercoil, 1950.
PHILIPOS, E. *The Syrian Christians of Malabar*. Oxford, 1869.
POPLEY, H. A. *K. T. Paul, Christian Leader*. YMCA, Calcutta, 1938.

RADHAKRISHNAN, S. *Indian Philosophy*. 2 vols., 2nd edn., London, 1929.
——— *The Bhagavadgita*. London, 1948.
RAJARIGAM, D. *The History of Tamil Christian Literature*. CLS, Madras, 1958.
——— 'Theological Content in Tamil Christian Poetical Works', in *Indian Journal of Theology* XI/4, XII/1, XII/2, 1962-64.
RAMABAI, PANDITA. *A Testimony*. 5th edn., Kedgaon, n.d. (1st edn. 1917).
RAO, MARK SUNDER. *Ananyatva* : Realization of Christian Non-Duality. CISRS, 1964.
RELTON, H. M. *A Study in Christology*. London, 1917.
'RETHINKING GROUP' (Chenchiah, Chakkarai etc.) *Rethinking Christianity in India*. Madras, 1938.
RIDDLE, T. E. *The Vision and the Call*; a Life of Sadhu Sundar Singh. Kharar, 1964.

ROBINSON, J. A. T. *Honest to God*. London, 1963.
——— *Exploration into God*. London, 1967.
——— AND EDWARDS, D. L. (eds.) *The Honest to God Debate*. London. 1963.
ROGERS, C. MURRAY. 'Hindu and Christian—a Moment Breaks', in *Religion and Society*. XII/1, (1965), pp. 35 ff.
ROY, RAM MOHAN. *The Precepts of Jesus*: the Guide to Peace and Happiness. Calcutta, 1820.
——— *An Appeal to the Christian Public in Defence of the Precepts of Jesus*. Calcutta, 1820.
——— *Second Appeal*. Calcutta, 1821.
——— *Final Appeal*. Calcutta, 1824.

SAMUEL, V. C. 'Were they Monophysites?' in *Indian Journal of Theology*, XI/1, (1962), p. 1. ff.
SARGANT, N. C. *The Lingayats*. CISRS, 1963.
SEN, KESHAB CHANDRA. *Keshub Chunder Sen's Lectures in India*. The Brahmo Samaj, Cassell, London, 1909.
SHARPE, ERIC, J. *J. N. Farquhar: a Memoir*. YMCA, Calcutta, 1963.
——— *Not to Destroy but to Fulfil*: the Contribution of J. N. Farquhar to Protestant Missionary Thought in India before 1914. Uppsala, 1965.
SINGH, BAKHT. *The Skill of His Loving Hands*. Gospel Lit. Service, Bombay, 1961.
SINGH, SUNDAR. *At the Master's Feet*. CLS, Madras, 1923.
——— *Visions of the Spiritual World*. London, 1926.
——— *The Real Pearl*. CLS, Madras, 1966.
SINGH, SURJIT. *Preface to Personality*: Christology in Relation to Radhakrishnan's Philosophy. CLS, Madras, 1952.
SMART, R. N. *Reasons and Faiths*: an Investigation of Religious Discourse, Christian and non-Christian. London, 1958.
——— *Doctrine and Argument in Indian Philosophy*. London, 1964.
——— *Philosophers and Religious Truth*. London, 1964.
SMITH, GEORGE. *The Life of William Carey*. London, 1885.
STEWART, JOHN. *Nestorian Missionary Enterprise*—the Story of a Church on Fire. CLS, Madras, 1928.
STREETER, B. H. AND APPASAMY, A. J. *The Sadhu*: a Study in Mysticism and Practical Religion. London, 1921.
SUDHAKAR, PAUL. *The Fourfold Ideal*. Gospel Lit. Service, Bombay, n.d.
SUNDKLER, BENGT. *CSI: the Movement towards Union, 1900-1947*. London, 1954.

THANGASAMY, D. A. 'Theology, the Church and the Gospel', in *S. India Churchman*, June, Sept., Oct. 1960.
——— 'Significance of Chenchiah and his Thought', in *Religion and Society*, X/3, 1963.
——— 'Chenchiah's Understanding of Jesus Christ' in *Religion and Society*, XI/3, 1964.
——— *The Theology of Chenchiah*. CISRS, 1967.
THOMAS, M. M. *The Christian Response to the Asian Revolution*. CISRS, 1966.
THOMAS, P. T. *The Theology of Chakkarai*. CISRS, 1968.
'T HOOFT, W. A. VISSER. *No Other Name*. London, 1963.
TISSERANT, EUGENE. *Eastern Christianity in India*: a History of the Syro-Malabar Church from the earliest Times to the present Day. Longmans Green, 1957.
TORRANCE, T. F. *Conflict and Agreement in the Church*. 2 vols., London, 1959-60.

VAN LEEUWEN, A. T. *Christianity in World History*. 1964.
VATH, A. *Im Kampfe mit der Zauberwelt des Hinduismus*. Berlin, 1928.

WAGNER, HERWIG. *Erstgestalten einer Einheimischen Theologie in Südindien.* München, 1963.

WARD, A. M. *Our Theological Task* : an Introduction to the Study of Theology in India. CLS, Madras, 1946.

——— *The Pilgrim Church* : an Account of the first Five Years in the Life of the CSI. London, 1953.

WHITEHURST, JAMES, E. 'Realization of Christian Non-Duality', in *Religion and Society*, XII/1, (1965), pp. 65 ff. (Review of M. S. Rao's *Ananyatva*).

WINSLOW, J. C. *Narayan Vaman Tilak* : the Christian Poet of Maharashtra. YMCA, Calcutta, 1930.

WOLFF, OTTO. *Mahatma und Christus.* Berlin, 1955.

——— *Christus unter den Hindus.* Gütersloh, 1965.

YESUDHAS, D. 'Indigenization or Adaptation ? A Brief Study of Roberto De Nobili's Attitude to Hinduism', in *Bangalore Theological Forum*, Sept. 1967, pp. 39 ff.

ZAEHNER, R. C. *At Sundry Times* : an Essay in the Comparison of Religions. London, 1958.

——— *The Convergent Spirit* : towards a Dialectics of Religion. London, 1963.

INDEX OF PROPER NAMES

INDEX OF SUBJECTS

SUPPLEMENTARY GLOSSARY
(for Chapters XIV-XVII)

ādhyātma	Universal Spirit; the Self, Reality.
akṛti	The uncreated (idea).
anāsakti	Detachment; freedom from the desire for fulfilment.
arcāvatāra	'Shining incarnation'.
ātmaniṣṭha	Intent, confident in contemplation of the Self.
Bhāgavata	Theist; one who worships the personal God, Bhagavan.
Brahma-sambandha	Relationship, fellowship with *Brahman*.
Brahmavidyā	Knowledge of *Brahman*; the science of the Supreme.
dvandva	Pair of opposites.
ekatvam	Unity, identity.
Khristādvaita	Non-separation from, i.e. unity with Christ.
Khristvidyā	Knowledge, science of Christ. Christology.
prajñāna	pre-knowledge, primeval intelligence.
puṣṭi	Fatness, nourishment, enjoyment; hence 'the way of pleasure' (Vallabhacharya).
Śabda	Word.
Śabda-Brahman	*Brahman* manifested as Word. 'God the Word'.
śuddhādvaita	'Pure non-dualism' (Vallabhacharya).
samabhāva	Equal feeling, respect (i.e. for all religions).
samanvaya	Harmony (e.g. of religions).
sampradāya	Tradition.
svadharmāgraha	Insistence on (the claims of) one's own religion.
vibhava	'Special being', greatness, glory (of the *avataras*).
viśvakarmā	Author (cause) of the universe.
viveka	Distinction, especially that between the realm of *karma* and that of *Brahman*.
vyuha	Battle-array, host; hence of Brahman's fourfold form.

SUPPLEMENTARY BIBLIOGRAPHY
(for Chapters XIV-XVII)

ABHISHIKTANANDA, SWAMI. (H. Le Saux). *Hindu-Christian Meeting Point within the Cave of the Heart.* Bombay, 1969.
——— *The Church in India.* Madras, 1969.
——— *Prayer.* Delhi, 1967.
AIRAN, C. D. *K. Subba Rao, the Mystic of Munipalle.* Secunderabad. n.d.
BAAGO, K. *The Movement around Subba Rao.* Madras, 1968.
——— *Pioneers of Indigenous Christianity.* Madras, 1969.
BANERJEA, K. M. *Dialogues on Hindu Philosophy.* Calcutta, 1861.
——— *The Arian Witness.* Calcutta, 1875.
BOYD, R. H. S. (ed.). *Manilal C. Parekh : Dhanjibhai Fakirbhai, a Selection.* Madras, 1974.
DEVANESEN, CHANDRAN. *The Making of the Mahatma.* Madras, 1969.
DHANJIBHAI FAKIRBHAI. *Shri Khrist Gita.* Delhi, 1969.
——— *Adhyatma Ḍarsana.* (unpublished MS).
KLOSTERMAIER, KLAUS. *Kristvidya : a Sketch of an Indian Christology.* Bangalore, 1967.
——— *Hindu and Christian in Vrindaban.* London, 1969.
KUNG, HANS. 'The World Religions in God's Plan of Salvation', in J. Neuner (ed.). *Christian Revelation and World Religions.* London, 1967.
MINZ, NIRMAL. *Mahatma Gandhi and Hindu-Christian Dialogue.* Madras 1969.
PANIKKAR, RAYMOND. *Kultmysterium in Hinduismus und Christentum.* Freiburg, 1964.
——— *Religion und die Religionen*, Munich, 1965.
——— *Maya e Apocalisse ; l'incontro del induismo et del Christianismo.* Rome, 1966.
——— *L'Homme qui devient Dieu ; la foi dimension constitutive de l'homme.* Aubier, 1969.
——— *The Trinity and World Religions.* Madras, 1970.
PAREKH, MANILAL, C. 'The Spiritual Significance and Value of Baptism', art. in *National Christian Council Review*, September 1924.
——— *The Brahma Samaj.* Rajkot, 1929.
——— *Sri Swami Narayana.* Rajkot, 1936.
——— *The Gospel of Zoroaster.* Rajkot, 1939.
——— *Sri Vallabhacharya.* Rajkot, 1943.
——— *Christian Proselytism in India : a Great and Growing Menace.* Rajkot, 1947.
——— *A Hindu's Portrait of Jesus Christ.* Rajkot, 1953.
——— *Autobiography of a Bhagavata.* (in Gujarati). Rajkot, 1963.
PAUL, R. D. *Chosen Vessels.* Madras, 1961.
PICKETT, J. W. *Christian Mass-Movements in India.* Abingdon, 1933.
RAO, K. SUBBA. *The Outpourings of my Heart.* Guntur, n.d.
——— *Translations of the New Songs.* Vijayawada, n.d.
——— *Retreat, Padri !* n.d.
SHARPE, ERIC J. *The Theology of A. G. Hogg.* Madras, 1971.
THOMAS, M. M. *Christians in the World Struggle* (with J. D. McCaughey). London, 1951.
——— *The Christian Response to the Asian Revolution.* London, 1966.
——— *The Indian Churches of St. Thomas* (with C. P. Mathew). Delhi, 1967.
——— *The Acknowledged Christ of the Indian Renaissance.* London, 1969.
——— *Joyful and Triumphant.* Madras, 1970.
——— *Salvation and Humanisation.* Bangalore, 1971.
——— *The Realization of the Cross.* Madras, 1972.

SUPPLEMENTARY INDEX OF PROPER NAMES

(for Chapters XIV-XVII)

SUPPLEMENTARY INDEX OF SUBJECTS

(for Chapters XIV-XVII)